CONSTITUTIONS
THAT MADE
HISTORY

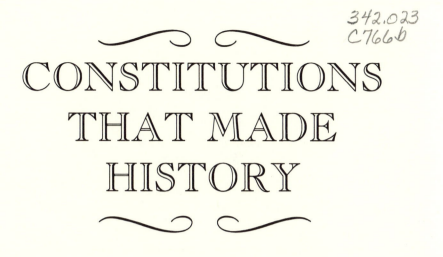

CONSTITUTIONS THAT MADE HISTORY

EDITED AND WITH AN INTRODUCTION BY

Albert P. Blaustein

Jay A. Sigler

PARAGON HOUSE PUBLISHERS

New York

First edition

Published in the United States by

Paragon House Publishers
90 Fifth Avenue
New York, NY 10011

Copyright © 1988 by Albert P. Blaustein and Jay A. Sigler
Published in cooperation with the Centre de Recherches pour le Droit
Constitutionnel, Fribourg, Switzerland.

Library of Congress Cataloging-in-Publication Data

Constitutions that made history / edited by Albert P. Blaustein, Jay A.
Sigler.—1st ed.
p. cm.
ISBN 0-913729-67-1
1. Constitutions. I. Blaustein, Albert P., 1921–
II. Sigler, Jay A.
K3157.E5C67 1988
342'.023—dc19   87-19381
[342.223]   CIP

To Phyllis
whose dedication and patience allowed the
completion of yet another book

CONTENTS

INTRODUCTION

There has never been a want of constitutional compilations. In fact, collections of constitutions date back to the first era of constitution-making. The world's first constitutions—those of the American states—had been translated into French and made available in Paris within weeks of their adoption. And their compilation (in French) was probably the first of the constitution anthologies. The work was *Constitutions des Treize Etats de l'Amerique*, whose publication in 1783 was officially authorized by the French ministry of foreign affairs at the behest of the then American Minister, Benjamin Franklin.

This constitution collection (supplemented by the United States Constitution of 1787) became the text and guidebook for the era of European constitution-making which was to follow. It began with the world's second constitution, the Polish Constitution of May 3, 1791, followed four months later by the French Constitution of September 3, 1791. It also provided background for the debates surrounding the passage of the French Constitutions of 1793 and 1795, and greatly influenced the delegates who drafted the important Spanish Constitution of 1812.

Constitutional compilations have continued to serve the needs of the delegates and draftsmen of the approximately one thousand constitutions subsequently promulgated. And they have continued to serve the needs of constitutional scholars. There are many such examples. The pioneer collector was Karl H. L. Pölitz, whose comprehensive four-volume work, *Die Constitutionen Der Europäischen Staaten Seit Den Letzten 25 Jahren*, was published in Leipzig by Brockhaus from 1817 to 1825.

For many decades after that the basic work was *Les Constitutions Modernes*, edited by F.R. and P. Dareste. The first edition was published in two volumes by Challamel Aine in Paris in 1883, but was expanded in subsequent editions as more and more nations became independent and drafted constitutions. The fourth edition in 1928 comprised six volumes.

There were also more limited international collections. Best known for many years in the United States was the two-volume work of W. F. Dodd, *Modern Constitutions, A Collection of Fundamental Laws of Twenty-Two of the Most Important Countries of the World, with Historical and Bibliographical Notes.* This was published in 1909 by the University of Chicago Press. A work of similar scope was the 1919 collection published by the United States Government Printing Office: *The Constitutions of the States at War 1914–1918.* This was the work of editor Herbert Francis Wright.

The most interesting of these international collections was the compilation prepared for the use of the Irish Parliament, the Dail Eireann, by order of the Irish Provisional Government. Entitled *Select Constitutions of the World*, this was published in Dublin by the government's Stationery Office in 1922 to meet the reference needs of Ireland's constitution-makers. A similar work, containing the constitutions of the nations with federal systems, was prepared for the use of the American occupation forces in helping to prepare Germany's post-World War II Constitution.

For some two decades, beginning with his Rumford Press edition in 1950, the most comprehensive collection was Amos J. Peaslee's *Constitutions of Nations.* The fourth edition, published at The Hague by Nijhoff in six volumes beginning in 1974 was under the editorship of his daughter, Dorothy Peaslee Xydis.

During the post World War II period there have been significant regional collections. Latin American anthologies include the Russell H. Fitzgibbon work, *The Constitutions of the Americas*, published by the University of Chicago Press in 1948, and Gerald E. Fitzgerald's *The Constitutions of Latin America*, published in Chicago by Regnery in 1968. Constitutions behind the Iron Curtain are in *Constitutions of the Communist Party States*, by Jan F. Triska, published at Stanford by the Hoover Institution in 1968, and *The Constitutions of the Communist World*, by William B. Simons, published in Leyden in the Netherlands by Sijthoff in 1979.

The most comprehensive constitution collection is *Constitutions of the Countries of the World* by Albert P. Blaustein and Gisbert H. Flanz, published by Oceana Publications in Dobbs Ferry, N.Y., beginning in 1971. This is a looseleaf collection, now housed in eighteen binders, and supplemented quarterly.

The principal (albeit unavoidable) defect of most of these constitutional collections has been their brief life span. Important to the study of constitutional contrast and comparison when first prepared, these collections soon become outdated and lost for scholarly use. For the prime focus has always been on collecting *current* constitutions. These are the ones needed by the practical people—the government officials, the journalists, the students of current affairs. And with three-quarters of the world's constitutions promulgated since 1970, modern constitution collecting has been unavoidably current. The old collections are soon discarded and become increasingly hard to find.

Blaustein and Flanz have tried to overcome this problem with their supplemental set of *Historic Constitutions*, now housed in thirty additional binders. As each new constitution pamphlet has been incorporated into the current set, the superseded constitution has been transferred into one of the historic binders. However, that only encompasses constitutions that were in effect since 1971. The older documents have been pushed further back into the dim light of "history." And when old collections are found, the researcher quickly realizes that the constitutional assortment consists largely of constitutions whose sole significance is that they were once current. There is no equality in the quality of old constitutions. The historic and research value of superseded constitutions varies widely.

But when these constitutions of the past are gathered together and studied, it is readily evident that some of them have had greater significance than the rest, and deserve special attention. These are the historic constitutions which have served a purpose beyond the time and place they were created. It is these historic constitutions which have been sought and collected for this constitutional anthology. They illustrate aspects of constitutional development which have permanent value. Each of the eighteen constitutions here represent important stages in the ever-continuous evolutionary process of manifesting the embodiment of constitutionalism. Each constitution played a significant role in reducing the abstractions of the political ideology of its age into a concrete reality. Each represents a step forward in the continuing process of describing the contours and dimensions of government. Once there were only the American constitutions. Now, all but six of the world's 168 nations either has or is committed to having a single-document written constitution. Those chosen for this compilation are the milestones in the forward progress of the idea of such a written constitution. As such they explain, support and expand the dominant political ideologies of modern times as well as their own eras.

The idea of constitutionalism is older than the existence of written constitutions. Constitutionalism places limits upon government, proscribing the means by which official power may be exercised. Constitutionalism establishes boundaries between the state and the individual, forbidding the state to trespass into certain areas reserved for private action. Constitutionalism also has a deeper and older connotation, demanding adherence by government to recognized customary procedures. The idea of a constitution in this procedural sense can be traced all the way back to Aristotle, who in his *Politics* and the *Constitution of Athens* described all the known political arrangements of ancient Greece. But neither Aristotle nor his constitutional successors prior to the age of American constitutionalism saw a single-document constitution as a means of securing individual liberty or of expressing popular sovereignty. This was the greatest American contribution to constitutionalism.

The United States Constitution proclaims its issuance in the name of "We the people." The idea that it is within the power of the people consciously to choose the means of their governance and to establish the modes of operation of their government is a modern concept, and largely an American idea. It was something America's revolutionary leaders wanted to incorporate into a constitution because a written constitution is, by its very nature, designed to be more lasting, more fundamental, than a mere statute. And this American idea soon captured the imaginations of constitutionalists everywhere. But the Americans had also studied and learned constitutional theory from the political philosophers of Europe.

The first written constitutions manifested two powerful political theories: social contract and natural law. These concepts had been given special meaning by political philosophers John Locke and Jean-Jacques Rousseau. They argued that government rested upon the will of the people, not an all-powerful monarch or an all-knowing God. According to Locke, government is legitimately established as a result of a compact in which individuals promise to accept the judgments of a common arbiter. Pursuant to this compact, government is formed, giving its promise to execute its authority on behalf of the people. At the same time, the people retain the right to rebel when the government fails to discharge its obligations under the social contract. Men would not rebel unless there were long and protracted abuses of power by government.

For the sake of government stability, it became apparent to those steeped in Lockean theory that some kind of written undertaking would be required in each country to establish the specific terms of such social contract. Colonial America provided an ideal testing ground for John Locke's ideas. The American colonists were already familiar with written documents framing government, having received specific charters from the monarchs of England or (as was the case with the Mayflower Compact) having written their own charters for their governments in the New World. Locke himself tried to write a constitution for Virginia.

The "natural law" element in constitutions gave them the sanctity of a higher law. For "the modern constitutional state at the time of its origins was justified and, to a large extent, legitimatized in terms of natural law theory."[1] While the ancient idea of a divinely inspired, immutable, eternal natural law had been secularized by the seventeenth century, it still provided a source of permanence in an ever unstable world. John Locke used natural law to support the natural rights of the individual, thus limiting the powers of government. The written constitutions which followed Locke's philosophy embodied such traditional natural rights in detailed provisions.

Rousseau, on the other hand, grounded his analysis of the social contract in the "general will," adopting a more radical version of natural law, less rooted in the customs of the past and accordingly more responsive to the desires of the multitude.

The precedent for written constitutions was "first developed in North America, was naturalized in France and from there transmitted to the continent of Europe, from which it has spread in our own day."[2] Despite its obvious forebears, Thomas Paine saw the American constitution as a fresh invention. In his view, "A constitution is not the act of a government, but of the people constituting a government, and a government without a constitution is power without right."[3] For Paine, as for most constitutionalists since his day, the conscious formulation by a people of its fundamental law was a new American contribution to the art or science of government. No longer were ancient customs or old statutes seen as the source of political authority. After the American experiment with written constitutions, there existed a model for constitutional development in all the nations of the world.

That is why this constitutional anthology begins with those first American constitutions.

The world's first conscious attempt to design a government for self-governance was made in Connecticut. Its Fundamental Orders of 1638–39 was essentially derived from the tenants of congregationalism to serve the needs of a secular community. Despite its religious origins, it served as a political constitution until 1818, long after the American Revolutionary era.

The Virginia Constitution of 1776 was a prime source for the Constitution of the United States. It adopted the Lockean ideas of natural rights and embodied them in the world's first Declaration of Rights. It provided an example and model to progressive forces in Europe, who saw a constitution as a means of securing individual liberty, as well as a plan for popular government.

The Pennsylvania Constitution of 1776 was even more influential in Europe, especially in France, where the constitutionalists mistakenly believed it had been drafted by the extremely popular Benjamin Franklin. It was also influential on the continent because it was the only American constitution which provided for a unicameral legislature. This was significant to revolutionaries who looked upon an upper house as representing and maintaining aristocracy.

The 1780 Massachusetts Constitution, based on the theory of "mixed constitutions" articulated by its primary author, John Adams, was the most developed state constitution prior to the adoption of the United States Constitution. Its provisions are both detailed and sophisticated, and it contains features studied and followed by subsequent constitutional draftsmen throughout the world.

The 1791 Constitution of Poland is one of the more obscure documents included in this collection. Although it was the world's second written national constitution, it is little-known outside of its homeland. Inspired by the American model, it was also influenced by French political theories and the English experience. It represented a compromise in achieving as much individual freedom as was possible in an heretofore absolute monarchy in central or eastern Europe. Yet, since the constitution retained both the monarchy and an inherited nobility, it failed to get the approbation of subsequent constitutionalists.

Four months later in 1791 came the adoption of the first French Constitution, incorporating the 1789 Declaration of the Rights of Man and the Citizen. Although the French endured great political instability in the years following the Revolution, the appeal of the short-lived constitution of 1791 was strong. For conservative reformers, the limited monarchy established by that constitution provided an acceptable compromise means of protecting popular rights, while curtailing royal privilege. The more radical reformers could tell their followers (and the world) that they had secured acceptance of human rights provisions which even exceeded those in the American Bill of Rights. They had put their Revolution into writing and provided a European constitutional model.

Spain's 1812 Cadiz Constitution, which borrowed much from the French precedent, was, for a time, Europe's most influential constitution. It was carried to Portugal, Naples, Russia and other hotbeds of political agitation in the post-Napoleonic era. In Latin America it was an inspiration and guide to revolutionary leaders seeking national independence. While they all knew and were influenced by the U.S. role model, they also wanted something European and Hispanic, and the Cadiz Constitution met that need.

For Latin American scholars, the most interesting of the early constitutions is Bolivia's 1826 Constitution. Prepared by the Great Liberator, Simon Bolivar, this document provided for a form of popular dictatorship which later became prevalent in the region.

In Europe, the Belgian Constitution of 1831 provided the chief model for constitutional reform for more than one hundred years after its adoption. While Belgians and constitutional historians still consider the 1831 document never to have been repealed and therefore still in force, it has been so changed by amendments that its significance and precedent value can only be understood by studying the original, hard-to-find document.

Federalism is one of the principal subjects of constitutional study and the princpial feature of the constitutions of many of the world's most important nations. The United States, Canada, Mexico, Brazil, Argentina, Venezuela, Germany, Austria, Switzerland, the Soviet Union, Yugoslavia, Nigeria, India and Australia are in that number. And every one of these nations has a detailed federalist constitution, grounded in the American system, but in some measure infuenced by the Swiss precedent. For even where the Swiss experience has not been followed, it has been studied and analyzed. The Swiss model is best understood by examining its 1848 Constitution. Especially important here are the provisions for ethnic, religious and lingustic rights.

1848 was Europe's year of revolution, and the year of many new constitutions. One of the victories of the spirit of 1848 was the proposed German Constitution, prepared by reformers assembled at Frankfurt. They raised the principles of popular sovereignty and individual rights to new heights, well beyond those set forth in other contemporary constitutions. Unfortunately, conditions in the Germany of that day precluded adoption of its progressive principles, but its spirit and influence have lived on.

Japan created its constitutional monarchy in 1889 with a constitution based upon the teachings of European scholars. That constitution ended the Japanese feudal system, but it fell far short of constructing a modern democracy. For Asia at the end of the nineteenth century, the Japanese Constitution was deemed enlightened, but the main features of authoritarian government were retained, albeit in a more modern form.

Republican ideals reached Asia in the form of the 1911 Constitution of the Republic of China. Democracy and individual rights were prominent in this Western-influenced Constitution. While the principles of constitutionalism were often not applied in Chinese practice, the ideals of that constitution are important subjects of study, not only in the People's Republic of China, Taiwan and Hong Kong, but throughout the non-Western world. Its contents and its history are significant in analyzing the exportability of the American and European constitutional models to the Third World.

The last constitution of the Russian Empire was promulgated in 1906 and was a vain and inadequate attempt to stem the tide of radical reform and revolution. The concessions exacted from the czar were an insufficient response to the call for more popular government. Had this constitution been less autocratic and more responsive to the needs of the Russian people, the chances in the future of so violent a revolution would have been lessened. But while this constitution was a failure, it was an important landmark in constitutional history, and features of the czarist constitution were echoed in the Lenin constitution which followed the Russian Revolution.

The Mexican Constitution of 1917 is one of the most infuential of modern constitutions, providing a non-Marxist source for social and economic rights. While the Mexican model has primarily inspired developments in Latin America, it deserves study by other reformers for its many progressive features. So frequently amended that its present version obscures its fundamental base, the original 1917 Constitution is provided here to illustrate its fundamental approaches.

Lenin's 1918 Constitution provided the world's first Marxist model. Since each Soviet Constitution is supposed to exemplify a stage in Marxist development, leading to the eventual disappearance of the state, it is important to understand the limited nature of the first Soviet Constitution.

By contrast, Germany's Weimar Constitution of 1919 embodied the highest development of liberal democratic thought in the post World War I era. Although the Weimar philosophy was in abeyance during the Nazi period, it was revived and played a role in the construction of Germany's post World War II Constitution, believed by many to be the most democratic constitution of that era. The 1919 document contains many features of significance to the practice of liberal democracy and has been studied widely in such disparate places as Brazil and South Korea even if it has not been implemented. In fact, the Basic Law of the Federal Republic of Germany retains five Articles of the Weimar Constitution.

Another European democracy which, like the Weimar Republic, was born in the ashes of the First World War, was Estonia, now incorporated by conquest into the Soviet Union. Its 1920 Constitution has faded in the memory of constitutional scholars, like the fate of that ill-starred democracy itself. Yet the Estonian Constitution is one of the most progressive liberal democratic constitutions of all times, and important in comparative study. Its greatest significance is its attention to a new classification of human rights—groups rights. In the constitutional formulation of this ideal (and in some of its other features), the Estonian document was and is ahead of its times.

These then are the constitutions that have not only made history but are continually making history, as their study continues to influence the ever-continuing course of constitution-making.

ALBERT P. BLAUSTEIN
JAY A. SIGLER

NOTES

1. William G. Andrews, *Constitutions and Constitutionalism* (Princeton: D. Van Nostrand Company, Inc., 1968), p. 15.
2. Charles Howard McIlwain, *Constitutionalism Ancient and Modern* (Ithaca, New York: Cornell University Press, 1947), p. 14.
3. From the *Rights of Man*, in *The Complete Works of Thomas Paine* (London: 1820), pp. 302–03.

CONSTITUTIONS
THAT MADE
HISTORY

Connecticut Constitution of 1638/39

Although a short document, the Fundamental Orders of Connecticut of 1638/39[1] is of major significance in the history of constitutionalism. This constitution was the first one that created a political state. Although constitutions had existed in ancient Greece and in Switzerland before the seventeenth century, they were more like treaties and were not conscious efforts to construct new forms of government.

On 14 January 1638/39, the freemen of the River Plantations of Hartford, Windsor, and Wethersfield adopted these Fundamental Orders. Containing a preamble and eleven brief "orders," their constitution outlined the structure of the commonwealth government of Connecticut. Little is known of the creative process that resulted in its formation, because the records or minutes of the constitutional session have never been uncovered.

Strict secrecy had been imposed on the delegates who attended the constitutional session—a prudent measure because the draftsmen were proposing to form a self-supporting community that would be independent of the Massachusetts Bay Colony as well as of the English Crown. Connecticut did not possess any printing presses at the time so it is probable that there was never more than one copy of the minutes.

It is known that Reverend Thomas Hooker, Connecticut's foremost pastor, was the inspiration behind the Fundamental Orders. On 31 May 1616, he led his congregation of approximately one hundred people from Newtown (now Cambridge), Massachusetts, on a two-week journey on foot into the Connecticut Valley and founded the river plantation[2] of Hartford. Until the adoption of the Fundamental Orders, Connecticut (which was essentially the three river communities of Hartford, Windsor, and Wethersfield) was technically governed by the authority of the provisional government instituted by the Massachusetts Bay Colony under the auspices of the eight-person Massachusetts Bay Commission. However, because of the difficulties of transportation and communication, Connecticut was an independent commonwealth from its inception. With the adoption of the Fundamental Orders, this benign neglect was formalized as independence.

Although Reverend Hooker provided the inspiration for the Fundamental Orders, Roger Ludlow was probably responsible for the actual drafting. Educated in England, Roger Ludlow was, at the time, the only man in Connecticut trained in law. It is thought that Ludlow took Hooker's tenets of Congregationalism and put them in a constitutional format. Based on Congregationalist polity, the Fundamental Orders was a civil constitution crafted to serve the secular needs of a religious community. The purpose of the Fundamental Orders was to supplement and support Congregationalism and to provide a legal guide for the government of the Congregationalists in the river plantations. By no means did the Fundamental Orders advocate religious liberty. Connecticut was founded for the express purpose of permitting the Congregationalists to worship God according to their polity and did not tolerate any deviations.

In the river plantations of Hartford, Windsor, and Wethersfield, people formed their churches (the foremost concern) before they adopted any political organization. Connecticut began with no written framework of government. It had no political covenant to correspond with the religious covenants on which their churches were founded. Congregation churches were united by covenants, and in Connecticut these covenants existed in three forms. First, and most important, the covenant of grace was the original agreement between God and the individual saint; made at God's discretion, this covenant bound the saint to God's authority alone. Second, the covenant of a particular church united saints together into a visible church body. Third, the Fundamental Orders was a civil covenant that bound people together in a political relationship. With this final covenant, Connecticut had the written instrument it needed to become a political entity.

Not all residents of Hartford, Windsor, and Wethersfield were granted benefits under the Fundamental Orders. Just as the church covenants pertained to only the saints, this document was a covenant to only those godly property owners. Civil rights were accorded exclusively to the privileged few. Although the Fundamental Orders listed no religious requirement for government officials[3] (other than the governor), church and state were virtually synonymous—those who were freemen of the Commonwealth tended to be brethren of the Congregational churches. This policy was taken from Thomas Hooker's sermon on Deuteronomy 1:13, preached 31 May 1638: "Choose wise, understanding, and experienced men, according to your tribes, and I will appoint them as your heads." The interpretation of this appeal was that people should select only those who had demonstrated leadership qualities to rule—prominent men of governing potential, who just happened to be leaders of the churches.

One of the most notable features of this constitution is the conspicuous absence of any reference to an earthly authority. The preamble ignored the English King completely. There was no separation of church and state under Connecticut's Fundamental Orders. God wielded sovereign authority over Connecticut's Congregationalists just as the Supreme Being exercised rule over their churches. Thus, Connecticut, under the Fundamental Orders, was a self-governing Commonwealth, not another colony of the English King.

Under the Fundamental Orders, the locus of power was with the General Court. Comprised of the governor, magistrates, and deputies, the General Court possessed the authority to enact orders governing the ecclesiastical, social, and moral aspects of the community as well as the criminal and constitutional ones. Although the Fundamental Orders did not explicitly provide for an amendment procedure, the constitution was altered several times between 1639 and 1661. Most of these amendments were effectuated by the General Court.

The government sanctioned by the Fundamental Orders ran smoothly for more than twenty years. The constitution contained flexibility to allow for the expansion of the Commonwealth and the admission of new towns. Moreover, the towns possessed sufficient local autonomy to govern their own affairs. Under the Fundamental Orders, the Commonwealth engaged in a regional confederation with Massachusetts Bay, Plymouth, and New Haven primarily for reasons of mutual security against the Indians. When Connecticut received its Royal Charter in October 1662, it was not a rejection of the Fundamental Orders because the Charter confirmed the government sanctioned by the Fundamental Orders. Rather, Connecticut became a royal colony to guarantee for itself the protection Great Britain could provide against hostile external forces—notably the Dutch and the Indians—that threatened the preservation of their Congregational state. Thus, even after the adoption of the Charter, the government formed by the Fundamental Orders remained essentially intact and remained so until 1818 when Connecticut adopted a state constitution to replace the Charter made obsolete by the American Revolution.

PATRICIA E. LARKIN
New Jersey Bar

NOTES

1. The English use of the Gregorian calendar did not commence until 1752. Before that year, time was recorded according to the Julian calendar whose new year

began on the Feast of the Annunciation (Lady Day), which fell on 25 March. When the Fundamental Orders were adopted, January was considered one of the closing months of the year. Thus, although Thomas Hooker would have considered his Fundamental Orders adopted on 14 January 1638, contemporary historians mark the year as 1639. Using both the Julian calendar year followed by the Gregorian calendar year, such dates as 14 January will be recorded as 1638/39.

2. References to town and river plantations are not synonymous. Connecticut had no towns at this time, although it did host several communities. It was not until early 1638/39, after the adoption of the Fundamental Orders, that the first town, Hartford, was incorporated.

3. The Fundamental Orders has been often mistaken as a democratic document because of this lack of a religious requirement for civil office. Although Connecticut might have been one step ahead of Massachusetts Bay on the road to democracy, it still had a long way to go. Connecticut's civil officers tended to be church members, and the close-knit church-state relationship lasted throughout the seventeenth and eighteenth centuries.

FUNDAMENTAL ORDERS OF CONNECTICUT—
1638/39[*][a][b]

FORASMUCH as it hath pleased the Allmighty God by the wise disposition of his diuyne pruidence so to Order and dispose of things that we the Inhabitants and Residents of Windsor, Harteford and Wethersfield are now cohabiting and dwelling in and vppon the River of Conectecotte and the Lands thereunto adioyneing; And well knowing where a people are gathered togather the word of God requires that to mayntayne the peace and vnion of such a people there should be an orderly and decent

The Federal and State Constitutions, Colonial Charters and Other Organic Laws of the States, Territories and Colonies Now or Heretofore Forming the United States of America. Vol. 1. Compiled and edited under the Act of Congress of 30 June 1906 by Francis Newton Thorpe (Washington, D.C.: Government Printing Office, 1909), 519.

[*] Hazard's State Papers, I, 437–41.

[a] A provisional government was instituted, under a commission from the General Court of Massachusetts (3 March 1635) to eight of the persons who "had resolved to transplant themselves and their estates unto the River of Connecticut . . . that commission taking rise from the desire of the people that removed, who judged it inconvenient to go away without any frame of government,—not from any claim of the Massachusetts of jurisdiction over them by virtue of Patent."

[b] Springfield withdrew in 1637 from the association, and the remaining towns—Windsor, Hartford, and Wethersfield—formed this voluntary compact or constitution on 14 January 1638/39.

Gouerment established according to God, to order and dispose of the affayres of the people at all seasons as occation shall require; doe therefore assotiate and conioyne our selues to be one Publike State or Comonwelth; and doe, for our selues and our Successors and such as shall be adioyned to vs att any tyme hereafter, enter into Combination and Confederation togather, to mayntayne and prsearue the liberty and purity of the gospell of our Lord Jesus wch we now prfesse, as also the disciplyne of the Churches, wch according to the truth of the said gospell is now practised amongst vs; As also in or Ciuell Affaires to be guided and gouerned according to such Lawes, Rules, Orders and decrees as shall be made, ordered & decreed, as followeth:—

1. It is Ordered, sentenced and decreed, that there shall be yerely two general Assemblies or Courts, the on the second thursday in Aprill, the other the second thursday in September, following; the first shall be called the Courte of Election, wherein shall be yerely Chosen fro tyme to tyme soe many Magestrats and other publike Officers shall be found requisite: Whereof one to be chosen Gouernor for the yeare ensueing and vntill another be chosen, and noe other Magistrate to be chosen for more then one yeare; pruided allwayes there be six chosen besids the Gouernour; wch being chosen and sworne according to an Oath recorded for that purpose shall haue power to administer iustice according to the Lawes here established, and for want thereof according to the rule of the word of God; wch choise shall be made by all that are admitted freemen and haue taken the Oath of Fidellity, and doe cohabitte within this Jurisdiction, (hauing beene admitted Inhabitants by the maior part of the Towne wherein they liue,ᶜ) or the mayor prte of such as shall be then prsent.

2. It is Ordered, sentensed and decreed, that the Election of the aforesaid Magestrats shall be on this manner: euery prson prsent and quallified for choyse shall bring in (to the prsons deputed to receaue the) one single papr wth the name of him written in yt whom he desires to haue Gouernour, and he that hath the greatest nuber of papers shall be Gouernor for that yeare. And the rest of the Magestrats or publike Officers to be chosen in this manner: The Secretary for the tyme being shall first read the names of all that are to be put to choise and then shall seuerally nominate them distinctly, and euery one that would haue the prson nominated to be chosen shall bring in one single paper written vppon, and he that would not haue him chosen shall bring in a blanke: and euery one that hath more written papers than blanks shall be a Magistrat for that yeare; wch papers shall be receaued and told by one or more that shall be then chosen by the court and sworne to be faythfull therein; but in case there should not be six chosen as aforesaid, besids the Gouernor, out of

ᶜ This clause has been interlined in a different handwriting, and at a more recent period.

those wch are nominated, then he or they wch haue the most written paprs shall be a Magestrate or Magestrats for the ensueing yeare, to make vp the aforesaid nuber.

3. It is Ordered, sentenced and decreed, that the Secretary shall not nominate any prson, nor shall any prson be chosen newly into the Magestracy wch was not prpownded in some Generall Courte before, to be nominated the next Election; and to that end yt shall be lawfull for ech of the Townes aforesaid by their deputyes to nominate any two who they conceaue fitte to be put to election; and the Court may ad so many more as they judge requisitt.

4. It is Ordered, sentenced and decreed that noe prson be chosen Gouernor aboue once in two yeares, and that the Gouernor be always a meber of some approved congregation, and formerly of the Magestracy wth in this Jurisdiction; and all the Magestrats Freemen of this Comonwelth: and that no Magestrate or other publike officer shall execute any prte of his or their Office before they are seuerally sworne, wch shall be done in the face of the Courte if they be prsent, and in case of absence by some deputed for that purpose.

5. It is Ordered, sentenced and decreed, that to the aforesaid Courte of Election the seuerall Townes shall send their deputyes, and when the Elections are ended they may prceed in any publike searuice as at other Courts. Also the other Generall Courte in September shall be for makeing of lawes, and any other publike occation, wch conserns the good of the Comonwelth.

6. It is Ordered, sentenced and decreed, that the Courner shall, ether by himselfe or by the secretary, send out sumons to the Constables of eur Towne for the cauleing of these two standing Courts, on month at lest before their seurall tymes: And also if the Gournor and the gretest prte of the Magestrats see cause vppon any spetiall occation to call a generall Courte, they may giue order to the secretary soe to doe wth in fowerteene dayes warneing; and if vrgent necessity so require, vppon a shorter notice, giueing sufficient grownds for yt to the deputyes when they meete, or els be questioned for the same; And if the Gournor and Mayor prte of Magestrats shall ether neglect or refuse to call the two Generall standing Courts or ether of the, as also at other tymes when the occasions of the Comonwelth require, the Freemen thereof, or the Mayor prte of them, shall petition to them soe to doe: if then yt be ether denyed or neglected the said Freemen or the Mayor prte of them shall haue power to giue order to the Constables of the seuerall Townes to doe the same, and so may meete togather, and chuse to themselues a Moderator, and may prceed to do any Acte of power, wch any other Generall Courte may.

7. It is Ordered, sentenced and decreed that after there are warrants giuen out for any of the said Generall Courts, the Constable or Constables of ech Towne shall forthwth give notice distinctly to the inhabitants of the

same, in some Publike Assembly or by goeing or sending fro howse to howse, that at a place and tyme by him or them lymited and sett, they meet and assemble the selues togather to elect and chuse certen deputyes to be att the Generall Courte then following to agitate the afayres of the comonwelth; wch said Deputyes shall be chosen by all that are admitted Inhabitants in the suerall Townes and haue taken the oath of fidellity; pruided that non be chosen a Deputy for any Generall Courte wch is not a Freeman of this Comonwelth.

The a-foresaid deputyes shall be chosen in manner following: euery person that is prsent and quallified as before exprssed, shall bring the names of such, written in seurrall papers as they desire to haue chosen for that Imployment, and these 3 or 4, more or lesse, being the nuber agreed on to be chosen for that tyme, that haue greatest nuber of papers written for the shall be deputyes for that Courte; whose names shall be endorsed on the backe side of the warrant and returned into the Courte, wth the Constable or Constables hand vnto the same.

8. It is Ordered, sentenced and decreed, that Wyndsor, Hartford and Wethersfield shall haue power, ech Towne, to send fower of their freemen as deputyes to euery Generall Courte; and whatsoeuer other Townes shall be hereafter added to this Jurisdiction, they shall send so many deputyes as the Courte shall judge meete, a resonable prportion to the nuber of Freemen that are in the said Townes being to be attended therein; wch deputyes shall have the power of the whole Towne to giue their voats and alowance to all such lawes and orders as may be for the publike good, and unto wch the said Townes are to be bownd.

9. It is ordered and decreed, that the deputyes thus chosen shall haue power and liberty to appoynt a tyme and a place of meeting togather before any Generall Courte to aduise and consult of all such things as may concerne the good of the publike, as also to examine their owne Elections, whether according to the order, and if they or the gretest prte of them find any election to be illegal they may seclud such for prsent fro their meeting, and returne the same and their resons to the Courte; and if yt proue true, the Courte may fyne the prty or prtyes so intruding and the Towne, if they see cause, and giue out a warrant to goe to a newe election in a legall way, either in whole or in prte. Also the said deputyes shall haue power to fyne any that shall be disorderly at their meetings, or for not coming in due tyme or place according to appoyntment; and they may returne the said fynes into the Courte if yt be refused to be paid, and the tresurer to take notice of yt, and to estreete or levy the same as he doth other fynes.

10. It is Ordered, sentenced and decreed, that euery Generall Courte, except such as through neglecte of the Fournor and the greatest prte of Magestrats the Freemen themselves doe call, shall consist of the Gouernor, or some one chosen to moderate the Court, and 4 other Magestrats at lest, wth the mayor prte of the deputyes of the seuerall Townes legally chosen;

and in case the Freemen or mayor prte of the through neglect or refusall of the Gouernor and mayor prte of the magestrats, shall call a Courte, that yt shall consist of the mayor prte of Freemen that are prsent or their deputyes, wth a Moderator chosen by the: In wch said Generall Courts shall consist the supreme power of the Comonwelth, and they shall haue power to make laws or repeale the, to graunt leuyes, to admitt of Freemen, dispose of lands vndisposed of, to seuerall Townes or prsons, and also shall haue power to call ether Courte or Magestrate or any other prson whatsoeuer into question for any misdemeanour, and may for just causes displace or deale otherwise according to the nature of the offence; and also may deale in any other matter that concerns the good of this comon welth, excepte election of Magestrats, wch shall be done by the whole boddy of Fremen: In wch Courte the Gouernour or Moderator shall haue power to order the Courte to giue liberty of spech, and silence vnceasonable and disorderly speakeings, to put all things to voate, and in case the vote be equall to haue the casting voice. But non of these Courts shall be adiorned or dissolued wthout the consent of the major prte of te Courte.

11. It is ordered, sentenced and decreed, that when any Generall Courte vppon the occations of the Comonwelth haue agreed vppon any sume or somes of mony to be leuyed vppon the seuerall Townes wthin this Jurisdiction, that a Comittee be chosen to sett out and appoynt wt shall be the prportion of euery Towne to pay of the said leuy, prvided the Comittees be made up of an equall nuber out of each Towne.

14th January, 1638, the 11 Orders abouesaid are voted.

Virginia Constitution of 1776

Promulgated in the same year as the American Declaration of Independence, the Virginia Constitution of 1776 was written in the same spirit. The idea of a bill of rights was first realized in this constitution.

Virginia's Constitution was one of the four colonial Constitutions actually in effect before the Declaration of Independence. Of the eight constitutions adopted by the various states in that year, it was by far the most important.

Authors of that document dominated the discussions that led to the framing of the U.S. Constitution in Philadelphia in 1787. The political philosophy of James Madison made this Virginian the Father of the Constitution; the Virginia Plan, presented by Edmund Randolph, formed the basis of the deliberations. The dissent of one of the Virginian delegates, George Mason, led to the subsequent adoption of the U.S. Bill of Rights in 1791.

Virginia had been the first permanent English settlement in North America, predating the Pilgrims' landing at Plymouth, Massachusetts, by fifteen years. The colony of Virginia had been settled under a grant of King James I in 1606. The Charter of 1606 represents the beginning of constitutionalism in America. The English Ordinance and Constitution of the Treasurer, Council, and Company in England for a Council of State and General Assembly, enacted in 1621, was the first document in history called a "constitution."

At the outbreak of the American Revolution, Virginia was without a popular government. On 15 May 1776 the provincial congress appointed "a committee to prepare a declaration of rights, and such a plan of government as will be most likely to maintain peace and order in this colony, and secure substantial and equal liberty to the people." The committee that was formed included, among others, Henry Lee, Patrick Henry, Edmund Randolph, Carter Braxton, James Madison, and George Mason; Mason played the leading role.

On 27 May 1776 an initital draft of the Declaration of Rights, prepared by George Mason, was read to the provincial congress. Two weeks of debate followed and unanimous approval was given on 12 June 1776. Only then did preparation of the Constitution itself begin.

Several plans of government were considered by the committee. Patrick Henry, with the advice of John Adams of Massachusetts, submitted the most democratic proposal. Carter Braxton, on the other hand, suggested an aristocratic model, based on the English parliamentary system. Thomas Jefferson, in Philadelphia for a meeting of the continental congress, was unable to present his draft in person, and it arrived too late for serious consideration. But of all the proposals, the one of George Mason—considered the father of the Virginia Constitution as well as its Declaration of Rights—received the most attention.

Even though the Virginia Declaration of Rights was the first manifestation and acknowledged progenitor of more than two centuries of bills of rights and declarations of human rights, it had several serious omissions. Absent was any provision on freedom of speech, assembly, or petition. It did not prohibit ex post facto legislation, bills of attainder, or the impairment of contracts. There was no definition of treason, no prohibition against suspension of habeas corpus, and no clear statement on due process of law. There was no reference to right to public trial, indictment by grand jury, or benefit of counsel.

Most significant was the statement that "all men are equally entitled to the free exercise of religion"—a message that became a fundamental part of all following constitutions. Freedom of the press was proclaimed to be "one of the great bulwarks of liberty." Popular sovereignty was recognized together with the right of "a majority of the community" to "alter or abolish" any existing government; all heredity offices were abolished.

The concept of inherent natural rights, set forth as the first principle of the Virginia Declaration of Rights influenced Thomas Jefferson in the formulation of the Declaration of Independence. The Virginia model guided other states in making bills of rights part of their constitutions.

The draftsmen of the Philadelphia Constitution deemed the entire document a guarantee of individual liberty and concluded that there was no need to spell out such rights in detail. Delegate Mason, however, objected to this omission and refused to sign the final draft on 17 September 1787. But the conclusion of the Founding Fathers was not the prevailing view in the new republic. Many of the states ratified the U.S. Constitution on the condition that a bill of rights be added. The first ten amendments, adopted in 1791, were the response to this demand. Author of the Bill of Rights, Virginian James Madison was heavily influenced by the Virginia Declaration of Rights. Such procedural guarantees as limitations on government searches and seizures, the right to confront an accuser, the right to bail, the right to a speedy trial, the right to a trial by jury, and the prohibition against cruel and unusual punishments all originated in the Virginia document.

Adhering to the basic principle of separation of powers, the Declaration of Rights also contained a provision "that the legislative and executive powers of the state should be separate and distinct from the judiciary; and that the members of the two first may be restrained from [acts of] oppression." This was the first time that a judiciary had been charged with the enforcement of human rights.

BRYAN McELVAINE
New Jersey Bar

THE CONSTITUTION OF VIRGINIA—1776*ᵃ

BILL OF RIGHTS

A declaration of rights made by the representatives of the good people of Virginia, assembled in full and free convention; which rights do pertain them and their posterity, as the basis and foundation of government.

Section 1. That all men are by nature equally free and independent,

The Federal and State Constitutions, Colonial Charters and Other Organic Laws of the States, Territories and Colonies Now or Heretofore Forming the United States of America. Vol. 1. Compiled and edited under the Act of Congress of 30 June 1906 by Francis Newton Thorpe (Washington, D.C.: Government Printing Office, 1909), 3812.

* Verified from "Ordinances Passed at a General Convention of Delegates and Representatives from the Several Counties and Corporations of Virginia," held at the capitol in the city of Williamsburg, on Monday, 6 May 1776. Reprinted by a Resolution of the House of Delegates, February 1816 (Richmond: Ritchie, Trueheart & Duval, Printers, 1816), 3–6.

Proceedings of the Convention of Delegates for the Counties and Corporations in the Colony of Virginia, held at Richmond Town, in the county of Henrico, on 20 March 1775. Reprinted by a Resolution of the House of Delegates, 24 February 1816 (Richmond: Ritchie, Trueheart & Duval, Printers, 1816), 1–8.

Proceedings of the Convention of Delegates for the Counties and Corporations in the Colony of Virginia, held at Richmond Town, in the county of Henrico, Monday, 17 July 1775. Reprinted by a Resolution of the House of Delegates, February 1816 (Richmond: Ritchie, Trueheart & Duval, Printers, 1816), 1–116.

Proceedings of the Convention of Delegates, held at the capitol in the city of Williamsburg, in the Colony of Virginia, Monday, 6 May 1776. Reprinted by a Resolution of the and have certain inherent rights, of which, when they enter into a state of society, they cannot, by any compact, deprive or divest their posterity; namely, the enjoyment of life and liberty, with the means of acquiring and possessing property, and pursuing and obtaining happiness and safety.

Section 2. That all power is vested in, and consequently derived from, the people; that magistrates are their trustees and servants, and at all times amenable to them.

Section 3. That government is, or ought to be, instituted for the common benefit, protection, and security of the people, nation, or community; of all the various modes and forms of government, that is best which is capable of producing the greatest degree of happiness and safety, and is most effectually secured against the danger of maladministration; and that, when any government shall be found inadequate or contrary to these purposes, a majority of the communty hath an indubitable, inalienable, and indefeasible right to reform, alter, or abolish it, in such manner as shall be judged most conducive to the public weal.

Section 4. That no man, or set of men, are entitled to exclusive or separate emoluments or privileges from the community, but in consideration of public services; which, not being descendible, neither ought the offices of magistrate, legislator, or judge to be herditary.

Section 5. That the legislative and executive powers of the State should be separate and distinct from the judiciary; and that the members of the two first may be restrained from oppression, by feeling and participating the burdens of the people, they should, at fixed periods, be reduced to a private station, return into that body from which they were originally taken, and the vacancies be supplied by frequent, certain, and regular elections, in which all, or any part of the former members, to be again eligible, or ineligible, as the laws shall direct.

Section 6. That elections of members to serve as representatives of the people, in assembly, ought to be free; and that all men, having sufficient evidence of permanent common interest with, and attachment to, the community, have the right of suffrage, and cannot be taxed or deprived of their property for public uses, without their own consent, or that of their rep-

---

House of Delegates, 24 February 1816 (Richmond: Ritchie, Trueheart & Duval, Printers, 1816) 1–86.

Ordinances passed at a General Convention of Delegates and Representatives, from the several Counties and Corporations of Virginia, held at the capitol in the city of Williamsburg, Monday, 6 May 1776. Reprinted by a Resolution of the House of Delegates, 24 February 1816 (Richmond: Ritchie, Trueheart & Duval, Printers, 1816), 19.

ª This Declaration of Rights was framed by a Convention, composed of forty-five members of the colonial house of burgesses, which met at Williamsburgh on 6 May 1776 and adopted this Declaration 12 June 1776.

This Constitution was framed by the convention that issued the Declaration of Rights, was adopted 29 June 1776, and was not submitted to the people for ratification.

resentatives so elected, nor bound by any law to which they have not, in like manner, assembled, for the public good.

Section 7. That all power of suspending laws, or the execution of laws, by any authority, without consent of the representatives of the people, is injurious to their rights, and ought not to be exercised.

Section 8. That in all capital or criminal prosecutions a man hath a right to demand the cause and nature of his accusation, to be confronted with the accusers and witnesses, to call for evidence in his favor, and to a speedy trial by an impartial jury of twelve men of his vicinage, without whose unanimous consent he cannot be found guilty; nor can he be compelled to give evidence against himself; that no man be deprived of his liberty, except by the law of the land or the judgment of his peers.

Section 9. That excessive bail ought not to be required, nor excessive fines imposed, nor cruel and unusual punishments inflicted.

Section 10. That general warrants, whereby an officer or messenger may be commanded to search suspected places without evidence of a fact committed, or to seize any person or persons not named, or whose offence is not particularly described and supported by evidence, are grievous and oppressive, and ought not to be granted.

Section 11. That in controversies respecting property, and in suits between man and man, the ancient trial by jury is preferable to any other, and ought to be held sacred.

Section 12. That the freedom of the press is one of the great bulwarks of liberty, and can never be restrained but by despotic governments.

Section 13. That a well-regulated militia, composed of the body of the people, trained to arms, is the proper, natural, and safe defence of a free State; that standing armies, in time of peace, should be avoided, as dangerous to liberty; and that in all cases the military should be under strict subordination to, and governed by, the civil power.

Section 14. That the people have a right to uniform government; and, therefore, that no government separate from, or independent of the government of Virginia, ought to be erected or established within the limits thereof.

Section 15. That no free government, or the blessings of liberty, can be preserved to any people, but by a firm adherence to justice, moderation, temperance, frugality, and virtue, and by frequent recurrence to fundamental principles.

Section 16. That religion, or the duty which we owe to our Creator, and the manner of discharging it, can be directed only by reason and conviction, not by force or violence; and therefore all men are equally entitled to the free exercise of religion, according to the dictates of conscience; and that it is the mutual duty of all to practise Christian forebearance, love, and charity towards each other.

THE CONSTITUTION OF FORM OF GOVERNMENT, AGREED TO AND RESOLVED UPON BY THE DELEGATES AND REPRESENTATIVES OF THE SEVERAL COUNTIES AND CORPORATIONS OF VIRGINIA

Whereas George the third, King of Great Britain and Ireland, and elector of Hanover, heretofore intrusted with the exercise of the kingly office in this government, hath endeavoured to prevent, the same into a detestable and insupportable tyranny, by putting his negative on laws the most wholesome and necessary for the public good:

By denying his Governors permission to pass laws of immediate and pressing importance, unless suspended in their operation for his assent, and, when so suppressed neglecting to attend to them for many years;

By refusing to pass certain other laws, unless the persons to be benefited by them would relinquish the inestimable right of representation in the legislature:

By dissolving legislative Assemblies repeatedly and continually for opposing with manly firmness his invasions of the rights of the people:

When dissolved, by refusing to call others for a long space of time thereby leaving the political system without any legislative head:

By endeavouring to prevent the population of our country, and, for that purpose, obstructing, the laws for the naturalization of foreigners:

By keeping among us, in times of peace, standing armies and ships of war:

By effecting to render the military independent of, and superior to, the civil power:

By combining with others to subject us to a foreign jurisdiction, giving his assent to their pretended acts of legislation:

For quartering large bodies of armed troops among us:

For cutting off our trade with all parts of the world:

For imposing taxes on us without our consent:

For depriving us of the benefits of trial by jury:

For transporting us beyond seas, to be tried for pretended offences:

For suspending our own legislatures, and declaring themselves invested with power to legislate for us in all cases whatsoever:

By plundering our seas, ravaging our coasts, burning our towns, and destroying the lives of our people:

By inciting insurrections of our fellow subjects, with the allurements of forfeiture and confiscation:

By prompting our negroes to rise in arms against us, those very negroes whom, by an inhuman use of his negative, he hath refused us permission to exclude by law:

By endeavouring to bring on the inhabitants of our frontiers the merciless Indian savages, whose known rule of warfare is an undistinguished destruction of all ages, sexes and conditions of existence:

By transporting, at this time, a large army of foreign mercenaries, to complete the works of death, desolation, and tyranny, already begun with circumstances of cruelty and perfidy unworthy the head of a civilized nation:

By answering our repeated petitions for redress with a repetition of injuries: And finally, by abandoning the helm of government and declaring us out of his allegiance and protection.

By which several acts of misrule, the government of this country, as formerly exercised under the crown of Great Britain, is TOTALLY DISSOLVED.

We therefore, the delegates and representatives of the good people of Virginia, having maturely considered the premises, and viewing with great concern the deplorable conditions to which this once happy country must be adopted, and in compliance with a recommendation of the General Congress, do ordain and declare the future form of government of Virginia to be as followeth:

The legislative, executive, and judiciary department, shall be separate and distinct, so that neither exercise the powers properly belonging to the other: nor shall any person exercise the powers of more than one of them, at the same time: except that the Justices of the County Courts shall be eligible to either House of Assembly.

The legislative shall be formed of two distinct branches, who, together, shall be a complete Legislature. They shall meet once, or oftener, every year, and shall be called, The General Assembly of Virginia. One of these shall be called, The House of Delegates, and consist of two Representatives, to be chosen for each county, and for the district of West-Augusta, annually, of such men as actually reside in, and are freeholders of the same, or duly qualified according to law, and also of one Delegate or Representative, to be chosen annually for the city of Williamsburg, and one for the borough of Norfolk, and a Representative for each of such other cities and boroughs, as may hereafter be allowed particular representation by the legislature; but when any city or borough shall so decrease, as that the number of persons, having right of suffrage therein, shall have been, for the space of seven years successively, less than half the number of votes in some one county in Virginia, such city or borough thenceforward shall cease to send a Delegate or Representative to the Assembly.

The other shall be called The Senate, and consist of twenty-four members, of whom thirteen shall constitute a House to proceed on business; for whose election, the different counties shall be divided into twenty-four districts; and each county of the respective district, at the time of the election of its Delegates, shall vote for one Senator, who is actually a resident and freeholder within the district, or duly qualified according to law, and is upwards of twenty-five years of age; and the Sheriffs of each county, within five days at farthest, after the last county election in the district, shall meet at some convenient place, and from the poll, so taken in their respective counties, return, as a Senator, the man who shall have the greatest number of votes in the whole district. To keep up this Assembly by rotation, the districts shall be equally divided into four classes and numbered by lot. At the end of one year after the general election, the six members, elected by the first division, shall be displaced, and the vacancies thereby occasioned supplied from such class or division, by new election, in the manner aforesaid. This rotation shall be applied to each division, according to its number, and continued in due order annually.

The right of suffrage in the election of members for both Houses shall remain as exercised at present; and each House shall choose its own Speaker, appoint its own officers, settle its own rules of proceeding, and direct writs of election, for the supplying intermediate vacancies.

All laws shall originate in the House of Delegates, to be approved of or rejected by the Senate, or to be amended, with consent of the House of Delegates; except money-bills, which in no instance shall be altered by the Senate, but wholly approved or rejected.

A Governor, or chief magistrate, shall be chosen annually by joint ballot of both Houses (to be taken in each House respectively) deposited in the conference room; the boxes examined jointly by a committee of each House, and the numbers severally reported to them, that the appointments may be entered (which shall be the mode of taking the joint ballot of both Houses, in all cases) who shall not continue in that office longer than three years successively, nor be eligible, until the expiration of four years after he shall have been out of that office. An adequate, but moderate salary shall be settled on him, during his continuance in office; and he shall, with the advice of a Council of State, exercise the executive powers of government, according to the laws of this Commonwealth; and shall not, under any pretence, exercise any power or prerogative, by virtue of any law, statute or custom of England. But he shall, with the advice of the Council of State, have the power of granting reprieves or pardons, except where the prosecution shall have been carried on by the House of Delegates, or the law shall otherwise particularly direct; in which cases, no reprieve or pardon shall be granted, but by resolve of the House of Delegates.

Either House of the General Assembly may adjourn themselves respectively. The Governor shall not prorogue or adjourn the Assembly, during their sitting, nor dissolve them at any time; but he shall, if necessary, either by advice of the Council of State, or on application of a majority of the House of Delegates, call them before the time to which they shall stand prorogued or adjourned.

A Privy Council, or Council of State, consisting of eight members, shall be chosen, by joint ballot of both Houses of Assembly, either from their own members of the people at large, to assist in the administration of government. They shall annually choose, out of their own members, a President, who, in case of death, inability, or absence of the Governor from the government, shall act as Lieutenant-Governor. Four members shall be sufficient to act, and their advice and proceedings shall be entered on record, and signed by the members present, (to any part whereof, any member may enter his dissent) to be laid before the General Assembly, when called for by them. This Council may appoint their own Clerk, who shall have a salary settled by law, and take an oath of secrecy, in such matters as he shall be directed by the board to conceal. A sum of money, appropriated to that purpose, shall be divided annually among the members, in proportion to their attendance; and they shall be incapable, during their continuance in office, of sitting in either House of Assembly. Two members shall be removed, by joint ballot of both Houses of Assembly, at the end of every three years, and be ineligible for the three next years. These vacancies, as well as those occasioned by death or incapacity, shall be supplied by new elections, in the same manner.

The Delegates for Virginia to the Continental Congress shall be chosen annually, or superseded in the mean time, by joint ballot of both Houses of Assembly.

The present militia officers shall be continued, and vacancies supplied by appointment of the Governor, with the advice of the Privy-Council, on recommendations from the respective County Courts; but the Governor and Council shall have a power of suspending any officer, and ordering a Court Martial, on complaint of misbehaviour or inability, or to supply vacancies of officers, happening when in actual service.

The Governor may embody the militia, with the advice of the Privy Council; and when embodied, shall alone have the direction of the militia, under the laws of the country.

The two Houses of Assembly shall, by joint ballot, appoint Judges of the Supreme Court of Appeals, and General Court, Judges in Chancery, Judges of Admiralty, Secretary, and the Attorney-General, to be commissioned by the Governor, and continue in office during good behaviour. In case of death, incapacity, or resignation, the Governor, with the advice of the Privy Council, shall appoint persons to succeed in office, to be approved or displaced by both Houses. These officers shall have fixed and adequate salaries, and, together with all others, holding lucrative offices, and all ministers of the gospel, of every denomination, be incapable of being elected members of either House of Assembly or the Privy Council.

The Governor, with the advice of the Privy Council, shall appoint Justice of the Peace for the counties; and in case of vacancies, or a necessity of increasing the number hereafter, such appointments to be made upon the recommendation of the respective County Courts. The present acting

Secretary in Virginia, and Clerks of all the County Courts, shall continue in office. In case of vacancies, either by death, incapacity, or resignation, a Secretary shall be appointed, as before directed; and the Clerks, by the respective Courts. The present and future Clerks shall hold their offices during good behaviour, to be judged of, and determined in the General Court. The Sheriffs and Coroners shall be nominated by the respective Courts, approved by the Governor, with the advice of the Privy Council, and commissioned by the Governor. The Justices shall appoint Constables; and all fees of the aforesaid officers be regulated by law.

The Governor, when he is out of office, and others, offending against the State, either by mal-administration, corruption, or other means, by which the safety of the State may be endangered, shall be impeachable by the House of Delegates. Such impeachment to be prosecuted by the Attorney-General, or such other person or persons, as the House may appoint in the General Court, according to the laws of the land. If found guilty, he or they shall be either forever disabled to hold any office under government, or be removed from such office pro tempore, or subjected to such pains or penalties as the laws shall direct.

If all or any of the Judges of the General Court should on good grounds (to be judged of by the House of Delegates) be accused of any of the crimes or offences above mentioned, such House of Delegates may, in like manner, impeach the Judge or Judges so accused, to be prosecuted in the Court of Appeals; and he or they, if found guilty, shall be punished in the same manner as is prescribed in the preceding clause.

Commissions and grants shall run, "In the name of the Commonwealth of Virginia," and bear test by the Governor, with the seal of the Commonwealth annexed. Writs shall run in the same manner, and bear test by the Clerks of the several Courts. Indictments shall conclude, "Against the peace and dignity of the Commonwealth."

A Treasurer shall be appointed annually, by joint ballot of both Houses.

All escheats, penalties, and forfeitures, heretofore going to the King, shall go to the Commonwealth, save only such as the Legislature may abolish, or otherwise provide for.

The territories, contained within the Charters, erecting the Colonies of Maryland, Pennsylvania, North and South Carolina, are hereby ceded, released, and forever confirmed, to the people of these Colonies respectively, with all the rights of property, jurisdiction and government, and all other rights whatsoever, which might, at any time heretofore, have been claimed by Virginia, except the free navigation and use of the rivers Patomaque and Pokomoke, with the property of the Virginia shores and strands, bordering on either of the said rivers, and all improvements, which have been, or shall be made thereon. The western and northern extent of Virginia shall, in all other respects, stand as fixed by the Charter of King James I in the year one thousand six hundred and nine, and by the public treaty of peace between the Courts of Britain and France, in the year one thousand seven hundred and sixty-three; unless by act of this Legislature, one or more governments be established westward of the Alleghany mountains. And no purchases of lands shall be made of the Indian natives, but on behalf of the public, by authority of the General Assembly.

In order to introduce this government, the Representatives of the people met in the convention shall choose a Governor and Privy Council, also such other officers directed to be chosen by both Houses as may be judged necessary to be immediately appointed. The Senate to be first chosen by the people, to continue until the last day of March next, and the other officers until the end of the succeeding session of Assembly. In case of vacancies, the Speaker of either House shall issue writs for new elections.

Pennsylvania Constitution
of 1776

The first Pennsylvania Constitution, adopted in September 1776, was among the first wave of Revolutionary state constitutions promulgated right after the Declaration of Independence. The Constitution was drafted by political outsiders, who seized control in an "internal revolution" that led Pennsylvania to join the independence movement and adopt major reforms to its prior colonial government. This Constitution, known as the most radical of the early state constitutions, remained in effect only until 1790. It did, however, greatly influence the writing of state constitutions from 1776–1786, primarily because of the interest in it among the delegates to the Continental Congress, which was located in Philadelphia during the Revolutionary years.[1]

Philadelphia became the national center of debate over state constitutions. The constitutions of other states, even draft versions, were published in Philadelphia newspapers and all of the well-known pamphlets on state constitutions were available in Philadelphia.[2] Also, the Pennsylvania Constitution and reports of controversy surrounding it, were widely disseminated throughout the states.

Tom Paine's *Common Sense* was published in Philadelphia on 9 January 1776. This pamphlet, together with its better-known call for independence, made a strong case for the establishment of republican governments in the states. These were to be "simple" governments, operating primarily through a unicameral legislature with a broad elective franchise. Because of a unique series of events in Pennsylvania, including opposition to independence and extra-legal activities by the colonial leaders, as well as their focus on national issues,[3] a group of Paine's relatively unknown associates found themselves with real power.[4] The elections for the Constitutional Convention of 1776 gave this same group, as well as many "plain countrymen," control of the constitutional convention.[5] Therefore, some of Paine's closest friends, including James Cannon, drafted Pennsylvania's "ultrademocratic" 1776 Constitution.[6] This Constitution was not submitted to the people for popular ratification.

The Pennsylvania Constitution of 1776 followed Paine's recommendation and established a "simple" government.[7] It contained a separate Declaration of Rights and Frame of Government. The Declaration of Rights was patterned after Virginia's, but Article XII contained among the broadest statements of speech and press freedom: "That the people have a right to freedom of speech, and of writing, and publishing their sentiments; therefore the freedom of the press ought not to be restrained." Interestingly, a number of other rights were protected under the Frame of Government (Sections 25, 26, 28, and 29).

Under the Frame of Government, legislative power was placed in a unicameral assembly (Section 2), with virtually no checks, such as veto power, given to the weak plural executive (headed by a "president") or the judiciary. Members of the Supreme Court could be removed by the legislature (Section 23). The Constitution contained provisions aimed at making the assembly accountable to the voters and an open, deliberative body (Sections 13–15). Such provisions were virtually unknown in other state constitutions of the period. The Constitution established the principle of apportionment by "the number of taxable inhabitants," with regular reapportionment (Section 17). Legislators served one-year terms and could serve no more than four out of seven years (Section 8). Bills had to be enacted by two successive legislative sessions before becoming law (Section 15). Property requirements for voting were eliminated, and the much broader requirement that a voter pay taxes was substituted in its place (Section 6). Finally, a Council of Censors was to be elected by the people every seven years to review legislative actions for conformity "to the principles of the constitution," and to propose necessary amendments (Section 47).[8]

From the moment it was implemented, controversy raged over whether the Constitution should be changed. This issue dominated most elections in Pennsylvania until a new constitution was substituted fourteen years later in 1790, as part of the overall movement leading to the federal Constitution.[9] This period generated a rich newspaper and pamphlet literature, with Paine contributing several newspaper articles in support of the Constitution.[10]

The political split in Pennsylvania, between what came to be known as the Constitutionalist and Republican "parties,"[11] reflected in a general sense the controversy that surrounded the new constitutions in other states.

Most of the same disputes about government structure such as unicameralism, executive veto power, suffrage, and elected as opposed to appointed officials occurred in the other states' constitutional conventions. Nowhere, however, were as many of these issues resolved in as radical a fashion as in Pennsylvania.

Historians and political scientists have universally concluded that the Pennsylvania Constitution of 1776 was a "failure."[12] However, this Constitution and Paine's *Common Sense* did provide both a popular and easily understood general theoretical basis for a simple, broad-based communitarian republic as well as a practical, enacted model reflecting the realization of the theory in written constitutional form.[13] These contributions, together with the political arguments supporting them, provided a basis for traditionally unrepresented people in other states to oppose "aristocratic" elements in the new state constitutions. The Pennsylvania example contributed to the "fiercely egalitarian and republican philosophy [that] swept the working classes."[14] Ideas similar to the prevailing ones in Pennsylvania in 1776 appeared in instructions, newspaper essays, pamphlets, and arguments in state constitutional conventions in all the other states. Vermont's Constitution of 1777 was patterned directly on Pennsylvania's.

The Pennsylvania Constitution of 1776 "marked the outer limits of the Revolution."[15] It was, therefore, influential during the founding decade, although this influence was not necessarily positive. Many established leaders were determined to avoid a constitution like Pennsylvania's. Even though the political philosophy and vision of government reflected in the Pennsylvania document did not prevail ultimately, it was at the time a well-known, if not widely adopted, alternative to the dominant political philosophy that prevailed in other states and in the U.S. Constitution. The early Pennsylvania ideas about the structure of government and the role of citizens in that government have now been largely forgotten.

ROBERT F. WILLIAMS
Associate Professor of Law
Rutgers University
Camden, New Jersey

NOTES

1. W. Adams, *The First American Constitutions: Republican Ideology and the Making of the State Constitutions in the Revolutionary Era* (Chapel Hill: University of North Carolina Press, 1980), 94 n. 111.
2. J. Paul Selsam, *The Pennsylvania Constitution of 1776: A Study in Revolutionary Democracy* (Philadelphia: University of Pennsylvania Press, 1936), 171; 172 n. 11; 173–75.

3. E. Foner, *Tom Paine and Revolutionary America* (New York: Oxford University Press, 1976), 108.
4. For a thorough review of these events, see R. Ryerson, "Republican Theory and Partisan Reality in Revolutionary Pennsylvania: Toward a New View of the Constitutionalist Party," in *Sovereign States in an Age of Uncertainty*. Edited by R. Hoffman and P. Albert (Charlottesville: University of Virginia Press, 1982), 95.
5. Foner, supra. n. 3, 131.
6. R. Ryerson, *The Revolution is Now Begun: The Radical Committees of Philadelphia, 1765–1776* (Philadelphia: University of Pennsylvania Press, 1978), 241. Historians agree that Pennsylvania's Constitution of 1776 was the most radical of the revolutionary state constitutions. See also Kenyon, "Constitutionalism in Revolutionary America," in *Nomos XX: Constitutionalism*. Edited by J. Pennock and J. Chapman (New York: New York University Press, 1979), 99.
7. A. O. Aldridge, *Thomas Paine's American Ideology* (Newark: University of Delaware Press, 1984), 69, observed: "Paine's proposals are simple, and they clearly favor the popular elements of society, particularly a provision for a single, democratically elected legislature, a provision which repelled men of property and conservative instincts."
8. See D. Lutz, *Popular Consent and Popular Control: Whig Political Theory in the Early State Constitutions* (Baton Rouge: Louisiana State University Press, 1980), which contains an entire chapter on the Council of Censors.
9. See generally Ryerson, supra note 4. See also Robert L. Brunhouse, *The Counter-Revolution in Pennsylvania 1776–1790* (Harrisburg, PA: Historical Commission, 1942), 17: "The Constitution became the center of the political warfare. . . ."
10. Foner, supra n. 3, 142–43.
11. Ryerson, supra n. 4; Selsam, supra n. 2; Brunhouse, supra n. 9.
12. See Ryerson, supra n. 4, 95–97, and materials cited 96, n. 1.
13. "The Pennsylvania constitution went farther than any other in putting the principles of the Revolution into specific constitutional form." M. Jensen, *The American Revolution Within America* (New York: New York University Press, 1974), 68. See also Robert Kelley, *The Cultural Pattern in American Politics: The First Century* (New York: Alfred A. Knopf, 1979), 77. ("Seen by many as the most radical in the colonies, the Pennsylvania government was designed to set an example of the democratic possibilities inherent in the new independence from royal rule.")
14. Kelley, supra n. 13, 75.
15. Ryerson, supra n. 4, 96.

CONSTITUTION OF PENNSYLVANIA—1776[*][a]

WHEREAS all government ought to be instituted and supported for the security and protection of the community as such, and to enable the individuals who compose it to enjoy their natural rights, and the other blessings which the Author of existence has bestowed upon man; and whenever these great ends of government are not obtained, the people have a right, by common consent to change it, and take such measures as to them may appear necessary to promote their safety and happiness. AND WHEREAS the inhabitants of this commonwealth have in consideration of protection only, heretofore acknowledged allegiance to the king of Great Britain; and the said king has not only withdrawn that protection, but commenced, and still continues to carry on, with unabated vengeance, a most cruel and unjust war against them, employing therein, not only the troops of Great Britain, but foreign mercenaries, savages and slaves, for the avowed purpose of reducing them to a total and abject submission to the despotic domination of the British parliament, with many other acts of tyranny, (more fully set forth in the declaration of Congress) whereby all allegiance and fealty to the said king and his successors, are dissolved and at an end, and all power and authority derived from him ceased in these colonies. AND WHEREAS it is absolutely necessary for the welfare and safety of the inhabitants of said colonies, that they be henceforth free

The Federal and State Constitutions, Colonial Charters and Other Organic Laws of the States, Territories and Colonies Now or Heretofore Forming the United States of America. Vol. 5. Compiled and edited under the Act of Congress of 30 June 1906 by Francis Newton Thorpe (Washington, Government Printing Office, 1909), 3081.

* The Proceedings Relative to Calling the Conventions 1776 and 1790, the Minutes of the Convention that formed the present Constitution of Pennsylvania, together with the Charter to William Penn, the Constitutions of 1776 and 1790, a view of the Proceedings of the Convention of 1776, and the Council of Censors (Harrisburg: John S. Wiestling, 1825), 384.

The Constitution of the Commonwealth of Pennsylvania, as established by the General Convention, carefully compared with the original, to which is added a Report of the Committee appointed to enquire, "Whether the Constitution has been preserved inviolate in every Part, and whether the legislative and executive branches of Government, have performed their duty as Guardians of the People, or assumed to themselves or exercised other or greater Powers, than they are entitled to by the Constitution."

As adopted by the Council of Censors, published by their Order (Philadelphia: Printed by Francis Bailey), 64.

a This constitution was framed by a convention (called in accordance with the expressed wish of the continental congress), which assembled in Philadelphia on 15 July 1776 and completed its labors 28 September 1776. This document was not submitted to the people for ratification.

and independent States, and that just, permanent, and proper forms of government exist in every part of them, derived from and founded on the authority of the people only, agreeable to the directions of the honourable American Congress. We, the representatives of the freemen of Pennsylvania, in general convention met, for the express purpose of framing such a government, confessing the goodness of the great Governor of the universe (who alone knows to what degree of earthly happiness mankind may attain, by perfecting the arts of government) in permitting the people of this State, by common consent, and without violence, deliberately to form for themselves such just rules as they shall think best, for governing their future society; and being fully convinced, that it is our indispensable duty to establish such original principles of government, as will best promote the general happiness of the people of this State, and their posterity, and provide for future improvements, without partiality for, or prejudice against any particular class, sect, or denomination of men whatever, do, by virtue of the authority vested in us by our constituents, ordain, declare, and establish, the following DECLARATION OF RIGHTS and FRAME OF GOVERNMENT, to be the CONSTITUTION of this commonwealth, and to remain in force therein for ever, unaltered, except in such articles as shall hereafter on experience be found to require improvement, and which shall by the same authority of the people, fairly delegated as this frame of government directs, be amended or improved for the more effectual obtaining and securing the great end and design of all government, herein before mentioned.

A DECLARATION OF THE RIGHTS OF THE INHABITANTS OF THE COMMONWEALTH, OR STATE OF PENNYLVANNIA

Article I. That all men are born equally free and independent, and have certain natural, inherent and inalienable rights, amongst which are, the enjoying and defending life and liberty, acquiring, possessing and protecting property, and pursuing and obtaining happiness and safety.

Article II. That all men have a natural and unalienable right to worship Almighty God according to the dictates of their own consciences and understanding: And that no man ought or of right can be compelled to attend any religious worship, or elect or support any place of worship, or maintain any ministry, contrary to, or against, his own free will and consent: Nor can any man, who acknowledges the being of a God, be justly deprived or abridged of any civil right as a citizen, on account of his religious sentiments or peculiar mode of religious worship: And that no authority can or ought to be vested in, or assumed by any power whatever, that shall in any case interfere with, or in any manner control, the right of conscience in the free exercise of religious worship.

Article III. That the people of this State have the sole, exclusive and inherent right of governing and regulating the internal police of the same.

Article IV. That all power being originally inherent in, and consequently derived from, the people; therefore all officers of government, whether legislative or executive, are their trustees and servants, and at all times accountable to them.

Article V. That government is, or ought to be, instituted for the common benefit, protection and security of the people, nation or community; and not for the particular emolument or advantage of any single man, family, or set of men, who are a part only of that community; And that the community hath an indubitable, unalienable and indefeasible right to reform, alter, or abolish government in such manner as shall be by that community judged most conducive to the public weal.

Article VI. That those who are employed in the legislative and executive business of the State, may be restrained from oppression, the people have a right, at such periods as they may think proper, to reduce their public officers to a private station, and supply the vacancies by certain and regular elections.

Article VII. That all elections ought to be free; and that all free men having a sufficient evident common interest with, and attachment to the community, have a right to elect officers, or to be elected into office.

Article VIII. That every member of society hath a right to be protected in the enjoyment of life, liberty and property, and therefore is bound to contribute his proportion towards the expense of that protection, and yield his personal service when necessary, or an equivalent thereto: But no part of a man's property can be justly taken from him, or applied to public uses, without his own consent, or that of his legal representatives: Nor can any man who is conscientiously scrupulous of bearing arms, be justly compelled thereto, if he will pay such equivalent, nor are the people bound by any laws, but such as they have in like manner assented to, for their common good.

Article IX. That in all prosecutions for criminal offences, a man hath a right to be heard by himself and his council, to demand the cause and nature of his accusation, to be confronted with the witnesses, to call for evidence in his favour, and a speedy public trial, by an impartial jury of the country, without the unanimous consent of which jury he cannot be found guilty; nor can he be compelled to give evidence against himself; nor can any man be justly deprived of his liberty except by the laws of the land, or the judgment of his peers.

Article X. That the people have a right to hold themselves, their houses, papers, and possessions free from search and seizure, and therefore warrants without oaths or affirmations first made, affording a sufficient foundation for them, and whereby any officer or messenger may be commanded or required to search suspected places, or to seize any person or persons, his or their property, not particularly described, are contrary to that right, and ought not to be granted.

Article XI. That in controversies respecting property, and in suits between man and man, the parties have a right to trial by jury, which ought to be held sacred.

Article XII. That the people have a right to freedom of speech, and of writing, and publishing their sentiments; therefore the freedom of the press ought not to be restrained.

Article XIII. That the people have a right to bear arms for the defence of themselves and the state; and as standing armies in the time of peace are dangerous to liberty, they ought not to be kept up; And that the military should be kept under strict subordination to, and governed by, the civil power.

Article XIV. That a frequent recurrence to fundamental principles, and a firm adherence to justice, moderation, temperance, industry, and frugality are absolutely necessary to preserve the blessings of liberty, and keep a government free: The people ought therefore to pay particular attention to these points in the choice of officers and representatives, and have a right to exact a due and constant regard to them, from their legislatures and magistrates, in the making and executing such laws as are necessary for the good government of the state.

Article XV. that all men have a natural inherent right to migrate from one state to another that will receive them, or to form a new state in vacant countries, or in such countries as they can purchase, whenever they think that thereby they may promote their own happiness.

Article XVI. That the people have a right to assemble together, to consult for their common good, to instruct their representatives, and to apply to the legislature for redress of grievances, by address, petition, or remonstrance.

PLAN OF FRAME OF GOVERNMENT FOR THE COMMONWEALTH OR STATE OF PENNSYLVANIA

Section 1. The commonwealth or state of Pennsylvania shall be governed thereafter by an assembly of the representatives of the freemen of the same, and a president and council, in manner and form following—

Section 2. The supreme legislative power shall be vested in a house of representatives of the freemen of the commonwealth or state of Pennsylvania.

Section 3. The supreme executive power shall be vested in a president and council.

Section 4. Courts of justice shall be established in the city of Philadelphia, and in every county of this state.

Section 5. The freemen of this commonwealth and their sons shall be trained and armed for its defence assembly shall be law direct, preserving always to the people the right of choosing their colonels and all commissioned officers under that rank, in such manner and as often as by the said laws shall be directed.

Section 6. Every freemen of the full age of twenty-one years, having resided in this state for the space of one whole year next before the day of election for representatives, and paid public taxes during that time, shall enjoy the right of an elector: Provided always, that sons of freeholders of the age of twenty-one years shall be entitled to vote although they have not paid taxes.

Section 7. The house of representatives of the freemen of this commonwealth shall consist of persons most noted for wisdom and virtue, to be chosen by the freemen of every city and county of this commonwealth respectively. And no person shall be elected unless he has resided in the city or county for which he shall be chosen two years immediately before the said election; nor shall any member, while he continues such, hold any other office, except in the militia.

Section 8. No person shall be capable of being elected a member to serve in the house of representatives of the freemen of this commonwealth more than four years in seven.

Section 9. The members of the house of representatives shall be chosen annually by ballot, by the freemen of the commonwealth, on the second Tuesday in October forever, (except this present year,) and shall meet on the fourth Monday of the same month, and shall be stiled, The general assembly of the representatives of the freemen of Pennsylvania, and shall have power to choose their speaker, the treasurer of the state, and their other officers; sit on their own adjournments; prepare bills and enact them into laws; judge of the elections and qualifications of their own members; they may expel a member, but not a second time for the same cause; they may administer oaths or affirmations on examination of witnesses; redress grievances; impeach state criminals; grant charters of incorporation; constitute towns, boroughs, cities, and counties; and shall have all other powers necessary for the legislature of a free state or commonwealth: But they shall have no power to add to, alter, abolish, or infringe any part of this constitution.

Section 10. A quorum of the house of representatives shall consist of two-thirds of the whole number of members elected; and having met and chosen their speaker, shall each of them before they proceed to business take and subscribe, as well the oath or affirmation of fidelity and allegiance hereinafter directed, as the following oath or affirmation, viz:

I _____ do swear (or affirm) that as a member of this assembly, I will not propose or assent to any bill, vote, or resolution, which shall appear to me injurious to the people; nor do or consent to any act or thing whatever, that shall have a tendency to lessen or abridge their rights and privileges, as declared in the constitution of this state; but will in all things conduct myself as a faithful honest representative and guardian of the people, according to the best of my judgment and abilities.

And each member, before he takes his seat, shall make and subscribe the following declaration, viz:

I do believe in one God, the creator and governor of the universe, the rewarder of the good and the punisher of the wicked. And I do acknowledge the Scriptures of the Old and New Testament to be given by Divine inspiration.

And no further or other religious test shall ever hereafter be required of any civil officer or magistrate in this State.

Section 11. Delegates to represent this state in congress shall be chosen by ballot by the future general assembly at their first meeting, and annually forever afterwards, as long as such representation shall be necessary. Any delegate may be superseded at any time, by the general assembly appointing another in his stead. No man shall sit in congress longer than two years successively, nor be capable of re-election for three years afterwards: and no person who holds any office in the gift of the congress shall hereafter be elected to represent this commonwealth in congress.

Section 12. If any city or cities, county or counties shall neglect or refuse to elect and send representatives to the general assembly, two-thirds of the members from the cities or counties that do elect and send representatives, provided they be a majority of the cities and counties of the whole state, when met, shall have all the powers of the general assembly, as fully and amply as if the whole were present.

Section 13. The doors of the house in which the representatives of the freemen of this state shall sit in general assembly, shall be and remain open for the admission of all persons who behave decently, except only when the welfare of this state may require the doors to be shut.

Section 14. The votes and proceedings of the general assembly shall be printed weekly during their sitting, with the yeas and nays, on any question, vote or resolution, where any two members require it, except when the vote is taken by ballot; and when the yeas and nays are so taken every member shall have a right to insert the reasons of his vote upon the minutes, if he desires it.

Section 15. To the end that laws before they are enacted may be more maturely considered, and the inconvenience of hasty determinations as much as possible prevented, all bills of public nature shall be printed for the consideration of the people, before they are read in general assembly the last time for debate and amendment; and, except on occasions of sudden necessity, shall not be passed into laws until the next session of assembly; and for the more perfect satisfaction of the public, the reasons and motives for making such laws shall be fully and clearly expressed in the preambles.

Section 16. The stile of the laws of this commonwealth shall be, "Be it enacted, and it is hereby enacted by the representatives of the freemen of the commonwealth of Pennsylvania in general assembly met, and by the authority of the same." And the general assembly shall affix their seal to every bill, as soon as it is enacted into a law, which seal shall be kept by the assembly, and shall be called, The seal of the laws of Pennsylvania, and shall not be used for any other purpose.

Section 17. The city of Philadelphia and each county of this commonwealth respectively, shall on the first Tuesday of November in this present year, and on the second Tuesday of October annually for the two next succeeding years, viz. the year one thousand seven hundred and seventy-seven, and the year one thousand seven hundred and seventy-eight, choose six persons to represent them in general assembly. But as representation in proportion to the number of taxable inhabitants is the only principle which can at all times secure liberty, and make the voice of a majority of the people the law of the land; therefore the general assembly shall cause complete lists of the taxable inhabitants in the city and each county in the commonwealth respectively, to be taken and returned to them, on or before the last meeting of the assembly elected in the year one thousand seven hundred and seventy-eight, who shall appoint a representation to each, in proportion to the number of taxables in such returns; which representation shall continue for the next seven years afterwards at the end of which, a new return of the taxable inhabitants shall be made, and a representation agreeable thereto appointed by the said assembly, and so on septennially forever. The wages of the representatives in general assembly, and all other state charges shall be paid out of the state treasury.

Section 18. In order that the freemen of this commonwealth may enjoy the benefit of election as equally as may be until the representation shall commence, as directed in the foregoing section, each county at its own choice may be divided into districts, hold elections therein, and elect their representatives in the county, and their other elective officers, as shall be hereafter regulated by the general assembly of this state. And no inhabitant of this state shall have more than one annual vote at the general election for representatives in assembly.

Section 19. For the present the supreme executive council of this state shall consist of twelve persons chosen in the following manner: The freeman of the city of Philadlephia, and of the counties of Philadelphia, Chester, and Bucks, respectively, shall choose by ballot one person for the city, and one for each county aforesaid, to serve for three years and no longer, at the time and place for electing representatives in general assembly. The freeman of the counties of Lancaster, York, Cumberland, and Berks, shall, in like manner elect one person for each county respectively, to serve as counsellors for two years and no longer. And the counties of Northampton, Bedford, Northumberland and Westmoreland, respectively, shall, in like manner, elect one person for each county, to serve as counsellors for one year, and no longer. And at the expiration of the time for which each counsellor was chosen to serve, the freemen of the city of Philadelphia, and of the several counties in this state, respectively, shall elect one person to serve as counsellor for three years and no longer; and so on every third year forever. By this mode of election and continual rotation, more men will be trained to public business, there will in every subsequent year be found in the council a number of persons acquainted with the proceedings of the foregoing years, whereby the business will be more consistently conducted, and moreover the danger of establishing an inconvenient aristocracy will be effectually prevented. All vacancies in the council that may happen by death, resignation, or otherwise, shall be filled at the next general election for representatives in general assembly, unless a particular election for that purpose shall be sooner appointed by the president and council. No member of the general assembly or delegate in congress, shall be chosen a member of the council. The president and vice-president shall be chosen annually by the joint ballot of the general assembly and council, of the members of the council. Any person having served as a counsellor for three successive years, shall be incapable of holding that office for four years afterwards. Every member of the council shall be a justice of the peace for the whole commonwealth, by virtue of his office.

In case new additional counties shall hereafter be erected in this state, such county or counties shall elect a counsellor, and such county or counties shall be annexed to the next neighbouring counties, and shall take rotation with such counties.

The council shall meet annually, at the same time and place with the general assembly.

The treasurer of the state, trustees of the loan office, naval officers, collectors of customs or excise, judge of the admiralty, attornies general, sheriffs, and prothonotaries, shall not be capable of a seat in the general assembly, executive council, or continental congress.

Section 20. The president, and in his absence the vice-president, with the council, five of whom shall be a quorum, shall have power to appoint and commission judges, naval officers, judge of the admiralty, attorney general and all other officers, civil and military, except such as are chosen by the general assembly or the people, agreeable to this frame of government, and the laws that may be made hereafter; and shall supply every vacancy in any office, occasioned by death, resignation, removal or disqualification, until the office can be filled in the time and manner directed by law or this constitution. They are to correspond with other states, and transact business with the officers of government, civil and military; and to prepare such business as may appear to them necessary to lay before the general assembly. They shall sit as judges, to hear and determine on impeachments, taking to their assistance for advice only, the justices of the supreme court. And shall have power to grant pardons, and remit fines, in all cases whatsoever, except in cases of impeachment; and in cases of treason and murder, shall have power to grant reprieves, but not to pardon, until the end of the next sessions of assembly; but there shall be no remission or mitigation of punishments on impeachments, except by act of the legislature; they are also to take care that the laws be faithfully executed; they are to expedite the execution of such measures as may be resolved upon by the general assembly; and they may draw upon the treasury for such sums as shall be appropriated by the house: They may also lay embargoes, or prohibit the exportation of any commodity, for any time, not exceeding thirty days, in the recess of the house only: They may grant such licences, as shall be directed by law, and shall have power to call together the general assembly when necessary, before the day to which they shall stand adjourned. The president shall be commander in chief of the forces of the state, but shall not command in person, except advised thereto by the council, and then only so long as they shall approve thereof. The president and council shall have a secretary, and keep fair books of their proceedings, wherein any counsellor may enter his dissent, with his reasons in support of it.

Section 21. All commissions shall be in the name, and by the authority of the freemen of the commonwealth of Pennsylvania, sealed with the state seal, signed by the president or vice-president, and attested by the secretary; which seal shall be kept by the council.

Section 22. Every officer of state, whether judicial or executive, shall be liable to be impeached by the general assembly, either when in office, or after his resignation or removal for mal-administration: All impeachments shall be before the president or vice-president and council, who shall hear and determine the same.

Section 23. The judges of the supreme court of judicature shall have fixed salaries, be commissioned for seven years only, though capable of re-appointment at the end of that term, but removable for misbehaviour at any time by the general assembly; they shall not be allowed to sit as members in the continental congress, executive council, or general assembly, nor to hold any other office civil or military, nor to take or receive fees or perquisites of any kind.

Section 24. The supreme court, and the several courts of common pleas of this commonwealth, shall, besides the powers usually exercised by such courts, have the powers of a court of chancery, so far as relates to the perpetuating testimony, obtaining evidence from places not within this state, and the care of the persons and estates of those who are non compos mentis, and such other powers as may be found necessary by future general assemblies, not inconsistent with this constitution.

Section 25. Trials shall be on jury as heretofore: And it is recommended to the legislature of this state, to provide by law against every corruption or partiality in the choice, return, or appointment of juries.

Section 26. Courts of sessions, common pleas, and orphans courts shall be held quarterly in each city and county; and the legislature shall have power to establish all such other courts as they may judge for the good of the inhabitants of the state. All courts shall be open, and justice shall be impartially administered without corruption or unnecessary delay: All their officers shall be paid an adequate but moderate compensation for their services; And if any officer shall take greater or other fees than the law allows him, either directly or indirectly, it shall ever after disqualify him from holding any office in this state.

Section 27. All prosecutions shall commence in the name and by the authority of the freeman of the commonwealth of Pennsylvania; and all indictments shall conclude with these words, "Against the peace and dignity of the same." The style of all process hereafter in this state shall be, The commonwealth of Pennsylvania.

Section 28. The person of a debtor, where there is not a strong presumption of fraud, shall not be continued in prison, after delivering up, bona fide, all his estate real and personal, for the use of his creditors, in such manner as shall be hereafter regulated by law. All prisoners shall be bailable by sufficient sureties, unless for capital offences, when the proof is evidence, or presumption great.

Section 29. Excessive bail shall not be exacted for bailable offences: And all fines shall be moderate.

Section 30. Justices of the peace shall be elected by the freeholders of each city and county respectively, that is to say, two or more persons may be chosen for each ward, township, or district, as the law shall hereafter direct: And their names shall be returned to the president in council, who shall commissionate one or more of them for each ward, township, or district so returning, for seven years, removable for misconduct by the general assembly. But if any city or county, ward, township, or district in this commonwealth, shall hereafter incline to change the manner of appointing their justices of the peace as settled in this article, the general assembly may make laws to regulate the same, agreeable to the desire of a majority of the freholders of the city or county, ward, township, or district so applying. No justice of the peace shall sit in the general assembly unless he first resigns his commission; nor shall he be allowed to take any fees, nor any salary allowance, except such as the future legislature may grant.

Section 31. Sheriffs and coroners shall be elected annually in each city or county, by the freemen; that is to say, two persons for each office, one of whom for each, is to be commissioned by the president in council. No person shall continue in the office of sheriff more than three successive years, or be capable of being again elected during four years afterwards. The election shall be held at the same time and place appointed for the election of representatives: And the commissioners and assessors, and other officers chosen by the people, shall also be then and there elected, as has been usual heretofore, until altered or otherwise regulated by the future legislature of this state.

Section 32. All elections, whether by the people or in general assembly, shall be by ballot, free and voluntary: And any elector, who shall receive any gift or reward for his vote, in meat, drink, monies, or otherwise, shall forfeit his right to elect for that time, and suffer such other penalties as future laws shall direct. And any persons who shall directly or indirectly give, promise, or bestow any such rewards to be elected, shall be thereby rendered incapable to serve for the ensuing year.

Section 33. All fees, licence money, fines and forfeitures heretofore granted, or paid to the governor, or his deputies for the support of government, shall hereafter be paid into the public treasury, unless altered or abolished by the future legislature.

Section 34. A register's office for the probate of wills and granting letters of administration, and an office for the recording of deeds, shall be kept in each city and county: The officers to be appointed by the general assembly, removable at their pleasure, and to be commissioned by the president in council.

Section 35. The printing presses shall be free to every person who undertakes to examine the proceedings of the legislature, or any part of government.

Section 36. As every freeman to preserve his independence, (if without a sufficient estate) ought to have some profession, calling, trade or farm, whereby he may honestly subsist, there can be no necessity for, nor use in establishing offices of profit, the usual effects of which are dependence and servility unbecoming freemen, in the possessors and expectants; faction, contention, corruption, and disorder among the peoople. But if any man is called into public service, to the prejudice of his private affairs, he has a right to a reasonable compensation: And whenever an office, through increase of fees or otherwise, becomes so profitable as to occasion many to apply for it, the profits ought to be lessened by the legislature.

Section 37. The future legislature of this state, shall regulate intails in such a manner as to prevent perpetuities.

Section 38. The penal laws as heretofore used shall be reformed by the legislature of the state, as soon as may be, and punishments made in some cases less sanguinary, and in general more proportionate to the crimes.

Section 39. To deter more effectually from the commission of crimes, by continued visible punishments of long duration, and to make sanguinary punishments less necessary; houses ought to be provided for punishing by hard labour, those who shall be convicted of crimes not capital; wherein the criminals shall be imployed for the benefit of the public, or for reparation of injuries done to private persons: And all persons at proper times shall be admitted to see the prisoners at their labour.

Section 40. Every officer, whether judicial, executive or military, in authority under this commonwealth, shall take the following oath or affirmation of allegiance, and general oath of office before he enters on the execution of his office.

THE OATH OR AFFIRMATION OF ALLEGIANCE

I _____ do swear (or affirm) that I will be true and faithful to the commonwealth of Pennsylvania: And that I will not directly or indirectly do any act or thing prejudicial or injurious to the constitution or government thereof, as established by the convention.

THE OATH OR AFFIRMATION OF OFFICE

I _____ do swear (or affirm) that I will faithfully execute the office of _____ for the _____ of_____ and will do equal right and justice to all men, to the best of my judgment and abilities, according to law.

Section 41. No public tax, custom or contribution shall be imposed upon, or paid by the people of this state, except by a law for that purpose: And before any law be made for raising it, the purpose for which any tax is to be raised ought to appear clearly to the legislature to be of more service to the community than the money would be, if not collected; which being well observed, taxes can never be burdens.

Section 42. Every foreigner of good character who comes to settle in this state, having first taken an oath or affirmation of allegiance to the same, may purchase, or by other just means acquire, hold, and transfer land or other real estate; and after one year's residence, shall be deemed a free denizen thereof, and entitled to all the rights of a natural born subject of this state, except that he shall not be capable of being elected a representative until after two years residence.

Section 43. The inhabitants of this state shall have liberty to fowl and hunt in seasonable time on the lands they hold, and on all other lands therein not enclosed; and in like manner to fish in all boatable waters; and others not private property.

Section 44. A school or schools shall be established in each county by the legislature, for the convenient instruction of youth, with such salaries to the masters paid by the public, as may enable them to instruct youth at low prices: And all useful learning shall be duly encouraged and promoted in one or more universities.

Section 45. Laws for the encouragement of virtue, and prevention of vice and immorality, shall be made and constantly kept in force, and provision shall be made for their due execution: And all religious societies or bodies of men heretofore united or incorporated for the advancement of religion or learning, or for other pious and charitable purposes, shall be encouraged and protected in the enjoyment of the privileges, immunities and estates which they were accustomed to enjoy, or could of right have enjoyed, under the laws and former constitution of this state.

Section 46. The declaration of rights is hereby declared to be a part of the constitution of this commonwealth, and ought never to be violated on any pretence whatever.

Section 47. In order that the freedom of the commonwealth may be preserved inviolate forever, there shall be chosen by ballot by the freemen in each city and county respectively, on the second Tuesday in October, in the year one thousand seven hundred and eighty-three, and on the second Tuesday in October, in every seventh year thereafter, two persons in each city and county of this state, to be called the COUNCIL OF CENSORS; who shall meet together on the second Monday of November next ensuing their election; the majority of whom shall be a quorum in every case, except as to calling a convention, in which two-thirds of the whole number elected shall agree: And whose duty it shall be to enquire whether the constitution has been preserved inviolate in every part; and whether the legislative and executive branches of government have performed their duty as guardians of the people, or assumed to themselves, or exercised other or greater powers than they are entitled to by the constitution: They are also to enquire whether the public taxes have been justly laid and collected in all parts of this commonwealth, in what manner the public monies have been disposed of, and whether the laws have been duly executed. For these purposes they shall have power to send for persons, papers, and records; they shall have authority to pass public censures, to order impeachments, and to recommend to the legislature the repealing of such laws as appear to them to have been enacted contrary to the principles of the constitution. These powers they shall continue to have, for and during the space of one year from the day of their election and no longer: The said council of censors shall also have power to call a convention, to meet within two years after their sitting, if there appear to them an absolute necessity of amending any article of the constitution which may be defective, explaining such as may be thought not clearly expressed, and of adding such as are necessary for the preservation of the rights and happiness of the people: But the articles to be amended, and the amendments proposed, and such articles as are proposed to be added or abolished, shall be promulgated at least six months before the day appointed for the election of such convention, for the previous consideration of the people, that they may have an opportunity of instructing their delegates on the subject.

Passed in Convention the 28th day of September, 1776, and signed by their order.

BENJ. FRANKLIN, Prest.

Massachusetts Constitution
of 1780

Historians[1] and political scientists[2] have identified two major "waves" of forming state constitutions during the founding decade. The key document in the first wave was the Pennsylvania Constitution of 1776; the Massachusetts Constitution of 1780 was the central feature of the second wave. According to Donald Lutz, the latter Constitution

> was the most important one written between 1776 and 1789 because it embodied the Whig theory of republican government, which came to dominate state level politics; the 1776 Pennsylvania Constitution was the second most important because it embodied the strongest alternative.[3]

Almost immediately after Tom Paine's *Common Sense* was published in 1776, John Adams of Massachusetts published *Thoughts on Government* as, among other objectives, a response to Paine.[4] Adams set forth an alternative, more traditional vision than Paine's of how the new state governments should be constituted. He proposed a model based on "balanced government," or separation of powers, to which bicameralism and executive power was central. He also advocated property requirements for office holding and voting.

Historian Elisha Douglass concluded that Adams's *Thoughts on Government* was probably the "paramount guide" for forming a constitution in at least five states.[5] "When it is considered that the state constitutions, particularly that of Massachusetts—were the greatest single influence on the Federal Constitution, the full importance of the pamphlet should be evident."[6]

The Massachusetts Constitution of 1780 was adopted toward the end of the Revolutionary War and, by contrast to the experience in Pennsylvania, was not related to the basic issue of whether the colony should declare independence. Also, unlike most of the other states,[7] the processes leading to the Massachusetts Constitution of 1780 were very well documented[8]—primarily because of the influence of local governments in the New England political structure at that time.[9] The responses of the towns in Massachusetts between 1776 and 1780 "on constitutional issues comprise the most important single source for any study of democratic ideas among the common people during the revolutionary period."[10] Willi Paul Adams has asserted that the intensity and sophistication of the public debate on Republican Constitutionalism in Massachusetts in 1778 rivaled that from 1787–1789 on the national level.[11]

As British authority continued to decline, in varying degrees, in the colonies during the year before the Declaration of Independence, a number of the colonies turned to the First Continental Congress for advice on developing alternative civil governments. Massachusetts was the first to seek advice on 16 May 1775, apparently as part of John Adams's plan to force a declaration of independence.[12] The Massachusetts request indicated that it could either draw up its own constitution or adopt one drafted by the Continental Congress.[13] Although several well-known Revolutionary leaders supported the idea of a "model constitution"[14] for the states, it was apparently not seriously considered by the Congress. Massachusetts was advised to modify its Charter of 1691 by eliminating the royal governor and lieutenant governor, holding elections, and proceeding with self-government.[15] Massachusetts took these measures temporarily, but they were surrounded by controversy.

As one historian has observed, in Massachusetts

> the overriding issue of the 1770s was the question of a state constitution. From the very moment the reins of government were taken up by a provincial congress in the fall of 1774, conservatives feared the unchecked democracy it seemed to represent, eagerly sought the reinstatement of the constitution of 1691 which gave coequal powers to a council and a house of representatives, and denounced the various reformist demands for a unicameral legislature and no governor.[16]

The more radical faction, on the other hand, argued that as a result of independence, the colony had returned to a "state of nature." They challenged the authority of the Continental Congress to dictate the resumption of the Charter of 1691.

The radicals fought not only for their views concerning the *content* of the state constitution but also for the proper *process* of adopting one. For example, the Pittsfield Petition of 29 May 1776 reasserted that Massachusetts had reverted to a state of nature, that the legislative power must conform to a higher source of law, and that the only legitimate source of a state constitution was the people themselves.[17]

The pressure for a legitimate state constitution led to the unsuccessful, legislatively proposed Massachusetts Constitution of 1778.[18] Ultimately, continuing pressure led to the famous Massachusetts Constitution of 1780, the oldest American Constitution, bearing the personal mark of John Adams.[19] Along the way, opposition to the substantive proposals of the radicals generated the Essex Result of 1778, "one of the most succinct statements of a conservative ideal in a free republic. . . ."[20] Although they lost their substantive arguments,[21] in the end, the radicals' process arguments prevailed in Massachusetts—helping to set one of the precedents leading to the Federal Constitutional Convention.[22]

The Massachusetts Constitution of 1780 was the first to be drafted by an elected convention and submitted to the people for popular ratification. It was separated into two parts: The Declaration of Rights and the Frame of Government. The Declaration of Rights was in many ways similar to those that came earlier, particularly in Virginia. However, this Constitution contained several complicated provisions on both religious freedom (Article II) and public support of religion (Article III).[23] Article XXX explicitly mandated separation of powers, "to the end it may be a government of laws, and not of men."[24] Other rights appeared in the Frame of Government (Chapter VI, Article VII).

The Frame of Government created a bicameral legislature consisting of a Senate and House of Representatives, "each of which shall have a negative on the other" (Chapter I, Section I, Article I). The governor was given the veto power, subject to being overriden by a two-thirds vote in the legislature (Chapter I, Section I, Article 2). Property requirements were imposed for voting for senators (Chapter I, Section 2, Article II), representatives (Chapter I, Section III, Article IV), and governor (Chapter II, Section I, Article III) as well as for serving as senators (Chapter I, Section II, Article V), representatives (Chapter I, Section III, Article III), and governor (Chapter II, Section I, Article II). The governor was to be elected annually.

Judges served during good behavior (Chapter III, Article I), and advisory opinions could be requested from the Supreme Judicial Court by either branch of the legislature, the governor, and council (Chapter III, Article II). Finally, the Constitution recognized Harvard College (Chapter V, Section I, Article I), and encouraged and mandated support of education (Chapter V, Section 2).

In 1914, the constitutional scholar Andrew McLaughlin, serving as president of the American Historical Association, said:

If I were called upon to select a single fact or enterprise which more nearly than any other single thing embraced the significance of the American Revolution I should select—not Saratoga or the French alliance, or even the Declaration of Independence—I should choose the formation of the Massachusetts Constitution of 1780, and I should do so because that constitution rested upon the fully developed convention, the greatest institution of government which America has produced, the institution which answered, in itself, the problem of how men could make government of their own free will.[25]

The Massachusetts Constitution of 1780 has played a influential role in the development of American constitutionalism and, although often amended, is still in effect. It reflects Adams's views of the need for checks and balances or in his terms, "balanced government."

ROBERT F. WILLIAMS
Associate Professor of Law
Rutgers University
Camden, New Jersey

NOTES

1. See, e.g., G. Wood, *The Creation of the American Republic 1776–1787* (Chapel Hill: University of North Carolina Press, 1969), 435.
2. D. Lutz, *Popular Consent and Popular Control: Whig Political Theory in the Early State Constitutions* (Baton Rouge: Louisiana State University Press, 1980), 44–45.
3. *Ibid.*, 129. See also C. Kenyon, *The Antifederalists* (1966), xxx. Note that some commentators focus on differences among state constitutions "emerging from sharp conflict between democratic and antidemocratic forces, with the constitutions at Pennsylvania and Massachusetts representing respectively victories of the two sides." See for example, Kenyon, "Constitutionalism in Revolutionary America," in *Nomos XX: Constitutionalism.* Edited by J. Pennock and J. Chapman (New York: New York University Press, 1979), 84, 92.
4. A. O. Aldridge, *Thomas Paine's American Ideology* (Newark: University of Delaware Press, 1984), 198.
5. E. Douglass, *Rebels and Democrats: The Struggle for Equal Political Rights and Majority Rule During the American Revolution* (Chapel Hill: University of North Carolina Press, 1955), 32.
6. *Ibid.* Lutz, supra n. 2, 84, noted: "The Massachusetts Constitution of 1780, written largely by John Adams, was extremely influential and became the model for most state constitutions written, down to the present."
7. Kenyon, supra n. 3 (1979), 84, 92.

8. See, e.g., O. & M. Handlin, *Popular Sources of Political Authority: Documents on the Massachusetts Constitution of 1780* (Cambridge: Harvard University Press, 1966).
9. Lutz, supra n. 2, 75–77.
10. Douglass, supra n. 5, 163.
11. W. Adams, *The First American Constitutions: Republican Ideology and the Making of the State Constitutions in the Revolutionary Era* (Chapel Hill: University of North Carolina Press, 1980), 5.
12. *Ibid.*, 51–55.
13. *Ibid.*, 53, 55.
14. This term is Adams's. *Ibid.*, 55.
15. *Ibid.*, 54.
16. S. Patterson, "The Roots of Massachusetts Federalism: Conservative Politics and Political Culture Before 1787," in *Sovereign States in an Age of Uncertainty* Edited by R. Hoffman and P. Albert (Charlottesville: University of Virginia Press, 1981), 31, 39. See also S. Patterson, *Political Parties in Revolutionary Massachusetts* (Madison: University of Wisconsin Press, 1973).
17. Handlin, supra n. 8, 88; Adams, supra n. 11, 88.
18. Handlin, supra n. 8, 190.
19. See generally R. Peters, *The Massachusetts Constitution of 1780: A Social Compact* (Amherst: University of Massachusetts Press, 1978).
20. Gerald Stourzh, *Alexander Hamilton and the Idea of Republican Government* (Stanford: Stanford University Press, 1970), 46 n. 26. See also Patterson, supra n. 16, 40: Essex Result was "one of the longest expositions of conservative principles during the war years. . . ."; and Adams, supra n. 11, 91: Essex Result was "an essay in political theory and constitutional practice comparable to *The Federalist* in the sophistication of its argument (and in its political outlook)."
21. Hammett, "Revolutionary Ideology in Massachusetts: Thomas Allen's 'Vindication' of the Berkshire Constitutionalists, 1778," *William and Mary Quarterly*, 3d ser., 3 (July 1976) 514, 516; G. Wood, supra n. 1, 339–41.
22. Hammett, supra n. 21, 517; Douglass, supra n. 5, 211.
23. On the question of public support for religion, see Peters, supra n. 19, 31–34.
24. This is discussed in Stourzh, supra n. 20, 56–57.
25. McLaughlin, "American History and American Democracy," *American Historical Review* 20 (January 1915) 255, 264.

CONSTITUTION OR FORM OF GOVERNMENT FOR THE COMMONWEALTH OF MASSACHUSETTS—1780*

PREAMBLE

The end of the institution, maintenance, and administration of government, is to secure the existence of the body politic, to protect it, and to furnish the individuals who compose it with the power of enjoying in safety and tranquility their natural rights, and the blessings of life: and whenever these great objects are not obtained, the people have a right to alter the government, and to take measures necessary for their safety, prosperity, and happiness.

The body politic is formed by a voluntary association of individuals; it is a social compact, by which the whole people covenants with each citizen, and each citizen with the whole people, that all shall be governed by certain laws for the common good. It is the duty of the people, therefore, in framing a constitution of government, to provide for an equitable mode of making laws, as well as for an impartial interpretation and a faithful execution of them; that every man may, at all times, find his security in them.

We, therefore, the people of Massachusetts, acknowledging, with grateful hearts, the goodness of the great Legislator of the universe, in affording us, in the course, of His providence, an opportunity, deliberately and peaceably, without fraud, violence, or surprise, of entering into an original, explicit, and solemn compact with each other; and of forming a new constitution of civil government, for ourselves and posterity; and devoutly imploring His direction in so interesting a design, do agree upon, ordain, and establish, the following Declaration of Rights, and Frame of Government, as the CONSTITUTION OF THE COMMONWEALTH OF MASSACHUSETTS.

The Federal and State Constitutions, Colonial Charters and Other Organic Laws of the States, Territories and Colonies Now or Heretofore Forming the United States of America. Vol. 3. Compiled and edited under the Act of Congress of 30 June 1906 by Francis Newton Thorpe (Washington, D.C.: Government Printing Office, 1909), 1888.

* Verified in *The Constitution of the Commonwealth of Massachusetts*, published by the Secretary of the Commonwealth (Boston: Wright & Potter Printing Co., 1902), 1–67.

PART THE FIRST

A DECLARATION OF THE RIGHTS OF THE INHABITANTS OF THE COMMONWEALTH OF MASSACHUSETTS

Article I. All men are born free and equal, and have certain natural, essential, and unalienable rights; among which may be reckoned the right of enjoying and defending their lives and liberties; that of acquiring, possessing, and protecting property; in fine, that of seeking and obtaining their safety and happiness.

Article II. It is the right as well as the duty of all men in society, publicly, and at stated seasons, to worship the SUPREME BEING, the great Creator and Preserver of the universe. And no subject shall be hurt, molested, or restrained, in his person, liberty, or estate, for worshipping God in the manner and season most agreeable to the dictates of his own conscience; or for his religious profession of sentiments; provided he doth not disturb the public peace, or obstruct others in their religious worship.

Article III.[a] As the happiness of a people, and the good order and preservation of civil government, essentially depend upon piety, religion, and morality; and as these cannot be generally diffused through a community but by the institution of the public worship of God, and of public instructions in piety, religion, and morality: Therefore, to promote their happiness, and to secure the good order and preservation of their government, the people of this commonwealth have a right to invest their legislature with the power to authorize and require, and the legislature shall, from time to time, authorize and require, the several towns, parishes, precincts, and other bodies politic, or religious societies, to make suitable provision, at their own expense, for the institution of the public worship of God, and for the support and maintenance of public Protestant teachers of piety, religion, and morality, in all cases where such provision shall not be made voluntarily.

And the people of this commonwealth have also a right to, and do, invest their legislature with authority to enjoin upon all the subjects an

---

[a] The constitution of Massachusetts was agreed upon by delegates of the people, in convention, begun and held at Cambridge, on the first day of September, 1779, and continued by adjournments to the second day of March 1780, when the convention adjourned to meet on the first Wednesday of the ensuing June. In the meantime the constitution was submitted to the people, to be adopted by them, provided two-thirds of the votes given should be in the affirmative. When the convention assembled, it was found that the constitution had been adopted by the requisite number of votes, and the convention accordingly resolved, "That the said Constitution or Frame of Government shall take place on the last Wednesday of October next; and not before, for any purpose, save only for that of making elections, agreeable to this resolution." The first legislature assembled at Boston, on the twenty-fifth day of October, 1780.

attendance upon the instructions of the public teachers aforesaid, at stated times and seasons, if there be any on whose instructions they can conscientiously and conveniently attend.

Provided, notwithstanding, that the several towns, parishes, precincts, and other bodies politic, or religious societies, shall, at all times, have the exclusive right of electing their public teachers, and of contracting with them for their support and maintenance.

And all moneys paid by the subject to the support of public worship, and of the public teachers aforesaid, shall, if he require it, be uniformly applied to the support of the public teacher or teachers of his own religious sect or denomination, provided there be any on whose instructions he attends; otherwise it may be paid towards the support of the teacher or teachers of the parish or precinct in which the said moneys are raised.

And every denomination of Christians, demeaning themselves peaceably, and as good subjects of the commonwealth, shall be equally under the protection of the law: and no subordination of any one sect or denomination to another shall ever be established by law.

Article IV. The people of this commonwealth have the sole and exclusive right of governing themselves, as a free, sovereign, and independent state; and do, and forever hereafter shall, exercise and enjoy every power, jurisdiction, and right, which is not, or may not hereafter be, by them expressly delegated to the United States of America, in Congress assembled.

Article V. All power residing originally in the people, and being derived from them, the several magistrates and officers of government, vested with authority, whether legislative, executive, or judicial, are their substitutes and agents, and are at all times accountable to them.

Article VI. No man, nor corporation, or association of men, have any other title to obtain advantages, or particular and exclusive privileges, distinct from those of the community, than what arises from the consideration of services rendered to the public; and this title being in nature neither hereditary, nor transmissable to children, or descendants, or relations by blood, the idea of a man born a magistrate, law-giver, or judge, is absurd and unnatural.

Article VII. Government is instituted for the common good; for the protection, safety, prosperity, and happiness of the people; and not for the profit, honor, or private interest of any one man, family, or class of men: Therefore the people alone have an incontestable, unalienable, and indefeasible right to institute government; and to reform, alter, or totally change the same, when their protection, safety, prosperity, and happiness require it.

Article VIII. In order to prevent those who are vested with authority from becoming oppressors, the people have a right, at such periods and in such manners as they shall establish by their frame of government, to cause their public officers to return to private life; and to fill up vacant places by certain and regular elections and appointments.

Article IX. All elections ought to be free; and all the inhabitants of this commnwealth, having such qualifications as they shall establish by their frame of government, have an equal right to elect officers, and to be elected, for public employments.

Article X. Each individual of the society has a right to be protected by it in the enjoyment of his life, liberty, and property, according to standing laws. He is obliged, consequently, to contribute his share to the expense of this protection; to give his personal service, or an equivalent, when necessary: but no part of the property of any individual can, with justice, be taken from him, or applied to public uses, without his own consent, or that of the representative body of the people. In fine, the people of this commonwealth are not controllable by any other laws than those to which their constitutional representative body have given their consent. And whenever the public exigencies require that the property of any individual should be appropriated to public uses, he shall receive a reasonable compensation therefore.

Article XI. Every subject of the commonwealth ought to find a certain remedy, by having recourse to the laws, for all injuries or wrongs which he may receive in his person, property, or character. He ought to obtain right and justice freely, and without being obliged to purchase it; completely, and without any denial; promptly, and without delay; comformably to the laws.

Article XII. No subject shall be held to answer for any crimes or offence, until the same is fully and plainly, substantially, and formally, described to him; or be compelled to accuse, or furnish evidence against himself. And every subject shall have a right to produce all proofs that may be favorable to him; to meet the witnesses against him face to face, and to be fully heard in his defence by himself, or his counsel, at his election. And no subject shall be arrested, imprisoned, despoiled, or deprived of his property, immunities, or privileges, put out of the protection of the law, exiled, or deprived of his life, liberty, or estate, but by the judgment of his peers, or the law of the land.

And the legislature shall not make any law that shall subject any person to a capital or infamous punishment, excepting for the government of the army and navy, without trial by jury.

Article XIII. In criminal prosecutions, the verification of facts, in the vicinity where they happen, is one of the greatest securities of the life, liberty, and property of the citizen.

Article XIV. Every subject has a right to be secure from all unreasonable searches, and seizures, of his person, his houses, his papers, and all his possessions. All warrants, therefore, are contrary to this right, if the cause or foundation of them be not previously supported by oath or affirmation, and if the order in the warrant to a civil officer, to make search in suspected places, or to arrest one or more suspected persons, or to seize their property, be not accompanied with a special designation of the persons or objects of search, arrest, or seizure; and no warrant ought to be issued but in cases, and with the formalities prescribed by the laws.

Article XV. In all controversies concerning property, and in all suits between two or more persons, except in cases in which it has heretofore been otherways used and practised, the parties have a right to a trial by jury; and this method of procedure shall be held sacred, unless, in causes arising on the high seas, and such as relate to mariners' wages; the legislature shall hereafter find it necessary to alter it.

Article XVI. The liberty of the press is essential to the security of freedom in a state; it ought not, therefore, to be restricted in this commonwealth.

Article XVII. The people have a right to keep and to bear arms for the common defence. And as, in time of peace, armies are dangerous to liberty, they ought not to be maintained without the consent of the legislature; and the military power shall always be held in an exact subordination to the civil authority, and be governed by it.

Article XVIII. A frequent recurrence to the fundamental principles of the constitution, and a constant adherence to those of piety, justice, moderation, temperance, industry, and frugality, are absolutely necessary to preserve the advantages of liberty, and to maintain a free government. The people ought, consequently, to have a particular attention to all those principles, in the choice of their officers and representatives; and they have a right to require of their lawgivers and magistrates an exact and constant observance of them, in the formation and execution of the laws necessary for the good administration of the commonwealth.

Article XIX. The people have a right, in an orderly and peaceable manner, to assemble to consult upon the common good; give instructions to their representatives, and to request of the legislative body, by the way of addresses, petitions, or remonstrances, redress of the wrongs done them, and of the grievances they suffer.

Article XX. The power of suspending the laws, or the execution of the laws, ought never to be exercised but by the legislature, or by authority derived from it, to be exercised in such particular cases only as the legislature shall expressly provide for.

Article XXI. The freedom of deliberation, speech, and debate, in either house of the legislature, is so essential to the rights of the people, that it cannot be the foundation of any accusation or prosecution, action or complaint, in any other court or place whatsoever.

Article XXII. The legislature ought frequently to assemble for the redress of grievances, for correcting, strengthening, and confirming the laws, and for making new laws, as the common good may require.

Article XXIII. No subsidy, charge, tax, impost, or duties ought to be established, fixed, laid, or levied, under any pretext whatsoever, without the consent of the people or their representatives in the legislature.

Article XXIV. Laws made to punish for actions done before the existence of such laws, and which have not been declared crimes by preceding laws, are unjust, oppressive, and inconsistent with the fundamental principles of a free government.

Article XXV. No subject ought, in any case, or in any time, to be declared guilty of treason or felony by the legislature.

Article XXVI. No magistrate or court of law shall demand excessive bail or sureties, impose excessive fines, or inflict cruel or unusual punishments.

Article XXVII. In time of peace, no soldier ought to be quartered in any house without the consent of the owner; and in time of war, such quarters ought not to be made but by the civil magistrate, in manner ordained by the legislature.

Article XXVIII. No person can in any case be subject to law-martial, or to any penalties or pains, by virtue of that law, except those employed in the army or navy, and except in the militia in actual service, but by authority of the legislature.

Article XXIX. It it essential to the preservation of the rights of every individual, his life, liberty, property, and character, that there be an impartial interpretation of the laws, and administration of justice. It is the right of every citizen to be tried by judges as free, impartial, and independent as the lot of humanity will admit. It is, therefore, not only the best policy, but for the security of the rights of the people, and of every citizen, that the judges of the supreme judicial court should hold their offices as long as they behave themselves well; and that they should have honorable salaries ascertained and established by standing laws.

Article XXX. In the government of this commonwealth, the legislative department shall never exercise the executive and judicial powers, or either of them: the executive shall never exercise the legislative and judicial powers, or either of them: the judicial shall never exercise the legislative and executive powers, or either of them: to the end it may be a government of laws and not of men.

PART THE SECOND

THE FRAME OF GOVERNMENT

The people, inhabiting the territory formerly called the Province of Massachusetts Bay, do hereby solemnly and mutually agree with each other, to form themselves into a free, sovereign, and independent body

politic, or state, by the name of THE COMMONWEALTH OF MAS-
SACHUSETTS.

CHAPTER I

THE LEGISLATIVE POWER

Section I. The General Court

Article I. The department of legislation shall be formed by two branches,
a Senate and House of Representatives; each of which shall have a negative
on the other.

The legislative body shall assemble every year on the last Wednesday
in May, and at such other times as they shall judge necessary; and shall
dissolve and be dissolved on the day next preceding the said last Wednesday
in May; and shall be styled, THE GENERAL COURT OF MASSA-
CHUSETTS.

Article II. No bill or resolve of the senate or house of representatives
shall become a law, and have force as such, until it shall have been laid
before the governor for his revisal; and if he, upon such revision, approve
thereof, he shall signify his approbation by signing the same. But if he
have any objection to the passing of such bill or resolve, he shall return
the same, together with his objections thereto, in writing, to the senate or
house of representatives, in whichsoever the same shall have originated;
who shall enter the objections sent down by the governor, at large, on
their records, and proceed to reconsider the said bill or resolve. But if
after such reconsideration, two-thirds of the said senate or house of representatives, shall, notwithstanding the said objections, agree to pass the
same, it shall, together with the objections, be sent to the other branch of
the legislature, where it shall also be reconsidered, and if approved by two-
thirds of the members present, shall have the force of law; but in all such
cases, the votes of both houses shall be determined by yeas and nays; and
the names of the persons voting for, or against, the said bill or resolve,
shall be entered upon the public records of the commonwealth.

And in order to prevent unnecessary delays, if any bill or resolve shall
not be returned by the governor within five days after it shall have been
presented, the same shall have the force of a law.

Article III. The general court shall forever have full power and authority to erect and constitute judicatories and courts of record, or other
courts, to be held in the name of the commonwealth, for the hearing,
trying, and determining of all manner of crimes, offences, pleas, processes,
plaints, actions, matters, causes, and things, whatsoever, arising or happening within the commonwealth, or between or concerning persons inhabiting, or residing, or brought within the same: whether the same be

criminal or civil, or whether the said crimes be capital or not capital, and whether the said pleas be real, personal, or mixed; and for the awarding and making out of execution thereupon. To which courts and judicatories are hereby given and granted full power and authority, from time to time, to administer oaths or affirmations, for the better discovery of truth in any matter in controversy or depending before them.

Article IV. And further, full power and authority are hereby given and granted to the said general court, from time to time, to make, ordain, and establish, all manner of wholesome and reasonable orders, laws, statutes, and ordinances, directions and instructions, either with penalties or without; so as the same be not repugnant or contrary to this constitution, as they shall judge to be for the good and welfare of this commonwealth, and for the government and ordering thereof, and of the subjects of the same, and for the necessary support and defence of the government thereof; and to name and settle annually, or provide by fixed laws for the naming and settling, all civil officers within the said commonwealth, the election and constitution of whom are not hereafter in this form of government otherwise provided for; and to set forth the several duties, powers, and limits, of the several civil and military officers of this commonwealth, and the forms of such oaths or affirmations as shall be respectively administered unto them for the execution of their several offices and places, so as the same be not repugnant or contrary to this constitution; and to impose and levy proportional and reasonable assessments, rates, and taxes, upon all the inhabitants of, and persons resident, and estates lying, within the said commonwealth; and also to impose and levy reasonable duties and excises upon any produce, goods, wares, merchandise, and commodities, whatsoever, brought into, produced, manufactured, or being within the same; to be issued and disposed of by warrant, under the hand of the governor of this commonwealth for the time being, with the advice and consent of the council, for the public service, in the necessary defence and support of the government of the said commonwealth, and the protection and preservation of the subjects thereof, according to such acts as are or shall be in force within the same.

And while the public charges of government, or any part thereof, shall be assessed on polls and estates, in the manner that has hitherto been practised, in order that such assessments may be made with equality, there shall be a valuation of estates within the commonwealth, taken anew once in every ten years at least, and as much oftener as the general court shall order.

CHAPTER I
Section II. Senate

Article I. There shall be annually elected, by the freeholders and other inhabitants of this commonwealth, qualified as in this constitution is provided, forty persons to be councillors and senators for the year ensuing their election; to be chosen by the inhabitants of the districts into which the commonwealth may, from time to time, be divided by the general court for that purpose; and the general court, in assigning the numbers to be elected by the respective districts, shall govern themselves by the proportion of the public taxes paid by the said districts; and timely make known to the inhabitants of the commonwealth the limits of each district, and the number of councillors and senators to be chosen therein; provided that the number of such districts shall never be less than thirteen; and that no district be so large as to entitle the same to choose more than six senators.

And the several counties in this commonwealth shall, until the general court shall determine it necessary to alter the said districts, be districts for the choice of councillors and senators, (except that the counties of Dukes County and Nantucket shall form one district for that purpose) and shall elect the following number for councillors and senators, viz.:—Suffolk, six; Essex, six; Middlesex, five; Hampshire, four; Plymouth, three; Barnstable, one; Bristol, three; York, two; Dukes County and Nantucket, one; Worcester, five; Cumberland, one; Lincoln, one; Berkshire, two.

Article II. The Senate shall be the first branch of the legislature; and the senators shall be chosen in the following manner, viz.: there shall be a meeting on the first Monday in April, annually, forever, of the inhabitants of each town in the several counties of this commonwealth, to be called by the selectmen, and warned in due course of law, at least seven days before the first Monday of April, for the purpose of electing persons to be senators and councillors; and at such meetings every male inhabitant of twenty-one years of age and upwards, having a freehold estate within the commonwealth, of the annual income of three pounds, or any estate of the value of sixty pounds, shall have a right to give in his vote for the senators for the district of which he is an inhabitant. And to remove all doubts concerning the meaning of the word "inhabitant" in this constitution, every person shall be considered as an inhabitant, for the purpose of electing and being elected into any office, or place within this state, in that town, district, or plantation where he dwelleth, or hath his home.

The selectmen of the several towns shall preside at such meetings impartially; and shall receive the votes of all the inhabitants of such towns present and qualified to vote for senators, and shall sort and count them in open town meeting, and in presence of the town clerk, who shall make a fair record, in presence of the selectmen, and in open town meeting, of the name of every person voted for, and of the number of votes against his name: and a fair copy of this record shall be attested by the selectmen and the town clerk, and shall be sealed up, directed to the secretary of the commonwealth for the time being, with a superscription, expressing the purport of the contents thereof, and delivered by the town clerk of such towns, to the sheriff of the county in which such town lies, thirty days at least before the last Wednesday in May annually; or it shall be delivered into the secretary's office seventeen days at least before the said last Wednesday in May: and the sheriff of each county shall deliver all such certificates by him received, into the secretary's office, seventeen days before the said last Wednesday in May.

And the inhabitants of plantations unincorporated, qualified as this constitution provides, who are or shall be empowered and required to assess taxes upon themselves toward the support of government, shall have the same privilege of voting for councillors and senators in the plantations where they reside,. as town inhabitants have in their respective towns; and the plantation meetings for that purpose shall be held annually on the same first Monday in April, at such place in the plantations, respectively, as the assessors thereof shall direct; which assessors shall have like authority for notifying the electors, collecting and returning the votes, as the selectmen and town clerks have in their several towns, by this constitution. And all other persons living in places unincorporated (qualified as aforesaid) who shall be assessed to the support of the government by the assessors of an adjacent town, shall have the privilege of giving in their votes for councillors and senators in the town where they shall be assessed, and be notified of the place of meeting by the selectmen of the town where they shall be assessed, for that purpose, accordingly.

Article III. And that there may be a due convention of senators on the last Wednesday in May annually, the governor with five of the council, for the time being, shall, as soon as may be, examine the returned copies of such records; and fourteen days before the said day he shall issue his summons to such persons as shall appear to be chosen by a majority of voters, to attend on that day, and take their seats accordingly; provided, nevertheless, that for the first year the said returned copies shall be examined by the president and five of the council of the former constitution of government; and the said president shall, in like manner, issue his summons to the persons so elected, that they may take their seats as aforesaid.

Article IV. The senate shall be the final judge of the elections, returns and qualifications of their own members, as pointed out in the constitution; and shall, on the said last Wednesday in May annually, determine and declare who are elected by each district to be senators by the majority of votes; and in case there shall not appear to be the full number of senators returned elected by a majority of votes for any district, the deficiency shall be supplied in the following manner, viz.: The members of the house of representatives, and such senators as shall be declared elected, shall take the names of such persons as shall be found to have the highest number of votes in such district, and not elected, amounting to twice the number of senators wanting, if there be so many voted for; and out of these shall elect by ballot a number of senators sufficient to fill up the vacancies in such district; and in this manner all such vacancies shall be filled up in every district of the commonwealth; and in like manner all vacancies in the senate, arising by death, removal out of the state, or otherwise, shall be supplied as soon as may be, after such vacancies shall happen.

Article V. Provided, nevertheless, that no person shall be capable of being elected as a senator, who is not seized of his own right of a freehold, within this commonwealth, of the value of three hundred pounds at least, or possessed of personal estate to the value of six hundred pounds at least, or both to the amount of the same sum, and who has not been an inhabitant of this commonwealth for the space of five years immediately preceding his election, and, at the time of his election, he shall be an inhabitant in the district for which he shall be chosen.

Article VI. The senate shall have the power to adjourn themselves, provided such adjournments do not exceed two days at a time.

Article VII. The senate shall choose its own president, appoint its own officers, and determine its own rules of proceedings.

Article VIII. The senate shall be a court with full authority to hear and determine all impeachments made by the house of representatives, against any officer or officers of the commonwealth, for misconduct and mal-administration in their offices. But previous to the trial of every impeachment the members of the senate shall respectively be sworn, truly and impartially to try and determine the charge in question, according to evidence. Their judgment, however, shall not extend further than to removal from office and disqualification to hold or enjoy any place of honor, trust, or profit, under this commonwealth; but the party so convicted shall be, nevertheless, liable to indictment, trial, judgment, and punishment, according to the laws of the land.

Article IX. Not less than sixteen members of the senate shall constitute a quorum for doing business.

CHAPTER I

Section III. House of Representatives

Article I. There shall be, in the legislature of this commonwealth, a representation of the people, annually elected, and founded upon the principle of equality.

Article II. And in order to provide for a representation of the citizens of this commonwealth, founded upon the principle of equality, every corporate town containing one hundred and fifty ratable polls may elect one representative; every corporate town containing three hundred and seventy-five ratable polls may elect two representatives; every corporate town containing six hundred ratable polls may elect three representatives; and proceeding in that manner, making two hundred and twenty-five ratable polls the mean increasing number for every additional representative.

Provided, nevertheless, that each town now incorporated, not having one hundred and fifty ratable polls, may elect one representative; but no place shall hereafter be incorporated with the privilege of electing a representative, unless there are within the same one hundred and fifty ratable polls.

And the house of representatives shall have power from time to time to impose fines upon such towns as shall neglect to choose and return members to the same, agreeably to this constitution.

The expenses of travelling to the general assembly, and returning home, once in every session, and no more, shall be paid by the government, out of the public treasury, to every member who shall attend as seasonably as he can, in the judgment of the house, and does not depart without leave.

Article III. Every member of the house of representatives shall be chosen by written votes; and, for one year at least next preceding his election, shall have been an inhabitant of, and have been seised in his own right of a freehold of the value of one hundred pounds within the town he shall be chosen to represent, or any ratable estate to the value of two hundred pounds; and he shall cease to represent the said town immediately on his ceasing to be qualified as aforesaid.

Article IV. Every male person, being twenty-one years of age, and resident in any particular town in this commonwealth for the space of one year preceding, having a freehold estate within the said town of the annual income of three pounds, or any estate of the value of sixty pounds, shall have a right to vote in the choice of a representative or representatives for the said town.

Article V. The members of the house of representatives shall be chosen annually in the month of May, ten days at least before the last Wednesday of that month.

Article VI. The house of representatives shall be the grand inquest of this commonwealth; and all impeachments made by them shall be heard and tried by the senate.

Article VII. All money bills shall originate in the house of representatives; but the senate may propose or concur with amendments, as on other bills.

Article VIII. The house of representatives shall have power to adjourn themselves; provided such adjournment shall not exceed two days at a time.

Article IX. Not less than sixty members of the house of representatives shall constitute a quorum for doing business.

Article X. The house of representatives shall be the judge of the returns, elections, and qualifications of its own members, as pointed out in the constitution; shall choose their own speaker; appoint their own officers, and settle the rules and orders of preceeding in their own house. They shall have authority to punish by imprisonment every person, not a member, who shall be guilty of disrespect to the house, by any disorderly or contemptuous behavior in its presence; or who, in the town where the general court is sitting, and during the time of its sitting, shall threaten harm to the body or estate of any of its members, for anything said or done in the house; or who shall assault any of them therefor; or who shall assault, or arrest, any witness, or other person, ordered to attend the house, in his way in going or returning; or who shall rescue any person arrested by the order of the house.

And no member of the house of representatives shall be arrested, or held to bail on mean process, during his going unto, returning from, or his attending the general assembly.

Article XI. The senate shall have the same powers in the like cases; and the governor and council shall have the same authority to punish in like cases; provided, that no imprisonment on the warrant or order of the governor, council, senate, or house of representatives, for either of the above described offences, be for a term exceeding thirty days.

And the senate and house of representatives may try and determine all cases where their rights and privileges are concerned, and which, by the constitution, they have authority to try and determine, by committees of their own members, or in such other way as they may respectively think best.

CHAPTER II

EXECUTIVE POWER

Section I. Governor

Article I. There shall be a supreme executive magistrate, who shall be styled—THE GOVERNOR OF THE COMMONWEALTH OF MASSACHUSETTS; and whose title shall be—HIS EXCELLENCY.

Article II. The governor shall be chosen annually; and no person shall be eligible to this office, unless, at the time of his election, he shall have been an inhabitant of this commonwealth for seven years next preceding; and unless he shall at the same time be seised, in his own right, of a freehold, within the commonwealth, of the value of one thousand pounds; and unless he shall declare himself to be of the Christian religion.

Article III. Those persons who shall be qualified to vote for senators and representatives within the several towns of this commonwealth shall, at a meeting to be called for that purpose, on the first Monday of April annually, give in their votes for a governor, to the selectmen, who shall preside at such meetings; and the town clerk, in the presence and with the assistance of the selectmen, shall, in open town meeting, sort and count the votes, and form a list of the persons voted for, with the number of votes for each person against his name; and shall make a fair record of the same in the town books, and a public declaration thereof in the said meeting; and shall, in the presence of the inhabitants, seal up copies of the said list, attested by him and the selectmen, and transmit the same to the sheriff of the county, thirty days at least before the said last Wednesday in May; or the selectmen may cause returns of the same to be made to the office of the secretary of the commonwealth, seventeen days at least before the said day; and the secretary shall lay the same before the senate and the house of representatives on the last Wednesday in May, to be by them examined; and in case of an election of a majority of the votes returned, the choice shall be by them declared and published; but if no person shall have a majority of votes, the house of representatives shall, by ballot, elect two out of four persons who had the highest number of votes, if so many shall have been voted for; but, if otherwise, out of the number voted for; and make return to the senate of the two persons so elected; on which the senate shall proceed, by ballot, to elect one, who shall be declared governor.

Article IV. The governor shall have authority, from time to time, at his discretion, to assemble and call together the councillors of this commonwealth for the time being; and the governor with the said councillors, or five of them at least, shall, and may, from time to time, hold and keep a council, for the ordering and directing the affairs of the commonwealth, agreeably to the constitution and the laws of the land.

Article V. The governor, with advice of council, shall have full power and authority, during the session of the general court, to adjourn or prorogue the same to any time the two houses shall desire; and to dissolve the same on the day next preceding the last Wednesday in May; and, in the recess of the said court, to prorogue the same from time to time, not exceeding ninety days in any one recess; and to call it together sooner than the time to which it may be adjourned or prorogued, if the welfare of the commonwealth shall require the same; and in case of any infectious distemper prevailing in the place where the said court is next at any time to convene, or any other cause happening, whereby danger may arise to the health or lives of the members from their attendance, he may direct the session to be held at some other, the most convenient place within the state.

And the governor shall dissolve the said general court on the day next preceding the last Wednesday in May.

Article VI. In cases of disagreement between the two houses, with regard to the necessity, expediency, or time of adjournment or prorogation, the governor, with advice of the council, shall have a right to adjourn or prorogue the general court, not exceeding ninety days, as he shall determine the public good shall require.

Article VII. The governor of this commonwealth, for the time being, shall be the commander-in-chief of the army and navy, and of all the military forces of the state, by sea and land; and shall have full power, by himself, or by any commander, or other officer or officers, from time to time, to train, instruct, exercise, and govern the militia and navy; and, for the special defence and safety of the commonwealth, to assemble in martial array, and put in warlike posture, the inhabitants thereof, and to lead and conduct them, and with them to encounter, repel, resist, expel, and pursue, by force of arms, as well by sea as by land, within or without the limits of this commonwealth, and also to kill, slay, and destroy, if necessary, and conquer, by all fitting ways, enterprises, and means whatsoever, all and every such person and persons as shall, at any time hereafter, in a hostile manner, attempt or enterprise the destruction, invasion, detriment, or annoyance of this commonwealth; and to use and exercise, over the army and navy, and over the militia in actual service, the law-martial, in time of war or invasion, and also in time of rebellion, declared by the legislature to exist, as occasion shall necessarily require; and to take and surprise, by all ways and means whatsoever, all and every such person or persons, with their ships, arms, ammunition, and other goods, as shall, in a hostile manner, invade, or attempt the invading, conquering, or annoying this commonwealth; and that the governor be intrusted with all these and other powers, incident to the offices of captain-general and commander-in-chief, and admiral, to be exercised agreeably to the rules and regulations of the constitution, and the laws of the land, and not otherwise.

Provided, that the said governor shall not, at any time hereafter, by virtue of any power by this constitution granted, or hereafter to be granted to him by the legislature, transport any of the inhabitants of this commonwealth, or oblige them to march out of the limits of the same, without their free and voluntary consent, or the consent of the general court; except so far as may be necessary to march or transport them by land or water, for the defence of such part of the state to which they cannot otherwise conveniently have access.

Article VIII. The power of pardoning offences, except such as persons may be convicted of before the senate by an impeachment of the house, shall be in the governor, by and with the advice of council; but no charter of pardon, granted by the governor, with advice of the council before conviction, shall avail the party pleading the same, notwithstanding any general or particular expressions contained therein, descriptive of the offence or offences intended to be pardoned.

Article IX. All judicial officers, the attorney-general, the solicitor-general, all sheriffs, coroners, and registers of probate, shall be nominated and appointed by the governor, by and with the advice and consent of the council; and every such nomination shall be made by the governor, and made at least seven days prior to such appointment.

Article X. The captains and subalterns of the militia shall be elected by the written votes of the train-band and alarm list of their respective companies, of twenty-one years of age and upwards; the field officers of regiments shall be elected by the written votes of the captains and subalterns of their respective regiments; the brigadiers shall be elected, in like manner, by the field officers of their respective brigades; and such officers, so elected, shall be commissioned by the governor, who shall determine their rank.

The legislature shall, by standing laws, direct the time and manner of convening the electors, and of collecting votes, and of certifying to the governor, the officers elected.

The major-generals shall be appointed by the senate and house of representatives, each having a negative upon the other; and be commissioned by the governor.

And if the electors of brigadiers, field officers, captains or subalterns, shall neglect or refuse to make such elections, after being duly notified, according to the laws for the time being, then the governor, with advice of council, shall appoint suitable persons to fill such offices.

And no officer, duly commissioned to command in the militia, shall be removed from his office, but by the address of both houses to the governor, or by fair trial in court-martial, pursuant to the laws of the commonwealth for the time being.

The commanding officers of regiments shall appoint their adjutants and quartermasters; the brigadiers their brigade-majors; and the major-generals their aids; and the governor shall appoint the adjutant-general.

The governor, with advice of council, shall appoint all officers of the continental army, whom by the confederation of the United States it is provided that this commonwealth shall appoint, as also all officers of forts and garrisons.

The divisions of the militia into brigades, regiments, and companies, made in pursuance of the militia laws now in force, shall be considered as the proper division of the militia of this commonwealth, until the same shall be altered in pursuance of some future law.

Article XI. No moneys shall be issued out of the treasury of this commonwealth, and disposed of (except such sums as may be appropriated for the redemption of bills of credit or treasurer's notes, or for the payment of interest arising thereon) but by warrant under the hand of the governor for the time being, with the advice and consent of the council, for the necessary defence and support of the commonwealth; and for the protection and preservation of the inhabitants thereof, agreeably to the acts and resolves of the general court.

Article XII. All public boards, the commissary-general, all superintending officers of public magazines and stores, belonging to this commonwealth, and all commanding officers of forts and garrisons within the same, shall once in every three months, officially, and without requisition, and at other times, when required by the governor, deliver to him an account of all goods, stores, provisions, ammunition, cannon with their appendages, and small arms with their accoutrements, and of all other public property whatever under their care respectively; distinguishing the quantity, number, quality and kind of each, as particularly as may be; together with the condition of such forts and garrisons; and the said commanding officer shall exhibit to the governor, when required by him, true and exact plans of such forts, and of the land and sea or harbor or harbors, adjacent.

And the said boards, and all public officers, shall communicate to the governor, as soon as may be after receiving the same, all letters, despatches, and intelligences of a public nature, which shall be directed to them respectively.

Article XIII. As the public good requires that the governor should not be under the undue influence of any of the members of the general court by a dependence on them for his support, that he should in all cases act with freedom for the benefit of the public, that he should not have his attention necessarily diverted from that object to his private concerns, and that he should maintain the dignity of the commonwealth in the character of its chief magistrate, it is necessary that he should have an honorable stated salary, of a fixed and permanent value, amply sufficient for those purposes, and established by standing laws; and it shall be among the first acts of the general court, after the commencement of this constitution, to establish such salary by law accordingly.

Permanent and honorable salaries shall also be established by law for the justices of the supreme judicial court.

And if it shall be found that any of the salaries aforesaid, so established, are insufficient, they shall, from time to time, be enlarged, as the general court shall judge proper.

CHAPTER II

Section II. Lieutenant-Governor

Article I. There shall be annually elected a lieutenant-governor of the commonwealth of Massachusetts, whose title shall be—His Honor; and who shall be qualified, in point of religion, property, and residence in the commonwealth, in the same manner with the governor; and the day and manner of his election, and the qualifications of the electors, shall be the same as are required in the election of a governor. The return of the votes for this officer, and the declaration of his election, shall be in the same manner; and if no one person shall be found to have a majority of all the votes returned, the vacancy shall be filled by the senate and house of representatives, in the same manner as the governor is to be elected, in case no one person shall have a majority of the votes of the people to be governor.

Article II. The governor, and in his absence the lieutenant-governor, shall be president of the council, but shall have no vote in council; and the lieutenant-governor shall always be a member of the council, except when the chair of the governor shall be vacant.

Article III. Whenever the chair of the governor shall be vacant, by reason of his death, or absence from the commonwealth, or otherwise, the lieutenant-governor, for the time being, shall, during such vacancy, perform all the duties incumbent upon the governor, and shall have and exercise all the powers and authorities, which by this constitution the governor is vested with, when personally present.

CHAPTER II

Section III. Council, and the Manner of Settling Elections by the Legislature

Article I. There shall be a council for advising the governor in the executive part of the government, to consist of nine persons besides the lieutenant-governor, whom the governor, for the time being, shall have full power and authority, from time to time, at his discretion, to assemble and call together; and the governor, with the said councillors, or five of them at least, shall and may, from time to time, hold and keep a council, for the ordering and directing the affairs of the commonwealth, according to the laws of the land.

Article III. Nine councillors shall be annually chosen from among the persons returned for councillors and senators, on the last Wednesday in May, by the joint ballot of the senators and representatives assembled in one room; and in case there shall be found upon the first choice, the whole number of nine persons who will accept a seat in the council, the deficiency shall be made up by the electors aforesaid from among the people at large; and the number of senators left shall constitute the senate for the year. The seats of the persons thus elected from the senate, and accepting the trust, shall be vacated in the senate.

Article III. The councillors, in the civil arrangements of the common-wealth, shall have rank next after the lieutenant-governor.

Article IV. Not more than two councillors shall be chosen out of any one district of this commonwealth.

Article V. The resolutions and advice of the council shall be recorded in a register, and signed by the members present; and this record may be called for at any time by either house of the legislature; and any member of the council may insert his opinion, contrary to the resolution of the majority.

Article VI. Whenever the office of the governor and lieutenant-governor shall be vacant, by reason of death, absence, or otherwise, then the council, or the major part of them, shall, during such vacancy, have full power and authority to do, and execute, all and every such acts, matters, and things, as the governor or the lieutenant-governor might or could, by virtue of this constitution, do or execute, if they, or either of them, were personally present.

Article VII. And whereas the elections appointed to be made, by this constitution, on the last Wednesday in May annually, by the two houses of the legislature, may not be completed on that day, the said elections may be adjourned from day to day until the same shall be completed. And the order of elections shall be as follows: the vacancies in the senate, if any, shall first be filled up; the governor and lieutenant-governor shall then be elected, provided there should be no choice of them by the people; and afterwards the two houses shall proceed to the election of the council.

CHAPTER II

Section IV. Secretary, Treasurer, Commissary, etc.

Article I. The secretary, treasurer, and receiver-general, and the com-missary-general, notaries public, and naval officers, shall be chosen an-nually, by joint ballot of the senators and representatives in one room. And, that the citizens of this commonwealth may be assured, from time to time, that the moneys remaining in the public treasury, upon the set-tlement and liquidation of the public accounts, are their property, no man shall be eligible as treasurer and receiver-general more than five years successively.

Article II. The records of the commonwealth shall be kept in the office of the secretary, who may appoint his deputies, for whose conduct he shall be accountable; and he shall attend the governor and council, the senate and house of representatives, in person, or by his deputies, as they shall respectively require.

CHAPTER III

JUDICIARY POWER

Article I. The tenure, that all commission officers shall by law have in their offices, shall be expressed in their respective commissions. All judicial officers, duly appointed, commissioned, and sworn, shall hold their offices during good behavior, excepting such concerning whom there is different provision made in this constitution; provided, nevertheless, the governor, with consent of the council, may remove them upon the address of both houses of the legislature.

Article II. Each branch of the legislature, as well as the governor and council, shall have authority to require the opinions of the justices of the supreme judicial court, upon important questions of law, and upon solemn occasions.

Article III. In order that the people may not suffer from the long continuance in place of any justice of the peace who shall fail of discharging the important duties of his office with ability or fidelity, all commissions of justices of the peace shall expire and become void, in the term of seven years from their respective dates; and, upon the expiration of any commission, the same may, if necessary, be renewed, or another person appointed, as shall most conduce to the well-being of the commonwealth.

Article IV. The judges of probate of wills, and for granting letters of administration, shall hold their courts at such place or places, on fixed days, as the convenience of the people shall require; and the legislature shall, from time to time, hereafter, appoint such times and places; until which appointments, the said courts shall be holden at the times and places which the respective judges shall direct.

Article V. All causes of marriage, divorce, and alimony, and all appeals from the judges of probate, shall be heard and determined by the governor and council, until the legislature shall, by law, make other provision.

CHAPTER IV

DELEGATES TO CONGRESS

The delegates of this commonwealth to the congress of the United States, shall, some time in the month of June, annually, be elected by the joint ballot of the senate and house of representatives, assembled together in one room; to serve in congress for one year, to commence on the first Monday in November then next ensuing. They shall have commissions under the hand of the governor, and the great seal of the commonwealth;

but may be recalled at any time within the year, and others chosen and commissioned, in the same manner, in their stead.

CHAPTER V

THE UNIVERSITY AT CAMBRIDGE AND ENCOURAGEMENT OF LITERATURE, ETC.

Section I. The University

Article I. Whereas our wise and pious ancestors, so early as the year one thousand six hundred and thirty-six, laid the foundation of Harvard College, in which university many persons of great eminence have, by the blessing of God, been initiated in those arts and sciences which qualified them for public employments, both in church and state; and whereas the encouragement of arts and sciences, and all good literature, tends to the honor of God, the advantage of the Christian religion, and the great benefit of this and the other United States of America,—it is declared, that the PRESIDENT AND FELLOWS OF HARVARD COLLEGE, in their corporate capacity, and their successors in that capacity, their officers and servants, shall have, hold, use, exercise, and enjoy, all the powers, authorities, rights, liberties, privileges, immunities, and franchises, which they now have, or are entitled to have, hold, use, exercise, and enjoy; and the same are hereby ratified and confirmed unto them, the said president and fellows of Harvard College, and to their successors, and to their officers and servants, respectively, forever.

Article II. And whereas there have been at sundry times, by diverse persons, gifts, grants, devises of houses, lands, tenements, goods, chattels, legacies, and conveyances, heretofore made, either to Harvard College in Cambridge, in New England, or to the president and fellows of Harvard College, or to the said college by some other description, under several charters, successively; it is declared, that all the said gifts, grants, devises, legacies, and conveyances, are hereby forever confirmed unto the president and fellows of Harvard College, and to their successors in the capacity aforesaid, according to the true intent and meaning of the donor or donors, grantor or grantors, devisor or devisors.

Article III. And whereas, by an act of the general court of the colony of Massachusetts Bay, passed in the year one thousand six hundred and forty-two, the governor and deputy-governor, for the time being, and all the magistrates of that jurisdiction, were, with the president, and a number of the clergy in the said act described, constituted the overseers of Harvard College; and it being necessary, in this new constitution of government to ascertain who shall be deemed successors to the said governor, deputy-governor, and magistrates; it is declared, that the governor, lieutenant-governor, council, and senate of this commonwealth are, and shall be deemed, their successors, who, with the president of Harvard College, for the time being, together with the ministers of the congregational churches in the towns of Cambridge, Watertown, Charlestown, Boston, Roxbury, and Dorchester, mentioned in the said act, shall be, and hereby are, vested with all the powers and authority belonging, or in any way appertaining to the overseers of Harvard College; provided, that nothing herein shall be construed to prevent the legislature of this commonwealth from making such alterations in the government of the said university, as shall be conducive to its advantage, and the interest of the republic of letters, in as full a manner as might have been done by the legislature of the late Province of the Massachusetts Bay.

CHAPTER V

Section II—The Encouragement of Literature, Etc.

Wisdom and knowledge, as well as virtue, diffused generally among the body of the people, being necessary for the preservation of their rights and liberties; and as these depend on spreading the opportunities and advantages of education in the various parts of the country, and among the different orders of the people, it shall be the duty of legislatures and magistrates, in all future periods of this commonwealth, to cherish the interests of literature and the sciences, and all seminaries of them; especially the university at Cambridge, public schools and grammar schools in the towns; to encourage private societies and public institutions, rewards and immunities, for the promotion of agriculture, arts, sciences, commerce, trades, manufactures, and a natural history of the country; to countenance and inculcate the principles of humanity and general benevolence, public and private charity, industry and frugality, honesty and punctuality in their dealings; sincerity, good humor, and all social affections, and generous sentiments, among the people.

CHAPTER VI

OATHS AND SUBSCRIPTIONS; INCOMPATABILITY OF AND
EXCLUSION FROM OFFICES; PECUNIARY QUALIFICATIONS;
COMMISSIONS; WRITS; CONFIRMATION OF LAWS; HABEAS CORPUS;
THE ENACTING STYLE; CONTINUANCE OF OFFICERS; PROVISION
FOR A FUTURE REVISAL OF THE CONSTITUTION, ETC.

Article I. Any person chosen governor, lieutenant-governor, councillor, senator, or representative, and accepting the trust, shall, before he proceed to execute the duties of his place or office, make and subscribe the following declaration, viz.:

"I, A.B., do declare, that I believe the Christian religion, and have a firm persuasion of its truth; and that I am seised and possessed, in my own right, of the property required by the constitution, as one qualification for the office or place to which I am elected."

And the governor, lieutenant-governor, and councillors, shall make and subscribe the said declaration, in the presence of the two houses of assembly; and the senators and representatives, first elected under this constitution, before the president and five of the council of the former constitution; and forever afterwards before the governor and council for the time being.

And every person chosen to either of the places or offices aforesaid, as also any person appointed or commissioned to any judicial, executive, military, or other office under the government, shall, before he enters on the discharge of the business of his place or office, take and subscribe the following declaration, and oaths or affirmations, viz.:

I, A.B., do truly and sincerely acknowledge, profess, testify, and declare, that the Commonwealth of Massachusetts is, and of right ought to be a free, sovereign, and independent state; and I do swear, that I will bear true faith and allegiance to the said commonwealth, and that I will defend the same against traitorous conspiracies and all hostile attempts whatsoever; and that I do renounce and abjure all allegiance, subjection, and obedience to the king, queen, or government of Great Britain (as the case may be), and every other foreign power whatsoever; and that no foreign prince, person, prelate, state, or potentate, hath, or ought to have, any jurisdiction, superiority, pre-eminence, authority, dispensing or other power, in any matter, civil, ecclesiastical, or spiritual, within this commonwealth, except the authority and power which is or may be vested by their constituents in the congress of the United States; and I do further testify and declare, that no man or body of men hath or can have any right to absolve or discharge me from the obligation of this oath, declaration, or affirmation; and that I do make this acknowledgment, profession, testimony, declaration, denial, renunciation, and abjuration, heartily and truly, according to the common meaning and acceptation of the foregoing words, without any equivocation, mental evasion, or secret reservation whatsoever. So help me, God."

"I, A.B., do solemnly swear and affirm, that I will faithfully and impartially discharge and perform all the duties incumbent on me as according to the best of my abilities and understand, agreeably to the rules and regulations of the constitution and the laws of the commonwealth. So help me, God."

Provided, always, that when any person chosen or appointed as aforesaid, shall be of the denomination of the people called Quakers, and shall decline taking the said oaths, he shall make his affirmation in the foregoing form, and subscribe the same, omitting the words, "I do swear," "and abjure," "Oath or," "and abjuration," in the first oath, and in the second oath, the words "swear and," and in each of them the words "So help me, God;" subjoining instead thereof, "This I do under the pains and penalties of perjury."

And the said oaths or affirmations shall be taken and subscribed by the governor, lieutenant-governor, and councillors, before the president of the senate, in the presence of the two houses of assembly; and by the senators and representatives first elected under this constitution, before the president and five of the council of the former constitution; and forever afterwards before the governor and council for the time being; and by the residue of the officers aforesaid, before such persons and in such manner as from time to time shall be prescribed by the legislature.

Article II. No governor, lieutenant-governor, or judge of the supreme judicial court, shall hold any other office or place, under the authority of this commonwealth, except such as by this constitution they are admitted to hold, saving that the judges of the said court may hold the offices of justices of peace through the state; nor shall they hold any other place or office, or receive any pension or salary from any other state or government or power whatever.

No person shall be capable of holding or exercising at the same time, within this state, more than one of the following offices, viz. judge of probate—sheriff—register of probate—or register of deeds; and never more than any two offices, which are to be held by appointment of the governor, or the governor and council, or the senate, or the house of representatives, or by the election of the people of the state at large, or of the people of any county, military offices, and the office of justices of the peace excepted, shall be held by one person.

No person holding the office of judge of the supreme judicial court—secretary—attorney-general—solicitor-general—treasurer or receiver-general—judge of probate—commissary-general—president, professor, or instructor of Harvard College—sheriff—clerk of the house of representatives—register of probate—register of deeds—clerk of the supreme judicial court—clerk of the inferior court of common pleas—or officer of the customs, including in this description naval officers—shall at the same time have a seat in the senate or house of representatives; but their being chosen or appointed to, and accepting the same, shall operate as a resignation of their seat in the senate or house of representatives; and the place so vacated shall be filled up.

And the same rule shall take place in case any judge of the said supreme judicial court, or judge of probate, shall accept a seat in council; or any councillor shall accept of either of those offices of places.

And no person shall ever be admitted to hold a seat in the legislature, or any office of trust or importance under the government of this commonwealth, who shall, in the due course of law, have been convicted of bribery or corruption in obtaining an election or appointment.

Article III. In all cases where sums of money are mentioned in this constitution, the value thereof shall be computed in silver, at six shillings and eight pence per ounce; and it shall be in the power of the legislature, from time to time, to increase such qualifications, as to property, of the persons to be elected to offices, as the circumstances of the comonwealth shall require.

Article IV. All commissions shall be in the name of the Commonwealth of Massachusetts, signed by the governor and attested by the secretary or his deputy, and have the great seal of the commonwealth affixed thereto.

Article V. All writs, issuing out of the clerk's office in any of the courts of law, shall be in the name of the Commonwealth of Massachusetts; they shall be under the seal of the court from whence they issue; they shall bear test of the first justice of the court to which they shall be returnable, who is not a party, and be signed by the clerk of such court.

Article VI. All the laws which have heretofore been adopted, used, and approved in the Province, Colony, or State of Massachusetts Bay, and usually practised on in the courts of law, shall still remain and be in full force, until altered or repealed by the legislature; such parts only excepted as are repugnant to the rights and liberties contained in this constitution.

Article VII. The privilege and benefit of the writ of habeas corpus shall be enjoyed in this commonwealth, in the most free, easy, cheap, expeditious, and ample manner; and shall not be suspended by the legislature, except upon the most urgent and pressing occasions, and for a limited time, not exceeding twelve months.

Article VIII. The enacting style, in making and passing all acts, statutes, and laws, shall be—"Be it enacted by the Senate and House of Representatives, in General Court assembled, and by the authority of the same."

Article IX. To the end there may be no failure of justice, or danger arise to the commonwealth from a change of the form of government, all officers, civil and military, holding commissions under the government and people of Massachusetts Bay in New England, and all other officers of the said government and people, at the time this constitution shall take effect, shall have, hold, use, exercise, and enjoy, all the powers and authority to them granted or committed, until other persons shall be appointed in their stead; and all courts of law shall proceed in the execution of the business of their respective departments; and all the executive and legislative officers, bodies, and powers shall continue in full force, in the enjoyment and exercise of all their trusts, employments, and authority; until the general court, and the supreme and executive officers under this constitution, are designated and invested with their respective trusts, powers, and authority.

Article X. In order the more effectually to adhere to the principles of the constitution, and to correct those violations which by any means may be made therein, as well as to form such alterations as from experience shall be found necessary, the general court which shall be in the year of our Lord one thousand seven hundred and ninety-five, shall issue precepts to the selectmen of the several towns, and to the assessors of the unincorporated plantations, directing them to convene the qualified voters of their respective towns and plantations, for the purpose of collecting their sentiments on the necessity or expedience of revising the constitution, in order to make amendments.

And if it shall appear, by the returns made, that two-thirds of the qualified voters throughout the state, who shall assemble and vote in consequence of the said precepts, are in favor of such revision or amendment, the general court shall issue precepts, or direct them to be issued from the secretary's office, to the several towns to elect delegates to meet in convention for the purpose aforesaid.

The said delegates to be chosen in the same manner and proportion as their representatives in the second branch of the legislature are by this constitution to be chosen.

Article XI. This form of government shall be enrolled on parchment, and deposited in the secretary's office, and be a part of the laws of the land; and printed copies thereof shall be prefixed to the book containing the laws of this commonwealth, in all future editions of the said laws.

ARTICLES OF AMENDMENT

Article I. If any bill or resolve shall be objected to, and not approved by the governor; and if the general court shall adjourn within five days after the same shall have been laid before the governor for his approbation, and thereby prevent his returning it with his objections, as provided by the constitution, such bill or resolve shall not become a law, nor have force as such.

Article II. The general court shall have full power and authority to erect and constitute municipal or city governments, in any corporate town or towns in this commonwealth, and to grant to the inhabitants thereof such powers, privileges, and immunities, not repugnant to the constitution, as the general court shall deem necessary or expedient for the regulation and government thereof, and to prescribe the manner of calling and holding public meetings of the inhabitants, inwards or otherwise, for the election of officers under the constitution, and the manner of returning the votes given at such meetings. Provided, that no such government shall be erected or constituted in any town not containing twelve thousand inhabitants, nor unless it be with the consent, and on the application of a majority of the inhabitants of such town, present and voting thereon, pursuant to a vote at a meeting duly warned and holden for that purpose. And provided, also, that all bylaws, made by such municipal or city government, shall be subject, at all times, to be annulled by the general court.

Article XXXIII. A majority of the members of each branch of the general court shall constitute a quorum for the transaction of business, but a less number may adjourn from day to day, and compel the attendance of absent members. All the provisions of the existing Constitution inconsistent with the provisions herein contained are hereby annulled.

Article XXXIV. So much of article two of section one of chapter two of part the second of the constitution of the Commonwealth as is contained in the following words: "and unless he shall at the same time, be seized in his own right, of a freehoold within the Commonwealth of the value of one thousand pounds;" is hereby annulled.

Article XXXV. So much of article two of section three of chapter one of the constitution of the commonwealth as is contained in the following words: "The expenses of travelling to the general assembly, and returning home, once in every session, and no more, shall be paid by the government, out of the public treasury, to every member who shall attend as seasonably as he can, in the judgment of the house, and does not depart without leave," is hereby annulled.

Article XXVI. So much of article nineteen of the articles of amendment ot the constitution of the commonwealth as is contained in the following words: "commissioners of insolvency" is hereby annulled.

Polish Constitution
of 1791

Unlike the world's first constitution, which is also the oldest in continuous existence, the world's second constitution is one of the shortest-lived. For unlike the U.S. Constitution of 1787, which marked the beginning of a new nation and ushered in the age of constitutionalism, the Polish Constitution of 3 May 1791 was a desperate and unsuccessful, effort to preserve the existence of a nation, which was founded in A.D. 966.

Both constitutions were products of the Age of Enlightenment. They represented (and still do) symbols of patriotism and hope for all subsequent generations. The dates are important. Most scholars of the Age of Enlightenment focus on its two great revolutions, the American Revolution of 1776 and the French Revolution of 1789. Many forget that the Polish Constitution preceded the French Constitution of 3 September 1791, the world's third constitution, by exactly four months. The lessons of the American and French Revolutions were well known to the Polish constitutionalists, who drew on their ideology as well as the technical aspects of the American and English Constitutions in preparing the Polish charter.

The dates are also important because of the historical setting of the Polish Constitution. In the preceding eight centuries Poland had become the largest country in Europe except for Russia, and its cultural achievements during the Polish Renaissance were hailed throughout the continent. In addition, Poland had become known for its military accomplishments. King Jan Sobiecki's defeat of the Turks at the Siege of Vienna in 1683 had marked the end of Turkish conquest and pressure on Europe.

But the military posture of Europe changed radically in less than a century. Russia, Prussia, and Austria joined forces in 1772 to seize large sections of Polish territory in the First Partition of Poland. The Second Partition occurred in 1793 and the Third Partition, which dissolved the state, in 1795. The Grand Duchy of Warsaw was established under Napoleon in 1807 and the government of "Congress Poland" was established by the Congress of Vienna in 1815. For practical purposes, there was no Poland again until after World War I—a period of more than a century in which the 3 May Constitution was regarded as a symbol of hope. The restored Poland immediately made 3 May a national holiday. Although the celebration of the holiday ended with World War II, the date is still one of inspiration throughout the nation.

The Polish Constitution was the product of the Great Four-Year Sejm (parliament) from 1788 to 1792, which was responsible for instituting many modern reforms reflecting the lessons of the Enlightenment. The members of the Sejm saw the Constitution as the first stage of reform that eventually would lead to the codification of all statutory law.

The first objective of the Polish Constitution, which the partitioning powers demanded in 1772, was to establish a hereditary constitutional monarchy to replace an elective one. The writers of the Constitution also wanted to end the *liberum veto*, the system that required a unanimous vote for the passage of any law by the Sejm. Finally, they sought to check the prerogatives of the nobility.

The English Constitution, consisting of a series of parliamentary enactments, could not serve as the sole model. But it was the English precedent, which led the Polish Constitution writers to provide for a king and for a parliamentary system in which government was responsible to parliament. The as yet unborn French Constitution of 1791 later influenced the thinking of the Polish Assembly, because the ideas of the French Revolution had become those of intellectuals throughout Europe.

Distant Poland also drew on the American experience. The Warsaw press had been carrying detailed accounts on current developments in the United States. Excerpts from the U.S. Constitution had appeared in Polish newspapers. *International Treaties*, a Polish journal, published in consecutive issues the Articles of Confederation and the text of the Treaty of Paris and, subsequently, the text of the Philadelphia Constitution and the first ten amendments.

The Polish Constitution, like the American model, recognized the sovereignty of the people as the source of all law. The Philadelphia document makes this point clear at the outset with the first words of the Preamble: "We the People of the United States. . . ." This phrase inspired Article V of the Polish document: "All power in civil society should be derived from the will of the people. . . ."

Further, the objectives of both Constitutions, as outlined in their respective Preambles, show great similarity in purpose. Like Americans, the Poles did "solemnly establish" their Constitution "free from the disgraceful shackles of foreign influence; prizing more than life the external independence and internal liberty of the nation; in order to exert our natural rights with zeal and firmness."

Both Constitutions are similar in the organization of the bicameral legislatures as well as in such technical matters as impeachment and executive clemency. Poland looked to the United States for guidelines in procedure as well as in substance, following the American precedent of preparing the Constitution in secret sessions.

Although the Age of Enlightment promoted some degree of equality— one of the proclaimed objectives of the American Declaration of Independence—it is conspicuously absent in both the U.S. and Polish Constitutions. The U.S. Constitution (Article I, Section 8, Clause 8) did prohibit granting any title of nobility—but that was all. The Polish document did not even go that far; in fact, Article II recognizes the special rights and privileges of the nobility. However, the nobility in Poland was 10 percent of the population compared with a nobility of less than 2 percent in England, France, or the German states. However, the Constitution provided ways for common citizens to be ennobled as rewards for military and civil accomplishments.

Specifically not adopted was the American system of federalism. Poland had lived for centuries under the federal Polish-Lithuanian Union, and the emphasis in 1791 was to ensure a unitary state.

The Polish Constitution of 3 May 1791 is an important historic document. This document manifests the compromise between the principles of monarchy and the ideals of the Enlightenment. The Polish Constitution remains a symbol of freedom and hope to people under foreign domination.

WACLAW SZYSZKOWSKI
Former Dean
Faculty of Law
Nicolas Copernicus University,
Torun, Poland.

NEW CONSTITUTION OF THE GOVERNMENT OF POLAND

As established by the Revolution May 3, 1791.
In the name of God, one in the Holy Trinity!

Stanislaus Augustius, by the grace of God, and the will of the nation, king of Poland, &c. &c. together with the Confederate States assembled in double number, to represent the Polish nation.

A History of Poland: From Its Origin as a Nation to the Commencement of the Year 1795 (London: Vernor and Hood, 1795), 375–90.

Convinced, by a long train of experience, of many defects in our government, and willing to profit by the favourable moment which has restored us to ourselves; free from the disgraceful shackles of foreign influence; prizing more than life the external independence and internal liberty of the nation; in order to exert our natural rights with zeal and firmness, we do solemnly establish the present constitution, which we declare wholly inviolable in every part, till such period as shall be prescribed by law; when the nation, if it should think fit, may alter by its express will such articles therein as shall be found inadequate.

Article I. The dominant national religion.—The holy Roman Catholic faith, with all its privileges and immunities, shall be the dominant national religion; but, as the same holy religion commands us to love our neighbours, we therefore owe to all people, of whatever persuasion, peace in matters of faith, and the protection of government; consequently we assure to all persuasions and religions freedom and liberty, according to the laws of the country, and in all dominions of the republic.

Article II. Nobility, or the equestrian order.—Revering the memory of our ancestors with gratitude, as the first founders of our liberties, it is but just to acknowledge, in a most solemn manner, that all the pre-eminence and prerogatives of liberty granted to this order by Casimir the Great, &c. &c. &c. are by the present act renewed, confirmed, and declared to be inviolable. We acknowledge the rank of the noble equestrian order in Poland to be equal to all degrees of nobility—all persons of that order to be equal among themselves, not only in the eligibility to all posts of honour, trust, or emolument, but in the enjoyment of all privileges and prerogatives; personal liberty, and security of territorial and moveable property; nor shall we ever suffer the least encroachment on either by the Supreme national power (on which the present form of government is established), under any pretext whatsoever; consequently, we regard the preservation of personal security and property, as by law ascertained, to be a tie of society, and the very essence of civil liberty, which ought to be considered and respected for ever.

Article III. Towns and citizens.—The law made by the present diet, intitled, "Our royal free towns within the dominions of the republic," we mean to consider as a part of the present constitution, and promise to maintain it as a new, additional, true, and effectual support of our common liberties and mutual defence.

Article IV. Peasants and villagers.—This agricultural class of people, the most numerous in the nation, consequently forming the most considerable part of its force, we receive under the protection of national law and government; enacting, that whatever liberties, grants, and conventions, between the proprietors and villagers, either individually or collectively, may be entered authentically into in future: such agreements shall import mutual and reciprocal obligations, binding not only the present contracting parties, but even their successors by inheritance or acquisition. Thus having insured to the proprietors every advantage they have a right to form their villages, and willing to encourage most effectually the population of our country, we publish and proclaim a perfect and entire liberty to all people, either who may be newly coming to settle, or those who, having emigrated, would return to their native country: and we declare most solemnly, that any person coming into Poland, from whatever part of the world, or returning from abroad, as soon as he sets his foot on the territory of the republic, becomes free, and at liberty to exercise his industry wherever and in whatever manner he pleases, to settle either in towns or villages, to farm and rent lands and houses, on tenures and contracts, for as long a term as may be agreed on; with liberty to remain, or to remove, after having fulfilled the obligations he may have voluntarily entered into.

Article V. Form of government.—All power in civil society should be derived from the will of the people, its end and object being the preservation and integrity of the state, the civil liberty, and the good order of society, on an equal scale, and on a lasting foundation. Three distinct powers shall compose the government of the Polish nation, according to the present constitution:

1. Legislative power in the states assembled.
2. Executive power in the king and the council of inspection. And,
3. Judicial power in jurisdictions existing, or to be established.

Article VI. The diet, or the legislative power.—The diet, or the assembly of states, shall be divided into two houses, the house of nuncios, or deputies, and the house of senate, where the king is to preside. The former, being the representative and central point of supreme national authority, shall possess the pre-eminence in the legislature; therefore all bills are to be decided first in this house.

1. All general laws, constitutional, civil, criminal, and perpetual taxes; concerning which matters, the king is to issue his propositions by the circular letters sent before the dietines to every palatinate and to every district for deliberation, which coming before the house with the opinion expressed in the instructions given to their representatives, shall be taken the first for decision.

2. Particular laws: temporal taxes; regulations of the mint; contracting public debts; creating nobles, and other casual recompences; reparation of public expenses, both ordinary and extraordinary; concerning war; peace; ratification of treaties, political and commercial; all diplomatic acts and conventions relative to the laws of nations; examining and acquitting different executive departments, and similar subjects arising from the accidental exigences and circumstances of the state; in which the propositions, coming directly from the throne into the house of nuncios, are to have preference in discussion before the private bills.

In regard to the house of Senate, it is to consist of bishops, palatines, castellans, and ministers, under the presidency of the king, who shall have but one vote, and the casting vote, in case of parity, which he may give either personally or by a message to the house. Its power and duty shall be,

1. Every general law that passes formally through the house of nuncios is to be sent immediately to this, which is either accepted, or suspended till farther national deliberation. If accepted, it becomes a law in all its force; if suspended, it shall be resumed at the next diet; and, if it is then agreed to again by the house of nuncios, the senate must submit to it.

2. Every particular law, as soon as it has been determined by the house of nuncios, and sent up to the senate, the votes of both houses shall be jointly computed, and the majority, as described by law, shall be considered as a decree and the will of the nation.

Those senators and ministers who, from their share in executive power, are accountable to the republic, cannot have an active voice in the diet, but may be present in order to give necessary explanations to the states.

These ordinary legislative diets shall have their uninterrupted existence, and be always ready to meet; renewable every two years. The length of sessions shall be determined by the law concerning diets. If convened out of ordinary session, upon some urgent occasion, they shall only deliberate on the subject which occasioned such a call, or on circumstances which may arise out of it.

The law concerning the dietines, or primary elections, as established by the present diet, shall be regarded as a most essential foundation of civil liberty.

The majority of votes shall decide everything, and everywhere; therefore we abolish and utterly annihilate, all sorts of confederacies, and confederate diets, as ruinous to society.

Willing to prevent, on one hand, violent and frequent changes in the national constitution, yet, considering on the other, the necessity of perfecting it, after experiencing its effects on public prosperity, we determine the period of every twenty-five years for an extraordinary constitutional diet, to be held purposely for the revision and such alterations of the constitution as may be found requisite.

Article VII. The kind, or executive power.—The most perfect government cannot exist without an effectual executive power. Experience has taught us that the neglecting of this essential part of government has overwhelmed Poland with disasters.

Having, therefore, secured to the free Polish nation the right of enacting laws for themselves, the supreme inspection over the executive power, and the choice of their magistrates, we intrust to the king and his council the highest power of executing the laws.

The council shall be called straz, or the council of inspection.

The duty of such executive power shall be to watch over the laws, and to see them strictly executed according to their import, even by the means of public force, should it be necessary.

The executive power cannot assume the right of making laws, or of their interpretation. It is expressly forbidden to contract public debts; to alter the repartition of the national income, as fixed by the diet; to declare war; to conclude definitively any treaty, or any diplomatic act: it is only allowed to carry on negociations with foreign courts and facilitate temporary occurrences, always with reference to the diet.

The crown of Poland we declare to be elective, in regard to families, and it is settled so for ever.

Having experienced the fatal effects of interregna, periodically subverting government, and being desirous of preventing for ever all foreign influence, as well as of insuring to every citizen a perfect tranquillity, we have, from prudent motives, resolved to adopt hereditary succession to our throne: therefore we enact and declare, that, after the expiration of our life, according to the gracious will of the Almighty, the present elector of Saxony shall reign over Poland.

The dynasty of future kings of Poland shall begin in the person of Frederic Augustus, elector of Saxony, with the right of inheritance to the crown to his male descendants. The eldest son of the reigning king is to succeed his father; and, in case the present elector of Saxony has no male issue, a husband chosen by him (with the consent and approbation of the republic) for his daughter, shall begin the said dynasty. Hence we declare the Princess Mary Augusta Nepomucena, only daughter of the elector of Saxony, to be infanta of Poland.

We reserve to the nation, however, the right of electing to the throne any other house or family, after the extinction of the first.

Every king, on his succession to the throne, shall take a solemn oath to God and the nation, to support the present constitution, to fulfil the pacta conventa, which will be settled with the present elector of Saxony, as appointed to the crown, and which shall bind him in the same manner as former ones.

The king's person is sacred and inviolable; as no act can proceed immediately from him, he cannot be in any manner responsible to the nation: he is not an absolute monarch, by the father and the head of the people; his revenues, as fixed by the pacta conventa, shall be sacredly preserved. All public acts, the acts of magistracies, and the coin of the kingdom, shall bear his name.

The king, who ought to possess every power of doing good, shall have the right of pardoning those that are condemned to death, except the crimes be against the state.

In time of war he shall have the supreme command of the national forces: he may appoint the commanders of the army, however, by the will of the states. It shall be his province to patentee officers in the army, and other dignitaries, consonant to the regulations hereafter to be expressed, to appoint bishops, senators, and ministers, as members of the executive power.

The king's council of inspection is to consist,

1. Of the primate, as the head of the clergy, and the president of the commission of education, or the first bishop in ordine.

2. Of five ministers: the minister of police, minister of justice, minister of war, minister of finances, and minister for foreign affairs.

3. Of two secretaries, to keep the protocols. The hereditary prince coming of age may assist at, but shall have not vote therein.

The marshal of the diet, being chosen for two years, has also a right to sit; for the end only of calling together the diet, always existing, if absolutely necessary, and the king refusing to do it.

The cases demanding such convocation of the diet are the following:

1. In a pressing necessity concerning the law of nations, and particularly in a cafe of a neighbouring war.

2. In case of an internal commotion.

3. In an evident danger of general famine.

4. In the orphan state of the country, or in case of the king's dangerous illness.

All resolutions of the council of inspection are to be examined by the rules above-mentioned.

The king's opinion, after that of every member of the council has been heard, shall decisively prevail.

Every resolution of this council shall be issued under the king's signature, countersigned by one of the ministers sitting therein.

Should all the members refuse their countersign, the king is obliged to forego his opinion.

Ministers composing this council cannot be employed at the same time in any other department.

If it should happen that two-thirds of secret votes in both houses demand the changing of any person, either in the council, or any executive department, the king is bound to nominate another.

Willing that the council of inspection should be responsible to the nation for their actions, we decree that, when accused of any transgression of positive law, they are answerable with their persons and fortunes.

Such impeachments shall be tried immediately by the comitial tribunal, and receive final judgment.

In order to form a necessary organization of the executive power, we establish hereby separate commissions, connected with the above councils, and subjected to obey its ordinations.

These commissions are—1st. of education—2d. of police—3d. of war—4th. of treasury.

Article VIII. Judicial power.—As judicial power is incompatible with the legislative, nor can be administered by the king, therefore tribunals and magistrates ought to be established and elected. It ought to have local existence, that every citizen should know where to seek justice, and every transgressor can discern the hand of national government. We establish, therefore,

1. Primary courts for each palatinate and district, composed of judges chosen at the dietine, which are always to be ready to administer justice. From these courts appeals are allowed to the high tribunals, erected one for each of three provinces, in which the kingdom is divided. Those courts, both primary and final, shall be for the equestrian order, and all proprietors of landed property.

2. We determine separate courts for the free royal towns.

3. Each province shall have a court of referendaries for the trial of causes relating to the peasantry, who are all hereby declared free.

4. Courts, curial and assessorial, tribunals for Courland, and relational, are hereby confirmed.

5. Executive commissions shall have judicial power in matters relative to their administration.

6. Besides all these, there shall be one supreme general tribunal or court, composed of persons chosen at the opening of every diet. This tribunal is to try all the persons accused of crimes against the state.

Lastly, we shall appoint a committee for the forming a civil and criminal code of laws, by persons whom the diet shall elect for that purpose.

Article IX. Regency.—The fame council of inspection is to compose the regency, with the queen at their head, or, in her absence, with the primate of the kingdom. The regency may take place only,

1. During the king's minority.

2. In case of the king's settled alienation of reason.

3. In case of the king's being made a prisoner of war.

Minority is to be considered till eighteen years are completed, and the malady must be declared in the existing diet by the plurality of three-fourths of the votes of both combined houses.

When the king comes of age, or recovers his health, or returns from capitivity, the regency shall cease, and shall be accountable to him, and responsible to the nation in their persons and fortunes, for their actions during their office.

Article X. Education of king's children.—The king's sons, being designed successors to the crown, are the first children of the country. Thence the care of their proper education, without encroaching, however, on the right of their parents, devolves naturally upon the nation.

During the king's life, the king himself, with the council, and a tutor appointed by the states, shall superintend the education of the princes.

In time of a regency, it shall be intrusted with this direction jointly with the above-mentioned tutor.

In both cases this tutor, named by the states, is to make his report before each ordinary diet of the education and progress of the princes.

Article XI. National force, or the army.—The nation is bound to preserve its possessions against invasion; therefore, all inhabitants are natural defenders of their country and its liberties.

The army is only an extract of defensive regular force from the general mass of national strength.

The nation owes to the army reward and respect, because of its devoting itself wholly for the defence of the country.

The army owes to the nation to guard the frontiers against enemies, and to maintain public tranquillity within. This national force, therefore, shall be employed for garrisoning fortresses, and assisting the civil power in the execution of the law against those that are refractory.

DECLARATION OF THE STATES ASSEMBLED

All laws and statutes, old and new, contrary to the present constitution, or to any part thereof, are hereby abolished; and every paragraph in the foregoing articles to be a competent part of the present constitution, is acknowledged. We recommend to the executive power to see the council of inspection immediately begin its office under the eye of the diet, and continue its duties without the least interruption.

We swear before God and the country to maintain and defend, with all possible human power, the present constitution; and considering this oath as a proof of real love of our country, we command all magistrates and troops here present to take it immediately. The commission of war shall issue orders to the rest of the army quartered in the kingdom, and in the grand duchy of Lithuania, to do the same within one month at farthest from the date of the present law.

We recommend to our bishops to appoint one and the same day of public thanksgiving to God Almighty in all churches over the kingdom; also, we appoint a day, N.N. for the solemn celebrating, by us and our posterity, of a commemoration anniversary for the mercies of the Supreme Being shewn to us so many public calamities.

And that future ages may know and feel that it is by the assistance of the Supreme Disposer of nations we have surmounted the greatest difficulties and obstacles, and effected this happy revolution, we decree, that a church shall be erected and consecrated to Divine Providence, in memory of this event, and at the expence of the states.

Having thus satisfied our general feelings on this event, we turn our attention towards securing the same constitution, by declaring and enacting, that whoever shall dare to oppose it, or to disturb the public tranquillity, either by exciting mistrust, or by perverse interpretation of this constitution, and much more, by forming insurrections and confederacies, either openly or secretly, such person or persons are declared to be enemies and traitors to their country, and shall be punished with the utmost rigour by the comitial tribunal. For this purpose, we order this tribunal to sit uninterruptedly at Warsaw, proroguing their session from day to day, and to try all persons so accused by any citizen of property, with the assistance of the attornies general of Poland and Lithuania, seizing all indicted persons with the aid of the national troops, which shall be ready to act on the first order from the executive power, as they shall be directed and occasion may require.

This restoration of liberty to the nation filled every mind with inexpressible joy. Even those who on the 3d had resolved to enter into a protest, and publish their manifesto, withdrew their opposition. They declared, "that by their instructions they deemed themselves obligated to it: but that the revolution having been consummated with the apparent applause of nearly the whole nation, fully persuaded of the patriotic intentions of the king, and those who were the chief agents in bringing about this great change; in fine, perceiving, by the form in which the king, the whole senate, and nearly all the chamber of nuncios, had already taken the oath, that it did not extend the royal power beyond its just bounds, but on the contrary guaranteed the full and entire liberty of every individual, by maintaining the sovereignty of the national assembled in the diet; they would no longer impede or retard by a vain resistance the effect of a revolution, commenced, conducted, and accomplished with so much good fortune; that they should heartily concur therein; that they should congratulate their country on the occassion; and should return their most sincere and unfeigned thanks to those who had contributed to the happy change, especially to the king, who had been the chief author and promoter of it."

The memory of this important event was ordered to be celebrated every year; and a church to be constructed at the expence of the public treasure, with this inscription, "To Divine Providence, in order to eternize the remembrance of a revolution effected almost unanimously, and without the loss of a single drop of blood!"

Oh! had this constitution, dictated by equity, enlightened by understanding, and founded on the imprescriptible rights of man, been suffered to operate its benign influence unmolested by the ruthless arms of insatiable ambition, the Polish nation might, after having vegetated so long in obscurity, and groaned under the yoke of oppression, have become one of the happiest nations of the universe!

French Constitution
of 1791

The world's third national constitution was promulgated in Paris on 3 September 1791. This document followed the one drafted in Philadelphia by four years and the Polish Constitution by four months. While it was in existence less than a year, the French Constitution was at the time of its adoption the most important and influential constitution in history. This document legalized the French Revolution and incorporated the Declaration of the Rights of Man and of the Citizen of 1789—giving constitutional and legal effect to the most important human rights statement ever drafted. It was as though the American Declaration of Independence had been made a part of the United States Constitution.

The French Constitution of 1791 must be seen in historical perspective. There were to be three constitutions promulgated during the French Revolution, the others in 1793 and 1795. But the first of the three had the greatest impact on the revolutionary movements of Europe. This document influenced the Spanish Constitution of 1812 (see following chapter), which in turn influenced the constitutions of many nations of Latin America.

Although the 1791 document constitutionalized the far-reaching Declaration of the Rights of Man and of the Citizen, it stopped short of establishing a republic, which the more radical revolutionaries had demanded. Many have criticized this Constitution as a bourgeois compromise preserving the monarchy; however, others think that such characterization is unfair. The existing monarchy was nothing like the absolute sovereignty long known in France. "L'Etat, c'est moi" was certainly at an end.

The French Constitution of 1791 sanctioned a British-type monarchy with qualifications. The king was required to take an oath to maintain and uphold the Constitution. Failing to honor this oath, leaving the country, or seeking the aid of other rulers was tantamount to abdication. The king could not dissolve the National Assembly and was subject to its will. He did have a suspensive veto, but not in either constitutional or financial matters. The king could not initiate legislation, and no order of the king was implemented unless countersigned by a minister with ultimate responsibility.

King Louis XVI took the necessary oath, saying:

> I accept then the constitution. I take the engagement to maintain it within, to defend it against attack from without, and to cause it to be executed by all the means which it places in my power. . . . I should be lacking in sincerity, however, if I said that I perceived in the means of execution and administration, all the energy which may be necessary in order to give motion to and preserve unity in all the parts of so vast an empire; but since opinions at present are divided upon these matters, I consent that experience alone remain judge therein.

The Declaration of the Rights of Man and of the Citizen, the introductory part of the Constitution, provided that "men are born and remain free and equal in rights." Yet the main body of the Constitution divided the citizenry into two categories: active and passive. The rights announced in the Declaration were guaranteed to all citizens, but political privileges such as voting and office holding were accorded to only those classified as "active." To achieve the preferred classification, a person had to be a property owner or a taxpayer. Membership in the National Assembly was restricted to active citizens who were designated on preferred lists.

Although the number of active citizens was 4 million, all could not vote. A complicated two-stage process for the choice of electors narrowed the actual number of voters for National Assembly seats to 50 thousand.

Despite the restrictions on the franchise, the Constitution itself incorporated more individual rights than even the U.S. Constitution of 1787 and the various documents that made up the British Constitution. Nor were such rights limited to the Declaration; they were in the body of the Constitution itself. This tabulation of rights advanced those in the U.S. Bill of Rights—a precedent that influenced French thinking—and in some respects exceeded most modern formulations.

The provision on freedom of speech and press surpasses the protection of the First Amendment to the U.S. Constitution. Title I sets forth those "natural and civil rights" that the government was to guarantee. Pursuant to these rights, Section 3 reads: "Liberty to every man to speak, to write, to print and publish his ideas without having his writings subjected to any censorship or inspection before their publication. . . ."

The French Constitution of 1791 also contained the first constitutional statement on economic or social rights. Also included in Title I, Section 3, was the statement: "There shall be created and organized a general establishment of public relief in order to bring up abandoned children, relieve infirm paupers, and provide work for the able-bodied poor who may not have been able to obtain it for themselves."

The same section also guaranteed free public education. In its desire to reduce the power of the Catholic Church, which once controlled one of the three estates making up the former French parliament, citizens were given the right "to elect or choose the ministers of their religious sects."

Yet this constitution was not destined to last. The king not only fought with the National Assembly, but also broke his pledge and sought support from other monarchs. Even if the king had been cooperative, the system established by the French Constitution of 1791 was doomed to failure. The public sentiment for a republic was far too strong. The monarchy fell on 10 August 1792, paving the path for the Constitutions of 1793 and 1795.

LEE CICCOTELI
New Jersey Bar

FRENCH CONSTITUTION OF 1791

DECLARATION OF THE RIGHTS OF MAN AND CITIZEN

The representatives of the French people, organized in National Assembly, considering that ignorance, forgetfulness or contempt of the rights of man, are the sole causes of the public miseries and of the corruption of governments, have resolved to set forth in a solemn declaration the natural, inalienable, and sacred rights of man, in order that this declaration, being present to all the members of the social body, may unceasingly remind them of their rights and their duties; in order that the acts of the legislative power and those of the executive power may be each moment compared with the aim of every political institution and thereby may be more respected; and in order that the demands of the citizens, grounded henceforth upon simple and incontestable principles, may always take the direction of maintaining the constitutions and the welfare of all.

In consequence, the National Assembly recognizes and declares, in the presence and under the auspices of the Supreme Being, the following rights of man and citizen.

Frank Maloy Anderson, *The Constitutions and Other Select Documents Illustrative of the History of France 1789–1907* (Minneapolis, H. W. Wilson Co., 1908).

1. Men are born and remain free and equal in rights. Social distinctions can be based only upon public utility.

2. The aim of every political association is the preservation of the natural and imprescriptible rights of man. These rights are liberty, property, security, and resistance to oppression.

3. The source of all sovereignty is essentially in the nation; no body, no individual can exercise authority that does not proceed from it in plain terms.

4. Liberty consists in the power to do anything that does not injure others; accordingly, the exercise of the natural rights of each man has no limits except those that secure to the other members of society the enjoyment of these same rights. These limits can be determined only by law.

5. The law has the right to forbid only such actions as are injurious to society. Nothing can be forbidden that is not interdicted by the law, and no one can be constrained to do that which it does not order.

6. Law is the expression of the general will. All citizens have the right to take part personally, or by their representatives, in its formation. It must be the same for all, whether it protects or punishes. All citizens being equal in its eyes, are equally eligible to all public dignities, places, and employments, according to their capacities, and without other distinction than that of their virtues and their talents.

7. No man can be accused, arrested, or detained, except in the cases determined by the law and according to the forms that it has prescribed. Those who procure, expedite, execute, or cause to be executed arbitrary orders ought to be punished: but every citizen summoned or seized in virtue of the law ought to render instant obedience; he makes himself guilty by resistance.

8. The law ought to establish only penalties that are strictly and obviously necessary, and no one can be punished except in virtue of a law established and promulgated prior to the offence and legally applied.

9. Every man being presumed innocent until he has been pronounced guilty, if it is though indispensable to arrest him, all severity that may not be necessary to secure his person ought to be strictly suppressed by law.

10. No one should be disturbed on account of his opinions, even religious, provided their manifestation does not derange the public order established by law.

11. The free communication of ideas and opinions is one of the most precious of the rights of man; every citizen then can freely speak, write, and print, subject to responsibility for the abuse of this freedom in the cases determined by law.

12. The guarantee of the rights of man and citizen requires a public force; this force then is instituted for the advantage of all and not for the personal benefit of those to whom it is entrusted.

13. For the maintenance of the public force and for the expenses of

administration a general tax is indispensable; it ought to be equally apportioned among all the citizens according to their means.

14. All the citizens have the right to ascertain, by themselves or by their representatives, the necessity of the public tax, to consent to it freely, to follow the employment of it, and to determine the quota, the assessment, the collection, and the duration of it.

15. Society has the right to call for an account of his administration from every public agent.

16. Any society in which the guarantee of the rights is not secured, or the separation of powers not determined, has no constitution at all.

17. Property being a sacred and inviolable right, no one can be deprived of it, unless a legally established public necessity evidently demands it, under the condition of a just and prior indemnity.

FRENCH CONSTITUTION

The National Assembly, wishing to establish the French constitution upon the principles which it has just recognized and declared, abolished irrevocably the institutions that have injured liberty and the equality of rights.

There is no longer nobility, nor peerage, nor hereditary distinctions, nor distinctions of orders, nor feudal regime, nor patrimonial jurisdictions, nor any titles, denominations, or prerogatives derived therefrom, nor any order of chivalry, nor any corporations or decorations which demanded proofs of nobility or that were grounded upon distinctions of birth, nor any superiority other than that of public officials in the exercise of their functions.

There is no longer either sale or inheritance of any public office.

There is no longer for any part of the nation nor for any individual any privilege or exception to the law that is common to all Frenchmen.

There are no longer jurandes, nor corporations of professions, arts, and crafts.

The law no longer recognizes religious vows, nor any other obligation which may be contrary to natural rights or to the constitution.

TITLE I. FUNDAMENTAL PROVISIONS
RECOGNIZED BY THE CONSTITUTION

The constitution guarantees as natural and civil rights:

1. That all the citizens are eligible to offices and employments, without any other distinction than that of virtue and talent;

2. That all the taxes shall be equally apportioned among all the citizens in proportion to their means;

3. That like offences shall be punished by like penalties, without any distinction of persons.

The constitution likewise guarantees as natural and civil rights:

Liberty to every man to move about, to remain, and to depart without liability to arrest or detention, except according to the forms determined by the constitution.

Liberty to every man to speak, to write, to print and publish his ideas without having his writings subjected to any censorship or inspection before their publication, and to follow the religious worship to which he is attached;

Liberty to the citizens to meet peaceably and without arms, in obedience to the police laws;

Liberty to address individually signed petitions to the constituted authorities.

The legislative power cannot make any law that attacks and impedes the exercise of the natural and civil rights contained in the present titled and guaranteed by the constitution; but as liberty consists only in the power to do anything that is not injurious to the rights of others or to the public security, the law can establish penalties against acts which, in attacking the public security or the rights of others, may be injurious to society.

The constitution guarantees the inviolability of property or a just and prior indemnity for that of which a legally established public necessity may demand the sacrifice.

Property intended for the expenses of worship and for all services of public utility belongs to the nation and is at all times at its disposal.

The constitution guarantees the alienations that have been or that shall be made under the forms established by law.

The citizens have the right to elect or choose the ministers of their religious sects.

There shall be created and organized a general establishment of public relief in order to bring up abandoned children, relieve infirm paupers, and provide work for the able-bodied poor who may not have been able to obtain it for themselves.

There shall be created and organized a system of public instruction, common to all citizens, gratuitous as regards the parts of education indispensable for all men, and whose establishments shall be gradually distributed in accordance with the division of the kingdom.

There shall be established national fetes to preserve the memory of the French revolution, to maintain fraternity among the citizens, and to attach them to the constitution, the fatherland, and the laws.

A code of civil laws common to all the kingdom shall be made.

TITLE II. OF THE DIVISION OF THE KINGDOM
AND OF THE CONDITION OF THE CITIZENS

1. The kingdom is one and indivisible; its territory is divided into eighty-three departments, each department into districts, each district into cantons.

2. French citizens are:

Those who are born in French of a French father;

Those who, born in France of a foreign father, have fixed their residence in the kingdom;

Those who, born in a foreign country of a French father, have become established in France and have taken the civic oath;

Lastly, those who, born in a foreign country and descended in any degree whatsoever from a French man or a French woman expatriated on account of religion, may come to live in France and take the civic oath.

3. Those residing in France, who are born outside of the kingdom from foreign parents, become French citizens after five years of continued domicile in the kingdom, if they have in addition acquired real estate, or married a French woman, or formed an agricultural or commercial establishment, and have taken the civic oath.

4. The legislative power shall be able, for important considerations, to give to a foreigner a certificate of naturalization, without other conditions than the fixing of his domicile in France and the taking of the civic oath.

5. The civil oath is: I swear to be faithful to the nation, the law, and the king, and to maintain with all my power the constitution of the kingdom decreed by the National Constituent Assembly in the years 1789, 1790, and 1791.

6. The title to French citizenship is lost:

1st. By naturalization in a foreign country;

2nd. By condemnation to the penalties which involve civic degradation, as long as the condemned is not rehabilitated;

3rd. By a judgment of contempt of court; as long as the judgment is not annulled;

4th. By affiliation with any foreign order of knighthood, or with any foreign organization which would imply proofs of nobility or distinctions of birth, or which would demand religious vows.

7. The law considers marriage as only a civil contract. The legislative power shall establish for all inhabitants, without distinction, the manner in which births, marriages, and deaths shall be recorded, and it shall designate the public officers who shall receive and preserve the records thereof.

8. French citizens, considered in their local relations arising from their union into cities and into certain districts of rural territory, form communes.

The legislative power shall fix the extent of the district of each commune.

9. The citizens who compose each commune have the right to elect at stated times and according to the forms fixed by law those among themselves, who, under the title of municipal officers, are charged with carrying on the particular affairs of the commune.

Some functions related to the interests of the state may be delegated to the municipal officers.

10. The regulations which the municipal officers shall be required to follow in the exercise of their municipal functions, as well as those which have been delegated to them for the general interest, shall be fixed by the laws.

TITLE III. OF THE PUBLIC POWERS

1. Sovereignty is one, indivisible, inalienable, and imprescriptible: it belongs to the nation: no section of the people nor any individual can attribute to himself the exercise thereof.

2. The nation, from which alone emanates all the powers, can exercise them only by delegation.

The French constitution is representative; the representatives are the legislative body and the king.

3. The legislative power is delegated to one National Assembly, composed of temporary representatives freely elected by the people, in order to be exercised by it with the sanction of the king in the manner which shall be determined hereafter.

4. The government is monarchical: the executive power is delegated to the king, in order to be exercised under his authority by ministers and other responsible agents, in the manner which shall be determined hereinafter.

5. The judicial power is delegated to judges elected at stated times by the people.

Chapter I. Of the National Legislative Assembly

1. The National Assembly, forming the legislative body, is permanent and is composed of only one chamber.

2. It shall be formed every two years by new elections. Each period of two years shall constitute a legislature.

3. The provisions of the preceding article shall not operate with respect to the next legislative body, whose powers shall cease the last day of April, 1973.

4. The renewal of the legislative body takes place ipso facto.

5. The legislative body shall not be dissolved by the king.

Section I. Number of the representatives—Basis of representation

1. The number of representatives in the legislative body is seven hundred and forty-five, by reason of the eighty-three departments of which the kingdom is composed, and apart from those which may be granted to the colonies.

2. The representatives shall be distributed among the eighty-three departments according to the three proportions of territory, population, and direct tax.

3. Of the seven hundred and forty-five representatives, two hundred and forty-seven are accredited for territory.

Each department shall select three of these, with the exception of the department of Paris which shall select but one.

4. Two hundred and forty-nine are accredited for population.

The total mass of the population of the kingdom is divided into two hundred and forty-nine parts, and each department selects as many deputies as it has parts of population.

5. Two hundred and forty-nine representatives are accredited for the direct tax.

The sum total of the direct tax of the kingdom is likewise divided into two hundred and forty-nine parts, and each department selects as many deputies as it pays part of the tax.

Section II. Primary Assemblies—Selection of the Electors

1. In order to form the National Legislative Assembly the active citizens shall meet every two years in primary assemblies in the cities and cantons.

The primary assemblies shall constitute themselves ipso factor on the second Sunday of March, if they have not been convoked earlier by the public functionaries designated by the law.

2. In order to be an active citizen it is necessary to be born or to become a Frenchman; to be fully twenty-five years of age; to be domiciled in the city or in the canton for the time fixed by the law;

To pay in some place within the kingdom a direct tax at the least equal to the value of three days of labor, and to present the receipt therefor;

Not to be in a state of domestic service, that is to say, not to be a servant for wages;

To be registered upon the roll of the national guards in the municipality of his domicile;

To have taken the civic oath.

3. Every six years the legislative body shall fix the minimum and maximum of the value of a day's labor, and the department administrators shall make the local determination thereof for each department.

4. No one may exercise the rights of an active citizen in more than one place, nor cause himself to be represented by another.

5. The following are excluded from the exercise of the rights of active citizenship:

Those who are under indictment;

Those who, after having been declared to be in a state of bankruptcy or insolvency, proven by authentic documents, do not procure a general discharge from their creditors.

6. The primary assemblies shall select electors in proportion to the number of active citizens domiciled in the city or canton.

There shall be one elector selected at the rate of one hundred active citizens, whether present at the assembly or not.

There shall be two selected for one hundred and fifty-one up to two hundred, and so on.

7. No one can be chosen an elector if he does not unite with the conditions necessary to be an active citizen, the following:

In the cities over six thousand souls, that of being proprietor or usufructuary of an estate valued upon the tax rolls at a revenue equal to the value of a hundred and fifty days of labor;

In cities under six thousand souls that of being proprietor or usufructuary of an estate valued upon the tax rolls at a revenue equal to the local value of a hundred and fifty days of labor, or of being the occupant of a habitation valued upon the same rolls at a revenue equal to the value of a hundred days of labor;

And in the country, that of being the proprietor of usufructuary of an estate valued upon the tax rolls at a revenue equal to the local value of one hundred and fifty day of labor, or that of being the farmer or metayer of estates valued upon the same rolls at the value of four hundred days of labor.

With respect to those who shall at the same time be proprietors or usufructuaries for one part and occupants, farmers or metayers for another, their means by these different titles shall be cumulated up to the amount necessary to establish their eligibility.

Section III. Electoral assemblies—Selection of representatives

1. The electors chosen in each department shall assemble in order to elect the number of representatives whose selection shall be assigned to their department and a number of substitutes equal to a third of that of the representatives.

The electoral assemblies shall constitute themselves ipso facto on the last Sunday in March, if they have not been convoked earlier by the public functionaries designated by the law.

2. The representatives and the substitutes shall be elected by majority of the votes, and they shall be chosen only from among the active citizens of the department.

3. All active citizens, whatever their condition, profession, or tax, can be elected representatives of the nation.

4. Nevertheless, the ministers and other agents of the executive power removable at pleasure, the commissioners of the national treasury, the collectors and receivers of the direct taxes, the overseers of the collection and administration of the indirect taxes and national domains, and those who, under any denomination whatsoever are attached to the military and civil household of the king, shall be obliged to choose [between their offices and that of representative].

The administrators, sub-administrators, municipal officers, and commandants of the national guards shall likewise be required to choose [between their offices and that of representative].

5. The exercise of judicial functions shall be incompatible with that of representative of the nation, for the entire duration of the legislature.

The judges shall be replaced by their substitutes, and the king shall provide by commissionary warrants for the replacement of his commissioners before the tribunals.

6. The members of the legislative body can be re-elected to the following legislature, and they can be elected thereafter only after the interval of one legislature.

7. The representatives selected in the department shall not be the representatives of one particular department, but of the entire nation, and no instructions can be given them.

Section IV. Meeting and government of the primary electoral assemblies

1. The functions of the primary and electoral assemblies are confined to election; they shall separate immediately after the elections have taken place and they shall not form themselves again unless they shall be convoked, except in the case of the 1st article of section II and of the 1st article of section III above.

2. No active citizen can enter or cast his vote in an assembly, if he is armed.

3. The armed force shall not be introduced into its midst without the express wish of the assembly, unless violence is committed there; in that case the order of the president shall suffice to summon in the public force.

4. Every two years there shall be drawn up in each district lists by cantons of the active citizens, and the list of each canton shall be published and posted there two months before the date of the primary assembly.

The complaints which shall arise, either to contest the qualifications of the citizens placed upon the list or on the part of those who shall allege that they are unjustly omitted, shall be brought before the tribunals in order to be passed upon there summarily.

The list shall serve as the rule for the admission of the citizens in the next primary assembly in everything that shall not have been rectified by the judgments rendered before the holding of the assembly.

5. The electoral assemblies have the right to verify the title and the credentials of those who shall present themselves there, and their decisions, shall be carried out provisionally, saving the judgment of the legislative body at the time of the verification of the credentials of the deputies.

6. In no case and under no circumstances shall the king or any of the agents appointed by him assume jurisdiction over questions relative to the regularity of the convocations, the holding of the assemblies, the form of the elections, or the political rights of the citizens, without prejudice to the functions of the commissioners of the king in the cases determined by the law where questions relative to the political rights of citizens must be brought before the tribunals.

Section V. Meeting of the representatives in National Legislative Assembly

1. The representatives shall meet on the first Monday of the month of May in the place of the sittings of the last legislature.

2. They shall form themselves provisionally in assembly under the presidency of the oldest member in point of age, in order to verify the credentials of the representative present.

3. As soon as there shall be verified members to the number of three hundred and seventy-three, they shall constitute themselves under the title of National Legislative Assembly; it shall name a president, a vice-president, and secretaries, and shall begin the exercise of its functions.

4. During the entire course of the month of May, if the number of the representatives present is under three hundred and seventy-three, the assembly shall not be able to perform any legislative act.

It can pass an order requiring the absent members to repair to their duties within the period of fifteen days at the latest, upon penalty of 3,000 livres fine, if they do not present an excuse which shall be pronounced legitimate by the assembly.

5. On the last day of May, whatever may be the number of the members present, they shall constitute themselves into National Legislative Assembly.

6. The representatives shall pronounce in unison, in the name of the French people, the oath to live free or to die.

They shall afterwards individually take the oath to maintain with all their power the constitution of the kingdom, decreed by the National Constituent Assembly, in the years 1789, 1790, and 1791; and not to propose nor to consent within the course of the legislature to anything which may injure it, and to be in everything faithful to the nation, the law, and the king.

7. The representatives of the nation are inviolable; they cannot be questioned, accused, nor tried at any time for what they have said, written, or done in the exercise of their functions as representatives.

8. They can, for criminal acts, be seized in the very act or in virtue of a warrant of arrest; but notice shall be given thereof without delay to the legislative body; and the prosecution can be continued only after the legislative body shall have decided that there is occasion for accusation.

Chapter II. Of the Royalty, the Regency, and the Ministers

Section I. Of the royalty and the king

1. Royalty is indivisible and is delegated hereditarily to the ruling family, from male to male, by order of primogeniture, to the perpetual exclusion of females and their descendants.

(Nothing is presumed about the effect of renunciations in the actually ruling family.)

2. The person of the king is inviolable and sacred: his only title is King of the French.

3. There is no authority in France superior to that of the law; the king reigns only by it and it is only in the name of the law that he can demand obedience.

4. The king, upon his accession to the throne or as soon as he shall have attained his majority, shall take to the nation, in the presence of the legislative body, the oath to be faithful to the nation and the law, to employ all the power which is delegated to him to maintain the constitution decreed by the National Constituent Assembly in the years 1789, 1790, and 1791, and to cause the laws to be executed.

If the legislative body is not assembled, the king shall cause a proclamation to be published, in which shall be set forth this oath and the promise to reiterate it as soon as the legislative body shall assemble.

5. If, one month after the invitation of the legislative body, the king shall not have taken this oath, or if, after having taken it, he retracts it, he shall be considered to have abdicated the throne.

6. If the king puts himself at the head of an army and directs the forces thereof against the nation, or if he does not by a formal instrument place himself in opposition to any such enterprise which may be conducted in his name, he shall be considered to have abdicated the throne.

7. If the king, having left the kingdom, should not return after the invitation which shall be made to him for that purpose by the legislative body and within the period which shall be fixed by the proclamation, which shall not be less than two months, he shall be considered to have abdicated the throne.

The period shall begin to run from the day when the proclamation of the legislative body shall have been published in the place of its sittings; and the ministers shall be required under their responsibility to perform all the acts of the executive power, whose exercise shall be suspended in the hands of the absent King.

8. After the express or legal abdication, the king shall be in the class of citizens and can be accused and tried like them for acts subsequent to his abdication.

9. The individual estates which the king possesses upon his accession to the throne are irrevocably united to the domain of the nation: he has the disposal of those which he acquires by personal title; if he does not dispose of them they are likewise united at the end of the reign.

10. The nation provides for the splendor of the throne by a civil list, of which the legislative body shall determine the sum at each change of reign for the entire duration of the reign.

11. The king shall appoint an administrator of the civil list, who shall conduct the judicial actions of the king, and against whom all the actions against the king shall be directed and judgments pronounced. The judgments obtained by the creditors of the civil list shall be executable against the adminstrator personally and upon his own estates.

12. The king shall have, apart from the guard of honor which shall be furnished him by the citizen national guards of the place of his residence, a guard paid out of the funds of the civil list; it shall not exceed the number of twelve hundred infantrymen and six hundred cavalrymen.

The grades and regulations for promotion in it shall be the same as in the troops of the line; but those who shall compose the guard of the king shall advance for all the grades exclusively among themselves, and they cannot obtain any of those in the army of the line.

The king can choose the men of his guard only from among those who are actually in active service in the troops of the line, or from among the citizens who for a year past have done service as national guards, provided they be residents of the kingdom and have previously taken the civic oath.

The guard of the king cannot be ordered or requisitioned for any other public service.

Section II. Of the regency

1. The king is a minor until he is fully eighteen years old; and during his minority there is a regent of the kingdom.

2. The regency belongs to the kinsman of the king nearest in degree, according to the order of inheritance to the throne, and fully twenty-five years of age, provided that he be French and native born, that he be not heir presumptive of another crown, and that he has previously taken the civic oath.

Women are excluded from the regency.

3. If a minor king has no kinsman uniting the qualifications above set forth, the regent of the kingdom shall be elected as provided in the following articles.

4. The legislative body cannot elect the regent.

5. The electors of each district shall meet at the headtown of the district, according to the proclamation which shall be made in the first week of the new reign by the legislative body, if it is assembled; and if it is separated, the minister of justice shall be required to issue this proclamation within the same week.

6. The electors in each district shall appoint, by individual ballot and majority of the votes, an eligible citizen domiciled within the district, to whom they shall give, by the minutes of the election, a special mandate limited to the single function of electing the citizen whom he shall judge, upon his soul and his conscience, the most worthy to be elected regent of the realm.

7. The mandatory citizens appointed by the districts shall be required to meet in the city where the legislative body is to hold its sitting, on the fortieth day at the latest from the accession of the minor king to the throne, and they shall form the electoral assembly which shall proceed to appointment of the regent.

8. The electoral assembly shall be able to occupy itself only with the election and shall separate as soon as the election shall be concluded; any other act which it may undertake to do is declared unconstitutional and void.

10. The electoral assembly shall cause the minutes of the election to be presented by its president to the legislative body, which, after having verified the regularity of the election, shall cause it to be published in all the kingdom by a proclamation.

11. The regent exercises, until the majority of the king, all the functions of royalty, and he is not personally responsible for acts of his administration.

12. The regent can begin the exercise of his functions only after having taken to the nation, in the presence of the legislative body, the oath to be faithful to the nation, the law, and the king; to employ all the power delegated to the king, and the exercise of which is confided to him during the minority of the king, to maintain the constitution decreed by the National Constituent Assembly in the years 1789, 1790, and 1791, and to cause the laws to be executed.

If the legislative body is not assembled, the regent shall cause a proclamation to be published in which shall be expressed his oath and the promise to repeat it as soon as the legislative body shall be assembled.

13. As long as the regent has not entered upon the exercise of his functions, the sanction of the laws remains suspended; the ministers continue to perform under their responsibility all acts of the executive power.

14. As soon as the regent shall have taken the oath, the legislative body shall determine his stipend, which cannot be changed during the continuance of the regency.

15. If, on account of the minority of the kinsman summoned to the regency, it shall have devolved upon a more remote kinsman, or shall have been bestowed by election, the regent who shall have entered upon the exercise of it shall continue his functions until the majority of the king.

16. The regency of the kingdom does not confer any right over the person of the minor king.

17. The custody of the minor king shall be confided to his mother; and if he has no mother, or if she has been married again at the time of the accession of her son to the throne, or if she marries again during the minority, the custody shall be bestowed by the legislative body.

Neither the regent and his descendants, nor women, can be elected to the guardianship of the minor king.

18. In case of notoriously recognized insanity of the king, legally established and declared by the legislative body after three deliberations taken successively from month to month, there shall be occasion for a regency as long as the insanity lasts.

Section III. Of the family of the king

1. The heir presumptive shall bear the name of Prince Royal.

He cannot leave the kingdom without a decree of the legislative body and the consent of the king.

If he does leave it, and if, having reached the age of eighteen years, he does not return to France after having been required to do so by a proclamation of the legislative body, he is considered to have abdicated the right of succession to the throne.

2. If the heir presumptive is a minor, the kinsman of full age first summoned to the regency is required to reside within the kingdom.

In case he may have left it and should not return upon the requisition of the legislative body, he shall be considered to have abdicated his right to the regency.

3. The mother of the minor king, having his custody, or the elected guardian, if they leave the kingdom, are deprived of the custody.

If the mother of the minor heir presumptive should leave the realm, she cannot, even after her return, have the custody of her minor son who has become king, except by a decree of the legislative body.

4. A law shall be made to govern the education of the minor king and that of the heir presumptive.

5. The members of the family of the king entitled to the eventual succession to the throne enjoy the rights of active citizenship, but they are not eligible to any of the places, employments, or functions which are at the disposal of the people.

With the exception of the departments of the ministry, they are eligible to the places and employments at the disposal of the king; nevertheless, they shall not command in chief any military or naval forces, nor fulfill the functions of ambassadors, except with the consent of the legislative body, granted upon the proposal of the king.

6. The members of the family of the king entitled to eventual succession to the throne shall add the denomination of French Prince to the name which shall have been given them in the civil certificate attesting their birth, and this name cannot be patronymical nor formed from any of the titles abolished by the present constitution.

The denomination of prince shall not be given to any other person and it shall not bestow any privileges nor any exception to the rights common to all Frenchmen.

7. The certificates by which shall be attested the births, marriages, and deaths of the French princes shall be presented to the legislative body, which shall order the deposit of them in its archives.

8. No real estate appanage shall be granted to members of the family of the king.

The younger sons of the king shall receive at the age of twenty-one years, or at the time of their marriage, an appanaged income which shall be fixed by the legislative body and shall terminate with the extinction of their masculine posterity.

Section IV. Of the ministers

1. The choice and dismissal of the ministers shall belong to the king alone.

2. The members of the present National Assembly and of the legislatures following, the members of the tribunal of cassation, and those who shall serve on the high jury, cannot be promoted to the ministry, nor receive any place, gift, pension, stipend, or commission from the executive power or from its agents, during the continuance of their functions, nor for two years after having ceased the exercise of them.

It shall be the same with those who are only enrolled upon the list of the high jury, during the time that their enrollment shall continue.

3. No one can enter upon the exercise of any employment either in the offices of the ministry or in those of the management or administration of the public revenues, nor in general any employment at the nomination of the executive power, without taking the civic oath, or without proving that he has taken it.

4. No order of the king can be excuted unless it is signed by him and countersigned by the minister or administrator of the department.

5. The ministers are responsible for all the offences committed by themselves against the national security and the constitution;

For every attack upon property and personal liberty;

For all waste of monies appropriated for the expenses of their departments.

6. In no case can the order of the king, verbal or in writing, shield a minister from his responsibility.

7. The ministers are required to present each year to the legislative body at the opening of the session an estimate of the expenditures to be made in their departments, to render account of the employment of the sums which were appropriated for them, and to indicate the abuses which may have been able to introduce themselves into the different parts of the government.

8. No minister, in office or out of office, can be prosecuted for any acts of his administration, without a decree of the legislative body.

Chapter III. Of the Exercise of the Legislative Power

Section I. Powers and Functions of the National Legislative Assembly

1. The constitution delegates exclusively to the legislative body the following powers and functions:

1st. To propose and enact laws; the king can only invite the legislative body to take the matter under consideration;

2d. To fix the public expenditures;

3d. To establish the public taxes, to determine the nature of them, the quota, the duration, and the mode of collection;

4th. To make the apportionment of the direct tax among the departments of the kingdom, to supervise the employment of all the public revenues, and to cause an account of them to be rendered;

5th. To decree the creation or suppression of public offices;

6th. To determine the title, weight, stamp, and denomination of the monies;

7th. To permit or forbid the introduction of foreign troops upon French soil and foreign naval forces in the ports of the kingdom;

8th. To determine annually, after the proposal of the king, the number of men and vessels of which the land and naval forces shall be composed; the pay and the number of persons of each grade; the rules for admission and promotion, the forms of enrollment and discharge, the formation of ship crews; the admission of troops or foreign forces into the service of France, and the treatment of troops in case of disbandment;

9th. To determine upon the administration and to order the alienation of the national lands;

10th. To institute before the High National Court legal proceedings for securing the responsibility of the ministers and the principal agents of the executive power;

To accuse and to prosecute before the same court those who shall be charged with attacks and conspiracies against the general security of the state or against the constitution;

11th. To establish laws according to which purely personal marks of honor or decorations shall be granted to those who have rendered services to the state;

12th. The legislative body alone has the right to award public honors to the memory of great men.

2. War can be declared only by a decree of the legislative body, rendered upon the formal and indispensable proposal of the king, and sanctioned by him.

In case hostilities are imminent or already begun, or in case of an alliance to sustain or a right to preserve by force of arms, the king shall give notification of it without delay to the legislative body and shall make known the causes thereof. If the legislative body is in recess the king shall convoke it immediately.

If the legislative body decides that war ought not to be made, the king shall take measures immediately to cause the cessation or prevention of all hostilities, the ministers remaining responsible for delays.

If the legislative body finds the hostilities already commenced to be a culpable aggression on the part of the ministers or of any other agent of the executive power, the author of the aggression shall be prosecuted criminally.

During the entire course of the war the legislative body can require the king to negotiate for peace; and the king is required to yield to this requisition.

As soon as the war shall have ceased the legislative body shall fix the period within which the troops raised in excess of the peace footing shall be discharged and the army reduced to its usual condition.

3. The ratification of treaties of peace, alliance, and commerce belongs to the legislative body; and no treaty shall have effect except by this ratification.

4. The legislative body has the right to determine the place of its sittings, to continue them as long as it shall judge necessary, and to adjourn. At the beginning of each reign, if it is not in session, it shall be required to reassemble without delay.

It has the right of police over the place of its sittings, and over the environs which it shall have determined.

It has the right of discipline over its members; but it cannot impose punishment more severe than censure, arrest for eight days, or imprisonment for three days.

It has the right, for its security and for the maintenance of the respect that is due to it, to dispose of the forces, which with its own consent shall be established in the city where it shall hold its sittings.

5. The executive power cannot cause any body of troops of the line to pass or sojourn within thirty thousand toises of the legislative body, except upon its requisition or with its authorisation.

Section II. Holding of the meetings and the form of deliberation

1. The deliberation of the legislative body shall be public and the minutes of its sittings shall be printed.

2. The legislative body, nevertheless, may at any time form itself into committee of the whole.

Fifty members shall have the right to require it.

During the continuance of the committee of the whole the clerks shall retire, the chair of the president shall be vacant; order shall be maintained by the vice-president.

3. No legislative act shall be deliberated upon or decreed, except in the following form.

4. There shall be three readings of the project for a decree at three intervals, each of which shall not be less than eight days.

5. The discussion shall be open after each reading; nevertheless, after the first or second reading, the legislative body may declare that there is need for adjournment or that there is no need for consideration of it; but in this case, the project for a decree can be presented again in the same session.

Every project for a decree shall be printed and distributed before the second reading of it can be given.

6. After the third reading, the president shall be required to put in deliberation and the legislative body shall decide whether it finds itself in condition to render a definitive decree or whether it wishes to postpone the decision to another time in order to receive more ample enlightenment.

7. The legislative body cannot deliberate unless the sitting is composed of at least two hundred members, and no decree shall be passed except by a majority of the votes.

8. No project of law which, submitted to discussion, shall have been rejected after the third reading can be presented again in the same session.

9. The preamble of every definitive decree shall announce expressly: 1st, the dates of the sittings at which the three readings of the project shall have occurred; 2d, the decree by which, after the third reading, it shall have been determined to decide definitively.

10. The king shall refuse his sanction to a decree whose preamble does not attest the observation of the above forms: if any of these decrees be sanctioned, the ministers shall not seal it and promulgate it, and their responsibility in this respect shall last for six years.

11. The decrees recognized and declared urgent by a prior declaration of the legislative body are excepted from the above provisions; but they can be modified or revoked in the course of the same session.

The decree by which the matter shall have been declared urgent shall set forth the motives thereof; and there shall be mention made of this prior decree in the preamble of the definitive decree.

Section III. Of the royal sanction

1. The decrees of the legislative body are presented to the king, who can refuse his consent to them.

2. In the case where the king refuses his consent, this refusal is only suspensive.

When the two legislatures following that which shall have presented the decree shall have again presented the same decree in the same terms, the king shall be considered to have given the sanction.

3. The consent of the king is expressed upon each decree by this formula signed by the king: The king consents and will cause it to be executed.

The suspensive refusal is expressed by this: The king will examine.

4. The king is required to express his consent or his refusal upon each decree within two months from the presentation.

5. No decree to which the king has refused his consent can be presented again by the same legislature.

6. The decrees sanctioned by the king and those which shall have been presented by three consecutive legislatures have the force of law, and bear the name and title of laws.

7. The following are executed as laws, without being subject to the sanction: The acts of the legislative body concerning its constitution in deliberative assembly;

Its internal police, and that which it is allowed to exercise in the environs which it shall have determined;

The verification of the credentials of its members in attendance;

Orders to the absent members;

The convocation of the primary assemblies which are late;

The exercise of the constitutional police over the administrators and the municipal officers;

Questions either of eligibility or of the validity of elections.

In like manner, neither the acts relative to the responsibility of the ministers, nor the decrees providing that there is cause for accusation are subject to the sanction.

8. The decrees of the legislative body concerning the establishment, the promulgation, and the collection of the public taxes shall bear the name and the title of laws. They shall be promulgated and executed without being subject to the sanction, except for the provisions which establish penalties other than fines and pecuniary constraints.

These decrees cannot be rendered except in accordance with the formalities prescribed by articles 4, 5, 6, 7, 8 and 9 of section II of the present chapter; and the legislative body shall not insert in them any provision foreign to their purpose.

Section IV. Relations of the Legislative Body with the King

1. When the legislative body is definitely constituted, it sends to the king a deputation in order to inform him thereof. The king can each year open the session and can bring forward the matters which he believes ought to be taken into consideration in the course of that session, without this formality, nevertheless, being considered as necessary for the activity of the legislative body.

2. When the legislative body wishes to adjourn beyond fifteen days, it is required to notify the king thereof by a deputation, at least eight days in advance.

3. At least eight days before the end of each session, the legislative body sends to the king a deputation, in order to announce to him the day whereon it proposes to terminate its sittings. The king can come to close the session.

4. If the king thinks it important for the welfare of the state that the session be continued, or that the adjournment should not occur, or that it should occur only for a shorter time, he can send a message to that effect, upon which the legislative body is required to deliberate.

5. The king shall convoke the legislative body during the intermission of its sessions, whenever the interest of the state appear to him to require it, as well as in the cases which have been provided for and determined by the legislative body before its adjournment.

6. Whenever the king repairs to the place of the sittings of the legislative body, he shall be received and conducted by a deputation; he cannot be accompanied within the interior of the hall except by the prince royal and the ministers.

7. In no case can the president make up part of a deputation.

8. The legislative body shall cease to be a deliberative body as long as the king shall be present.

9. The documents of the correspondence of the king with the legislative body shall always be countersigned by a minister.

10. The ministers of the king shall have entrance into the National Legislative Assembly; they shall have a designated place there.

They shall be heard, whenever they shall demand it, upon matters relative to their administrations or when they shall be required to give information.

They shall likewise be heard upon matters foreign to their administration when the National Assembly shall grant them the word.

Chapter IV. Of the Exercise of the Executive Power

1. The supreme executive power resides exclusively in the hands of the king.

The king is the supreme head of the general administration of the kingdom; the task of looking after the maintenance of public order and tranquility is confided to him.

The king is the supreme head of the army and navy.

The task of looking after the external security of the kingdom and of maintaining its rights and possessions is delegated to the king.

2. The king appoints the ambassadors and other agents of political negotiations.

He confers the command of the armies and fleets, and the grades of marshall and admiral.

He appoints two-thirds of the rear-admirals, half of the lieutenant generals, camp-marshals, ship-captains, and colonels of the national gendarmerie.

He appoints two-thirds of the colonels and lieutenant colonels, and a sixth of the ship-lieutenants.

All of these conforming to the laws upon promotion.

He appoints in the civil administration of the navy the managers, comptrollers, treasurers of the arsenals, heads of the works, under-chiefs of civil buildings, and half of the heads of administration and under-chiefs of construction.

He appoints the commissioners before the tribunals.

He appoints the officers-in-chief for the administrations of the indirect taxes and for the administration of the national lands.

He superintends the coining of monies, and appoints the officers charged with the exercise of this surveillance in the general commission and in the mints.

The image of the king is stamped upon all the monies of the kingdom.

3. The king causes to be delivered the letters-patent, warrants, and commissions, to public functionaries or others who ought to receive them.

4. The king causes to be drawn up the list of the pensions and gratuities, in order to be presented to the legislative body at each of its sessions and to be decreed, if there is need thereof.

Section I. Of the promulgation of the laws

1. The executive power is charged to cause the laws to be sealed with the seal of the state and to cause them to be promulgated.

It is likewise charged to cause to be promulgated and to be executed the acts of the legislative body which do not need the sanction of the king.

2. There shall be made two original copies of each law, both signed by the king, countersigned by the minister of justice, and sealed with the seal of the state.

One shall remain on deposit in the archives of the seal, and the other shall be placed in the archives of the legislative body.

3. The promulgation shall be thus expressed:

"N. (the name of the king), by the grace of God, and by the constitutional law of the state, King of the French, to all present and to come, greeting. The National Assembly has decreed, and we wish and order as follows:"

(A literal copy of the decree shall be inserted without any change.)

"We command and order to all the administrative bodies and the tribunals that they cause these presents to be recorded in their registers, read, published, and posted in their respective departments and jurisdictions, and executed as law of the kingdom. In testimony whereof we have signed these presents, to which we have caused to be affixed the seal of the state."

4. If the king is a minor, the laws, proclamations, and other documents emanating from the royal authority during the regency shall be expressed as follows:

"N. (the name of the regent), regent of the kingdom, in the name of N. (the name of the king), by the grace of God and by the constitutional law of the state, King of the French, etc., etc."

5. The executive power is required to send the laws to the administrative bodies and the tribunals, to cause the transmission to be certified, and to give proof thereof to the legislative body.

6. The executive power cannot make any law, even provisionally, but only proclamations in conformity with the laws to order or call to mind the execution of them.

Section II. Of the internal administration

1. In each department there is a superior administration, and in each district a subordinate administration.

2. The administrators do not have any representative character.

They are agents elected at stated times by the people to exercise, under the surveillance and authority of the king, the administrative functions.

3. They cannot interfere in the exercise of the legislative power, not suspend the execution of the laws, nor encroach in any manner upon the judiciary, nor upon the military arrangements or operations.

4. The administrators are essentially charged with the apportionment of the direct taxes and the surveillance of the monies arising from all the public taxes and revenues in their territory.

It belongs to the legislative power to determine the regulations and the mode of their functions, upon the matters above expressed as well as upon all the other parts of the internal administration.

5. The king has the right to annul the acts of the department administrators which are contrary to the laws or to the orders which shall have been addressed to them.

He can suspend them from their functions, in case of persistent disobedience, or if they compromise by their acts the public security of tranquility.

6. The department administrators, likewise, have the right to annul the acts of the district sub-administrators which are contrary to the laws, or to the decisions of the department administrators, or to the orders which these latter shall have given or transmitted. They can, likewise, suspend them from their functions in case of persistent disobedience, or if these latter compromise by their acts the public security or tranquility, provided that notification thereof be given to the king who can remove or confirm the suspension.

7. When the department administrators shall not have used the power which is delegated to them in the article above, the king can annul directly the acts of the sub-administrators and suspend them in the same cases.

8. Whenever the king shall have pronounced or confirmed the suspension of administrators or sub-administrators, he shall give notice thereof to the legislative body.

This [body] may remove the suspension or confirm it, or even dissolve the guilty administration and, if there is need, send all the administrators or any of them in the criminal tribunals, or bring against them the decree of accusation.

Section III. Of the external relations

1. The king alone can enter upon political relations abroad, conduct negotiations, make preparations for war proportioned to those of the neighboring states, distribute the forces of the army and the navy as he shall deem suitable and control the direction thereof in case of war.

2. Every declaration of war shall be made in these terms: On the part of the King of the French, in the name of the nation.

3. It belongs to the king to conclude and sign with all foreign powers all treaties of peace, alliance, and commerce, and all other conventions which he shall deem necessary for the welfare of the state, subject to the ratification of the legislative body.

Chapter V. Of the Judicial Power

1. The judicial power cannot in any case be exercised by the legislative body nor the king.

2. Justice shall be rendered gratuitously by judges elected at stated times by the people and instituted by letters patent of the king, who cannot refuse them.

They cannot be removed except for duly pronounced forfeiture, nor suspended save by an accepted accusation.

The public accuser shall be chosen by the people.

3. The tribunals cannot interfere in the exercise of the legislative power, nor suspend the execution of the laws, nor encroach upon the

administrative functions, nor cite before them the administrator on account of their functions.

4. Citizens cannot be deprived of the judges whom the law assigns to them by any commission, nor by other attributions and evocations that those determined by the laws.

5. The right of citizens to terminate definitively their controversies by means of arbitration cannot be impaired by the acts of the legislative power.

6. The ordinary tribunals cannot entertain any civil action unless it should be shown to them that the parties have appeared, or that the plaintiff has cited the adverse party before mediators, in order to obtain a conciliation.

7. There shall be one or several justices of the peace in the cantons and cities; the number thereof shall be determined by the legislative power.

8. It belongs to the legislative power to regulate the number and the district of the tribunals, and the number of the judges of which each tribunal shall be composed.

9. In criminal matters no citizen can be tried except upon an accusation received by the jurors or decreed by the legislative body, in the cases where the preferring of the accusation belongs to it.

After the accusation has been accepted, the facts shall be recognized and declared by the jurors.

The accused shall have the right to reject up to twenty of these without giving reasons.

The jurors who shall declare the facts shall not be less than twelve in number.

The application of the law shall be made by the judges.

The proceedings shall be public and the assistance of counsel shall not be refused to the accused.

Nor man acquitted by a legal jury can be taken again or accused on account of the same act.

10. No man can be seized except in order to be brought before the police officer; and no man can be put under arrest or detained, except in virtue of a warrant from police officers, an order of arrest from a tribunal, a decree of accusation of the legislative body, in case the decision belongs to it, or of a sentence of condemnation to prison or correctional detention.

11. Every man seized and brought before the police officers shall be examined immediately, or at the latest within twenty-four hours.

If the examination shows that there is no ground for incrimination, he shall be set at liberty immediately; or if there is occasion for sending him to jail, he shall be taken there within the briefest possible interval, which in any case shall not exceed three days.

12. No arrested man can be kept in confinement in any case in which the law permits remaining free under bail, if he gives sufficient bail.

13. No man, in a case in which his detention is authorised by law, can

be brought to or confined anywhere except in the places legally and publicly designated to serve as jail, court house, or prison.

14. No custodian nor jailer can receive or confine any man, except in virtue of a warrant or order of arrest, decree of accusation or sentence mentioned in article 10 above, and unless the transcript thereof has been made upon his register.

15. Every custodian or jailer is required, without any order being able to dispense therewith, to present the person of the prisoner to the civil officer having the police of the jail, whenever it shall be required by him.

In like manner the presentation of the person of the prisoner cannot be refused to his kinsmen and friends bearing the order of the civil officer, who shall always be required to grant it, unless the custodian or jailer presents an order of the judge, transcribed upon his register, to keep the accused in secret.

16. Any man, whatever may be his place or his employment, other than those to whom the law gives the right of arrest, who shall give, sign, execute or cause to be executed an order or arrest for a citizen, or anyone, who, even in the case of arrest authorized by law, shall conduct, receive, or retain a citizen in a place of detention not publicly and legally designated, and any custodian or jailer who shall contravene the provisions of articles 14 and 15 above, shall be guilty of the crime of arbitrary imprisonment.

17. No man can be questioned or prosecuted on account of writings which he shall have cause to be printed or published upon any matter whatsoever, unless he has intentionally instigated disobedience to the law, contempt for the constituted authorities, resistance to their acts, or any of the acts declared crimes or offences by the law.

Criticism upon the acts of the constituted authorities is permitted; but wilful calumnies against the probity of the public functionaries and the rectitude of their intentions in the exercise of their functions can be prosecuted by those who are the object of them.

Calumnies and injuries against any persons whatsoever relative acts of their private life shall be punished upon their prosecutions.

18. No one can be tried either by civil or criminal process for written, printed, or published facts, unless it has been recognized and declared by a jury: 1st, whether there is an offence in the writing denounced, 2d, whether the prosecuted person is guilty.

19. There shall be for all the kingdom a single tribunal of cassation, established near the legislative body. Its functions shall be to pronounce:

Upon petitions in cassation against the judgments rendered in the last resort by the tribunals;

Upon petitions for transfer from one tribunal to another, on account of legitimate suspicion;

Upon orders of judges and the charges of prejudice against an entire tribunal.

20. In matters of cassation the tribunal of cassation shall never be able to take jurisdiction over the facts of suits; but after having quashed the judgment rendered upon a proceeding in which the forms shall have been violated, or which shall contain an express contravention of the law, it shall remand the facts of the trial to the tribunal which ought to have jurisdiction therein.

21. When after two cassations, the judgment of the third tribunal shall be attacked by the same means as the first two, the question shall not be further discussed in the tribunal of cassation without having been submitted to the legislative body, which shall pass a decree declaratory of the law, to which the tribunal of cassation shall be required to conform.

22. Each year the tribunal of cassation shall be required to send to the bar of the legislative body a deputation of eight of its members, who shall present to it a list of the judgments rendered, along with each of which shall be a condensed account of the suit and the text of the law which shall have determined the decision.

23. A high national court, formed of members of the tribunal of cassation and of high jurors, shall have jurisdiction over the offences of the ministers and principal agents of the executive power, and over crimes which shall assail the general security of the state, when the legislative body shall have rendered a decree of accusation.

It shall not assemble except upon the decree of the legislative body, and only at a distance of at least thirty thousand toises from the place where the legislative body shall hold its sittings.

24. The writs of execution of the tribunals shall be expressed as follows:

"N. (the name of the king), by the grace of God and by the constitutional law of the state, King of the French, to all present and to come, greeting. The tribunal of . . . has rendered the following judgment:

(Here shall be copied the judgment, in which mention shall be made of the names of the judges.)

"We command and order to all bailiffs, upon this requisition, to put the said judgment into execution; to our commissioners before the tribunals, to support them; and to all commandants and officers of the public forces, to lend assistance, when they shall be legally summoned thereto. In testimony of which, the present judgment has been signed by the president of the tribunal and the clerk."

25. The functions of the commissioners of the king before the tribunals shall be to require the observation of the laws in the judgments rendered, and to cause the judgments rendered to be executed.

They shall not be public accusers, but they shall be heard upon all accusations and shall make demand for the regularity of the forms, during the course of the proceedings, and for the application of the law before the sentence.

26. The commissioners of the king before the tribunals shall denounce to the foreman of the jury, either ex-officio or in consequence of the orders which shall be given them by the king:

Attacks upon the personal liberty of the citizens, against the free circulation of provisions and other articles of commerce, and against the collection of the taxes;

Offences by which the execution of the orders given by the king in the exercise of the functions which are delegated to him may be disturbed or interfered with;

Attacks upon international law;

And revolts against the execution of the judgments and of all the executory acts emanating from the constituted authorities.

27. The minister of justice shall denounce to the tribunal of cassation, by means of the commissioner of the king, and without prejudice to the rights of the interested parties, the acts which the judges may have exceeded the limits of their power.

The tribunal shall annul them; and, if they give occasion for forfeiture, the fact shall be denounced to the legislative body, which shall render the decree of accusation, if there is need, and shall send the accused before the high national court.

TITLE IV. OF THE PUBLIC FORCE

1. The public force is instituted in order to defend the state against enemies from abroad, and to assure within the maintenance of order and the execution of the laws.

2. It is composed of the army and the navy, of the troops especially intended for internal service, and subsidiarly of the active citizens and their children, in condition to bear arms, registered upon the roll of the national guard.

3. The national guards form neither a military body nor an institution within the state; they are the citizens themselves summoned to service in the public force.

4. The citizens shall never take the form nor act as national guards, except in virtue of a requisition or of a legal authorisation.

5. They are subject in this capacity to an organization determined by the law.

They can have but one common discipline and one common uniform in the whole kingdom.

The distinctions of rank and subordination exist only in relation to the service and during its continuance.

6. The officers are elected at stated times and they can be re-elected only after an interval of service as soldiers.

No one shall command the national guard of more than one district.

7. All parts of the public force employed for the security of the state against enemies from abroad shall act under the orders of the king.

8. No corps nor detachment of troops of the line can act in the interior of the kingdom without a legal requisition.

9. No agent of the public force can enter into the house of a citizen, except for the execution of the warrants of police and justice, or in the cases expressly provided for by law.

10. The requisition of the public force within the interior of the realm belongs to the civil officers, according to the regulations determined by the legislative power.

11. If disorders disturb an entire department, the king, under the responsibility of his ministers, shall give the necessary orders for the execution of the laws and for the re-establishment of order, but subject to informing the legislative body thereof, if it is assembled, and at convoking it, if it is in recess.

12. The public force is essentially obedient; no armed body can deliberate.

13. The army and navy and the troops designed for the internal security are subject to special laws, in the matter of military offences, both for the maintenance of discipline and for the form of the trials and the nature of the penalties.

TITLE V. OF THE PUBLIC TAXES

1. The public taxes are considered and fixed each year by the legislative body and they shall not remain in force beyond the last day of the following session, unless they have been expressly renewed.

2. Under no pretext shall the funds necessary for the discharge of the national debt and the payment of the civil list be refused or suspended.

The compensation of the ministers of the Catholic worship, pensioned, maintained, elected, or appointed in virtue of the decrees of the National Assembly, makes part of the national debt.

The legislative body shall not in any case charge the nation with the payment of the debts of any person.

3. The detailed accounts of the expenditure of the ministerial departments, signed and certified by the ministers or ordainers-general, shall be made public by being printed at the beginning of the sessions of each legislature.

Likewise there shall be lists of the receipts from the different taxes and of all the public revenues.

The lists of these expenses and receipts shall be distinguished according to their nature, and shall show the sums received and expended year by year in each district.

The particular expenses of each department relative to the tribunals, the administrative bodies and other establishments, shall likewise be made public.

4. The department administrators and sub-administrators shall not establish any public tax, nor make any apportionment beyond the time and sums fixed by the legislative body, nor consider or permit, without being authorised by it, any local loan at the expense of the citizens of the department.

5. The executive department directs and supervises the collection and disbursement of the taxes and gives all the necessary orders for that purpose.

TITLE VI. OF THE RELATION OF THE FRENCH
NATION WITH FOREIGN NATIONS

The French nation renounces the undertaking of any war with a view to making conquests, and will never employ its forces against the liberty of any people.

The constitution does not admit the right of aubaine.

Foreigners, established in France or not, inherit from their French or foreign kinsmen.

They can contract for, acquire, and receive estates situated in France and dispose of them just as any French citizen by all the methods authorised by the laws.

Foreigners who chance to be in France are subject to the same criminal and police laws as the French citizens, saving the conventions arranged with the foreign powers; their persons, their estates, their business, their religion, and likewise protected by the law.

TITLE VII. OF THE REVISION OF THE CONSTITUTIONAL DECREES

1. The National Constituent Assembly declares that the nation has the imprescriptible right to change its constitution: nevertheless, considering that it is more conformable to the national interests to make use of the right only to reform, by the means provided in the constitution itself, the articles of which experience shall have made the inconveniences felt, decrees that it shall proceed by an assembly of revision in the following form.

2. When three consecutive legislatures shall have expressed a uniform wish for the amendment of some constitutional article, the revision demanded shall take place.

3. The next legislature and the one following shall not propose the alteration of any constitutional article.

4. Of the three legislatures which may one after another propose any changes, the first two shall occupy themselves with that matter only in the

last two months of their last session and the third only at the end of its first session or at the beginning of the second.

Their deliberations upon this matter shall be subject to the same forms as the legislative acts; but the decrees by which they shall have expressed their wish shall not be subject to the sanction of the king.

5. The fourth legislature, augmented by two hundred and forty-nine members selected in each department by doubling the usual number which it furnishes for its population, shall form the assembly of revision.

These two hundred and forty-nine members shall be elected after the selection of the representatives of the legislative body shall have been concluded and there shall be a separate record made of it.

The assembly of revision shall be composed of only one chamber.

6. The members of the third legislature which shall have requested the alteration cannot be elected to the assembly of revision.

7. The members of the assembly of revision, after having pronounced in unison the oath to live free or to die, shall take individually that "to confine themselves to pass upon the matters which shall have been submitted to them by the uniform wish of the three preceding legislatures; to maintain, besides, with all their power the constitution of the kingdom, decreed by the National Constituent Assembly in the years 1789, 1790, and 1791, and in everything to be faithful to the nation, the law, and the king."

8. The assembly of revision shall be required to occupy itself afterwards and without delay with the matters which shall have been submitted, to its examination: as soon as its work shall be concluded, the two hundred forty-nine members in augmentation shall retire, without power to take part in any case in legislative acts.

[MISCELLANEOUS PROVISIONS]

The French colonies and possessions in Asia, Africa, and America, although they form part of the French dominion, are not included in the present constitution.

None of the authorities instituted by the constitution has the right to change it in its entirety or in its parts, saving the alterations which may be made in it by way of revision in conformity with the provisions of title VII above.

The National Constituent Assembly delivers it as a trust to the fidelity of the legislative body, the king, and the judges, to the vigilance of the fathers of families, to the wives and the mothers, to the affection of the young citizens, to the courage of all the French.

The decrees rendered by the National Constituent Assembly which are not included in the constitutional act, shall be executed as laws, and the prior laws which have not been abrogated shall likewise be observed, in so far as the one or the other have not been revoked or modified by the legislative power.

The National Assembly having heard the reading of the above constitutional act, and after having approved it, declared that the constitution is completed and that it cannot be further changed.

Spanish Constitution of 1812

The Spanish Constitution proclaimed in Cadiz on 19 March 1812, was Europe's most influential constitution until the promulgation of the Belgian Constitution in 1831. This Constitution was created not only as a weapon against France and Napoleon but also as a "benevolent symbol of unity" and an attempted solution to the problems then besetting the country.[1] Ideologically, it was also an effort to establish revolutionary principles, and to bring new individualistic and egalitarian concepts to the traditional society characterizing the Spanish nation.[2]

In March 1808, France invaded Spain with a force of 100,000 troops on the pretext of protecting the coast from the English. A month later in Bayonne, France, Napoleon forced Ferdinand VII, the Spanish king who was a captive in France, to abdicate the crown to Joseph Bonapart, the emperor's brother. Patriotic uprisings resulted throughout Spain, and un-occupied Spanish territory soon became a mosaic of autonomous provinces ruled by local committees called juntas. Delegates from the provincial committees also formed a short-lived Junta Suprema Central followed by the Regency of Five, which called for the convening of a single-chamber parliament called the Cortes.

Deputies to the Cortes were elected by a system of indirect household suffrage, which disregarded the past practice that had provided separate representation for both the aristocracy and the Church. Significantly, delegates from the Spanish colonies were included. Although besieged by French troops, the Cortes met on the Isla de Leon in the Bay of Cadiz on 24 September 1810, primarily to reorganize the defense of the nation. In its initial session, it declared that "national sovereignty resides in the Cortes," and on 9 December a commission was established to draft a constitution.

The constitution project was discussed from 18 August to 26 December 1811; the first Spanish Constitution was signed on 18 March 1812 and promulgated on the following day.

This Constitution was in effect from 1812 to 1814, from 1820 to 1823, and from 1836 to 1837. Napoleon permitted Ferdinand VII to return to Spain as king on 4 May 1814, and the absolutist government was restored. However, after an army revolt led by Major Riego in 1820, the Constitution of 1812 was again proclaimed and King Ferdinand gave his oath of support. The so-called Constitutional Triennium followed. This ended with the invasion of the peninsula by the Sons of Saint Louis, an army of some 100,000 sent by the powers of the Holy Alliance to restore absolutism once again. An uprising of the Royal Guards restored the Constitution of Cadiz briefly on 13 August 1836. However, another revolt, the Tumult of La Granja, led to the promulgation of a new constitution in 1837, largely influenced by the Belgian Constitution of 1831.[3]

The sources of the Constitution of Cadiz are many, and the exact borrowings are still a matter of debate. The constitutional thought of the Age of Enlightenment as well as the writings of Locke, Montesquieu, and the other *philosophes* certainly influenced members of the Cortes. Of far more significance were the U.S. Constitution of 1787 and the French Constitution of 1791. Technically, the French document was much more important, and the pattern is obvious. Yet there was a different spirit guiding the Spanish document, which hearkened back to the U.S. Declaration of Independence for its Article 13 on the "pursuit of happiness." The document also emphasized its religious roots in Article 12: "The religion of the Spanish nation is, and shall be perpetually, Apostolic Roman Catholic, the only true religion." However, Spanish tradition is present in Article 16, which maintained the monarchy by declaring that "the power of executing laws resides in the King." Article 1 provides that the Spanish nation consists of all Spaniards in both hemispheres, and Article 3 states that "sovereignty resides essentially in the nation."

Perhaps the most important public liberties, as understood by the Cortes, were those involving property rights. The recognition of the right to property was a constitutional confirmation of a new liberal economic order. This order was put into effect after the abolition in August 1911 of the *señoríos*, important enclaves of private or seignorial jurisdiction within the juridical and economic framework of the old regime. The constitutional concept of private property included the rights of people to dispose of their property as they saw fit—a right that was deemed the essential foundation of a liberal economy and a bourgeois society. These rights are in Article 4 and are incorporated into Article 131 on the powers of the Cortes. Section 21 of the same article calls on the Cortes "to promote and encourage all kinds of industry and to remove obstacles impeding it"; Section 24 calls on the Cortes "to protect the political liberty of the press." A more detailed statement of press freedom is in Article 371 under the general heading of Public Instruction.

The Spanish Constitution of 1812 became the banner for revolutionary movements throughout Europe and Latin America. Spanish military liberalism served as a model for such disparate groups as the Decembrists in Russia and the revolutionary military in the Piedmont. The Naples Revolution in 1820 used the Spanish document as its rallying point; the patriots in the Milan uprising proclaimed this Constitution as their own the following year. It was also a basic symbol in the Portuguese Revolution of 1822 and had a significant influence in framing the Portuguese Constitution of 1826.

The significance of the Spanish Constitution in Latin America was enormous. At the time of its 1812 promulgation, it was also the Constitution of the Spanish colonies overseas who were represented in the Cortes by thirty deputies. Thus, the document was well known to the leaders of the South and Central American independence movements and was considered along with the U.S. Constitution of 1787 in the preparation of constitutions in the newly created states. The early texts of the Columbia Constitution of 1821 at Cundinamarca and the Mexico Constitution of 1824 drawn up at Chiapas reflect the influence of the Spanish Constitution of 1812 as well as that of the U.S. Constitution of 1787.[4]

PROFESSOR ANTONIO LÓPEZ PINA
Universidad Complutense de Madrid
Madrid, Spain

PROFESSOR GLORIA N. MORAN
Universidad de Santiago
Santiago, Spain

NOTES

1. R. Solis, "Cara y cruz. La primera Constitución española. Cadiz 1812." *Revista de Estudios Politicos* (1962), 148 n. 126.
2. F. Fernandez-Segado, *Las constituciones históricas españolas.* (Madrid: 1981), 21.
3. V. Palacio Atard, *España del siglo XIX, 1808–1898* (Madrid: 1978); R. De la Cierva, *Historia básica de la España actual, 1800–1975* (Barcelona: 1976); L. Sanchez Agesta, *Historia del Constitucionalismo español* (Madrid: 1964).
4. C. M. De Bustamante, *La Constitución de Cadiz o motives de mi afecto a la Constitución* (Mexico: 1971).

POLITICAL CONSTITUTION OF THE SPANISH NATION PROCLAIMED IN CADIZ, 19 MARCH, 1812

PREAMBLE

In the name of God Almighty, Father, Son, and Holy Ghost, Author and Supreme Legislator of society:

The general and extraordinary Cortes of the Spanish nation, well convinced, after very close examination and mature deliberation, that the ancient fundamental laws of the monarchy, accompanied by the opportune provisions and precautions which assure their entire fulfillment in a stable and permanent manner, will worthily achieve the great object of promoting the glory, prosperity, and welfare of the entire nation, decree the following political constitution for the good government and just administration of the state.

TITLE I. THE SPANISH NATION AND SPANIARDS

CHAPTER I. THE SPANISH NATION

Article 1. The Spanish nation consists of all Spaniards in both hemispheres.

Article 2. The Spanish nation is free and independent, and is not, nor can it be, the patrimony of any family or person.

Article 3. Sovereignty resides essentially in the nation, and therefore the right of establishing its fundamental laws belong to it exclusively.

Article 4. The nation is obliged to preserve and protect by just and wise laws, the civil liberty, the property, and the other legitimate rights of all individuals belonging to it.

CHAPTER II. SPANIARDS

Article 5. The following are Spaniards:

1) All free men born and resident in Spanish dominions and their children;

From *Manual of Spanish Constitutions, 1808–1931*. Edited by Arnold Verduin (Ypsilanti, Michigan: University Lithoprinters, 1941).

2) Foreigners who have obtained certificates of naturalization from the Cortes;

3) Foreigners who, without such certificate, reside ten years in a district, may obtain it, according to law, in any town of the monarchy;

4) Freedmen as soon as they obtain their liberty in Spain.

Article 6. Love of his country is one of the principal obligations of all Spaniards, as well as justice and beneficence.

Article 7. Every Spaniard is bound to be faithful to the constitution, to obey the laws, and to respect established authorities.

Article 8. Every Spaniard is likewise bound, without any distinction, to contribute in proportion to his means, to the expenses of the state.

Article 9. Every Spaniard is also bound to defend his fatherland by bearing arms when called upon by law.

TITLE II. THE TERRITORY OF SPAIN, ITS RELIGION AND GOVERNMENT, AND SPANISH CITIZENS

CHAPTER I. THE TERRITORY OF SPAIN

Article 10. Spanish territory in the peninsula with its possessions and adjacent islands comprises: Aragon, Asturias, Old Castile, New Castile, Catalonia, Cordova, Extremadura, Galicia, Granada, Jaen, Leon, Molina, Murcia, Navarre, the Basque Provinces, Seville and Valencia, the Canary and Balearic Islands, with other possessions in Africa. In North America, it comprises New Spain with New Galicia, the peninsula of Yucatan, Guatemala, the internal eastern and western provinces, the island of Cuba, the two Floridas, the Spanish part of the island of Santo Domingo, the island of Puerto-Rico, and the islands adjacent thereto and to the continent in both oceans. In South America it comprises New Granada, Venezuela, Peru, Chile, the provinces of the Plata River, and all the islands adjacent in the Pacific and Atlantic Oceans. In Asia it comprises the Philippine Islands and their dependencies.

Article 11. A more convenient division of Spanish territory shall be made by a constitutional law as soon as the political circumstances of the nation permit.

CHAPTER II. RELIGION

Article 12. The religion of the Spanish nation is, and shall be perpetually, Apostolic Roman Catholic, the only true religion. The nation protects it by wise and just laws and prohibits the exercise of any other, whatsoever.

CHAPTER III. GOVERNMENT

Article 13. The object of the government is the happiness of the nation since the end of all political society is only the well being of the individuals who compose it.

Article 14. The government of the Spanish nation is a limited, hereditary monarchy.

Article 15. The power of making laws reside in the Cortes and the King.

Article 16. The power of executing laws resides in the King.

Article 17. The power of applying laws in civil and criminal cases resides in the courts established by law.

CHAPTER IV. SPANISH CITIZENS

Article 18. Those are Spanish citizens who, in both family lines, trace their origin to the Spanish dominions in both hemispheres, and are resident in some town of the dominions.

Article 19. That foreigner is also a citizen who, already enjoying the rights of a Spaniard, obtains a special certificate of citizenship from the Cortes.

Article 20. In order that the foreigner may obtain such special certificate from the Cortes, he must have married a Spanish woman, and have brought into, and established in, Spain some invention or valuable industry, or have acquired property on which he pays a direct tax, or have established himself in trade with an adequate and considerable capital, in the judgment of the Cortes, or have performed distinguished services for the welfare and defense of the nation.

Article 21. Those also are citizens who are the legitimate children of foreigners resident in Spain who, born in Spanish dominions, have never left them without the permission of the government, and having attained twenty-one years of age, have resided in a town of the same dominions, pursuing in it some profession, office or useful industry.

Article 22. The channels of virtue and merit are left open for Spaniards reputed of African origin on either side to attain citizenship; consequently, the Cortes shall grant a certificate of citizenship to those who may perform reasonable services for the fatherland, or those who distinguish themselves by their talents, diligence, and good conduct, on condition that they are children in lawful marriage of fathers naturally free, that they are married to a woman naturally free, that they are settled in the Spanish dominions, and pursue some profession, office or useful industry with adequate capital.

Article 23. Only citizens may obtain municipal offices and vote for them in the cases designated by law.

Article 24. Spanish citizenship is lost by:

1) Naturalization in a foreign country;

2) Receiving employment under another government;

3) Any sentence imposing severe or infamous penalties so long as it is unrevoked;

4) Residence for five consecutive years outside of Spanish territory without a commission or permit from the government.

Article 25. The exercise of the same rights is suspended:

1) By virtue of any judicial prohibition because of moral or physical incapacity;

2) In case of bankruptcy or indebtedness to the public treasury;

3) In the status of domestic servitude;

4) From failure to have any employment, office, or known means of living;

5) From having undergone criminal prosecution.

6) From the year 1830, all those who enter upon the rights of citizenship must be able to read and write.

Article 26. The rights of citizenship may be lost or suspended only for the reasons designated in the two preceding articles, and for no other reasons.

TITLE III. THE CORTES

CHAPTER I. THE MANNER OF FORMING THE CORTES

Article 27. The Cortes is the assembly of all the Deputies who represent the nation, elected by the citizens in the manner given below.

Article 28. The basis for national representation is the same in both hemispheres.

Article 29. This basis is the population consisting of the natives who, on both sides, have originated in Spanish dominions and of those who have received a certificate of citizenship from the Cortes as well as those comprehended in art. 21.

Article 30. The last census of the year 1797, shall serve for the computation of the population of the dominions in Europe, until a new one can be taken, and a corresponding census shall be made for the computation of the population of the overseas dominions, using, in the meantime, the most authentic census of those recently taken.

Article 31. There shall be a Deputy to the Cortes for every 70,000 souls of population, composed according to the explanation in art. 29.

Article 32. After the population has been distributed among the several provinces, if an excess beyond 35,000 souls appears, another Deputy shall be elected as though the number amounted to 70,000; if the excess does not pass 35,000, it shall be ignored.

Article 33. Should there be any province whose population does not amount to 70,000 souls but which is not under 60,000, it shall elect a Deputy; if there are less than 60,000 souls, the province shall be united to the one adjoining, to complete the requisite number of 70,000. Excepted from this rule is the island of Santo Domingo which shall elect a Deputy, regardless of its population.

CHAPTER II. THE ELECTION OF DEPUTIES TO CORTES

Article 34. For the election of Deputies parish, district, and provincial meetings shall be held.

CHAPTER III. THE PARISH ELECTORAL MEETINGS

Article 35. The parish electoral meetings shall be composed of all citizens settled and resident in the respective parish, including secular ecclesiastics.

Article 36. These meetings shall always be held in the Spanish peninsula, the islands, and the adjoining possessions on the first Sunday in October of the year before that of the meeting of the Cortes.

Article 37. In the overseas provinces they shall be held on the first Sunday in December, fifteen months before the meeting of the Cortes; the magistrates shall always give previous notice for both.

Article 38. The parish meeting shall choose one parish elector for each 200 inhabitants.

Article 39. If the number of inhabitants in the parish exceeds 300 but does not amount to 400, two electors shall be chosen; if the number exceeds 500 but does not amount to 600, three shall be chosen, and thus progressively.

Article 40. In parishes whose number of inhabitants does not amount to 200, but exceeds 150, one elector shall be chosen; and in those that have not 150 inhabitants, the residents shall be united with those of the next adjoining parish in order to choose the elector or electors, according to their numbers.

Article 41. The parish meeting shall elect by a majority of votes, eleven commissioners to nominate the parish elector.

Article 42. If two parish electors are to be chosen in the meeting, twenty-one commissioners shall be chosen; if three, thirty-one; but in no case shall the last number be exceeded, in order to save confusion.

Article 43. For the greater convenience of small places, it shall be observed that parishes containing twenty inhabitants shall elect one commissioner; those containing from thirty to forty shall elect two, those containing from fifty to sixty shall elect three, and thus progressively. Parishes containing less than twenty shall unite with the next nearest parish to elect commissioners.

Article 44. Commissioners of small places thus elected, shall meet in the most convenient towns, and numbering eleven, or at least nine, shall choose a parish elector; numbering twenty-one or at least seventeen, shall choose two electors; numbering thirty-one, or at least twenty-five, shall choose three electors or the electors according to their numbers.

Article 45. To become a parish elector, one must be a citizen, above twenty-five years of age, settled and resident in the parish.

Article 46. The parish meetings shall be presided over by the principal civil official or the magistrate (*alcalde*) of the city, town or village where the meeting is held; the parish curate shall attend in order to give greater solemnity to the election; and if one town holds two or more meetings because of the number of parishes, one shall be presided over by the principal civil officer or the magistrate, another by the other magistrate, and the other meetings by the alderman, chosen by lot.

Article 47. The voters, assembled in the town hall or in the customary place, at the hour appointed shall proceed to the parish church, headed by the president; there a solemn mass to the Holy Ghost shall be celebrated by the parish priest, who shall deliver an address suitable to the occasion.

Article 48. After mass, they shall return to their meeting place, and the meeting shall be opened there with the appointment of two inspectors and a secretary from among those present; all this shall be in open session.

Article 49. Then the president shall ask whether any voter has a complaint to make relative to bribery or corruption in order to elect any particular person; if there is, a public and verbal accusation must be made. If the charge is proved, those who have offended shall be deprived of their suffrage. Calumniators shall suffer the same penalty, and no recourse is allowed from this judgment.

Article 50. Should any doubts arise concerning the qualifications of those who are to vote, the meeting shall decide on them straightway, and its decisions shall be executed without recourse for this instance and for this effect.

Article 51. The election of commissioners shall follow, each voter designating the number of persons equal to that of the commissioners required; for that purpose he shall go to the table placed before the president, the inspectors, and the secretary, and the latter shall write the names in a list in the voter's presence; no voter shall inscribe his own name on the list of candidates in any election on pain of losing the right to vote.

Article 52. When this has been done, the president, the inspectors and the secretary shall inspect the lists; the president shall announce in an audible voice the names of the citizens who, by a majority of votes, have been elected commissioners.

Article 53. Before the adjournment of the meeting, the commissioners elected shall withdraw to a private room and, in conference there, shall choose the elector or electors for the parish; the person or persons obtaining more than one-half of the votes, shall be elected, and the election shall be published in the meeting immediately.

Article 54. The secretary shall make a record thereof, which shall be signed by the president and the commissioners, and a copy similarly signed shall be delivered to the person or persons elected, as evidence of their election.

Article 55. No citizen may excuse himself from these duties under any pretext or reason.

Article 56. No citizen may present himself at the parish meeting bearing arms.

Article 57. After the verification of the selection of electors, the meeting shall be adjourned immediately. Every other act shall be null and void.

Article 58. The members of the meeting shall proceed to the parish church wherein a solemn *Te Deum* shall be sung. The elector or electors shall be placed among the president, inspectors, and secretary.

CHAPTER IV. DISTRICT ELECTOR MEETINGS

Article 59. The district electoral meetings shall be composed of the parish electors who shall assemble in the chief town of the district in order to choose the elector or electors who shall proceed, when they have assembled in the provincial capital, to the election of Deputies to the Cortes.

Article 60. In the peninsula and adjacent islands, these meetings shall always be held on the first Sunday of November in the year preceding the opening of a new Cortes.

Article 61. In the overseas provinces, they shall be held on the first Sunday of January following the parish electoral meetings held in December.

Article 62. In order to ascertain the number of electors to be chosen by each district, the following regulations shall be observed.

Article 63. The number of district electors shall be three times as great as the number of Deputies to be elected.

Article 64. If the number of districts in the province should be greater than the number of electors required by the previous article for the election of Deputies, nevertheless, each district shall have one elector.

Article 65. If the number of districts be less than that of the electors, each district shall elect one, two, or more to complete the required number; but if one elector be still lacking, the district with the largest population shall elect him; if two be needed the next most populous district shall elect the second, and so on progressively.

Article 66. In conformity with the provisions in articles 31, 32, 33, and articles 63, 64, 65, the census shall determine the number of Deputies belonging to each province and the number of electors for each district.

Article 67. The district electoral meetings shall be presided over by the principal civil officer or by the first magistrate of the chief town of the district, to whom the parish electors shall present themselves with the documents authenticating their election, so that their names may be inscribed in the record book of the meeting.

Article 68. On the appointed day, the parish electors shall assemble with their president in the consistorial hall in open session; they shall proceed to the appointment of a secretary and two inspectors, from among their own number.

Article 69. Then the electors shall present their certificate of election for examination by the secretary and the inspectors, who shall report on the following day whether the certificates are in order. The certificates of the secretary and of the inspectors shall be examined by a commission of three members of the meeting, appointed for this purpose; the latter shall report on the following day.

Article 70. On the same day, the parish electors being assembled, the reports on the certificates shall be read, and if there is an objection to the certificates or to the electors because of lack of necessary qualifications, the meeting shall decide the matter in the same sitting; the decision shall be executed without recourse.

Article 71. After this act, the parish electors, headed by their president, shall proceed to the principal church, where a solemn mass to the Holy Ghost shall be sung by the highest ecclesiastical dignitary of the district; the latter shall give a discourse appropriate to the circumstances.

Article 72. After divine service, they shall return to the consistorial hall and shall take seats without any preference; the secretary shall read this chapter of the constitution, and the president shall put the question contained in article 49 and every particular of its contents shall be observed.

Article 73. Immediately afterward, they shall proceed to the selection of one or more district electors; the latter shall be chosen singly by secret ballot, using votes upon which is written the name of the person whom each elector nominates.

Article 74. After the balloting, the president, secretary, and inspectors shall count the votes and he shall be elected who receives one more than one half the votes cast; the president shall announce each election. If no one has a majority of votes, the two receiving the highest number of votes in the second balloting shall be elected. In case of a tie, it shall be decided by drawing lots.

Article 75. To become a district elector, one must be a citizen in full exercise of his rights, above twenty-five years of age, a resident of the district, either a layman or one of the secular clergy. The election may fall upon citizens either in or out of the meeting.

Article 76. The secretary shall make a record of the proceedings, which shall be signed by the president and the inspectors; a copy similarly signed shall be given to the person or persons elected as evidence of their election. The president of this meeting shall deliver another copy signed by himself and by the secretary to the president of the provincial meeting who shall publish the election in the public papers.

Article 77. All the provisions for parish electoral meetings prescribed in article 55, 56, 57, and 58 shall be observed in the district electoral meetings.

CHAPTER V. THE PROVINCIAL ELECTORAL MEETINGS

Article 78. The provincial electoral meetings shall be composed of all the district electors of the province who shall assemble in its capital to elect the respective number of Deputies in the Cortes as representatives of the nation.

Article 79. In the peninsula and adjacent islands, these meetings shall be held on the first Sunday of December of the year preceding the opening of the new Cortes.

Article 80. In the overseas provinces they shall be held on the second Sunday of March of the same year in which the district meetings are held.

Article 81. They shall be presided over by the governor of the province to whom the district electors shall present themselves with the documents of their election so that their names may be inscribed in the record book of the meeting.

Article 82. On the appointed day the district electors shall meet with their president in the consistorial hall or in the building most suitable for the solemnity of the proceedings, in open session; they shall proceed to select by a majority of votes, a secretary, and two inspectors from among their own numbers.

Article 83. If a province has only one Deputy to elect, at least five electors must concur in his election, distributing that number among the districts into which the province is divided, or forming new districts for that special purpose.

Article 84. The four chapters of this constitution relating to elections shall be read. After this, the records of the proceedings of the district electoral meetings, forwarded by the respective presidents, shall be read; the electors shall present the certificates of election for examination by the secretary and inspectors who shall report on the following day whether they are in order. The certificates of the secretary and inspectors shall be examined by a commission of three members of the meeting, appointed for this purpose and the commission shall report on the following day.

Article 85. When the district electors are assembled, the reports on the certificates shall be read, and if there is an objection to the certificates or to the electors because of lack of necessary qualifications, the meeting shall decide the matter in the same sitting; the judgment shall be executed without recourse.

Article 86. Thereupon the district electors, headed by their president, shall proceed to the cathedral or largest church where a solemn mass to the Holy Ghost shall be sung, and the bishop, or in default of him, the highest ecclesiastical dignitary, shall give a discourse appropriate to the circumstances.

Article 87. After divine service they shall return to the place of meeting and in open session, the electors occupying seats without any preference, the president shall put the question contained in article 49 and every particular detail of its contents shall be observed.

Article 88. The electors present shall proceed to the election of one or more Deputies who shall be chosen singly; the electors shall go to the table placed before the president, inspectors, and secretary and the latter shall inscribe on a list in the elector's presence, the nomination made by him. The secretary and inspectors shall vote first.

Article 89. After the balloting the president, secretary, and inspectors shall count the votes, and he shall be elected who receives at least one more than one-half of the votes. If no one has a majority of votes, the two receiving the highest number of votes shall be voted upon, and the one receiving the larger number of votes in the second balloting shall be elected. In case of a tie, it shall be decided by drawing lots; the president shall publish the result of each election.

Article 90. After the election of Deputies, alternates shall be elected in the same manner and their number shall be one-third of the number of Deputies assigned to the province. If any province elects only one or two Deputies, nevertheless, one alternate shall be elected. These alternates shall enter the Cortes in case of the death of a Deputy to the Cortes or of his incapacity, as judged by the Cortes, at whatever time either event occurs after the election.

Article 91. To become a Deputy to the Cortes, one must be a citizen in the full exercise of his rights, above twenty-five years of age, a native of the province or a resident of it for at least seven years, either a layman or one of the secular clergy; the election may fall on citizens either in or out of the meeting.

Article 92. No one may be elected Deputy to the Cortes who does not have an adequate annual income derived from his own property.

Article 93. The provision of the previous article shall remain suspended until the next Cortes shall have decided when it is to have full effect, and shall have determined the amount of income, and the kind of property from which it must be derived; their resolution shall be considered as constitutional law, as though inserted here.

Article 94. If it should happen that the same person is elected by the province in which he was born and also by the province where he resides, his election by the latter shall prevail, and the alternate from the province in which he was born, shall take his place in the Cortes.

Article 95. The ministers of state, the Councillors of State, and those holding office in the royal household may not be elected Deputies to the Cortes.

Article 96. Foreigners, even though they have obtained certificates of citizenship from the Cortes, may not be elected Deputies to the Cortes.

Article 97. No public official appointed by the government may be elected Deputy to the Cortes for the province in which he holds office.

Article 98. The secretary shall make a record of the elections, which must be signed by himself, by the president, and by the electors.

Article 99. Afterwards all the electors without any excuse shall grant to all and each of the Deputies full powers according to the following formula, each Deputy being given his respective powers for presentation in the Cortes.

Article 100. The powers shall be expressed in these terms: In the city or town of _____ , on _____ day of the month of _____ in the hall of _____ before me, the undersigned notary, and the witness called for this purpose, appeared (here shall be inserted the names of the president and the district electors composing the provincial electoral meeting) who, being convened in constitutional form, declared that the elections for parish and district electors having been duly made, according to the Constitution of the Spanish Monarchy, and with all the solemnities therein prescribed, as appears by the original certificates inscribed in the records, the said electors of the districts of the province of _____ on the day of _____ of the month of _____ of the present year, have nominated the Deputies who, in the name and representation of this province, are to assemble in the Cortes and who were elected Deputies to it for this province, to wit, N.N.N., as shown by the records drawn up and signed by N.N.; and that consequently they grant full powers to them as a group and severally to fulfill and discharge the august functions of their office, and in order that they, with the other Deputies, as representatives of the Spanish nation, may agree to and propose all that they may seem conducive to the national welfare, by virtue of powers vested in them by the constitution, and within the limits therein prescribed, without the power to derogate, alter, or vary in any manner the articles thereof for any reason; that they, the said constituents, by virtue of the powers granted them as electors appointed for the selection of Deputies, do bind themselves, as well in their own names as in the name of all inhabitants of the province, to support, obey, and comply with all that the said Deputies enact and resolve in accordance with the Political Constitution of the Spanish Monarchy. Done in the presence of N.N. witnesses, who, together with the said constituents, have signed these present, which I certify.

Article 101. The president, inspectors and secretary shall send a copy of the record of the elections, signed by themselves, to the Permanent Committee of the Cortes, and they shall cause the result of the elections to be printed, sending a copy thereof to each town of the province.

Article 102. The salaries of the Deputies shall be paid by their respective provinces, to the amount stipulated by the general Cortes in the second year of each term, for the succeeding term; the overseas provinces shall allow their Deputies such sums as they deem necessary for the expenses of the outward and homeward journey.

Article 103. In the provincial electoral meetings all the provisions of articles 55, 56, 57, and 58 shall be observed, with the exception mentioned in article 328.

CHAPTER VI. THE ASSEMBLING OF THE CORTES

Article 104. The Cortes shall assemble every year in the capital of the kingdom in a building assigned for that purpose.

Article 105. When the Cortes considers it convenient to remove to another place, it may do so, provided that the town is not more than twelve leagues from the capital, and provided that two-thirds of the Deputies present shall agree to the removal.

Article 106. The sessions of Cortes each year shall be held in three successive months, beginning on 1 March.

Article 107. The Cortes may prolong its sessions for another month in only two cases: upon royal petition, and upon resolution of two-thirds of the Deputies, if the Cortes shall deem it necessary.

Article 108. All the Deputies shall be renewed every two years.

Article 109. If war or enemy occupation of some part of the territory of the monarchy should prevent the timely appearance of all or some of the Deputies from one or more provinces, the former Deputies of the respective provinces shall supply in their places; lots shall be drawn among them to complete the number required.

Article 110. Deputies may not be re-elected unless a term has elapsed since their previous term of office.

Article 111. The Deputies, upon arriving at the capital, shall present themselves before the permanent Committee of the Cortes for the registration of their names and the provinces electing them in the records of the secretariat of that Cortes.

Article 112. In the year of the renewal of Deputies, the first preliminary meeting shall be held in open session on 12 February. Its president shall be the president of the Permanent Committee and the committee shall select from its own members the secretaries and inspectors.

Article 113. At the first meeting, all the Deputies shall present their powers and they shall select, by a majority of votes, two commissions, one of five members to examine the powers of all the Deputies, and the other of three members to examine the powers of the five commissioners.

Article 114. On 20 February of the same year a second preliminary meeting shall be held in open sessions; at this meeting the two commissions shall report on the regularity of the powers, having, at hand, copies of the records of the provincial elections.

Article 115. In this meeting, and in the others which are necessary until 25 February, doubts concerning the regularity of the powers and qualifications of the Deputies shall be decided definitely by majority vote.

Article 116. In the year following that of the renewal of the Deputies, the first preliminary meeting shall be held on 20 February, and whatever other meetings are deemed necessary, shall be held until 25 February to decide, in the manner and form expressed in the three preceding articles, on the regularity of the powers presented by new Deputies.

Article 117. On 25 February every year, the final preliminary meeting shall be held, in which the Deputies shall take the following oath, placing their hands on the Holy Gospels:

"Do you swear to defend and preserve the Apostolic Roman Catholic religion without admitting any other in the kingdom?"

R: "I do."

"Do you swear to support, and cause to be observed the political constitution of the Spanish Monarchy sanctioned by the general and extraordinary Cortes of the nation in 1812?"

R: "I do."

"Do you swear to discharge faithfully the duties of the office entrusted to you by the nation and to have always in view, the welfare and prosperity of the same nation?"

R: "I do."

"If you observe your oath, may God reward you, if you do not, may He hold you to account."

Article 118. The Deputies shall then proceed by secret ballot to choose from their own number, a president, vice-president, and four secretaries; thereupon the Cortes shall be considered duly organized and constituted and the Permanent Committee shall cease in all its functions.

Article 119. A committee of twenty-two members and of two secretaries shall be chosen on the same day to inform the King of the constitution of the Cortes and of their election of a president so that the King may make known whether he will attend the opening of the Cortes which shall take place on 1 March.

Article 120. If the King is out of the capital, he shall be informed in writing and he shall answer in the same manner.

Article 121. The King shall personally attend the opening of the Cortes; if he should be unable to do so, the president shall open it on the appointed day which may not be postponed for any reason. The same formalities shall be observed at the closing of the Cortes.

Article 122. The King shall enter the hall of the Cortes without a guard; he shall be accompanied only by the persons who shall be designated by the regulations of the internal government of the Cortes concerning the ceremony observed at the reception and departure of the King.

Article 123. The King shall deliver a speech, proposing to the Cortes whatever seems suitable, to which the president shall respond in general terms. If the King does not attend personally, he shall send his speech to the president for the latter to read in the Cortes.

Article 124. The Cortes may not deliberate in the presence of the King.

Article 125. When the ministers of state shall make proposals to the Cortes in the name of the King, they shall attend the discussions at such times, and in such manner as the Cortes prescribes, and they may speak in the Cortes; but they may not be present when the votes are taken.

Article 126. The sessions of the Cortes shall be public and only in cases demanding privacy shall secret sessions be held.

Article 127. In the discussions of the Cortes and in all other matters pertaining to its government and internal order, the regulations which shall be made by this general and extraordinary Cortes shall be observed without prejudice to reforms which succeeding Cortes shall think proper to make.

Article 128. Deputies shall be inviolable, and at no time and in no case may they be held responsible for their opinions by any authority. In criminal cases commenced against them, they shall be judged only by the court of the Cortes in the manner prescribed in the regulation for the internal government of the Cortes. During the sessions of the Cortes and the month following, Deputies may not be sued nor arrested for debts.

Article 129. No deputy, during the term of his office, which shall be reckoned from the reception of the notification of his election by the Permanent Committee of the Cortes, shall receive for himself or shall seek for another, an office at the King's disposal or a promotion (unless it be governed by the strict rules of seniority) in his respective career.

Article 130. Likewise he may not, during his term in the Cortes or during the year succeeding the end of his term, obtain for himself, or solicit for another, any pension or honour at the disposal of the King.

CHAPTER VII. THE POWERS OF THE CORTES

Article 131. The Cortes has the following powers:

1) To propose and decree laws and to interpret and alter them when necessary;

2) To receive the oath from the King, the Prince of Asturias, and the regency as provided in their places;

3) To settle any doubt of fact or right occuring in the order of succession to the crown;

4) To elect a regency or regent of the kingdom, as provided by the constitution and to designate the limits within which the regency or regent may exercise the royal authority;

5) To recognize publicly the Prince of Austurias;

6) To appoint a guardian for the minor King as provided by the constitution;

7) To approve before ratification, treaties of offensive alliance, of subsidies, and special treaties of commerce;

8) To grant or refuse the admission of foreign troops in the kingdom;

9) To decree the creation and suppression of offices in the courts established by the constitution and also the creation and suppression of public offices;

10) To fix annually upon royal proposal, the forces on land and sea, determining the establishment in time of peace, and the increase in time of war;

11) To issue ordinances to the army, navy, and national militia in all their branches;

12) To fix the expenses of the public administration;

13) To establish annually the taxes and imposts;

14) To obtain loans, in cases of necessity, on national credit;

15) To approve the division of taxes among the provinces;

16) To examine and approve the accounts of the inversion of public funds;

17) To establish customs-houses and the duties paid therein;

18) To order what is expedient for the administration, preservation, and alienation of national property;

19) To determine the value, weight, standard, type, and denomination of money;

20) To adopt the system of weights and measures that it considers most suitable and just;

21) To promote and encourage all kinds of industry and to remove obstacles impeding it;

22) To establish a general plan of public instruction in all the monarchy, and to approve what is planned for the education of the Prince of Asturias;

23) To approve the general regulation for the police and sanitation of the kindgom;

24) To protect the political liberty of the press;

25) To render effective the responsibility of the secretaries of state and other public employees;

26) To grant or refuse its consent in all those cases and acts which the constitution prescribes as necessary.

CHAPTER VIII. THE FORMATION OF LAWS AND THE ROYAL SANCTION

Article 132. Every Deputy possesses the power of proposing to the Cortes projects of law in writing, explaining the reasons on which they are founded.

Article 133. Two days at least after the presentation and reading of a project of law, it shall be read a second time; the Cortes shall deliberate whether it should be admitted to discussion.

Article 134. After admission to discussion, if the gravity of the matter, in the judgment of the Cortes, requires that it pass first to a committee, it shall be done thus.

Article 135. Four days at least after the admission to discussion of the project, it shall be read a third time, and the day may be set for opening discussion on it.

Article 136. On the day appointed for discussion the Cortes shall examine the project in its totality and every one of its articles.

Article 137. The Cortes shall decide when the matter has been sufficiently discussed, and if so, it shall decide whether to proceed to a vote.

Article 138. If it is decided to proceed to a vote, the voting shall commence immediately, the Cortes admitting or rejecting the project as a whole, or in part, or varying or modifying according to the observations made in discussion.

Article 139. Decisions shall be given by an absolute majority of votes and the presence of one more than one-half of the total number of Deputies composing the Cortes shall be necessary for passing a law.

Article 140. If the Cortes rejects a project of law in any stage of its examination, or resolves that it shall not be put to a vote, the project cannot be proposed again in the same year.

Article 141. If it has been adopted, it shall be drawn up in duplicate form of a law and shall be read to the Cortes; after this, the two originals, signed by the president and two secretaries, shall be presented at once to the King by a committee.

Article 142. The King sanctions the law.

Article 143. The King sanctions in the following form, signed by his own hand, "Publish this as law."

Article 144. The King refuses his sanction in the following form, also signed by his own hand, "Let it be returned to the Cortes," accompanying it with an exposition of the reasons for refusal.

Article 145. The King shall have thirty days for the use of the prerogative; if within that time, he has not granted or refused this sanction, it shall be understood thereby that he has given his sanction and, he shall give it.

Article 146. After the King gives or refuses his sanction, one of the two original copies, with its respective formula, shall be returned to the Cortes for its formation. This copy shall be preserved in the archives of the Cortes and the other copy shall be kept by the King.

Article 147. If the King refuses his sanction, the bill may not be revived in the Cortes of that year; it may be revived in the Cortes of the next year.

Article 148. If the same bill is proposed, admitted, and approved in the Cortes of the following year, it shall be presented to the King who may give his sanction or refuse it again in the form mentioned in articles 143 and 144; in the latter case, the bill shall not be revived in that year.

Article 149. If, for the third time the bill is proposed, admitted, and approved by the Cortes of the following year, by this act, the bill is considered sanctioned, and when it is presented to the King, he shall give his sanction using the formula expressed in article 143.

Article 150. If before the expiration of the term of thirty days, in which the King gives or refuses his sanction, the Cortes should close its sessions, the King shall give or refuse it in the first eight days of the sessions of the succeeding Cortes; should he not have done so in that amount of time, it shall thereby be considered as given and he shall give it, in fact, according to the prescribed form; but if the King refuses his sanction, the same Cortes may debate the same bill.

Article 151. Although one or more years elapse since the King has refused his sanction to a bill without its being brought up again, yet if such a bill be brought up in the same legislature which adopted it, or in the two succeeding legislatures, it shall be considered always as the same bill with respect to the King's sanction as treated in the three preceding articles; but, if during the terms of the aforementioned legislatures, it is not brought up again in the same words, it shall be considered a new bill with respect to the King's sanction.

Article 152. If, at the second or third time that the bill be brought up within the term prescribed by the preceding article, it should be rejected by the Cortes, it shall be considered a new bill whenever it is afterwards revived.

Article 153. Laws are repealed with the same formalities and in the same manner that they are made.

CHAPTER IX. PROMULGATION OF THE LAWS

Article 154. After a law has been published in the Cortes, the King shall be informed thereof, so that he may proceed immediately to its solemn promulgation.

Article 155. The King shall promulgate the laws in the following terms:

"N. (the name of the King) by the grace of God and by the Constitution of the Spanish Monarchy, King of Spain, to all who shall see and hear these present, be it known that: The Cortes has decreed and We have sanctioned the following (here the literal text of the law). Therefore, We order all courts, magistrates, chief officials, governors and other civil, military, and ecclesiastical authorities of every class and dignity to observe, and cause to be observed, this present law and to see it executed and complied with, in all its parts. You shall take measures to carry it into effect and arrange for its printing, publication, and circulation. (It is directed to the respective minister of the state.)

Article 156. All laws shall be circulated by the royal command, through the respective ministers of state directly to every supreme court and every province and to the other superior authorities who shall transmit them to their subordinates.

CHAPTER X. THE PERMANENT COMMITTEE OF THE CORTES

Article 157. The Cortes, before closing its sessions, shall appoint a committee called the Permanent Committee of the Cortes, composed of seven of its own members, three from the peninsula, three from the overseas provinces; the seventh shall be chosen by lot between a European Deputy and an overseas Deputy.

Article 158. At the same time the Cortes shall appoint two alternates to this committee, one from Europe and the other from overseas.

Article 159. The Permanent Committee shall continue in its function from the end of one session to the beginning of the next session of the Cortes.

Article 160. The Committee shall have the following powers:

1) To watch over the observance of the constitution and the laws in order to render an account to the Cortes of the infractions which they have noticed;

2) To convoke extraordinary Cortes in the cases prescribed by this constitution;

3) To discharge the functions prescribed in articles 111 and 112;

4) To give notice to alternate Deputies to fill the positions vacated by

Deputies; and in case of the death or absolute incapacity of the Deputies and alternates of a province, to transmit the proper orders for a new election in the province.

CHAPTER XI. THE EXTRAORDINARY CORTES

Article 161. The extraordinary Cortes shall be composed of the same Deputies who constitute the ordinary Cortes during the two years of their term of office.

Article 162. The Permanent Committee of the Cortes shall convoke the extraordinary Cortes on an appointed day in the three following cases:

1) When the crown shall be vacant;

2) When the King is incapacitated in any way for governing, or when he wishes to abdicate the crown in favor of his successor; in the first case, the Committee is authorized to take all suitable measures to ascertain the incapacity of the King;

3) When, in critical circumstances and concerning arduous business, the King shall deem it necessary that it assemble and shall thus inform the Permanent Committee of the Cortes.

Article 163. The extraordinary Cortes shall take cognizance of no other matters than those for which it was convoked.

Article 164. The sessions of the extraordinary Cortes shall commence and close with the same formalities as those prescribed for the ordinary Cortes.

Article 165. The assembly of extraordinary Cortes shall not prevent the election of new Deputies at the time prescribed.

Article 166. If the extraordinary Cortes shall not have closed its sessions on the day appointed for the assembly of ordinary Cortes, the former shall cease its functions and the latter shall continue the matter for which the former was assembled.

Article 167. The Permanent Committee of the Cortes shall continue in the functions designated in articles 111 and 112, in the case mentioned in article 166.

TITLE IV. THE KING

CHAPTER I. THE INVIOLABILITY OF
THE KING AND HIS AUTHORITY

Article 168. The person of a King is sacred and inviolable and he is not subject to responsibility.

Article 169. The King shall bear the title of Catholic Majesty.

Article 170. The power of executing the laws rests exclusively in the

King, and his authority extends to everything that conduces to the preservation of public order at home and to the security of the state abroad,
in conformity with the constitution and the laws.

Article 171. In addition to the royal prerogative of sanctioning and
promulgating laws, the King has the following powers:

1) To issue decrees, regulations and instructions that he considers
conducive to the execution of the laws;

2) To see that speedy and full justice is administered in all the kingdom;

3) To declare war and make peace, giving a documented account
thereof afterward to the Cortes;

4) To appoint the magistrates of all the civil and criminal courts at
the proposal of the Council of State;

5) To appoint to all civil and military offices;

6) To present for all the bishoprics and for all the ecclesiastical dignities and benefices under royal patronage, at the proposal of the Council
of State;

7) To grant honours and distinctions of every class according to law;

8) To command the armies and fleets and to appoint generals;

9) To direct the armed force, distributing it as may be most suitable;

10) To direct diplomatic and commercial relations;

11) To supervise the coining of money on which his head and name
shall be placed;

12) To decree the inversion of funds appropriated for each branch of
the public administration;

13) To pardon criminals according to law;

14) To propose to the Cortes, laws or reforms that he may consider
conducive to the national welfare, for their deliberation according to prescribed form;

15) To allow to circulate or to retain the conciliar decrees and pontifical bulls with consent of the Cortes, if they contain general provisions;
if they deal with local or governmental affairs, the Council of State must
be consulted; if they contain contentious points, they shall pass to the
Supreme Court of Justice for their decision according to law;

16) To appoint and dismiss ministers of state freely.

Article 172. The restrictions upon the authority of the King are as
follows:

1) The King shall not, under any pretext, prevent the celebration of
the Cortes at the periods and in the cases prescribed in the constitution,
nor suspend or dissolve it, nor embarrass, in any way whatever, its sessions
and deliberations. Those who advise or assist in any attempt at such acts
are declared traitors and shall be prosecuted as such;

2) The King may not absent himself from the kingdom without consent
of the Cortes, or else he shall be understood to have abdicated the crown;

3) The King may not alienate, grant, or renounce, or transfer in any way, the royal authority or any of his prerogatives; if, for any reason, he should wish to abdicate the throne in favour of his immediate successor, he must obtain the consent of the Cortes;

4) The King may not alienate, grant, or exchange any province, city, town, or village, however small, of Spanish territory;

5) The King may not enter into offensive alliance, nor make a special treaty of commerce with any foreign power without the consent of the Cortes;

6) Neither may he engage by treaty to grant subsidies to a foreign power without the consent of the Cortes;

7) The King may not grant or alienate the national property without consent of the Cortes;

8) He may not, upon his own authority, impose taxes, either direct or indirect, nor demand supplies under any name or for any purpose; all imposts must be authorized by the Cortes;

9) The King may not grant any exclusive right to any person or corporation;

10) The King may not take the property of any individual or corporation, nor disturb them in the possession, free use, and benefit thereof; and in any case, if it should be necessary, for an object of recognized public utility, to take the property of an individual, that person shall be indemnified, and given a fair sum according to the judgment of upright men;

11) The King may not, upon his own authority, deprive anyone of his liberty or impose any penalty upon him. The minister of state who signs such an order, and the judge executing it, shall be responsible to the nation and shall be prosecuted as violators of personal liberty;

12) The King, before contracting marriage, shall inform the Cortes thereof in order to obtain its consent; if he fails in this respect, he shall be understood to have abdicated the crown.

Article 173. The King upon his accession to the throne, or if he has been under age, upon his assumption of the government of the kingdom, shall take the following oath before the Cortes:

N (here his name) by the grace of God, and the Constitution of the Spanish Monarchy, King of Spain: I swear by God and the Holy Gospels that I shall protect and preserve the Apostolic Roman Catholic religion without permitting any other in the kingdom; that I shall defend and cause to be supported, the political constitution and the laws of the Spanish monarchy and that all my actions shall be directed to its good and welfare; that I shall not alienate, grant, or dismember any part of the kingdom; that I shall not exact any produce, money, or anything else which has not been decreed by the Cortes; that I shall never deprive anyone of his property and that I shall respect, above all, the political liberty of the nation and the personal liberty of the individual; if I shall act in opposition to what I have sworn, or any part thereof, I ought not to be obeyed, and such acts shall be null and void. May God help me and defend me if I keep my oath; otherwise, may He call me to account.

CHAPTER II. THE SUCCESSION TO THE CROWN

Article 174. The kingdom of Spain is indivisible, and from the promulgation of the constitution, the succession shall always be among the lawful descendants, male and female, in regular order of primogeniture and representation of lines mentioned hereafter.

Article 175. No one shall be King of Spain who was not born in lawful wedlock.

Article 176. In the same degree of kinship, males shall be preferred to females, and the elder to the younger always; but females, of a nearer line or nearer degree within the same line shall be preferred to males of more remote line or degree.

Article 177. The son or daughter of the eldest son of the King, in case of the death of the eldest son before succeeding to the crown, shall be preferred to the uncles and shall succeed to his grandfather immediately by right of representation.

Article 178. So long as the direct line of succession shall exist, the collateral branches shall not succeed.

Article 179. The King of Spain is our lord, Don Ferdinand VII of Bourbon, who now reigns.

Article 180. After our lord, Don Ferdinand VII of Bourbon, his legitimate descendants, both male and female, shall succeed him; in their default, there shall succeed his brothers and sisters and his father's brothers and sisters, both male and female, and their legitimate descendants in the order provided, preserving always the right of representation and the preference of the nearer line to the more remote ones.

Article 181. The Cortes shall exclude from the succession that or those persons who are incapable of governing or who have committed an act for which they deserve to lose the right to the crown.

Article 182. If all the lines herein designated become extinct, the Cortes shall make new choices as may be most suitable to the nation, following always the order and rules of succession herein established.

Article 183. When the crown shall devolve, or has devolved upon a female, she may not select a husband without consent of the Cortes; otherwise she shall be considered to have abdicated the crown.

Article 184. When a female reigns, the prince consort shall have no authority in the kingdom and shall take no part in the government.

CHAPTER III. THE MINORITY OF THE KING AND THE REGENCY

Article 185. The King is a minor until he attains eighteen years of age.

Article 186. During the minority of the King, the kingdom shall be governed by a regency.

Article 187. It shall be so ruled when the King is incapacitated for the exercise of his authority for any physical or moral cause.

Article 188. If the King has been incapacitated for more than two years, and the immediate successor is of age, the Cortes may appoint him regent in place of a regency.

Article 189. In those cases in which the crown shall be vacated during the minority of the Prince of Asturias, until such time as the extraordinary Cortes assembles, if the ordinary Cortes is not in session, there shall be a provisional regency composed as follows: the queen mother, if she be alive; two Deputies of the Permanent Committee of the Cortes, the oldest in order of their election; the two oldest Councillors of State, the dean and the next senior member; if the queen mother be dead, then the third senior Councillor of State shall be one of the regency.

Article 190. The provisional regency shall be presided over by the queen mother, if she be living; in default of her, by the eldest member of the Permanent Committee in order of election to it.

Article 191. The provisional regency shall dispatch no business save that which admits no delay, and shall not remove or appoint civil employees except temporarily.

Article 192. When the extraordinary Cortes is assembled it shall choose a regency of three or five persons.

Article 193. To become a member of the regency, one must be a citizen in the exercise of his rights; foreigners although they may have certificate of citizenship, are excluded.

Article 194. The regency shall be presided over by one of its members upon the nomination of the Cortes which shall decide, if necessary, whether the presidency shall be held by turns and with what limitations.

Article 195. The regency shall discharge the authority of the King within the limitations to be prescribed by the Cortes.

Article 196. Both the provisional and permanent regencies shall take the oath prescribed in article 173, adding the clause that they shall be faithful to the King; the permanent regency shall add further: that it observe the conditions imposed by the Cortes for the exercise of its authority, and that when the King shall be of age or his incapacity ceases, they shall turn over the government of the kingdom to him, under the penalty of being punished as traitors if they delay a moment in doing so.

Article 197. All acts of the regency shall be published in the name of the King.

Article 198. The guardian of the minor King shall be the person appointed by the late King in his will. In default of such appointment the queen mother shall be the guardian but only until remarriage. In default of her, the Cortes shall name the guardian. In the first and third cases, the guardian must be a native of the kingdom.

Article 199. The regency shall see that the education of the minor King shall be suited to his high dignity, and that it be carried out according to the plan approved by the Cortes.

Article 200. The Cortes shall assign the salary that the members of the regency shall receive.

CHAPTER IV. THE ROYAL FAMILY AND THE RECOGNITION OF THE PRINCE OF ASTURIAS

Article 201. The King's eldest son shall bear the title of Prince of Asturias.

Article 202. The other sons and daughters of the King shall bear the title of *Infantes* of Spain.

Article 203. The sons and daughters of the Prince of Asturias shall likewise bear the title of *Infantes* of Spain.

Article 204. No other persons but the above mentioned may bear the title of *Infante* of Spain.

Article 205. Infantes of Spain shall enjoy the distinctions and honours which they have hitherto enjoyed; they may be appointed to any offices except those of judicature and that of Deputy to the Cortes.

Article 206. The Prince of Asturias may not leave the kingdom without the consent of the Cortes; otherwise, he is thereby excluded from the succession to the crown.

Article 207. He shall likewise lose his right to the crown by remaining abroad longer than permitted, and by refusing to comply with the summons within the time set by the Cortes when it requires his re-entry.

Article 208. The Prince of Asturias, the *Infantes*, and their children and descendants who are subjects of the King, may not contract marriage without the consent of the King and of the Cortes under the pain of being excluded from the succession to the crown.

Article 209. An authentic copy of the certificate of birth, marriage, and death of all persons of the royal family shall be delivered to the Cortes, or if it is not assembled, to the Permanent Committee, for preservation in its archives.

Article 210. The Prince of Asturias shall be recognized by the Cortes with the formalities provided by the regulation for its internal government.

Article 211. This recognition shall be made in the first Cortes assembled after his birth.

Article 212. The Prince of Asturias, upon attaining the age of fourteen years, shall take an oath before the Cortes as follows:

N (here his name) Prince of Asturias: I swear by God and the Holy Gospels that I will defend and preserve the Apostolic Roman Catholic religion without permitting any other in the kingdom; that I will support the political constitution of the Spanish monarchy, and that I will be faithful and obedient to the King. So help me God.

CHAPTER V. THE REVENUE OF THE ROYAL FAMILY

Article 213. The Cortes shall assign to the King the annual revenue of his household, which will be commensurate with his high dignity.

Article 214. All those palaces possessed by his predecessors shall belong to the King, and the Cortes shall assign such lands as they consider most convenient for his recreation.

Article 215. The Cortes shall assign to the Prince of Asturias from the day of his birth, and to the *Infantes* from their seventh year of age, the annual sum for their establishments, which sum must be commensurate with their respective dignities.

Article 216. The Cortes shall assign the sum which it determines as dowry for the *Infantes*, when they marry; when this has been given, the annual sums shall cease.

Article 217. If the *Infantes* marry and live in the kingdom they shall continue to receive the annual sums assigned them; if they marry and live abroad, their allowance shall cease and the gross sum, as determined by the Cortes, shall be given them.

Article 218. The Cortes shall assign the annual sum for the establishment of the dowager-queen.

Article 219. The salaries of the members of the regency shall be taken from the revenue allotted to the royal household.

Article 220. At the beginning of each reign, the Cortes shall assign the revenue of the royal household and of the establishments of his family, as mentioned in the preceding articles; no alteration may be made during the reign.

Article 221. All the sums shall be paid out of the national treasury to the administrator appointed by the King, and all the accounts shall be settled by the said administrator.

CHAPTER VI. THE MINISTERS OF STATE

Article 222. There shall be seven ministers of state, viz:

1) Foreign Relations;
2) Internal Affairs of the Peninsula and Adjacent Islands;
3) Overseas Provinces;
4) Grace and Justice;

5) Finance;
6) War;
7) Navy.

Successive Cortes may make in this system of ministries of state such variation as circumstances and experience demand.

Article 223. To become a minister of state, one must be a citizen in the exercise of his rights; foreigners, though they may have certificates of citizenship, are excluded.

Article 224. A special regulation approved by the Cortes shall determine the kind of affairs which belong to each department.

Article 225. All the King's orders must be signed by the minister of state of the corresponding department. No court, or public official shall execute an order which lacks this requisite.

Article 226. The ministers of state shall be responsible to the Cortes for the orders that they authorize contrary to the constitution and the laws, and their having been ordered to do so by the King shall not serve as an excuse.

Article 227. The ministers of state shall every year produce an estimate of the expense of their respective departments of the public administrations, and shall render accounts of their expenditures, according to the manner prescribed.

Article 228. In order to enforce the responsibility of the ministers, the Cortes shall first decree that there is cause for accusation.

Article 229. After this decree has been given, the minister of state shall be suspended, and the Cortes shall send to the Supreme Court of Justice all the documents concerning the case. That court shall have cognizance of the case and shall decide it according to the laws.

Article 230. The Cortes shall assign the salaries that the ministers of state shall receive during their actual service.

CHAPTER VII. THE COUNCIL OF STATE

Article 231. The Council of State shall be composed of forty persons who are citizens in the full exercise of their rights; foreigners, although they possess a certificate of citizenship, are excluded.

Article 232. The Councillors shall be precisely of the following description, to wit: only four ecclesiastics of acknowledged and distinguished talent and merit, of which number two shall be bishops; only four grandees of Spain of reputed virtue, talent, and necessary knowledge; and the remainder shall be chosen from those subjects who have distinguished themselves most by their brilliance and attainments, or by their signal service in one of the principal branches of the administration and government of the state. The Cortes may not propose for these offices, any person who is a Deputy to the Cortes at the time of the selection. At least twelve of the members of the Council of State shall be natives of the overseas provinces.

Article 233. All the Councillors of State shall be appointed by the King upon the proposal of the Cortes.

Article 234. For the formation of this council, the Cortes shall prepare a triple list for the three classes aforementioned, in the proper proportion, and from this list the King shall select the forty members for the Council of State, selecting the ecclesiastics from the list of their class, the grandees from their list, and the others from their list.

Article 235. When a vacancy occurs in the Council of State, the first Cortes which assembles thereafter shall present to the King three persons of the class in which the vacancy occurs; the King shall select one of the three.

Article 236. The Council of State is the only council of the King; he shall consult it in grave affairs of state especially in granting or refusing his sanction to laws, and in declaring war and making peace treaties.

Article 237. The Council shall have the privilege of presenting to the King three candidates for each ecclesiastical benefice and judicial office.

Article 238. The King shall frame regulations for the government of the Council of State after consulting with it, and the regulations shall be presented to the Cortes for its approval.

Article 239. Councillors of State may not be removed from office without lawful cause substantiated before the Supreme Court of Justice.

Article 240. Salaries for the Councillors of State shall be fixed by the Cortes.

Article 241. Upon taking office the Councillors of State shall take oath before the King to support the constitution, to be faithful to the King, and to advise him, looking to the best interests of the nation, without regard to personal interests or private views.

TITLE V. THE COURTS AND THE ADMINISTRATION OF JUSTICE IN CIVIL AND CRIMINAL CASES

CHAPTER I. THE COURTS

Article 242. The power of applying laws in civil and criminal cases belongs exclusively to the courts.

Article 243. Neither the Cortes or the King may perform judicial functions in any case, nor prevent the trial of pending cases, nor order the reopening of adjudged cases.

Article 244. The laws shall determine the order and formalities of procedure which shall be uniform in all courts, and neither the Cortes or the King may cause them to be dispensed with.

Article 245. The courts may not exercise any other functions than those of judging and of enforcing their judgments.

Article 246. The courts may not suspend the execution of laws nor make any rules for the administration of justice.

Article 247. No Spaniard may be tried in civil and criminal cases by any commission, but only by a competent court, previously authorized by law.

Article 248. There shall be only one jurisdiction for all classes of persons in public civil and criminal cases.

Article 249. The ecclesiastics shall continue under ecclesiastical jurisdiction within the limits that the ordinance prescribes or shall prescribe.

Article 250. The military shall likewise remain under their own jurisdiction within the limits that the ordinance prescribes or shall prescribe.

Article 251. In order to be appointed judge or magistrate, one must be a native Spaniard and have attained twenty-five years of age. The other necessary qualifications shall be determined by law.

Article 252. Magistrates and judges may not be deposed from their offices, whether selected for a limited or permanent term, except for cause legally proven and adjudged, nor may they be suspended except for an accusation legally charged.

Article 253. If any complaints against a magistrate shall be brought to the King, and if after investigation, they seem to him to be well founded, he may, upon consultation with the Council of State, suspend him, referring the case to the Supreme Court of Justice for its decision according to the law.

Article 254. Judges shall be responsible personally for their failure to observe the laws governing procedure in criminal and civil cases,

Article 255. Popular action shall lie against magistrates and judges who commit bribery, corruption, and prevarication.

Article 256. The Cortes shall assign an adequate compensation for magistrates and judges.

Article 257. Justice shall be administered in the name of the King, and executory sentences and provisions of the superior courts shall be issued in his name.

Article 258. The civil and criminal code and the code of commerce shall be the same throughout the monarchy without prejudice to the variations that the Cortes may make in certain circumstances.

Article 259. In the capital of the kingdom there shall be a court called the Supreme Court of Justice.

Article 260. The Cortes shall determine the number of magistrates who are to compose the court and the chambers in which they may be placed.

Article 261. The Supreme Court of Justice shall have power:

1) To arrange the jurisdiction of the courts of audience (*audiencia*) among themselves in all Spanish territory and the jurisdictions of the courts of audience with those of the special courts in the peninsula and adjacent islands. In the overseas provinces they shall be adjusted as the law shall direct;

2) To judge ministers of state after the Cortes has declared that there is cause of accusation against them;

3) To take cognizance of all cases of removal and suspensions of councillors and magistrates of courts of audience;

4) To take cognizance of criminal cases brought against ministers of state, Councillors of State, and magistrates of the courts of audience; the preparatory proceedings shall be held before the highest civil officer who shall report them to the court;

5) To take cognizance of all criminal cases brought against members of the Supreme Court. Should it be necessary to enforce the responsibility of this Supreme Court, the Cortes after the formality established in article 228, shall proceed to appoint for this purpose a court composed of nine judges, selected by lot from eighteen nominees;

6) To take cognizance of the investigation of administration of every public employee subject to the court, according to law;

7) To take cognizance of all litigious matters pertaining to the royal patronage;

8) To take cognizance of the recourses to force by any of the higher ecclesiastical courts;

9) To take cognizance of appeals from errors interposed against sentences, given in the court of last instance, for the purpose of retrial of the original case, and to enforce the responsibility mentioned in article 254. In the overseas provinces, the courts of audience shall have cognizance of these appeals in the manner described below;

10) To receive expressions of doubt from other courts concerning the proper interpretation of a law and to consult with the King about such expressions, laying before him the available documents thereof, so that he may suggest a proper decision in the Cortes;

11) To examine the lists of civil and criminal cases which the courts of audience must remit to it, in order to promote the prompt administration of justice, to send copies to the government for the same purpose, and to cause them to be printed.

Article 262. All civil and criminal cases shall be terminated within the jurisdiction of each court of audience.

Article 263. The courts of audience shall take cognizance of all civil and criminal cases, in the second or third instance, of the lower courts of their jurisdiction, as the laws determine, and also of the cases of suspension and removal of the inferior judges of their jurisdictions in the manner prescribed by law, giving account thereof to the King.

Article 264. Magistrates who have heard a case in second instance may not sit as judges on the review of the case in third instance.

Article 265. The courts of audience shall also have cognizance of the jurisdictions of the inferior judges of their territory.

Article 266. They likewise shall have cognizance of recourse to force which are introduced by the ecclesiastical courts and authorities of the territory.

Article 267. They shall also receive from all inferior judges of their territory, punctual notice of cases of criminal prosecution and lists of civil and criminal cases pending in their jurisdictions, with a report on the progress of both kinds of cases, in order to promote the promptest administration of justice.

Article 268. The courts of audience overseas shall also have cognizance of the appeals for errors in law; such appeals must be presented to those courts of audience that have enough judges for the formation of three courts and have not in any instance had cognizance of the case. In the courts of audience that do not have this number of judges, the appeals shall be interposed from one court to another of those comprehended in the same district of the same superior government; if there is only one court of audience, appeals shall go to the nearest court of audience in the nearest district.

Article 269. After the court of audience, having cognizance thereof, has declared that there is error in the proceedings appealed from, account thereof shall be given to the Supreme Court of Justice, along with the proper documents, in order to enforce the responsibility mentioned in article 254.

Article 270. The courts of audience shall send each year to the Supreme Court of Justice, correct lists of the civil cases, and, every six months, the criminal cases, either decided or pending, with an indication of the stage of progress in each case, including also, those reports received from inferior judges.

Article 271. Special laws and regulations shall determine the number of judges of the courts of audience, such number not to be less than seven, the form of these courts, and their places of establishment.

Article 272. When the proper division of Spanish territory mentioned in article 11 has been made, the number of courts of audience shall be regulated accordingly and the territory for each shall be designated.

Article 273. Districts proportionately equal shall be established, and in the chief town of each district there shall be a judge with a corresponding jurisdiction.

Article 274. The powers of these judges shall be limited to litigated cases, and the law shall determine which cases shall come under their jurisdiction in the chief city and in the towns of the district, as well as the amount to which they can give judgment in civil cases, without appeal.

Article 275. Magistrates shall be established in every town and the law shall determine the limits of their powers in both litigious and economic matters.

Article 276. All judges of inferior courts must give account within three days to their respective courts of audience of their criminal cases and afterwards shall report on the progress thereof at the times prescribed by the court of audience.

Article 277. They must likewise send to their respective courts of audience general lists of the civil cases every six months; every three months they must send a list of the criminal cases pending, with information on the progress of such cases.

Article 278. The laws shall decide whether special courts shall be established to take cognizance of special legal business.

Article 279. Magistrates and judges, upon assuming office, shall swear to support the constitution, to be faithful to the King, to observe the laws, and to administer justice impartially.

CHAPTER II. THE ADMINISTRATION OF JUSTICE IN CIVIL CASES

Article 280. No Spaniard may be deprived of the right of having his differences terminated by arbiters chosen by both parties.

Article 281. The judgment given by the arbiters shall be executed unless the parties have reserved the right of appealing it.

Article 282. The magistrate of each town shall exercise therein the office of conciliator; whoever has a case of civil suit or of injuries received, must appear before him for that purpose.

Article 283. The magistrate with two honest men, one appointed by each party, shall hear the argument of the plaintiff and of the defendant; after consulting his associates, the magistrate shall reach the decision best calculated to terminate the suit without further litigation; the suit shall be terminated if the parties agree to this extrajudicial decision.

Article 284. No law suit shall be commenced unless it appears that conciliatory measures have been tried previously.

Article 285. Lawsuits, regardless of their character, shall have, at most, three trials and three definitive judgments pronounced upon them. When two like sentences have been given and the suit is brought to a third trial, the number of judges on the third trial must exceed the number of judges on the second trial according to the provisions of law; the law shall also determine on general principles concerning the nature of the several courts and the cases to be brought before them, how and in what cases their sentences are to be put in execution.

CHAPTER III. THE ADMINISTRATION OF
JUSTICE IN CRIMINAL CASES

Article 286. The laws shall direct the administration of justice in criminal cases so that the trials may be brief and regular and that the offenders may be brought promptly to punishment.

Article 287. No Spaniard may be arrested without the preceding formalities of a summary inquest of the deed for which he lawfully deserves corporal punishment, and of the written order of judge, which shall be communicated to the person upon his arrest.

Article 288. Every person must obey these mandates; any resistance shall be considered a grave crime.

Article 289. If resistance is offered or flight is attempted by the offender, force may be used to secure him;

Article 290. The person arrested, before commitment to jail, shall be brought before a judge, whenever that is possible, for examination; otherwise he shall be jailed as an offender and shall be examined by the judge within twenty-four hours thereafter.

Article 291. The prisoner shall not be examined upon oath; in criminal cases, no oath shall be taken by any one in his own cause.

Article 292. Anyone may arrest an offender seized *in flagrante delicto* and bring him before a judge; when the offender has been brought before a judge, or jailed, the case shall be proceeded with as prescribed in the two preceding articles.

Article 293. If there is reason for commitment to jail, the judge shall issue a warrant to that effect, and a copy of it shall be delivered to the jail keeper for registration in his records; without such writ, no jail keeper may receive a person as a prisoner, under the strictest responsibility.

Article 294. The property of an offender shall be attached only in cases of pecuniary responsibility, and in proportion to the extent of such responsibility.

Article 295. No person shall be jailed who shall give sufficient bail unless it is as expressly provided by law.

Article 296. When, in any stage of the case, it appears that corporal punishment will not be suffered by the offender, he shall be put at liberty upon giving bail.

Article 297. The jails shall be regulated so as to secure the prisoners but not molest them; the jail keepers shall keep them in good order and shall separate those to whom the judges have forbidden communication, but never in subterranean dungeons or unhealthful cells.

Article 298. The frequency of prison inspection shall be determined by law and no prisoner shall fail to present himself under any pretext.

Article 299. The judge and the jail keeper who fail to conform to the provisions of the preceding articles shall be punished as guilty of arbitrary detention, which shall be considered a crime in the criminal code.

Article 300. Within twenty-four hours, the accused shall be informed of the cause of the detention and the name of his accuser, if there be any.

Article 301. Upon examination of the accused, all the documents and the depositions of the witnesses, together with their names, shall be read to him; and if he does not know the witnesses, he shall be given as much information as he asks in order to learn their identity.

Article 302. The remainder of the prosecution shall be public in the manner prescribed by law.

Article 303. The penalty of confiscation of property may not be imposed.

Article 304. Torture and other means of compulsion shall never be used.

Article 305. No punishment for any crime shall extend to the family of the offender for any period of time; the culprit alone shall bear the entire punishment.

Article 306. The house of a Spaniard shall not be forcibly entered except in the cases determined by law for the good order and security of the state.

Article 307. If, at a later time, the Cortes should consider it desirable to make a distinction between judges of fact and judges of law, it shall establish such distinctions as is deemed suitable.

Article 308. If, in extraordinary circumstances, the security of the state should demand the suspension of some of the formalities of the arrest of offenders, as described in this chapter, throughout the monarchy, or in any part thereof, the Cortes may decree it for a limited time.

TITLE VI. THE INTERNAL GOVERNMENT OF THE PROVINCES AND OF THE TOWNS

CHAPTER I. THE MUNICIPAL COUNCILS

Article 309. For the internal government of the towns there shall be municipal councils (*ayuntamientos*) composed of the chief magistrates (*alcaldes*), the aldermen (*regidores*), and the town proctor (*procurador sindico*); they shall be presided over by the principal civil officer, in default of him, by the magistrate or if there be two magistrates, by the first elected.

Article 310. Municipal councils shall be established in the towns lacking them; wherever it is suitable, one shall be set up. Towns that, with or without their surrounding district, have a population of 1,000 souls must have municipal councils; proper limits shall be determined for each district.

Article 311. The number of members of each class who are to compose the municipal councils shall be determined by law, according to the population.

Article 312. The chief magistrates, aldermen, and town proctors shall be chosen by election in the towns; those aldermen and others who hold perpetual office in the municipal council, whatever their title or position, lose their offices.

Article 313. The citizens of each town shall assemble every year in December to elect by a majority of votes and according to the population, the specified number of electors, who must reside in that town, and be in the full exercise of their rights of citizenship.

Article 314. In the same month, the electors shall choose by absolute majority of votes, the magistrate or magistrates, the aldermen, and the town proctor or proctors in order that they may take office on 1 January of the following year.

Article 315. The magistrates shall be changed each year as well as one-half of the aldermen and of the town proctors whenever there are two of the latter; if there is only one proctor, he shall be changed annually.

Article 316. The above named officers may not be re-elected until at least two years have elapsed, wherever the population permits.

Article 317. To become a magistrate, alderman, or town proctor, one must not only be a citizen in full exercise of his rights, but also be above twenty-five years of age and have resided in the town for at least five years. Other qualifications for these officers shall be determined by law.

Article 318. No incumbent of public office appointed by the King may be a magistrate, alderman, or town proctor; those serving in the National Militia are not comprehended in this ruling.

Article 319. No citizen may excuse himself, without legal cause, from the assumption of the above-mentioned offices.

Article 320. Each municipal council shall elect, by absolute majority of votes, a secretary, who shall be paid out of public funds.

Article 321. The municipal councils shall have the following duties:

1) To preserve the cleanliness and health of the town;

2) To assist the magistrate in everything pertaining to the security of the inhabitants and their property and to the preservation of public order;

3) To collect and administer the revenue and excise duties according to law and to regulations, appointing a treasurer under the responsibility of those who appoint him;

4) To assess and collect the taxes and to remit them to the proper treasury;

5) To supervise all primary schools and other educational institutions supported by community funds;

6) To oversee hospitals, foundling's homes, hospices, and other charitable institutions according to the rules prescribed;

7) To direct the construction and repair of roads, causeways, bridges, and prisons; to take care of woods and forests belonging to the town, and of all public works of necessity, utility, and ornament.

8) To frame municipal ordinances for the town and to present them to the Cortes for approval, through the provincial council which shall forward them accompanied by its own opinion thereon.

9) To promote agriculture, industry, and commerce according to the locality and circumstances of the town and whatever else which might be advantageous to it.

Article 322. If some works or other objects of public utility should be wanted, and if, through lack of funds, it should be necessary to resort to taxation, these taxes may not be levied without consent of the Cortes, obtained through the provincial council. In case of urgency of such works, the municipal council with the approval of the provincial council may levy such taxes *pro tempore* until the decision of the Cortes shall be made. These shall be administered like the regular revenue.

Article 323. The municipal councils shall discharge their duties under the inspection of the provincial council to which an authenticated account of receipts and expenditures shall be transmitted annually.

CHAPTER II. THE CIVIL GOVERNMENT OF THE PROVINCES AND THE PROVINCIAL COUNCILS

Article 324. The civil government of the provinces shall be vested in a governor whom the King appoints in each province.

Article 325. To promote its prosperity, each province shall have a provincial council presided over by the governor.

Article 326. This provincial council shall be composed of its president, of the intendant and seven individuals elected as shall be later described, without prejudice to the variations in number which the Cortes may think suitable, or circumstances may require, after the new partition of provinces mention in Article 11.

Article 327. One-half of the members of the provincial council shall be renewed every two years; after the first two years, the larger number shall leave their seats, and the lesser number shall leave at the end of the second term of the two years, and so on progressively.

Article 328. The elective members of the provincial council shall be chosen by the district electors on the day following their election of Deputies to the Cortes and in the same manner.

Article 329. Three alternates for each council shall be similarly elected at the same time.

Article 330. To become a member of the provincial council, one must be a citizen in the exercise of his rights, above twenty-five years of age, a native or inhabitant of the province with at least seven years of residence therein, and must have sufficient means to maintain himself decently; no royal appointee, as mentioned above, in article 318, may be a member of the council.

Article 331. No one may be re-elected until four years have elapsed from the time at which he ceased his functions in the provincial council.

Article 332. When the governor cannot preside over the council, the intendant shall do so, and in default of the latter, the first elected member of the council.

Article 333. The council shall appoint a secretary to be paid by provincial funds.

Article 334. The councils shall hold their sessions ninety days, at most, each year, according to their convenience. In the peninsula they must assemble on 1 March; overseas, on 1 June.

Article 335. The provincial councils shall have power:

1) To examine and approve of the assessment of taxes for the various towns from the provincial quota;

2) To watch over the proper inversion of the public funds of the towns and to examine their accounts so that, being authenticated by the provincial councils, they may gain the superior approval, conforming themselves in every detail to the laws and regulations;

3) To see that municipal councils are established where they should be according to Article 310;

4) To propose to the government the levy of suitable excise duties to be used for the construction of new works of public utility in the province, or for the repair of old ones, in order to obtain the approval of the Cortes for it; In the overseas provinces, if the urgency of the public works does not permit waiting for the resolution of the Cortes, the council, with the express assent of the governor, may levy excise duties temporarily, giving immediate account thereof to the government for the approval of the Cortes. The council, upon its own responsibility, shall appoint a treasurer for the collection of the excise duties; and the accounts of expenditure, after examination by the council, shall be transmitted to the government for its recognition and examination, and finally shall pass to the Cortes for its approval.

5) To promote the education of youth according to the plans approved, to encourage agriculture, industry, and commerce, and to protect those who have made new discoveries in these branches;

6) To inform the government of abuses which they have noted in the administration of public funds;

7) To take the census and prepare statistical reports of the provinces;

8) To see that charitable institutions fulfill their respective purposes,

and to propose to the government the regulations that they consider suitable for the reform of abuses noted;

9) To inform the Cortes of the infringements upon the constitution that they observe in the province;

10) The overseas provincial councils shall oversee the economy, order, and progress of the missions for the conversion of heathen Indians; the superintendents of the missions shall give accounts of their operations so that abuses may be prevented; these accounts shall be transmitted to the government.

Article 336. If any council exceeds its powers, the king may suspend the elective members thereof, informing the Cortes of this disposition and the reasons for it, so that the Cortes may make the proper decision upon the matter; during the suspension, the alternates shall take up the functions of the council.

Article 337. All members of the municipal and provincial councils upon assuming office shall take an oath, the former upon the hands of the chief civil officer of the jurisdiction, or in default of him, of the magistrate first elected, the latter upon the hands of the governor of the provinces, to support the political constitution of the Spanish Monarchy, to observe the laws, to be faithful to the King and to discharge religiously the duties of office.

TITLE VII. TAXATION

CHAPTER I

Article 338. The Cortes shall establish or confirm annually the taxes, either direct or indirect, general, provincial, or municipal; those already established shall continue until their rejection or the imposition of new taxes shall be announced.

Article 339. Taxes shall be apportioned among all Spaniards according to their ability, without any exception or privilege.

Article 340. The taxes shall be proportioned to the appropriations decreed by the Cortes for public service in all branches.

Article 341. In order to enable the Cortes to fix the sums necessary in all branches of the public service, and the taxes needed to raise such sums, the minister of finance shall present to the Cortes upon its assembly the general estimate of sums deemed necessary, after he has received the estimates from the other departments.

Article 342. The finance minister shall likewise present, along with the estimates of expenses, the plan of taxation necessary to raise such sums.

Article 343. If the King should consider any tax burdensome or prejudicial, he shall so notify the Cortes through the minister of finance, presenting at the same time, such substitute for it as he considers most suitable.

Article 344. After the quota of direct taxes has been fixed, the Cortes shall assign the proper share to each province according to its wealth; the minister of finance shall also furnish the necessary estimates for this assignment.

Article 345. There shall be a national treasury charged with the disposal of the funds apportioned to the service of each State.

Article 346. Each province shall have a treasury for the safekeeping of funds collected for the public treasury. The provincial treasuries shall be in correspondence with the national treasury, at whose disposition the funds shall be kept.

Article 347. No payment shall be admitted to the account of the national treasury except by virtue of a royal decree signed by the finance minister, in which decree shall be stated for what service the payment is required, together with the decree of the Cortes authorizing it.

Article 348. To insure correctness in the account of the national treasury, the income and expenditures must be examined, respectively, by the Auditing Committee on Assessments and by that on Distribution of Public Taxes.

Article 349. A special regulation shall direct those committees so that they may serve the purpose of their institution.

Article 350. A general auditing committee, to be established by a special law, shall examine all the accounts of public funds.

Article 351. As soon as the account of the national treasury, comprising the annual revenue from taxes and duties and their inversion, shall be approved definitely by the Cortes, such account shall be printed, published, and circulated among the provincial and municipal councils.

Article 352. The accounts of the expenditures in each department, rendered by the respective ministers, shall likewise be printed, published, and circulated.

Article 353. The management of the public funds shall always be independent of any authority other than that to which it is confided.

Article 354. No customs houses shall be established except in sea ports and at the frontiers; this disposition shall not be in effect until the Cortes so decrees it.

Article 355. The public debt shall be one of the first considerations of the Cortes, and the Cortes shall devise the best means for its gradual extinction and the payment of interest which is due; it shall arrange everything concerning the direction of this important branch, as much the agencies to be established, which must be managed separately from the general treasury, as the supervision of accounts and auditing.

TITLE VIII. THE NATIONAL MILITARY FORCE

CHAPTER I. TROOPS IN CONTINUAL SERVICE

Article 356. There shall be a permanent national force on land and sea for the defense of the state abroad and the preservation of order at home.

Article 357. The Cortes shall fix annually the number of troops necessary, according to circumstances, and shall determine the most convenient method of raising them.

Article 358. The Cortes shall also fix annually the number of ships of military marine which are to be armed or to be kept armed.

Article 359. The Cortes, by means of respective ordinances, shall establish everything relative to discipline, order of promotion, salaries, administration, and whatever else conduces to the good condition of the army and navy.

Article 360. Military schools shall be established for instruction and training in all the different branches of the army and navy.

Article 361. No Spaniard may be excused from military service whenever he is properly called upon by law.

CHAPTER II. NATIONAL MILITIA

Article 362. Each province shall have a corps of National Militia composed of its own inhabitants, in proportion to its population and circumstances.

Article 363. An ordinance shall regulate the manner of formation of the corps, its number, and especial constitution in all its branches.

Article 364. The service of the militia shall not be continuous, and shall take place only when circumstances require it.

Article 365. When necessary, the King may dispose of this force within the respective province; but he may not employ it outside the province without consent of the Cortes.

TITLE IX. PUBLIC INSTRUCTION

CHAPTER I

Article 366. In every town of the monarchy there shall be established primary schools in which children shall be taught reading, writing and counting, the catechism of the Catholic religion and a brief exposition of civil obligations.

Article 367. Likewise, an adequate number of universities and other establishments of instruction considered necessary for the teaching of all sciences, literature, and fine arts, shall be created and regulated.

Article 368. The general plan of instruction shall be uniform throughout the kingdom; the political constitution of the monarchy must be explained in all the universities and literary establishments where ecclesiastical and political sciences are taught.

Article 369. There shall be a general directorate of studies, composed of persons of recognized academic standing, who shall be charged under government authority, with the inspection of public education.

Article 370. The Cortes, by means of plans and special statutes, shall regulate whatever pertains to the important object of public instruction.

Article 371. All Spaniards have the freedom of writing, printing, and publishing their political ideas without need of license, revision, or any approval previous to publication, subject to the restrictions and responsibility by law.

TITLE X. THE OBSERVANCE OF THE CONSTITUTION
AND THE MANNER OF AMENDING IT

Article 372. In its first sessions, the Cortes shall consider the infractions of the constitution of which it is informed, in order to apply the suitable remedy, and to enforce the responsibility of those persons contravening it.

Article 373. Every Spaniard has the right to petition the Cortes or the King, claiming the proper observance of the constitution.

Article 374. Every public, civil, military, or ecclesiastical officer upon assuming office, shall promise, on oath, to preserve the constitution, to be faithful to the King, and to discharge the duties of his office properly.

Article 375. No alteration, addition or reform in any articles of the constitution may be proposed until eight years shall have elapsed from the time at which the constitution shall have been put fully into execution.

Article 376. In order to make an alteration, addition, or reform in the constitution, the deputation which is to decree it definitively, must be authorized by special powers for this purpose.

Article 377. Any proposal of reform in any article of the constitution must be made in writing and must be supported and signed by twenty deputies at least.

Article 378. The proposal of reform shall be read three times with an interval of six days between readings, and after the third reading, the Cortes shall determine whether it should be admitted to discussion.

Article 379. If admitted to discussion, it shall be treated with the same formalities and methods prescribed for the formation of laws; after these, the Cortes shall vote whether the same shall be discussed again in the next general Cortes; an agreement of two-thirds of the votes is necessary for such declaration.

Article 380. The next general Cortes, after the same formalities have been observed, may declare with the concurrence of two-thirds of its sessions, that there is cause for granting special powers to make such amendment.

Article 381. This declaration made, it shall be published in, and communicated to, all the provinces and according to the time of declaration, the Cortes shall decide whether the delegates to the next general Cortes, or to the one next immediately succeeding, shall be granted the special powers.

Article 382. Such powers shall be granted by the provincial electoral meetings, there shall be added to the ordinary powers, the following clause:

Likewise, they grant them special power of making in the constitution the reform mentioned in the decree of Cortes (here the literal decree), the whole according to the provisions of the said constitution. They bind themselves to recognize and consider constitutional, all that shall be decree by virtue thereof.

Article 383. The proposed reform shall be discussed anew, and if approved by two-thirds of the Deputies, it shall become a constitutional law and as such shall be published in the Cortes.

Article 384. A committee shall present the decree of reform to the King and he shall cause it to be published and circulated to all the authorities and towns of the Monarchy.

Bolivian Constitution
of 1826

Latin America's great Liberador, Simon Bolívar (1783–1830), was also Latin America's first great Constitutionalist. Although the other Constitutionalists of the region were influenced by the U.S. Constitution of 1787 and the Spanish Constitution of 1812, Bolívar was obsessed with the problems of political instability that had plagued the early revolutionary states south of the Rio Grande. He was, at the same time, a fierce opponent of monarchy and a strong believer in republicanism. Well educated in the classics and classical history, his conception of a constitution was in part inspired by patterns established in Ancient Rome. Unfortunately, the authoritarian base that he established set a confused precedent for dictatorship as an alternative to democracy in Latin America.

Liberador Bolívar was a soldier, statesman, political philosopher, and eventually the liberator of five Latin American nations. Educated in Spain, he derived his own concept of republicanism from both his studies and experiences as a revolutionary leader. For more than fifteen years, he fought against Spanish colonialism, eventually managing to liberate from Spanish rule Venezuela, Ecuador, Colombia, Peru, and the country bearing his name.

At various times in his career, Bolívar headed the revolutionary governments of all five countries. As a statesman, he repeatedly faced the transitional problem of turning a revolutionary government into a working, stable nation-state. He regarded these new governments as "infant"[1]—too inexperienced to afford the luxury of popular government. Thus, in the first constitution of Bolivia he sought arrangements and structures to compensate for what he saw as the inadequacies of the population.

"Our citizens lack the political virtues of true republicans,"[2] declared Bolívar in his Cartagena Manifesto of 1812, which followed the collapse of the First Republic of Venezuela. This Manifesto was one of the four documents that set forth his political ideas. The other three were the Jamaica Letter of 1815, the Angostura Address of 1819, and the Address on the Bolivian Constitution of 1826.

Each of the four, in varying degrees, revealed Bolívar's distrust of democracy and his belief in a strong national leader. In the Jamaica Letter and Angostura Address, he discusses those aspects of the structure of the U.S. Constitution that might be suitable for a Latin American republic. He argued that the executive should be patterned after the U.S. presidency. He also believed in the separation of powers between and among the executive, legislative, and judiciary; however, he rejected the concept of a federal system, contending that it would unnecessarily weaken the central government.

Nine months after the creation of the Republic of Bolivia in 1825, Bolívar submitted a draft constitution. In his Address on the Bolivian Constitution, which accompanied the submission of the draft, Bolívar again summarized his political philosophy. The key provision of his constitution established a life term for the chief executive. As he explained it, the life-term president is "the sun . . . which imparts life to the political universe." He cited Haiti as proof of the success of such a presidency. Bolívar believed that the president should appoint the vice-president, thus avoiding "elections which result in that great scourge of republics—anarchy."[3]

The legislature was to have three chambers, so that one would always be the arbiter between the other two. These three houses were divided among the Censors, the Tribunes, and the Senators. He attempted to establish a system in which every potentially useful law would have to be reviewed three times before being acted on.

The Censors, who had life terms, were to supervise public morality and instruction. They also were charged with bringing to the attention of the Senate any constitutional or other illegal infractions of the executive.

The Tribunes constituted the popular branch of government. Elected for four-year terms, they exercised general legislative power, including the power to tax and to make public expenditures.

The Senators, who were to be elected for eight-year terms, were to be responsible for writing the civil, criminal, procedural, and commercial codes as well as ecclesiastical regulations. They were also charged with initiating all laws relative to judicial matters. In addition, the Senators were to hear the charges brought by the Censors against the executive.

The least democratic features of the Bolivian Constitution were in the electoral provisions. An Electoral Body, which constituted a fourth branch of government, was composed of one-tenth of the population and chosen by popular vote. This electoral college was to select the legislators of all three chambers. In Bolívar's view, electors should be "skilled in some trade or useful art that assures an honest living."[4]

Human rights are provided for in the Bolivian Constitution either as restrictions on the powers of the president, as rules for the administration of justice, or as separate guarantees. The president is specifically prohibited from depriving any Bolivian of his or her freedom or property unless the public interest so demands. The judiciary may not prescribe torture as a punishment (an unusual prohibition in that period), nor could any Bolivian be arrested without being informed of the reason for apprehension in a written judicial order of the judge before whom he would be tried. A limited right to trial by jury in criminal cases also was guaranteed. In addition, the Constitution provided for freedom to communicate thoughts by word or in writing and to publish them without prior censorship.

The Bolivian Constitution of 1826 was operative for little more than a year. The elaborate structure of the legislature, the limited size of the electorate, and the life-time presidency revealed not only the Liberador's deep distrust, but also his confused perception of both popular democracy and republicanism. He had hoped to build an institutional structure that would be simultaneously popular, nonmonarchial, and strong in leadership; however, the formula that he conceived was not equal to the task. Bolivia, which has had more constitutions than any other country in the world, is still seeking constitutional solutions.

MARTIN ROSENBERG

NOTES

1. "The Cartagena Manifesto," as found in Vincente Lecuna and Harold Bierck, Jr. *Selected Writings of Bolívar* (New York: 1951), 7.
2. Ibid., 8.
3. Quoted in David Bushnell, *The Liberator Simon Bolívar* (New York: 1970), 40.
4. Ibid., 39.

CONSTITUTION OF THE BOLIVIAN REPUBLIC— CHUQUISACA, NOVEMBER 6, 1826.

In the Name of God.

The General Constituent Congress of the Bolivian Republic, appointed by the Nation for the purpose of framing the Constitution of the State, Decrees as follows:

TITLE I. OF THE NATION

CHAPTER I. OF THE BOLIVIAN NATION

Art. I. The Bolivian Nation is the aggregate of all Bolivians.

II. Bolivia is, and always shall be, independent of every foreign domination, and cannot be the patrimony of any person or family whatsoever.

CHAPTER II. OF THE TERRITORY

III. The territory of the Bolivian Republic comprehends the Departments of Potosi, Chuquisaca, La Paz, Santa-Cruz, Cochabamba, and Oruro.

IV. It is divided into departments, provinces, and cantons.

V. A more convenient division shall be made by a law: while another law shall fix its boundaries in concurrence with the adjoining States.

TITLE II. OF RELIGION

SOLE CHAPTER

VI. The Catholic Apostolic Roman Religion is that of the Republic, to the exclusion of every other. The Government will protect it, and cause it to be respected; recognizing the principle of freedom of conscience.

Translated from *British and Foreign State Papers*, Vol. 23 (London: James Ridgway and Sons, 1852), 5-24.

TITLE III. OF THE GOVERNMENT

CHAPTER I. FORMS OF THE GOVERNMENT

VII. The Government of Bolivia is popular Representative.

VIII. The Sovereignty emanates from the People, and its exercise resides in the Powers established by this Constitution.

IX. The Supreme Power is divided for its exercise into 4 sections or branches: Electoral, Legislative, Executive, and Judicial.

X. Each Power, Section, or Branch, shall exercise the functions assigned to it by this Constitution, without transgressing the limits assigned to it.

CHAPTER II. OF THE BOLIVIANS

XI. Bolivians are:

1. All who are born in the territory of the Republic.

2. The children of a Bolivian father or mother born out of the territory, when they legally express their wish to become domiciliated in Bolivia.

3. Those who fought for liberty in Junin or Ayacucho.

4. Foreigners who obtain letters of naturalization, or who have resided 3 years in the territory of the Republic.

5. All those who until this day have been Slaves, acquire the right of freedom, by the act itself of publishing the Constitution; but they cannot quit the residence of their former masters, except in the manner which shall be determined by a special law.

XII. The duties of every Bolivian are:

1. To live subject to the Constitution and the Laws.

2. To respect and obey the constituted authorities.

3. To contribute to the public burdens.

4. To sacrifice his property, and even his life, when the safety of the Republic requires it.

5. To watch over the preservation of the public liberties.

XIII. Bolivians who are deprived of the exercise of the Electoral Power shall enjoy all the civil rights granted to the Citizens.

XIV. The qualifications for Citizenship are:

1. To be a Bolivian.

2. To be married, or to have attained his majority, that is, 21 years of age.

3. To know how to read and write; although this qualification shall be required only after the year 1836.

4. To have some employment or trade, or to profess some science or

art, without subjection to any other person in the capacity of menial servant (sirviente domestico).

XV. Citizens are:

1. Those who fought for liberty at Junin and Ayacucho.

2. Foreigners who have obtained Letters of Citizenship.

3. Foreigners married to a Bolivian woman, and who possess the qualifications 3 and 4 of Art. XIV.

4. Foreigners unmarried, provided they have resided 4 years in the Republic, and possess the same qualifications.

XVI. The Citizens of those Nations which were formerly Spanish America, shall enjoy the rights of Citizenship in Bolivia, agreeably to the Treaties entered into with them.

XVII. Only such as are Citizens in the exercise of Citizenship can obtain employments and offices in the Public Service.

XVIII. The exercise of Citizenship is suspended:

1. In the case of insanity.

2. For the crime of fraudulent bankruptcy.

3. For having been the object of a criminal prosecution.

4. For being a notorious drunkard, gambler, or beggar.

5. For buying or selling votes at elections, or disturbing their regular proceedings.

XIX. The right of Citizenship is forfeited:

1. By treason to the Public Cause.

2. By naturalization in a foreign country.

3. By having suffered infamous or corporeal punishment, by virtue of a judicial sentence, and not having obtained a restitution of rights from the Legislative Body.

4. By accepting employments, honors, or emoluments from another Government, without the consent of the Chamber of Censors.

TITLE IV. OF THE ELECTORAL POWER

CHAPTER I. OF THE ELECTIONS

XX. The Electoral Power is immediately exercised by Citizens having the rights of Citizenship, naming 1 Elector for every 100 souls.

XXI. The exercise of the Electoral Power can never be suspended; and the Civil Magistrates, without awaiting any order, must convoke the People precisely at the time indicated by law.

XXII. A Special Law shall lay down the Regulations to be observed at Elections.

CHAPTER II. OF THE ELECTORAL BODY

XXIII. The Electoral Body is composed of the Electors named by those who are entitled to vote.

XXIV. In order to be an Elector it is indispensable to be a Citizen in the exercise of Citizenship, and who can read and write.

XXV. Each Electoral Body shall last 4 years, at the end of which it shall terminate, its place being filled up by that which succeeds it.

XXVI. The Electors shall assemble every year in the capital of their respective province, on the 1st, 2nd, 3rd, 4th, 5th, and 6th days of April, in order to exercise the following powers:

1. To examine the qualifications of the Citizens who enter upon the exercise of their rights, and declare the inability of those who are in the cases comprehended in Articles XVIII, XIX.

2. To name, in the first instance, the individuals who are to compose the Chambers.

3. To elect and propose, in ternary: 1. to the respective Chambers, the Members destined to renew them, or to fill up their vacancies; 2. to the Senate, the Members of the Courts of the Judicial district to which they belong, and the Judges of the First Instance; 3. to the Prefect of the Department, the Justices of the Peace who should be appointed.

4. To propose: 1. to the Executive Power, from 6 to 10 candidates for the Prefecture of their department; as many others for the Government of their province, and for the Corregidors of their cantons and towns; 2. to the Ecclesiastical Government, a list of Curates and Vicars for the Vacancies which occur in their province.

5. To receive the Returns (Actas) of the popular elections; examine the identity of the newly elected, and declare them constitutionally appointed.

6. To petition the Chamber for whatever they believe to be conducive to the welfare of the Citizens; and to complain of the wrongs and injuries which they may receive from the constituted authorities.

TITLE V. OF THE LEGISLATIVE POWER

CHAPTER I. OF THE DIVISION, POWERS, AND RESTRICTIONS OF THIS BRANCH

XXVII. The Legislative Power emanates immediately from the electoral bodies named by the People: its exercise resides in 3 Chambers: 1. Of Tribunes. 2. Of Senators. 3. Of Censors.

XXVIII. Each Chamber shall be composed of 20 Members, for the first 20 years.

XXIX. On the 6th day of August of each year, the Legislative Body shall assemble of itself, without waiting for being convoked.

XXX. The particular powers of each Chamber shall be enumerated in their proper place. Those which the Chambers possess in common, are:

1. To appoint the President of the Republic, and confirm his successors by an absolute plurality.

2. To approve of the Vice-President, on the proposition of the President.

3. To select the town which is to be the seat of Government, and to transfer it to another town, when important circumstances require it, and when such change is decreed by two-thirds of the Members composing the 3 Chambers.

4. To decide, in a National Judicial Assembly (Juicio Nacional), whether or not there be just cause for prosecuting the Members of the Chambers, the Vice-President, or the Ministers of State.

5. To invest, in time of war, or of extraordinary danger, the President of the Republic with the powers deemed indispensable for the salvation of the State.

6. To choose from among the candidates which are presented in ternary by the Electoral bodies, the Members destined to supply the vacancies in each Chamber.

XXXI. The Members of the Legislative Body may be appointed Vice-President of the Republic, or Ministers of State, in which cease to be Members of their respective Chambers.

XXXII. No individual of the Legislative Body can be arrested during the term of his deputation, but by a warrant from his respective chamber; unless he be taken in the actual commission of a crime deserving capital punishment.

XXXIII. The Members of the Legislative Body shall be inviolable for the opinions which they express within their Chambers, in the exercise of their function.

XXXIV. Each Legislative Parliament shall last 4 years; and each annual Session, 2 months. All the 3 Chambers shall open and shall close simultaneously.

XXXV. The Opening of the Sessions shall annually take place in the presence of the President of the Republic, the Vice-President, and the Ministers of State.

XXXVI. The Sittings shall be public, and only such business of the State as requires secrecy shall be discussed with closed doors.

XXXVII. The business in each Chamber shall be determined by the absolute Majority of votes of the Members present.

XXXVIII. Official persons who are named Deputies for the Legislative Body, shall, in the interim, be replaced in the exercise of their employments by other individuals.

XXXIX. The restrictions upon the Legislative Body are:

1. No Sitting can be held in any of the Chambers, without there being present the two-third parts of the respective Members composing them: and the absentees must be compelled to attend and fulfil their duties.

2. No one of the Chambers can initiate or introduce a Bill (Projecto de Ley) connected with affairs committed by the Constitution to another Chamber; but it may invite the others to take under their consideration the motions which they refer to them.

3. Upon an extraordinary union of the Chambers, they can discuss no other subjects than those for which they were convoked by the President of the Republic, or those which that authority shall lay before them.

4. No Member of the Chambers can obtain during the period of his deputation, any promotion except the graduated one attached to his profession.

XL. The Chambers shall unite:

1. At the opening and closing of its Sessions.

2. For the purpose of examining the conduct of the Ministry, when the latter is impeached by the Chamber of Censors.

3. To revise the laws returned to them by the Executive Power.

4. When required to unite, upon sufficient grounds, by any one of the Chambers, as in the case, for instance, of Art. XXX, power 3rd.

5. For the purpose of confirming the Vice-President in the office of President.

XLI. Whenever the Chambers are united, one of their Presidents shall preside in turn.

The union shall take place in the Chamber of Censors, in which also the Presidency shall commence.

CHAPTER II. OF THE CHAMBER OF TRIBUNES

XLII. To be a Tribune are required:

1. The same qualifications as for an Elector.

2. To be born in Bolivia, or to have resided within it for 6 years.

3. The not having ever been condemned as a criminal.

4. To be 25 years of age.

XLIII. The Chamber of Tribunes has the initiative:

1. In the settlement of the territorial division of the Republic.

2. In the annual taxes and public expenses.

3. In authorizing the Executive Power to negotiate loans and adopt the necessary means for liquidating the Public Debt.

4. In the value, type, alloy, weight, and denomination of the coin; and in the regulation of weights and measures.

5. In making every class of ports free.

6. In constructing roads, highways, bridges, and public edifices, and in improving the police and every branch of industry.

7. In fixing the salaries of persons employed in the State.

8. In the reforms which they consider necessary in the Finance and War departments.

9. In making war or peace, on proposition of the Government.

10. In alliances.

11. In granting a passage to foreign troops.

12. In fixing the armed naval and military force for the service of the current year, on the proposition of the Government.

13. In issuing ordinances and regulations for the Navy, the Army, and the Militia, on the proposition of the Government.

14. In foreign affairs.

15. In granting letters of naturalization and citizenship.

16. In granting general pardons.

XLIV. The Chamber of Tribunes shall be renewed every 2 years, in the proportion of one-half, and its duration shall be for 4 years.

In the first Legislature, the half which is to be renewed at the end of the 2 years, shall be determined by lot.

XLV. The Tribunes may be re-elected.

CHAPTER III. OF THE CHAMBER OF SENATORS

XXLVI. To be a Senator it is necessary to possess:

1. The qualifications required for Tribunes.

2. The age of 30 years, completed.

XLVII. The powers of the Senate are:

1. To form the Civil and Criminal Codes, the Code of Prosecutions, that of Commerce, and the Ecclesiastical regulations.

2. To initiate or introduce the Laws relative to reforms in judicial affairs.

3. To watch over the prompt administration of justice, in civil and criminal affairs.

4. To initiate the laws for the repression of infractions of the Constitution and of the Laws, by magistrates, judges, and ecclesiastics.

5. To secure the responsibility of the Superior Courts of Justice, of the Prefects, Magistrates, and inferior Judges.

6. To propose in ternary, to the Chamber of Censors, the individuals who are to compose the Supreme Court of Justice, the Archbishops, Bishops, Dignitaries, Canons, and Prebendaries of Cathedrals.

7. To approve, or disapprove, of the Prefects, Governors, and Magistrates which the Government proposes to them out of those named by the Electoral Bodies.

8. To elect from the ternary presented to them by the Electoral Bod-

ies, the District Judges, and the subordinates belonging to every department of justice.

9. To regulate the exercise of presentation to ecclesiastical preferments, and to introduce Bills (Projectos de Ley) upon all the ecclesiastical affairs which are connected with the Government.

10. To examine the decrees of Councils, bulls, rescripts, and pontifical briefs, and to approve of them, or not.

XLVIII. The duration of the functions of Members of the Senate shall be for 8 years, and that Body shall be renewed in the proportion of one-half every fourth year. The removal of the first half of the first Legislature must be determined by lot.

XLIX. The Members of the Senate may be re-elected.

CHAPTER IV. OF THE CHAMBER OF CENSORS

L. It is necessary in order to be a Censor:

1. To possess the qualifications required for a Senator.

2. To have completed 35 years of age.

3. Never to have been condemned, even of a misdemeanour (falta leve).

LI. The powers of the Chamber of Censors are:

1. To take care that the Government fulfil and cause to be fulfilled, the Constitution, the Laws, and the public Treaties.

2. To give information to the Senate, of the infractions which the Executive shall commit, of the Constitution, the Laws, and the Public Treaties.

3. To require of the Senate the suspension of the Vice-President of Ministers of State, if the safety of the Republic urgently demand it.

LII. It belongs exclusively to the Chamber of Censors to impeach the Vice-President and Ministers of State before the Senate, in cases to treason, extortion, or open violation of the fundamental Laws of the State.

LIII. Should the Senate consider that there are sufficient grounds for the accusation brought by the Chamber of Census, the Court of National Judicature (Juicio Nacional) shall be assembled; if, on the contrary, the opinion of the Senate should be in the negative, the accusation shall be passed to the Chamber of Tribunes.

LIV. Should 2 of the Chambers agree in opinion, the Court of National Judicature shall be opened.

LV. The 3 Chambers shall then unite together, and, after an investigation of the documents laid before them by the Chamber of Censors, shall decide by an absolute plurality of votes, if there be or be not, grounds for impeaching the President and the Ministers of State.

LVI. So soon as the National court of Judicature shall determine that there are grounds for the impeachment of the Vice-President or Ministers of State, they shall be forthwith suspended from their functions, and the Chambers shall hand over all the legal documents to the Supreme Court of Justice, which alone shall take cognizance of the case; and the sentence which it pronounces shall be executed without appeal.

LVII. So soon as the Chambers shall declare that there is ground for the impeachment of the Vice-President and Ministers of State, the President of the Republic shall present to the united Chamber, a Candidate for the Vice-Presidentship, ad interim, and shall name provisionally the Ministers of State. If the first candidate should be rejected by an absolute majority of the Legislative Body, the President shall present a second and if he should be rejected, he shall present a third, and in case of his rejection also, the Chambers shall then elect by an absolute majority of votes, within the space of 24 hours, one of the 3 Candidates proposed by the President.

LVIII. The Vice-President, ad interim, shall from that time exercise his functions, until the result of the proceedings against the person for whom he is substitute, be known.

LIX. By a Law which shall originate in the Chamber of Censors, the cases shall be determined, in which the Vice-President and Ministers of State are responsible, collectively or individually.

LX. It also belongs to the Chambers of Censors:

1. To select from the ternary proposed by the Senate, the individuals who are to compose the Supreme Court of Justice, as well as those who are recommended for the vacant Archbishopries, Bishopries, Canonries, and Prebends.

2. To originate all the Laws concerning the Press, the Government, the plan of studies, and method of public education.

3. To protect the Liberty of the Press, and to appoint the Judges who are to try causes respecting it, without appeal.

4. To propose Regulations for the encouragement of the Arts and Sciences.

5. To grant National rewards and recompense to those who have deserved them, by services rendered to the Republic.

6. To decree public honours to the memory of great men, and to the virtues and services of Citizens.

7. To condemn to eternal infamy the usurpers of the Public Authority, and all traitors and delinquents who have obtained disgraceful notoriety in crime.

8. To grant to all Bolivians admission into public employments, and permission to enjoy the titles and emoluments conferred upon them by other Governments, when they have merited the same by their services.

LXI. The Censors shall be for life.

CHAPTER V. OF THE FORMATION AND
PROMULGATION OF THE LAWS

LXII. The Government may propose to the Chambers the Bills (Projectos de Ley) which it considers necessary.

LXIII. The Vice-President and the Ministers of State may be present at the Sittings, and join in the discussions upon laws and other matters; but they can neither vote, nor be present while the sense of the Chamber is taken (votacion).

LXIV. When the Chamber of Tribunes agrees to the introduction of a Bill, the said Bill shall be passed to the Senate with the following formula:—"The Chamber of Tribunes transmit the accompanying bill to the Chamber of Senators, and is of opinion that it should be passed into a Law."

LXV. If the Chamber of Senators approve of the Bill, it shall be returned to the Chamber of Tribunes with the following formula:—"The Senate returns to the Chamber of Tribunes the Bill (with amendments or not, as the case may be), and is of opinion that it should be passed to the Executive, in order to be carried into effect."

LXVI. All the chambers shall, under the like circumstances, observe the same formula.

LXVII. If one Chamber should not approve of the amendments or additions made by the other, and if the Chamber in which the Bill originated should still consider it, in its original form, advantageous, it may by a deputation of 3 Members, invite the other 2 Chambers to a discussion upon the said Bill, and upon the amendments to or negative put upon it. The only object of the union of the Chambers shall be, that of coming to an understanding, and each Chamber shall afterwards proceed to adopt whatever resolutions it may consider expedient.

LXVIII. The Bill having been approved of by 2 Chambers, 2 copies thereof, signed by the President and Secretaries of the Chamber which introduced the law, shall be forwarded to the President of the Republic, with the following formula:—"The Chamber with the approbation of the transmits to the Executive Power the law upon in order that it may be promulgated."

LXIX. Should the Chamber of Senators decline adopting the Bill proposed by that of the Tribunes, it shall be passed to that of the Censors, with the following formula:—"The Chamber of Senators forwards to that of the Censors the annexed Bill; and is of opinion that it is not expedient." The resolution thereupon of the Chamber of Censors shall then be definitive.

LXX. The Bills which originate in the Senate shall be passed to the Chamber of Tribunes; and its decision shall be given in the form already prescribed with respect to that Chamber.

LXXI. The Bills initiated in the Chamber of Censors shall be passed to the Senate, the sanction of which shall have the force of law, but should the latter refuse its assent, the Bill shall be passed to the Chamber of Tribunes, which shall give or refuse its assent, as provided in the preceding Articles.

LXXII. If the President of the Republic should be of opinion that the law is not required, he must, within the space of 101 full days, return it to the Chamber which transmitted it to him, together with his observations upon it, with the following formula:—"The Executive is of opinion that the Bill should be reconsidered."

LXXIII. The Laws which shall be passed within the 10 last days of the Session may be retained by the Executive Power until the next ensuing Session, but must then be returned, with his observations.

LXXIV. Upon the Executive Power returning the Laws, accompanied by observations, to the Chambers, these shall unite; and their decision, by a majority of votes, shall be adopted without further discussion or remark.

LXXV. Should the Executive Power have no observation to make upon the Laws, it shall order them to be published with this formula:— "Let it be executed."

LXXVI. The Laws shall be promulgated with this formula:—"N. of N., Constitutional President of the Bolivian Republic: We make known to all Bolivians, that the Legislative Body has decreed, and that we publish, the following Law [here the text of the Law is to be inserted]: and, in pursuance thereof, we enjoin all and every Authorities of the Republic to execute and fulfil the same, and to cause it to be fulfilled and executed."

"The Vice-President shall cause this Law to be printed, published, and distributed to all whom it may concern."

The Law must be signed by the President, Vice-President, and Minister of State of the Department connected with the Law.

TITLE VI. OF THE EXECUTIVE POWER

LXXVII. The exercise of the Executive Power resides in a President, holding office for life, a Vice-President, and 3 Ministers of State.

CHAPTER I. OF THE PRESIDENT

LXXVIII. The President of the Republic shall be appointed, the first time, by the Constituent Congress, on the proposition of the Electoral Colleges.

LXXIX. In order to be appointed President of the Republic, it is required:

1. To be a citizen in the exercise of citizenship, and a Bolivian by birth.

2. To profess the religion of the Republic.

3. To be above 30 years of age.

4. To have performed important services to the Republic.

5. To possess acknowledged ability in the Government of the state.

6. Never to have been condemned by any tribunal, not even for a misdemeanor.

LXXX. The President of the Republic is the Head of the Government of the State, without being responsible for the acts of the Administration.

LXXXI. In case of the resignation, death, illness, or absence of the President of the Republic the Vice-President shall succeed him instanter.

LXXXII. In default of the President and Vice-President of the Republic, the Government shall be administered, ad interim, by the 3 Ministers of State, and of these Ministers, he who has been longest in office shall preside until such time as the Legislative Body be united.

LXXXIII. The powers of the President of the Republic are:

1. To open the Sessions of the Chambers, and to address to them a message upon the state of the Republic.

2. To propose the Vice-President to the Chambers, and to appoint, at his own pleasure, the Ministers of State.

3. To dismiss, at his pleasure, the Vice-President and the Ministers of State, whenever he considers it necessary.

4. To order the Laws to be published, circulated, and observed.

5. To sanction the Regulations and Orders required to insure the better observance of the Constitution, the Laws, and the Public Treaties.

6. To carry into execution and cause to be executed the Sentences of the tribunals.

7. To require from the Legislative Body the extension of its ordinary Sessions for 30 days.

8. To convoke the Legislative Body for extraordinary Sessions on case of absolute necessity.

9. To dispose of the permanent Land and Sea Forces for the external defence of the Republic.

10. To command the Armies of the Republic in peace and war, and in person when considered requisite. When the President absents himself from the Capital, in order to command the army, the vice-President shall take upon himself the Government of the Republic.

11. To reside in any territory occupied by the National arms, whenever the President directs the war in person.

12. To dispose of the National Militia for internal security, within the limits of their respective departmented, and beyond them, with the consent of the Legislative Body.

13. To appoint all the persons employed in a civil capacity in the Army and Navy.

14. To establish Military and naval Schools.

15. To order the establishment of Military Hospitals and Asylums for the wounded and superannuated.

16. To grant Discharges and Licences of Leave (Licencias), to assign Pensions to Soldiers and their families, conformably to the Laws, and to settle in accordance with them all the other matters connected with that branch.

17. To declare war, in the name of the Republic, in consequence of a decree of the Legislative Body.

18. To grant letters of marque.

19. To supervise the collection and disbursement of the taxes, conformably to the laws.

20. To appoint the persons employed in the Finance department.

21. To direct diplomatic negotiations, and conclude treaties of peace, friendship, league, alliance, truce, neutrality, armament, commerce and others, of whatever description; the previous approval of the Legislative Body being always understood.

22. To appoint the Public Ministers and Consuls, and the Subordinates of the Department for Foreign Affairs.

23. To receive the Foreign Minister.

24. To allow, or to suspend the introduction of, the decisions of Councils, pontifical bulls, briefs, and rescripts, with the consent of the authority whose duty it is to take cognizance thereof.

25. To present to the Senate for its approbation, one of the candidates proposed by the Electoral Body for Prefects, Governors, and Corregidors.

26. To present to the Ecclesiastical Government, one of the 3 persons proposed by it, from among the candidates recommended by the Electoral Body, for the curates and vicars of its provinces.

27. To suspend Government functionaries for the space of 3 months, whenever there is sufficient cause for so doing.

28. To commute capital punishment into transportation for 10 years, or for life.

29. To confer, in the name of the Republic, diplomas and commissions upon all those who are employed in the Public Service.

LXXXIV. The restrictions upon the President of the Republic are:

1. He cannot, upon his sole authority deprive any Bolivian of his liberty, or inflict any punishment whatever upon him.

2. Should the security of the Republic require the arrest, by his order, of one or more citizens, 48 hours must not elapse before the accused is brought before the competent tribunal or judge.

3. He cannot deprive any individual of his property, except the public

interest urgently require it; in which case a full indemnification must be previously given to the owner.

4. He cannot obstruct the elections, nor any other matters which by law appertain to the powers of the Republic.

5. He cannot absent himself from the territory of the Republic, without the permission of the Legislative Body.

CHAPTER II. OF THE VICE-PRESIDENT

LXXXV. The Vice-President is named by the President of the Republic, and approved by the Legislative Body in the case provided for in Article LVII.

LXXXVI. A special law shall comprise all the cases that can occur.

LXXXVII. In order to be Vice-President, it is required to have been born in Bolivia, and to possess the other qualifications necessary for the President.

LXXXIX. He, together with the Minister of State for the respective department, shall be responsible for the Government of the State.

XC. He, together with the Minister of State for the respective department, shall transact and sign, in the name of the Republic and of the President, all the business of the Government.

XCI. He cannot absent himself from the territory of the Republic, without the permission of the Legislative Body.

CHAPTER III. OF THE MINISTERS OF STATE

XCII. There shall be 3 Ministers of State. One of them shall take upon himself the Home Department, another that of Finance, and the third that of War and Marine.

XCIII. These 3 Ministers shall transact the public business under the immediate orders of the Vice-President.

XCIV. No tribunal nor any public functionary shall carry into execution any orders of the Executive, which are not signed by the Vice-President and the Minister of the respective department.

XCV. In case of impediment on the part of the Vice-President, the orders of the Executive shall be signed by the President.

XCVI. The Ministers of State shall, together with Vice-President, be responsible for all the orders which are issued by their authority, in violation of the Constitution, the Laws, and public Treaties.

XCVII. They shall make out the annual Estimates of the expenses to be incurred in their respective department, and shall render an account of expenditure of the preceding year.

XCVIII. In order to be a Minister of State, it is required:

1. To be a Citizen in the exercise of Citizenship.

2. To be 30 years of age.

3. Never to have been condemned in any criminal case.

TITLE VII. OF THE JUDICIAL POWER

CHAPTER I. POWERS OF THIS DEPARTMENT

XCIX. The power of deciding all questions, civil or criminal (facultad de juzgar), belongs exclusively to the tribunals established by law.

C. The Magistrates and Judges shall continue in office during their good behaviour.

CI. The Magistrates and Judges cannot be suspended from their employments, except in cases determined by the laws.

CII. Any grave fault committed by Magistrates and Judges in the discharge of their respective duties, shall be visited by a public prosecution, which may be instituted any time within the term of 1 year, either by the Electoral Body collectively, or by any Bolivian.

CIII. The Magistrates and Judges are personally responsible. A special law shall determine in what way this responsibility shall be rendered effective.

CIV. Neither the Government nor the tribunals can in any case alter or dispense with the orders and forms already prescribed, or which shall hereafter be prescribed, by the laws, for the different kinds of cases which are decided by them.

CV. No Bolivian can be tried in civil and criminal cases, except by the competent tribunal previously appointed by the law.

CVI. Justice shall be administered in the name of the Nation; and the Judgments and Decrees of the Superior Tribunals shall have a heading to that effect.

CHAPTER II. OF THE SUPREME COURT

CVII. The Chief Judicial Magistracy of the State shall reside in the Supreme Court of Justice.

CVIII. The court shall be composed of a President, 6 Members, and Registrar, divided into a convenient number of Chambers.

CIX. The requisites for being a Member of the Supreme Court of Justice are:

1. To be 35 years of age.

2. To be a Citizen in the exercise of Citizenship

3. To have been a Member of one of the Judicial district Courts, and during the time that these Courts are being organized, to have been an advocate of 10 year's standing and credit.

CX. The powers of the Supreme Court of Justice are:

1. To take cognizance of criminal prosecutions against the Vice-President of the Republic, Ministers of State, and Members of the Chambers, upon the decree of the Legislative Body that there are good grounds for such prosecution.

2. To take cognizance of all disputed cases of ecclesiastical patronage belonging to the Nation.

3. To examine bills, briefs, and rescripts, when they relate to civil matters.

4. To take cognizance of disputed cases between Ambassadors, Resident Ministers, Consuls, and Diplomatic Agents.

5. To take cognizance of the causes of removal of the Magistrates of the District Judicial Courts and Prefects of the department.

6. To settle disputes between the District Courts, as well as their differences with the other authorities.

7. To take cognizance, in the third instance, of the account of his administration rendered by every Government officer.

8. To hear the doubts of the other tribunals, respecting the real meaning of any law, and to consult with the executive, that a proper explanation thereon may be given in the Chambers.

9. To take cognizance of the appeals for annulling sentences pronounced, in the last instance, by the District Courts.

10. To examine the state and progress of the civil and criminal causes pending in the District Courts, by the means provided by law.

11. And lastly, to exercise the supreme directive, administrative, and correctional power over the National Tribunals and Courts of Justice.

CHAPTER III. OF THE JUDICIAL DISTRICT COURTS

CXI. Judicial district Courts shall be formed in such departments as the Legislative Body may think fit.

CXII. To be a Member of these Courts, it is necessary:

1. To be 30 years of age.

2. To be a Citizen in the exercise of Citizenship.

3. To have been a regular Judge (Juez de Letras*), or to have exercised with credit, during 8 years, the profession of an advocate.

CXIII. The powers of the Judicial District Courts are:

1. To take cognizance, in the second and third degree, of all the civil and criminal cases of the common law, public revenue, commerce, mining, seizures, and confiscations; being for this purpose associated, in each case,

---

* A person regularly brought up to the law, distinguished from the Juez de Paz who is not so.

with an individual from one of those professions, calling, &c., in the capacity of assessor.

2. To take cognizance of appeals made on account of the Judge's misconduct, from the Ecclesiastical Tribunals and authorities of their territory.

CHAPTER IV. JUDICIAL DISTRICTS

CXIV. There shall be established in the provinces Judicial districts, proportioned to the extent of the said provinces; and in each chief town of the district there shall be a regular Judge, having the Jurisdiction to be determined by law.

CXV. The powers of these Judges are confined to matters of dispute, and they can take cognizance, without appeal, in all civil matters, up to the amount of 200 dollars.

CXVI. To be a regular Judge, it is required:

1. To be 28 years of age.
2. To be a Citizen in the exercise of Citizenship.
3. To be an admitted advocate of some tribunal of the Republic.
4. To have exercised the profession with credit for 6 years.

CHAPTER V. OF THE ADMINISTRATION OF JUSTICE

CXVII. There shall be Justices of the Peace in each town, for reconciling or settling disputes; no application for redress in any civil or criminal case being admissible without this previous requisite.

CXVIII. The functions of the Conciliators are limited to hearing the complaints of the parties, instructing them in their rights, and effecting a reasonable accommodation between them.

CXIX. Actions connected with the Treasury or Exchequer admit of no conciliation.

CXX. Not more than 3 instances are admitted in the trials.

CXXI. The appeal for notorious injustice is abolished.

CXXII. No Bolivian can be arrested, without previous information being given of any act for which he may merit corporeal punishment, and a written warrant of the Judge before whom he is to be brought; except in the cases of Article LXXXIV, restriction 2, and Articles CXXIV and CXXXIX.

CXXIII. If possible, the declaration, without oath, of the Justice of the Peace, should be given in the same sitting, but in no case must it be deferred beyond 48 hours.

CXXIV. Any delinquent discovered in the actual commission of a crime, may be arrested by any person whatever, and brought before the Judge.

CXXV. In criminal cases the trial shall be public; the alleged act shall be examined into and decided upon by a Jury (when Juries are established); and the law applied by the Judges.

CXXVI. No torture shall ever be applied, nor shall confession be obtained by judicial compulsion.

CXXVII. All confiscation of property is abolished, as well every punishment characterized by cruelty or infamy in the last degree. The Criminal Code shall restrict as far as possible the application of capital punishment.

CXXVIII. If, under extraordinary circumstances, the security of the Republic should require the suspension of any of the forms prescribed in this chapter, the Chambers may decree that measure; and should these not be assembled, the executive may order the same, provisionally, and shall render an account thereof, upon the next opening of the Sittings, being at the same time responsible for any abuses it may have committed.

TITLE VIII. OF THE INTERNAL GOVERNMENT
OF THE REPUBLIC

CXXIX. The superior political government of each department shall reside in a Prefect.

CXXX. That of each province in a Governor.

CXXXI. That of the cantons in a Corregidor.

CXXXII. In order to be a Prefect or Governor, it is required:

1. To be a Citizen in the exercise of citizenship.
2. To be 30 years of age.
3. Never to have been condemned for any crime.

CXXXIII. In every town, in which the number of inhabitants together with that of its district, is not less than 100 souls nor more than 2000, there shall be a Justice of the Peace.

CXXXIV. Wherever the number of inhabitants in the town and its district exceeds 2000 souls, there shall be, for each 2000, a Justice of the Peace; should the fraction exceed 500, another Justice shall be added.

CXXXV. It is the duty of the Justice of the Peace to give advice, and no Citizen can, without sufficient cause, excuse himself from discharging it.

CXXXVII. The Justices of the Peace shall be renewed every year, nor can they be re-elected until after the expiration of 2 years.

CXXXVIII. The powers of the Prefects, Governors and Corregidors shall be determined by the law, for the purpose of maintaining the public order and security, and upon the principle of a graduated subordination to the Supreme Government.

CXXXIX. The Justices of the Peace have no judicial cognizance; but if the public tranquility should require the arrest of any individual, and circumstances not permit them to apply to the respective Judge for a warrant, they can order his immediate apprehension, giving information of the same to the proper Judge within 48 hours. Any abuse committed by these functionaries with respect to individual security, or that of private dwellings, shall be liable to a public prosecution.

CXL. All persons employed in the Public Service are strictly responsible for the abuses which they commit in the exercise of their functions.

TITLE IX. OF THE ARMED FORCE

CXLI. There shall be a permanent armed Force maintained in the Republic.

CXLII. The armed Force shall be composed of Troops of the Line and a Navy.

CXLIII. There shall be in each province a corps of Militia, composed of its inhabitants.

CXLIV. There shall be a Military Preventive Force, the principal duty of which shall be to suppress smuggling and all contraband trade. The organization and particular constitution of this corps shall be declared in detail by a special regulation.

TITLE X. REFORM OF THE CONSTITUTION

CXLV. If after the expiration of 10 years from the time of swearing to the Constitution, it be found that some of its Articles require reform or amendment, the proposition or motion to that effect shall be made in writing, signed by a third part at least of the Chamber of Tribunes, and supported by two-third parts of the Members present in the Chamber.

CXLVI. The Proposition shall be read 3 times, with an interval of 6 days between each reading; and after the third, the Chamber of Tribunes shall determine whether the Proposition shall or shall not be admitted; in every other respect, conforming itself to the regulations already prescribed for the formation of the laws.

CXLVII. The Proposition being admitted, and the Chambers being convinced of the necessity of reforming the Constitution, a law shall be passed, by which the Electoral Bodies shall be ordered to confer upon the Deputies of the 3 Chambers, special powers for altering or reforming the Constitution: the said law shall also point out the principles upon which the reform is to be effected.

CXLVIII. In the first sitting of the Legislature, following the one in which the motion shall have been made for altering or reforming the Constitution, the matter shall be proposed and discussed, and whatever the Chambers shall decide shall be carried into effect, the Executive Power having been previously consulted touching the propriety of the reform.

TITLE XI. OF THE GUARANTEES

SOLE CHAPTER

CXLIX. The Constitution guarantees to all Bolivians their civil liberty and personal security, their property, and their equality in the eye of the law, whether for reward or punishment.

CL. Every one may communicate his thoughts, either by word of mouth or by writing, and publish them by means of the Press, without previous exercise of censorship, subject, however, to the responsibility determined by law.

CLI. Every Bolivian may remain in or quit the territory of the Republic, at his convenience, taking with him his property, provided the regulations of Police be observed, and the rights of others not infringed.

CLII. Every Bolivian's house in inviolable. It cannot be entered at night, but by the owner's consent; nor by day, except under the circumstances and in the manner determined by the law.

CLIII. The Taxes shall be fairly imposed, without either exception or privilege.

CLIV. Hereditary employments and privileges, together with entails, are abolished; and all estates whatsoever, even those belonging to charitable institutions, religious communities, &c., are alienable.

CLV. No kind of work, industry, or commerce is prohibited, unless the same be contrary to public morality, security, or health.

CLVI. Every inventor shall enjoy the fruits of his discoveries or inventions. The law shall secure to him an exclusive right therein for a given space of time, or shall indemnify him for any loss he may incur by their being made public.

CLVII. The Constitutional Powers can suspend neither the Constitution nor the rights belonging to Bolivians, except in the cases necessary, it is indispensable that the time that the said suspension is to last, be fixed and declared.

Given in the Hall of Sessions, November 6, 1892.

EUSEBIO GUTIERREZ, PRESIDENT

MARIANO DEL CALLEJO,
JOSE MARIA PEREZ DE URDININEA,
Vice-Presidents
(Signatures of 38 Deputies)
MARIANO CALVIMONTES,
JOSE MARIA SALINAS,
Secretaries

Palace of the Government in Chuquisaxa, November 19, 1892. 16th of Independence.

Let it be printed, published and circulated. The Civil and Military Authorities of the Republic, the Tribunals, Corporations, and all Bolivians of whatsoever class and dignity, shall defend and cause to be defended, and shall fulfil and accomplish the said Constitution here annexed, as a fundamental law of the Bolivian Republic.

Given, signed, sealed with the Seal of the Republic, and counter signed by the Ministers of State.

(Seal)   The President,
                    ANTONIO JOSE DE SUCRE
                    The Minister of the Interior and of Foreign Affairs,
                    FACUNDO INFANTE
                    The Minister of War,
                    AGUSTIN JERALDINO
                    The Minister of Finance,
                    JUAN DE BERNABE Y MADERO

Belgian Constitution of 1831

Throughout the nineteenth century, the Belgian Constitution of 1831 served as the principal European constitutional model. The Spanish Constitution of 1833, the Greek Constitution of 1844 and 1864, the Luxembourg Constitution of 1848, the Prussian Constitution of 1850, and the Bulgarian Constitution of 1864 were among those directly patterned after the Belgian example.

The longevity of this document is also noteworthy. Only the U.S. Constitution of 1787 and the Norwegian Constitution of 1814 have longer histories of continuous existence. Because the Belgian Constitution was significantly amended by provisions on linguistic rights in 1970 and 1980, it is essential to look at the original document—the well-organized, democratic version of 1831, which, by any standard, has met the test of time. The Belgian Constitution of 1831 envisaged a unitary state, whereas the recent amendments have dramatically created a quasi-federal structure.

The Constitution itself drew on earlier constitutional formulations in both the United States and Europe. Its basic structure resembled that of the French Constitution of 3 September 1791. In addition, a number of sections were taken almost verbatim from the French Constitution of 14 August 1830. Fifteen sections of the Dutch Constitution of 1815 were also incorporated in much the same form. Yet the British constitutional scholar A. V. Dicey claimed that "the Belgian constitution . . . comes very near to a written reproduction of the English constitution."[1]

The Belgian Constitution was drafted by its National Congress, sitting as a constituent assembly from November 1830, until February 1831. The document was a product of the political philosophy of the men who led the July 1830 secession from Holland. It was also the result of a compromise between conservative Catholic forces and the liberal middle classes, led by lawyers and tradespeople.

Two generations of turmoil preceded these events. Although part of the Austrian Empire since the Reformation and at the time of the 1789 French Revolution, Belgium had a pervasive spirit of local autonomy. Thus the Belgians greeted the troops of the French Directory as liberators from the hated Austrians. But local autonomy was tested once again when Belgium was practically annexed to the French Republic and administered as part of France. Napoleon inherited and continued this status; however, the Congress of Vienna convened after the defeat of Napoleon joined the Belgian Provinces to those of Holland under the name of the Kingdom of the Netherlands. A working constitution was established for this new monarchy in 1815. It provided for a legislative assembly in which both countries were to be equally represented, although Belgium at that time had a much larger population. The Belgian Revolution of 1830 ended this constitutional arrangement, and the independent Kingdom of Belgium was proclaimed.

The prevailing constitutional ideology of the 1831 document upheld such principles as the supremacy of the legislative branch, limited monarchial powers, extensive protections of civil liberties and of private property, and the separation of church and state. Suspicion of the king and the executive branch in general is evident—the most appealing feature of the Constitution to the forces of republicanism throughout Europe.

Although the Constitution did recognize the role of a hereditary monarch, it gave the parliament considerable authority over him. The Constitution itself designated Leopold I of Saxe-Coburg as monarch and his male descendants as successors. It also provided that if there were no male descendants, the king could not name his successor without the consent of parliament. Nor could the king be head of another state at the same time without parliamentary approval. The Constitution also provided that if the king's ministers deemed him incapacitated, the parliament had to be convened immediately to provide for an appropriate regency and guardianship. Article 78, the most telling one concerning the limitation of the monarch, provides that "the king has no other powers than those which the constitution, and the special laws enacted under the constitution, formally confer upon him."

Hailed as one of the world's most democratic constitutions at the time of its promulgation, the Belgian Constitution was certainly not democratic by today's standards. Both houses of parliament were elected by the citizens; however, women were denied the right to vote, and the franchise was not made universal to all men until 1921. In addition, the Constitution itself provided for a poll tax, and the electoral requirements established pursuant to the Constitution favored the wealthy. The Senate particularly came to represent the propertied classes: "Un corps aristocratique, une institution conciliatrice et un pouvoir moderateur."[2]

The combination of prior democratic European precedent and Belgian innovation made for a remarkably consistent institutionalization of the basic principles of a liberal, monarchial form of government, which was to characterize so many of the European constitutions for most of the next hundred years. In addition, the Belgian constitutional structure permitted modernizing adaptations through laws and practice without the necessity of amendments. This inherent flexibility in its application was in marked contrast with the rigidity of the constitutional amendment procedure. Such procedure required first the dissolution of parliament and then a subsequent two-thirds majority of the next parliament. Thus, the Constitution has been amended in only 1893, 1921, 1970, and 1980.

F. REYNTJENS
Lecturer in Law
The Universities of Antwerp and Louvain
Antwerp and Louvain, Belgium

NOTES

1. A. V. Dicey, *An Introduction to the Study of the Law of the Constitution* (1885), 90.
2. G. Smets, *La reforme du Senat* (1919), 19: "An aristocratic body, a conciliating institution and a moderating power."

THE CONSTITUTION OF BELGIUM

In the name of the Belgian people, the National Congress:

TITLE I

THE TERRITORY AND ITS DIVISIONS

Article 1. Belgium is divided into provinces. These provinces are: Antwerp, Brabant, West Flanders, East Flanders, Hainaut, Liege, Limbourg, Luxembourg, Namur, except for the relations of Luxembourg to

Translated by John Martin Vincent, Ph.D., Associate Professor of History, Johns Hopkins University, and Ada S. Vincent *Annals* (Philadelphia: American Academy of Political and Social Science, 1896).

the Germanic Confederation. If required, the territory may be divided by law into a greater number of provinces.

Article 2. Subdivisions of the provinces cannot be made except by law.

Article 3. The boundaries of the state, or of the provinces, or of the communities cannot be changed or rectified except by law.

TITLE II

BELGIAN CITIZENS AND THEIR RIGHTS

Article 4. Belgian citizenship is acquired, maintained and lost according to regulations established by the civil law.

The present constitution and the other laws relating to political rights determine what other conditions are necessary for the exercise of these rights.

Article 5. Naturalization is granted by the Legislative power.

Full naturalization alone admits foreigners to equality with Belgians in the exercise of political rights.

Article 6. There shall be no distinction of classes in the state.

Belgian citizens are equal before the law; they alone are admissible to civil and military offices, with such exceptions as may be established by law for particular cases.

Article 7. Individual liberty is guaranteed.

No one may be prosecuted except in cases provided for by law and in the form therein prescribed.

Except in the case of flagrant offense no one may be arrested without a warrant issued by a magistrate, which ought to be shown at the time of arrest, or at the latest within twenty-four hours thereafter.

Article 8. No person shall be removed against his will from the jurisdiction of the judge to whom the law assigns him.

Article 9. No penalty shall be established or enforced except in pursuance of law.

Article 10. The private domicile is inviolable; no search of premises can take place except in cases provided for by law and according to the form therein prescribed.

Article 11. No one may be deprived of his property except for the public good and according to the forms established by law, and in consideration of a just compensation previously determined.

Article 12. Punishment by confiscation of property shall not be established.

Article 13. Total deprivation of civil rights (mort civile) is abolished and shall not be reestablished.

Article 14. Religious liberty and the freedom of public worship, as well as free expression of opinion in all matters, are guaranteed, unless crimes are committed in the use of these liberties.

Article 15. No one shall be compelled to join in any manner whatever in the forms or ceremonies of any religion, nor to observe its days of rest.

Article 16. The state shall not interfere either in the appointment or in the installation of the ministers of any religion whatever, nor shall it forbid them to correspond with their superiors or publish their proceedings, subject to the ordinary responsibility of the press and of publication.

Civil marriage shall always proceed the religious ceremony, except in cases to be established by law if found necessary.

Article 17. There shall be freedom of opinion in teaching; all measures preventing this are forbidden; the repression of offenses shall be regulated only by law.

Public instruction given at the exposure of the state shall likewise be regulated by law.

Article 18. The press is free; no censorship shall ever be established; no caution money shall be exacted of writers, publishers or printers.

In case the writer is known and is a resident of Belgium, the publisher, printer or distributor can not be prosecuted.

Article 19. Belgian citizens have the right to assemble peaceably and without arms, when conforming to the laws which regulate this right, and without previous authorization.

This provision does not apply to assemblies in the open air, which remain entirely under the police laws.

Article 20. Belgian citizens have the right of association; this right shall not be restricted by any preventive measure.

Article 21. Any one has the right to address petitions to the public authorities, signed by one or more persons.

The constituted authorities alone have the right to address petitions in the name of the people collectively.

Article 22. The privacy of correspondence is inviolable.

The law shall determine who are the agents responsible for the violation of the secrecy of letters entrusted to the post.

Article 23. The use of the languages spoken in Belgium is optional. This may be regulated only by law and only for acts of public authority and for judicial proceedings.

Article 24. No previous authorization is necessary to bring action against public officials for the acts of the acts of their adminstration, except as provided for cabinet ministers.

TITLE III

CONCERNING POWERS

Article 25. All powers emanate from the people.

They are to be exercised in the manner established by the constitution.

Article 26. The Legislative power is exercised collectively by the king, the Chamber of Representatives and the Senate.

Article 27. Each of the three branches of the Legislative power has the right of initiative.

Nevertheless, all laws relative to the revenues or expenditures of the state or to the army contingent must be voted first by the Chamber of Representatives.

Article 28. The authoritative interpretation of the laws belongs only to the Legislative power.

Article 29. The Executive power is vested in the King, subject to the regulations of the constitution.

Article 30. The Judicial power is exercised by the courts and the tribunals.

Decrees and judgments are executed in the name of the King.

Article 31. Affairs exclusively communal or provincial are regulated by the communal or provincial councils, according to the principles established by the constitution.

CHAPTER I

THE CHAMBERS

Article 32. The members of the two Chambers represent the nation, and not the province alone, nor the subdivision of the province which has elected them.

Article 33. The sessions of the Chambers shall be public. Nevertheless each Chamber may resolve itself into a secret committee upon the demand of its president or ten members.

It may then decide by vote of an absolute majority, whether the session shall be resumed in public upon the same subject.

Article 34. Each Chamber shall judge of the qualifications of its own members, and shall decide all contests which arise upon that subject.

Article 35. No person can at the same time be a member of both Chambers.

Article 36. Any member of either of the two Chambers, who shall be appointed by the Government to any other salaried office except that of minister, and who accepts the same, shall give up his seat immediately, and may resume his duties only by virtue of a new election.

Article 37. At each session, each of the Chambers shall elect its president, its vice-presidents, and shall form its secretariat.

Article 38. All resolutions shall be made by the absolute majority of votes; except for those that will be established by the rules of the Chambers with regard to elections and presentations.

In a case where the votes are evenly divided, the proposal that is being deliberated, is rejected.

Neither one of the two Chambers can pass a resolution without the Concurrence of the majority of its members.

Article 39. Votes are indicated either aloud, or by sitting and standing. When a decision is being made on laws, voting is always done by calling by name with responses aloud.

Elections and presentations of candidates are made by secret ballot.

Article 40. Each Chamber has the right of investigation.

Article 41. A project of law can not be adopted by one of the Chambers, except having been voted on, article by article.

Article 42. The Chambers have the right to amend and to divide the articles and proposed amendments.

Article 43. It is forbidden to present petitions to the Chambers in person.

Each Chamber has the right to return to the Ministers, petitions that are addressed to them. The ministers must give explanations as to their content, every time that the Chamber requires it.

Article 44. No member of either Chamber can be prosecuted or sought out because of the opinions or votes that he expressed in the exercise of his functions.

Articles 45. No member of either Chamber can be prosecuted or arrested in a manner of restraint except with the authorization of the Chamber of which he is a member, except in cases of flagrant misdemeanor.

No member of either Chamber shall be arrested during the session, except by the same authority.

The detention or the prosecution of a member of either Chamber is suspended during the session and for the entire term, if the Chamber so demands.

Article 46. Each Chamber determines by its own rules the mode in which it is to exercise its powers.

SECTION I

THE CHAMBER OF REPRESENTATIVES

Article 47. The Chamber of Representatives shall be composed of deputies, elected directly by the citizens paying a poll tax determined by the electoral law. The poll tax shall not exceed 100 florins of direct tax nor be under 20 florins.

Article 48. Elections are conducted according to provincial divisions and such places that the law shall determine.

Article 49. The electoral law shall fix the number of deputies according to the population.

This number shall not exceed the proportion of one deputy per 40,000 inhabitants. The law likewise determines the prerequisites required to be a voter as well as the steps of the electoral procedures.

Article 50. To be eligible it is necessary:

1. To be a Belgian citizen by birth, or to have received full naturalization;
2. To enjoy civil and political rights;
3. To have reached the age of twenty-five years;
4. To be a resident of Belgium.

No other condition of eligibility shall be required.

Article 51. The members of the Chamber of Representatives shall be elected for a term of four years; one-half being elected every two years, in the order determined by the electoral law.

In case of dissolution the Chamber shall be entirely renewed.

Article 52. Each member of the Chamber of Representatives shall receive an annual compensation of 200 florins. Those who reside in the Capital will not receive any compensation.

He shall have, in addition, the right of free transportation upon all state and concessionary railways from the place of his residence to the city where the session is held.

SECTION II

THE SENATE

Article 53. Members of the Senate shall be elected by the citizens who elect the members of the Chamber of representatives in accordance with the population of each province.

Article 54. The Senate shall be composed of a number of members equal to one-half of the deputies of the other Chamber.

Article 55. Senators shall be elected for a term of eight years; one-half being elected every four years in the order determined by the electoral law.

In case of dissolution, the Senate shall be entirely renewed.

Article 56. To be a Senator, it is necessary:

1. To be a Belgian citizen by birth, or to have received full naturalization;

2. To enjoy civil and political rights;

3. To be a resident of Belgium;

4. To be at least forty years of age;

5. To pay in Belgium at least 1000 florins of direct taxes, including licenses.

In the provinces where the number of citizens paying 1000 florins in direct taxes does not reach the proportion of one for every 6000 inhabitants, the list shall be completed by those residents of the province paying the highest taxes.

Article 57. Senators shall receive neither salary nor emolument.

Article 58. The sons of the King, or if there are none, the Belgian princes of the branch of the royal family designated to succeed to the throne, are by right Senators at the age of eighteen years. They have no deliberative vote until twenty-five years of age.

Article 59. Any assembly of the Senate which may be held at any other time than during the session of the Chamber of Representatives, is null and void.

CHAPTER II

THE KING AND THE MINISTERS

Section I. The King

Article 60. The constitutional powers of the King are hereditary in the direct descendants, natural and legitimate, of His Majesty Leopold-George-Christian-Frederick of Saxe-Coburg, from male to male in the order of primogeniture, and to the perpetual exclusion of the females and of their descendants.

Article 61. In default of male descendants of His Majesty Leopold-George-Christian-Frederick of Saxe-Coburg, the King may name his successor, with the consent of the Chambers expressed in the manner prescribed by the following article.

If no nomination has been made after the manner described below, the throne shall be vacant.

Article 62. The King cannot be at the same time be the head of another state without the consent of the two Chambers.

Neither of the Chambers can deliberate upon this point unless two-thirds, at least, of the members who compose it are present, and the resolution must be adopted by at least two-thirds of the votes cast.

Article 63. The person of the King is inviolable; his ministers are responsible.

Article 64. No decree of the King can take effect unless it is countersigned by a minister, who, by that act alone, renders himself responsible for it.

Article 65. The King appoints and dismisses his ministers.

Article 66. He confers the grades in the army.

He appoints the officers of the general administration and for foreign relations, except as otherwise established by law.

He appoints other governmental officials only by virtue of an express provision of law.

Article 67. He issues all regulation and decrees necessary for the execution of the laws, without power to suspend the laws themselves, or to dispense with their execution.

Article 68. The King commands the forces both by land and sea, declares war, makes treaties of peace, of alliance and of commerce. He notifies the two Chambers of these acts as soon as the interest and safety of the state permit, adding thereto suitable comments.

Treaties of commerce, and treaties which might burden the state, or bind Belgian citizens individually, shall take effect only after having received the approval of the two Chambers.

No cession, no exchange and no addition of territory can take place except by law. In no case can the secret articles of a treaty be destructive of those openly expressed.

Article 69. The King sanctions and promulgates the laws.

Article 70. The Chambers shall assemble each year, the second Tuesday in November, unless they shall have been previously summoned by the King.

The Chambers shall remain in session at least forty days each year.

The King announces the closing of the session.

The King has the right to convoke the Chambers in extra session.

Article 71. The King has the right to dissolve the Chambers either simultaneously or separately. The act of dissolution shall order a new election within forty days, and summon the Chambers within two months.

Article 72. The King may adjourn the Chambers. In no case shall the adjournment exceed the term of one month, nor shall it be renewed in the same session, without the consent of the Chambers.

Article 73. He has the right to remit or reduce the penalties pronounced by the judges of courts except such as are fixed by law in the case of ministers.

Article 74. He has the right to coin money as regulated by law.

Article 75. He has the right to confer titles of nobility, but without the power of attaching to them any privilege.

Article 76. He may confer military orders in accordance with the provisions of the law.

Article 77. The civil list is to be fixed by law for the duration of each reign.

Article 78. The King has no other powers than those which the constitution, and the special laws enacted under the constitution, formally confer upon him.

Article 79. At the death of the King, the Chambers shall assemble without a summons, at the latest on the tenth day after his decease. If the Chambers shall have been previously dissolved, and if in the act of dissolution the reassembling had been fixed for a day later than the tenth day, the former members shall resume duties until the assembling of those who should replace them.

If only one Chamber shall have been dissolved, the same rule shall be followed in regard to that Chamber.

From the date of the death of the King and until the taking of the oath by his successor to the throne, or by the regent, the constitutional powers of the King shall be exercised, in the name of the Belgian people, by the ministers united in council, and upon their responsibility.

Article 80. The King is of age when he shall have completed the age of eighteen years.

He shall not take possession of the throne until he shall have solemnly taken, before the united Chambers, the following oath:

"I swear to observe the constitution and the laws of the Belgian people, to maintain the national independence and the integrity of the territory."

Article 81. If, at the death of the King, his successor is a minor, the two Chambers shall unite in one assembly, for the purpose of providing for the regency and guardianship.

Article 82. If the King becomes incapacitated to reign, the ministers, after having ascertained this incapacity, shall immediately convoke the Chambers. The Chambers assembled together shall provide for the regency and guardianship.

Article 83. The regency can be conferred upon only one person.

The regent can enter upon his duties only after having taken the oath prescribed by Article 80.

Article 84. No change in the constitution can be made during a regency.

Article 85. In case there is a vacancy of the throne, the Chambers deliberating together, shall arrange provisionally for the regency, until the first meeting of the Chambers after they have been wholly re-elected. That meeting shall take place at the latest within two months. The new Chambers deliberating together shall provide definitely for the vacancy.

SECTION II

THE MINISTERS

Article 86. No person can be a minister unless he is a Belgian citizen by birth, or has received full naturalization.

Article 87. No member of the royal family can be a minister.

Article 88. Ministers have no deliberative vote in either Chamber unless they are members of it.

They shall have admission to either Chamber, and are entitled to be heard when they so request.

The Chambers have the right to demand the presence of ministers.

Article 89. In no case shall the verbal or written order of the King relieve a minister of responsibility.

Article 90. The Chamber of Representatives has the right to accuse ministers and to arraign them before the Court of Cassation, which, sitting in full bench, alone has the right to judge them, except in such matters as shall be established by law respecting a civil suit by an aggrieved party and respecting crimes and misdemenaors committed by ministers when not in the performance of their duties.

The law shall determine the responsibility of ministers, the penalties to be inflicted on them, and the method of proceeding against them, whether upon accusation accepted by the Chamber of Representatives or by prosecution by the aggrieved parties.

Article 91. The King can grant pardon to a minister sentenced by the Court of Cassation only upon request of one of the two Chambers.

CHAPTER III

THE JUDICIARY

Article 92. Actions which involve questions of civil rights belong exclusively to the jurisdiction of the tribunals.

Article 93. Actions which involve questions of political rights belong to the jurisdiction of the tribunals, except as otherwise determined by law.

Article 94. No tribunal nor contentious jurisdiction shall be established except by law. No commissions nor extraordinary tribunals under any title whatever can be established.

Article 95. There shall be a Court of Cassation for all Belgium.

This Court shall not consider questions of fact except in the trial of ministers.

Article 96. The sessions of the tribunals shall be public, unless this publicity is declared by a judgment of the Court to be dangerous to public order or morals.

In cases of political and press-law offences, closed doors can be enforced only by a unanimous vote of the tribunal.

Article 97. Every judgment shall be pronounced in open court, and the reasons therefor stated.

Article 98. The right of trial by jury is guaranteed in all criminal cases and for all political and press-law offences.

Article 99. The justices of the peace and the judges of the tribunals shall be appointed directly by the King.

The councillors of the courts of appeal and the presidents and vice-presidents of the courts of original jurisdiction shall be appointed by the King from two double lists presented the one by these courts and the other by the provincial councils.

The councillors of the Court of Cassation shall be appointed by the King from two double lists presented one by the Senate and one by the Court of Cassation.

In both cases the candidates named upon one list can be named also upon the other.

All the names shall be published at least fifteen days before the appointment.

The courts shall choose their presidents and vice-presidents from among their own number.

Article 100. Judges shall be appointed for life.

No judge can be deprived of his office nor suspended until after trial and judgment.

The removal of a judge from one place to another can take place only by means of a new appointment and with his consent.

Article 101. The King appoints and removes the state officials serving in the courts and tribunals.

Article 102. The salaries of the members of the judiciary shall be fixed by law.

Article 103. No judge shall accept from the government any salaried office, unless he shall perform the duties thereof gratuitously, and not then if it is contrary to the law of incompatibility.

Article 104. There shall be three courts of appeal in Belgium.

Their jurisdiction and the places where they shall be held shall be determined by law.

Article 105. Special laws shall govern the organization of military tribunals, their powers, the rights and obligations of the members of these tribunals, and the duration of their functions,

There shall be tribunals of commerce in places which shall be designated by law. Their organization, powers, the method of appointment of their members and the duration of their term of office shall also be determined by law.

Article 106. The Court of Cassation shall decide conflicts of jurisdiction, according to the method prescribed by law.

Article 107. The courts and tribunals shall enforce executive decrees and ordinances, whether general, provincial or local, only so far as they shall conform to the laws.

CHAPTER IV

PROVINCIAL AND COMMUNAL INSTITUTIONS

Article 108. Provincial and communal institutions shall be regulated by law.

The law shall establish the application of the following principles:

1. Direct election, except in the cases which may be established by law in regard to the chiefs of the communal administration, and government commissioners acting in the provincial councils.

2. The relegation to provincial and communal councils of all provincial and communal affairs, without prejudice to the approval of their acts in the cases and according to the procedure determined by law.

3. The publicity of the sittings of the provincial and communal councils within the limits established by law.

4. The publicity of budgets and accounts.

5. The intervention of the King or of the Legislative power to prevent provincial and communal councils from exceeding their powers and from acting against the general welfare.

Article 109. The keeping of the civil register is exclusively the duty of the communal authorities.

TITLE IV

FINANCES

Article 110. No tax for the benefit of the state shall be imposed except by law.

No public charge, nor any provincial assessment shall be imposed without the consent of the provincial council.

No public charge, nor any communal assessment shall be imposed without the consent of the communal council.

The law shall determine the exceptions which experience shall show to be necessary in regard to provincial and communal taxes.

Article 111. Taxes for the benefit of the state shall be voted annually.

The laws which impose such taxes shall remain in force for one year only unless they are re-enacted.

Article 112. No privilege shall be established in regard to taxes.

No exemption or abatement of taxes shall be established, except by law.

Article 113. Beyond the cases expressly excepted by law, no payment shall be exacted of any citizen other than taxes levied for the benefit of the state, of the province or of the community. No change shall be made in the existing system of polders[1] and wateringen,[2] which remain subject to ordinary legislation.

Article 114. No pension or gratuity shall be paid out of the public treasury without the authority of law.

Article 115. Each year the Chambers shall fix the law of accounts and vote the budget.

All the receipts and expenditures of the state must be contained in the budget and in the accounts.

Article 116. The members of the Court of Accounts shall be appointed by the Chamber of Representatives, and for a term fixed by law.

This court is intrusted with the examination and settlement of the accounts of the general administration, and of all persons accountable to the public treasury. It shall guard that no item of the expenditures of the budget shall be overdrawn and that no transfer shall take place.

It shall audit the accounts of the different administrations of the state, and it shall be its duty to gather for this purpose all information and all necessary vouchers.

The general accounts of the state shall be submitted to the Chambers with the comments of the Court of Accounts.

This court shall be organized by law.

Article 117. The salaries and pensions of the ministers of religion shall be paid by the state; the sums necessary to meet this expenditure shall be entered annually in the budget.

---

1. Polders are lands reclaimed from the sea by dikes.
2. Wateringen are canals.

TITLE V

THE ARMY

Article 118. The method of recruiting the army shall be determined by law. The laws shall also regulate the promotion, the rights and the duties of soldiers.

Article 119. The army contingent shall be voted annually. The law which fixes this shall remain in force for one year only, unless re-enacted.

Article 120. The organization and the duties of the constabulary shall be regulated by law.

Article 121. No foreign troops shall be admitted to the service of the state, to occupy or to cross its territory except by provision of law.

Article 122. There shall be a citizen militia, the organization of which shall be regulated by law.

The officers of all grades, at least as high as that of captain, shall be chosen by the militia, with such exceptions as may be judged necessary for accountants.

Article 123. The militia cannnot be brought into active service, except when authorized by law.

Article 124. Soldiers shall not be deprived of their grades, honors and pensions except in the manner prescribed by law.

TITLE VI

GENERAL PROVISIONS

Article 125. The Belgian nation adopts for its colors red, yellow and black, and for the coat of arms of the kingdom, the Belgian lion, with the motto, "UNION GIVES STRENGTH."

Article 126. The city of Brussels is the capital of Belgium and the seat of government.

Article 127. No oath shall be imposed except by law. The law shall determine its format.

Article 128. All foreigners, who find themselves in the territory of Belgium, shall enjoy the protection accorded to both people and property, except for the exceptions established by the law.

Article 129. No law, no arrest, nor any rule of general administration in the provinces or in the community shall be effective until having been published in the form determined by the law.

TITLE VII

REVISION OF THE CONSTITUTION

Article 131. The legislative power has the authority to declare if there is room for the revision of a constitutional provision that they designate.

After such declaration, the two Chambers shall be dissolved of full rights.

Two new Chambers shall then be summoned, in conformance with Article 71.

The Chambers shall hand down a ruling, with common agreement from the King, on the points subject to the revision.

In such instance, the Chambers cannot deliberate; if at least two-thirds of the members who compose each one of them are not present, and no change shall be adopted with less than a two-thirds vote.

TITLE VIII

TRANSITORY PROVISIONS

Article 132. For the first appointee as Secretary of State, the first provision of Article 80 can be waived.

Article 133. Foreigners, who settled in Belgium before January 1, 1814, and who continue to reside there, are considered to as Belgians at birth, conditioned upon their declaring their intention to enjoy the benefit of this present provision.

The declaration must be made within six months, starting from the day that the present constitution shall be obligatory, if they are of the age of majority, and in the year that will follow reaching the age of majority if they are minors.

This declaration shall take place before the provincial authority having jurisdiction over the locale where they reside. It will be made in person or by a proxy, bearer of a special and authentic power-of-attorney.

Article 134. Until there is authority established by law, the Chamber of Representatives shall have discretionary power to accuse a minister, and the Court of Cassation to judge him, in characterizing the crime and determining the penalty.

Nevertheless, the penalty cannot excede imprisonment [Reclusion] without prejudice to a provision expressly provided for in the penal laws.

Article 135. The personnel of the Courts and the tribunals shall remain in existing office, subject to change by law.

This law must be proposed during the first legislative session.

Article 136. A law proposed in the same session will determine the method for the first nomination of members of the Court of Cassation.

Article 137. The Fundamental law of August 24, 1815 is abolished as well as its provincial and local statutes.

However, the provincial and local authorities shall hold their assignments until the law provides otherwise.

Article 138. Starting from the day when the Constitution shall be promulgated, all of the laws, decrees, ordinances rules and other acts which are contrary to it shall be repealed.

SUPPLEMENTARY PROVISIONS

Article 139. The National Congress declares that it is necessary to provide separate laws, and with the shortest possible delay, to the following subjects:

1) The press.

2) The organization of the jury.

3) Finances.

4) Provincial and communal organization.

5) The responsibility of the Ministers and other agents of power.

6) The organization of the judiciary.

7) The revision of the pensions list.

8) The proper measures to prevent the abuse of holding more than one office.

9) The revision of legislation on bankruptcy and deferment.

10) The organization of the army, the rights of advancement and retirement, and the military penal Code.

11) The revision of the Codes.

German Constitution
of 1848

The year 1848 was the one of European revolutions. The economic crises that had swept Europe in the 1840s reached their height in 1848 and precipitated revolutions in Austria, France, Italy, Switzerland, and Germany.

As a result of these revolutions, five new constitutions were written. The new Austrian Constitution of 4 May 1848 reasserted the unity of the Hapsburg Empire and removed Austria from possible inclusion in a German confederation. The new French Constitution marked the end of constitutional monarchy and restored the republic. The new Italian Constitution recognized the union of the Italian states under Mazzini and Cavour. The new Swiss Constitution (see next chapter) embodied nationalism and national unity. And the new German confederation Constitution—known in history as both the German Reich Constitution and the Frankfurt Constitution—provided the best expression of the revolutionary ideals of 1848, although it never went into effect.

After the disintegration of the Holy Roman Empire of the German Nation in 1806, the next attempt to unify Germany was the establishment of the German confederation by the Congress of Vienna in 1815. This decree was followed in the same year by the German Federal Act, which in turn was followed by the Vienna Final Act of 1820. However, the result of these enactments was a very weak and still disunited Germany. In the interests of further unification, Prussia in 1833 created a *zollverein*, a general customs union, in order to remove obstructions to trade. Many Germans believed that this would eventually lead to economic and political unification; however, the rivalry between Prussia and Austria precluded such an attempt.

German unification seemed a practical possibility in 1848. Revolutionary forces, demanding a constitution that would incorporate civil liberties, the abolition of feudalism, and the strengthening of the German confederation, had triumphed in many of the smaller German states. In the Prussian capital of Berlin, similar forces were erecting barricades in the streets to express their demands. King Frederick William IV yielded to some of these demands and, under the pressure of mob rioting, summoned an assembly to draw up a constitution. He declared Prussia "merged in Germany" and proclaimed himself "King of the free regenerated German nation."[1]

But the Constitutional Assembly that was to meet in Frankfurt in 1848 to draft such a constitution was not selected by the king. Rather, the members were chosen in a series of elections by methods that varied from state to state. Although all 838 members were selected by voters, none of the delegates were government representatives or officials. Chosen for the Assembly was Germany's intellectual elite, including 223 judges and lawyers, 49 university professors, 57 school teachers, 18 physicians, 33 clergymen, and 140 businessmen. There were only four blue-collar workers and a single farmer.

The opening session was held in the Church of St. Paul in Frankfurt in May 1848. Its first task was to determine the geographical limits of Germany, an issue that sharply divided the delegates. The majority wanted to exclude Bohemia and Prussian Poland because their natives did not speak German. German national sentiment, however, demanded their inclusion as long as these areas were under German domination.

The second major issue was one of federalism. The delegates had to determine the apportionment of power to the central government and the states. A compromise solution between the British and American systems was reached. The new federal legislature would consist of a lower house elected by universal male suffrage, and an upper house chosen by the governments and the legislatures of the constituent states. However, there would be no election of the executive; the legislature would choose all ministers, and a constitutional monarch would preside.

Thus, the third issue before the Assembly was the selection of a constitutional monarch. Frederick William IV of Prussia, whose original concessions had led to the election of the Assembly in the first place, was selected; however, he refused the offer. The king objected to the Assembly because he had no part in its selection and criticized its constitution as "a bastard product." He disdained a crown bestowed by the people: "The crown is no crown," he said, "the crown which a Hohenzollern could accept . . . is not one created by an assembly born of revolutionary seed."[2]

One month later, the king of Prussia invited the leaders of the several independent German states to a conference in Berlin—an undisguised attempt to create a Prussian-dominated national union in opposition to the government devised by the Frankfurt Constitution. Because twenty-nine of the roughly fifty states had already accepted the Frankfurt Constitution, a contest arose between Berlin and Frankfurt. However, this struggle was actually between ancient feudal rights and the new liberal ideal as well as monarchical privilege and popular sovereignty. In the short run, victory went to the king and the old established order; however, in the final analysis, the constitutional ideas and principles of Frankfurt prevailed.

The Frankfurt Constitution sought to enshrine constitutionalism and popular sovereignty throughout Germany. Paragraph 186 read: "Every German state is to have a constitution with popular representation. The ministers are responsible to the popular representatives of the people."

The civil liberties incorporated into the Frankfurt document soon became an essential part of the constitutions of the German states, although they were not to be included in a national German constitution until the Weimar Constitution of 1919 (see later section). However, the constitutional provisions created at Frankfurt for the enforcement of civil rights did not become a reality in Germany until the Bonn Basic Law of 1949.[3]

Section VI of this Constitution is entitled "The Basic Rights of the German People." Paragraph 130 of this section is designed as a preamble to the objectives of the framers: "The following basic rights are to be guaranteed to the German people. They are to serve as the norm for the constitutions of the individual German states, and no constitution or legislation of an individual German state may ever abolish or limit them."

The enumeration of these rights went beyond the listings in the U.S., Polish, and French Constitutions, which exemplified the rights of the people as understood at the end of the eighteenth century. These additional rights included the right to a free public education, the right to a civil marriage, freedom of emigration, and the right of any citizen to engage in any form of occupation. This Constitution was also the first to limit the death penalty; capital punishment "except where prescribed by martial law or allowed by maritime law in cases of mutinies" was abolished as well as pillory, branding, and corporal punishment.

CHRISTIAN STARCK
Professor
Georg-August-Universät
Göttingen, Germany

NOTES

1. Quoted in Crane Brinton, John B. Christopher, and Robert Lee Wolff, *A History of Civilization* (Englewood Cliffs, N.J.: Prentice-Hall, 1976), 557.

2. Quoted in J. G. Legge, *Rhyme and Revolution in Germany* (London: 1918), 516–17.
3. The Bonn Basic Law is the present constitution of the Federal Republic of Germany or West Germany. It is called the Basic Law because its framers decided to reserve "constitution" for a reunited Germany.

GERMAN CONSTITUTION OF 1848

SECTION I: THE REICH

ARTICLE I

§ 1. The German Reich consists of the area of the heretofore existing German Confederation. The stipulation of the position of the Duchy of Schleswig remains reserved [for future arrangement].

§ 2. If a German territory has the same head of state as a non-German one, then the German territory must have its own constitution, government and administration separate from the non-German one. Only German citizens may be appointed to the government and administration of a German territory.

The Reich constitution and Reich legislation have the same binding force in such a German territory as in the other German lands.

§ 3. If a German territory has the same head of state as a non-German one, then the head of state must either reside in his German lands, or a regency must be installed in a constitutional manner to which only Germans may be appointed.

§ 4. Apart from already existing associations of German and non-German lands, no head of state of a non-German territory may at the same time take over the government of a German territory, nor may a prince governing in Germany, without resigning his German government, accept a foreign crown.

§ 5. The individual German states retain their independence in so far as it is not limited by the Reich constitution; they have all the state sovereignty and rights in so far as these are not expressly assigned to the Reich Authority.

Translation from *The Revolutions of 1848–49*. Edited by Frank Eyck (Edinburgh: Oliver and Boyd, 1972), 149–165.

SECTION II. THE REICH AUTHORITY

ARTICLE I

§ 6. The Reich Authority exercises the exclusive international representation of Germany and of the individual German states towards foreign countries. . . .

§ 7. The individual German governments do not have the right to receive or to maintain resident ministers. They may also not maintain any special consuls. . . .

ARTICLE II

§ 10. The Reich Authority has the exclusive right of war and peace.

ARTICLE III

§ 11. The Reich Authority has at its disposal the whole armed force of Germany.

§ 12. The Reich army consists of the entire land forces of the individual German states designated for the purpose of war. . . . Those German states which have less than 500,000 inhabitants are to be united by the Reich Authority to a greater military whole which will then be under the direct command of the Reich Authority or will not be attached to an adjoining greater state. . . .

§ 14. The military oath is to contain in the first place the obligation of loyalty to the Head of the Reich and to the Reich constitution. . . .

§ 17. The appointment of commanders and officers of their troops, in so far as their strength demands it, is left to the Governments of the individual states. For the greater military units to which the troops of several states are united, the Reich authority appoints the common commanders. For war the Reich authority appoints the commanding generals of the independent corps as well as the personnel of headquarters. . . .

§ 19. The Navy is exclusively a matter for the Reich. No individual state is allowed to maintain warships or to issue letters of marque. . . .

ARTICLE VI

§ 28. Over railways and their operation, in so far as the protection of the Reich or the interest of general traffic demands it, the Reich Authority has superintendence and the right of legislation. . . .

ARTICLE VII

§ 33. The German Reich shall form one customs and trading area, surrounded by a common customs frontier, with the abolition of all internal border dues. The exclusion of individual places and areas from the customs area remains reserved to the Reich Authority. It remains further reserved to the Reich Authority to attach even territories . . . not belonging to the Reich to the German customs area by means of special treaties.

§ 34. The Reich Authority has exclusive legislation over customs as well as over common production and consumption duties. . . .

§ 35. The levying and administration of customs duties, as well as of the common production and consumption duties, takes place on the orders and under the supervision of the Reich Authority. From the proceeds a certain part will, according to the ordinary budget, be allotted for the expenditure of the Reich, the rest will be distributed to the individual states. . . .

§ 36. On what objects the individual states may put production or consumption duties for the benefit of the state or of individual municipalities . . . will be determined by Reich legislation.

§ 37. The individual German states are not entitled to levy customs duties on commodities which pass into or out of the Reich frontiers.

§ 38. The Reich Authority has the right of legislation about trade and shipping and supervises the execution of the Reich laws issued about these. . . .

ARTICLE IX

§ 45. The Reich Authority has the exclusive legislation and supervision of the monetary system. It is incumbent upon it to introduce the same monetary system for the whole of Germany. . . .

§ 46. The Reich Authority is obliged to establish in the whole of Germany the same system of weights and measures. . . .

§ 47. The Reich Authority has the right to regulate banking and the issue of paper money by legislation. . . .

ARTICLE X

§ 49. To cover its expenditure, the Reich Authority is in the first instance dependent on its share of the revenue from customs and from the common production and consumption duties.

§ 50. The Reich Authority has the right, in so far as the other revenues are not sufficient, to levy contributions from the individual states [*Matrikularbeiträge*].

§ 51. The Reich Authority is empowered to levy Reich taxes in extraordinary cases . . . as well as to contract loans or other debts.

ARTICLE XII

§ 53. It is incumbent upon the Reich Authority to maintain a supervisory watch over the rights guaranteed to all Germans by the Reich constitution.

§ 54. The Reich Authority is charged with the maintenance of the Reich peace. It has to take the measures required for the maintenance of internal security and order:

(1) if a German state is disturbed in its peace or endangered by another German state;

(2) if in a German state security and order is disturbed or endangered by natives or strangers. But in this case the Reich Authority should only intervene if the Government concerned invites it to do so, unless the State Government concerned is notoriously incapable of doing so, or unless the general Reich peace appears to be threatened;

(3) if the constitution of a German state is forcibly or unilaterally abolished or changed, and if immediate help cannot be secured by appealing to the Supreme Reich Court [*Reichsgericht*].

§ 55. The measures which may be taken by the Reich Authority for the preservation of the Reich peace are:

(1) Decrees

(2) The dispatch of commissioners

(3) The use of armed force. . . .

§56. The Reich Authority is charged with determining by a Reich law the cases and forms in which armed force should be used against disturbances of the public order.

§57. The Reich Authority has the task of fixing the legal norms for the acquisition and forfeiture of Reich and state citizenship.

§58. The Reich Authority is competent to issue Reich laws about the law of domicile and to watch over their execution. . . .

ARTICLE XIII

§62. The Reich Authority has the power of legislation necessary for the execution of the tasks entrusted to it by the constitution and for the protection of the institutions made over to it.

§63. The Reich Authority is empowered, if it finds common institutions and measures necessary in the general interest of Germany, to issue the laws necessary for their establishment in the forms prescribed for the change of the constitution. . . .

§64. The Reich Authority is charged with establishing unity of law in the German people by the issue of general law codes. . . .

§66. Reich laws have precedence over the laws of the individual states, in so far as they are not expressly given only a subsidiary validity. . . .

SECTION III: THE HEAD OF THE REICH

ARTICLE I

§68. The dignity of Head of the Reich will be assigned to one of the reigning German princes.

§69. This dignity is hereditary in the house of the prince to whom it is assigned. It devolves in the male line according to the right of primogeniture.

§70. The head of the Reich has the title: Emperor of the Germans.

§71. The residence of the Emperor is at the seat of the Reich Government. . . .

ARTICLE II

§73. The person of the Emperor is inviolable. The Emperor exercises the authority assigned to him through responsible ministers appointed by him.

§74. All government actions of the Emperor require for their validity the countersignature of at least one of the Reich Ministers, who thus assumes responsibility.

ARTICLE III

§75. The Emperor exercises the international representation of the German Reich and of the individual German states. He appoints the Reich ministers [resident] and the consuls and conducts diplomatic relations.

§76. The Emperor declares war and concludes peace.

§77. The Emperor concludes alliances and treaties with foreign powers, with the collaboration of the Reichstag in so far as this is reserved to it in the constitution. . . .

§79. The Emperor summons and closes the Reichstag; he has the right of dissolving the popular chamber [*Volkshaus*].

§80. The Emperor has the right of proposing bills. He exercises the legislative power in common with the Reichstag under the constitutional limitations. He proclaims Reich laws and issues the decrees necessary for their execution. . . .

§82. The Emperor is charged with the preservation of the peace of the Reich.

§83. The Emperor has the right of disposal over the armed forces. . . .

SECTION IV: THE REICHSTAG

ARTICLE I

§85. The Reichstag consists of two houses, the House of States [*Staatenhaus*] and the House of the People [*Volkshaus*].

ARTICLE II

§86. The House of States will be formed from the representatives of the German states.

§87. The number of members is as follows:

Prussia	40
Austria	38
Bavaria	18
Saxony, Hanover, Wurtemberg, 10 each	30
Baden	9
Electoral Hesse, Grand-Duchy of Hesse, Holstein, 6 each	18
Mecklenburg-Schwerin	4
Luxemburg–Limburg, Nassau, 3 each	6
Brunswick, Oldenburg, Saxe-Weimar, 2 each	6
The 23 others, 1 each	23
	192 members.[1]

§88. Members of the House of States are appointed one-half by the governments and one-half by the popular representation of the particular states. . . .

§92. The members of the House of States are elected for six years. One-half of the seats are filled every three years. . . .

[1] There were to be certain modifications so long as Austria did not join.

ARTICLE III

§93. The House of the People consists of the deputies of the German people.

§94. The members of the House of the People are elected initially for four years, thereafter for three years. The election is to be in accordance with the regulations contained in the Reich electoral law.[2]

ARTICLE IV

§95. The members of the Reichstag draw from the Reich exchequer uniform daily allowances and compensation for their travelling expenses.

§96. The members of both houses may not be committed by instructions.

§97. Nobody may at the same time be a member of both houses.

ARTICLE V

§98. For a resolution of each house of the Reichstag the participation of at least one-half of the legal number of its members and a simple majority are required. . . .

§99. Each house has the right of initiation, of legislation, of complaint, of address and of the investigation of facts, as well as of the impeachment of ministers.

§100. A resolution of the Reichstag can only validly be made by agreement of both houses.

§101. A resolution of the Reichstag which has not obtained the consent of the Reich Government may not be repeated in the same session. If the Reichstag in three immediately consecutive ordinary sessions makes the same resolution without change, it becomes law with the end of the third Reichstag, even if the Reich Government does not give its consent. . . .

§102. A resolution of the Reichstag is necessary in the following cases:

(1) if it is a matter of the issue, abolition, alteration, or interpretation of Reich laws.

(2) when the Reich budget is fixed, when loans are contracted, when the Reich takes over expenditure for which provision has not been made in the budget, or levies contributions from the states [Matrikularbeiträge] or taxes.

(6) if territories not belonging to the Reich are included in the German custom area or particular places or areas are excluded from it.

(7) if German territories are ceded, or non-German territories incor-

---

[2] See document V.2.C.

porated in the Reich or to be associated with it in some other manner.

§103. . . . (3) the length of the financial period and of the grant of the budget is one year. . . .

ARTICLE VI

§104. The Reichstag assembles each year at the seat of the Reich Government. . . .

§106. The House of the People may be dissolved by the Head of the Reich. In case of dissolution, the Reichstag is to be re-assembled within three months. . . .

ARTICLE VII

§111. The sessions of both houses are public. . . .

ARTICLE VIII

§117. A member of the Reichstag may be neither arrested nor investigated because of criminal accusations during the session without approval of the house to which he belongs, with the sole exception of his being caught red-handed. . . .

§120. No member of the Reichstag may at any time be prosecuted or disciplined or otherwise called to account outside the assembly because of his vote or because of utterances made in the exercise of his profession.

ARTICLE IX

§121. The Reich Ministers are entitled to be present at the proceedings of both Houses of the Reichstag and to be heard by it at any time.

§122. The Reich Ministers are obliged at the request of either house of the Reichstag to appear in it and to give information, or to indicate the reason why it cannot be given.

§123. The Reich Ministers may not be members of the House of States.

§124. If a member of the House of the People accepts an office or a promotion in the service of the Reich, he must submit to a new election; he keeps his seat until the new election has taken place.

SECTION V: THE SUPREME REICH COURT
[*REICHSGERICHT*]

ARTICLE I

§125. The jurisdiction belonging to the Reich is exercised by the *Reichsgericht*. . . .

SECTION VI: THE BASIC RIGHTS OF THE GERMAN
PEOPLE

§130. The following basic rights are to be guaranteed to the German people. They are to serve as the norm for the constitutions of the individual German states, and no constitution or legislation of an individual German state may ever abolish or limit them.

ARTICLE I

§131. The German people consists of the members of the states which form the German Reich.

§132. Every German has German Reich citizenship. He can exercise the rights arising from it in every German state. . . .

§133. Every German has the right to stay and reside at any place in the area of the Reich, to acquire immovables of any kind and to dispose of them, to engage in any form of livelihood, to gain municipal citizenship. . . .

§134. No German state may make a difference in civil and criminal law or in any litigation between its citizens and other Germans which discriminates against the latter as foreigners. . . .

§136. The state does not limit the freedom of emigration; duties on removal may not be levied. . . .

ARTICLE II

§137. The law does not recognise any difference between estates. The nobility as an estate is abolished. All privileges of estates are abolished. All Germans are equal before the law. All titles, in so far as they are not connected with an office, are abolished and may not be reintroduced. . . . Public offices are equally accessible to all who are qualified. Military service is the same for all; performance of service by a deputy is not permitted.

ARTICLE III

§138. The freedom of the person is inviolable. The arrest of a person, except when caught red-handed, may only take place by virtue of an order from a judge stating the reasons. This order must be handed to the arrested person at the time of the arrest or within the following twenty-four hours. The police must either release or hand over to the judicial authority in the course of the following day every person whom it has taken into custody. . . .

§139. The death penalty—except where prescribed by martial law or allowed by maritime law in case of mutinies—as well as the penalties of the pillory, of branding and of corporal punishment, are abolished.

§140. The home is inviolable. . . .

ARTICLE IV

§143. Every German has the right of free expression by word, writing, printing and picture. Freedom of the press may not in any circumstances and in any way . . . be limited, suspended or abolished. . . .

ARTICLE V

§144. Every German has full freedom of faith and conscience. . . .

§146. The enjoyment of civil . . . rights does not depend on a religious confession and is not limited by it. The duties of the citizen may not be hindered by it.

§147. Every religious society . . . administers in affairs independently but remains subject to the general state laws. No religious society is given preference by the state over others; there is no state church. . . .

§150. The civil validity of marriage is dependent only on the execution of the civil act; church marriage may only take place after the civil act. Difference in religion is no obstacle to civil marriage. . . .

ARTICLE VI

§152. Learning and its instruction is free.

§153. Education is under the superintendence of the state and is, apart from religious instruction, removed from the supervision of the clergy as such. . . .

§157. No fees are payable for instruction in elementary schools and in the lower trade schools. Those without means will be instructed free of charge in all public educational institutions. . . .

. . .

ARTICLE VIII

§161. The Germans have the right to assemble peacefully and without weapons; special permission for this is not necessary. Assemblies of the people out-of-doors may be prohibited in case of urgent danger to public order and security.

ARTICLE IX

§164. Property is inviolable. . . .

§166. All serfdom . . . is abolished forever.

§167. Abolished without compensation are:

(1) patrimonial jurisdiction and the seignorial police, including all powers, exemptions and dues flowing from these rights. . . .

§168. All dues and labour tariffs attached to the soil are commutable. . . .

ARTICLE X

§174. All jurisdiction is derived from the State. There are to be no patrimonial courts.

§175. The judicial authority is exercised independently by the courts . . . ministerial justice is not permissible. Nobody may be withdrawn from his legal judge. Emergency courts may never be held.

§176. There must be no privileged judicial estate or persons or property. . . .

§177. No judge may, except by judgement and law, be removed from his office or be prejudiced in rank and salary. . . .

§178. Court procedure is to be public and oral. . . .

§179. Criminal cases are dealt with through prosecution. In more serious criminal cases at any rate and in all political offences there is to be a trial by jury. . . .

§181. Justice and administration are to be separate and independent from each other. . . .

ARTICLE XII

§186. Every German state is to have a constitution with popular representation. The ministers are responsible to the popular representatives of the people.

§187. The representation of the people has a decisive voice in legislation, in taxation, in the ordering of the budget; also it has—where two Chambers exist, each Chamber separately—the right of making proposals for laws, of complaint, of address, as well as that of impeachment of ministers. As a rule the sittings of the state parliaments are public.

ARTICLE XIII

§188. The non-German speaking peoples of Germany are guaranteed their national development, especially equality of the rights of their languages, as far as their areas extend, in church matters, in [school] instruction, in internal administration and jurisdiction. . . .

SECTION VII: THE GUARANTEE OF THE CONSTITUTION

ARTICLE I

§190. At the beginning of a new reign, the Reichstag meets without being summoned—unless it is already assembled—in the manner in which it was composed the last time. The Emperor, before he takes over the Government, swears in a united session of both houses of the Reichstag an oath to the constitution. The oath reads: 'I swear to protect the Reich and the rights of the German people, to maintain the Reich constitution and to execute it conscientiously. So help me God'. Only after having sworn the oath is the Emperor entitled to carry out acts of government. . . .

ARTICLE III

§196. Changes in the Reich constitution may only be made by a resolution of both houses and with the consent of the Head of the Reich. Such a resolution requires in each of the houses:
(1) The presence of at least two-thirds of the members;
(2) two votes, at least eight days from each other;
(3) a majority of at least two-thirds of the members present at each of the two votes.
   The consent of the Head of the Reich is not necessary, if in three immediately following ordinary sessions the same resolution of the Reichstag is passed unchanged. . . .

V.2.c   The 'democratic' male franchise formed part of a deal between the moderates and a section of the Left in the Frankfurt Parliament to permit the 'Little German' solution under the King of Prussia as hereditary German Emperor. Extract translated from the German text in Huber, *Dokumente*, pp. 324 ff.

ARTICLE I

§I. Every German of good repute who has completed his twenty-fifth year has the vote. . . .

ARTICLE II

§5. Every German entitled to vote who has completed his twenty-fifth year and has belonged for at least three years to a German state is eligible as a deputy of the House of the People.

ARTICLE III

§7. In every state, constituencies are to be formed each containing one hundred thousand souls according to the last census. . . .

ARTICLE V

§13. The electoral act is public. . . . The vote is exercised in person by voting paper without signature.

§14. The election is direct. It takes place by absolute majority of all the votes cast in a constituency. If there is no absolute majority at the election, a second ballot is to take place. If here, too, an absolute majority of the votes is not achieved, a third vote is to be taken on the two candidates who received most votes in the second ballot. . . .

V.3 THE AUSTRIAN CONSTITUTION OF MARCH 1849
Following the example of the King of Prussia in December, 1848, the new Emperor of Austria, Francis Joseph, in March 1849, unilaterally granted a constitution, instead of agreeing it with parliament.
V.3.A

Extracts from the centralist Austrian constitution of 4th March 1849, weakening Magyar control, are from *Annual Register*, 1848, pp. 318 ff.

. . . *Section 1.* The full enjoyment of political liberty, and the right of domestic exercise of the religious confession, are guaranteed to every one. The enjoyment of civil and political rights is independent of religious confession, but religious confession shall not be allowed to interfere with the political duties of the citizens. . . .

Section 2. Every church and religious society, if recognised by law, has the right of a common public exercise of its religion. . . .

Section 5. Everybody has the right of a free expression of his opinion, by words, by writing, by print, and by drawings or paintings. The press may not be put under censorship. Supervisory laws shall be published against abuses of the press. . . .

Section 7. Austrian citizens have the right to assemble, and to form associations, if the end or the means and the manner of the meeting or association are not opposed to the law, or dangerous to the State.

Section 8. Individual liberty is guaranteed.

Section 9. The police are bound to liberate persons whom they have taken into custody within forty-eight hours, or to deliver them into the hands of the judge of the district.

Section 10. A man's domicile is inviolable.

Section 11. The secrecy of correspondence shall not be violated, and letters shall not be seized unless in time of war, or on the strength of a judicial warrant. . . .

Swiss Constitution
of 1848

The Swiss confederation (not the United States) is the world's oldest federal state. Founded in the thirteenth century, it expanded (coincidentally) to thirteen states—the number existing in the confederation when the 1648 Treaty of Westphalia recognized it as an independent sovereignty. Further, "in some respects the Swiss Confederation affords an even more striking example than the United States of how conflicting state interests can be overcome, without annihilating state identity, by the political device called federalism."[1]

Swiss constitutionalism has not been static. Although the present constitution was promulgated in 1874, it has been the subject of many amendments. Formal constitutions date back to the Helvetic Republic Constitution, which the invading French Revolutionary armies imposed on the Swiss in 1798. Two constitutions dictated by Napoleon followed in 1802 and 1803 as well as a Federal Agreement in 1815 after the Congress of Vienna, acknowledging the right of the cantons to promulgate their own constitutions.

It was not until 1848, the year of social revolution, that Switzerland was to adopt a constitution that established a national central government. This document was created after a short, bloodless civil war in 1846 in which seven Catholic cantons attempted secession, but were forced to return to the confederation. The year 1848 also marked the promulgation of four other constitutions, including the Frankfurt Constitution (see preceding section) and new constitutions in Austria, France, and Italy. Unlike the other constitutions, however, the basic principles of the Swiss Constitution survived. Although this document was revised in 1874, its fundamental, democratic character was retained.

Switzerland in 1848 was surrounded by powerful monarchies, and it was only in the cantons and in the confederation itself in all of Europe that regimes existed based on democratic republicanism. The Constitution of 1848 managed to achieve what was then impossible elsewhere on the continent: a central government that permitted both popular sovereignty and local autonomy.

To the Swiss, local autonomy meant dual sovereignty and cantonal autonomy. Article III states this point in definite terms: "The Cantons are sovereign, so far as their sovereignty is not limited by the Federal Constitution, and accordingly they exercise all rights which are not delegated to the Federal Power."

The Swiss legislature created by the Constitution of 1848 was organized along the lines of American-style federalism. The federal assembly, sitting in two chambers, would exercise the "Supreme Power of the confederacy" (Article LX). A national council would have a membership composed of one delegate for every 20 thousand members of the population. The states council of forty-four delegates would have two from each canton. Apparently, "the writings of Toqueville had made the Swiss to a great extent familiar with the American bicameral system as the solution of the conflict of claims between the greater and lesser cantons."[2]

Switzerland's most original contribution to governmental organization was a new kind of executive, a collegial federal council. This was a seven-member body, appointed by the federal assembly for three-year terms, with the qualification that no more than one person might be selected from the same canton. In addition, the federal assembly was to designate the president (also to be president of the confederacy) and vice-president of the federal council who would serve for one year and be ineligible for a successive term.

Although chosen by the federal assembly, the federal council was not (and is not) responsible for its decisions to the legislative body. It has proved to be a stable body, impervious to changing parliamentary majorities. During the 140 years of its history, there are virtually no cases in which an ex-president who sought another term on the federal council was not selected. No other nation has ever modeled its executive on the Swiss pattern, but it continues to be studied as a model constitutional arrangement for power sharing.

Like the Frankfurt Constitution (and to a lesser extent the other 1848 constitutions), the Swiss Constitution incorporated provisions on human rights that were known at that time in the United States only. Unlike the other 1848 constitutions, which either never went into effect or were short-lived, these provisions have remained in effect for nearly a century and a half. The free exercise of religious worship is guaranteed although only to "the acknowledged Christian professions." Freedom of the press is also guaranteed as is the right to form associations and the right of petition. Of particular interest in that monarchial age was Article LIV: "No sentence inflicting capital punishment for political offences is permitted to be passed."

Also unique in the Swiss Constitution of 1848 are the many provisions dealing with the military. "Every Swiss is subject to military duty" (Article XVIII) and yet "the Confederacy has no right to maintain Standing Armies" (Article XIII). A complicated system was devised to create a federal army composed "of the contingents of the Cantons"—three men for every hundred in its population, with a reserve of half that number (Article XIX). In the event of threatened danger from abroad, another canton, or civil disturbances, procedures were developed for notifying the federal council, which would then call on the other cantons for assistance. According to Article XV, "the notified Cantons are bound to render aid." The system is such that some Constitutionalists have classified Switzerland as a "military democracy."

THOMAS FLEINER
Professor
Institut du Fédéralisme
Université de Fribourg
Fribourg, Switzerland

NOTES

1. C. F. Strong, *A History of Modern Political Constitutions* (New York: Capricorn Books, 1963), 114.
2. Ramesh Chandra Ghosh, *The Government of the Swiss Republic* (Calcutta: The World Press, 1953), 149.

THE FEDERAL CONSTITUTION OF THE SWISS CONFEDERATION

September 12, 1848
IN THE NAME OF ALMIGHTY GOD!
The Swiss Confederation,

Desirous of confirming the Alliance of the Confederates, of maintaining and consolidating the unity, power, and honor of the Swiss nation, has adopted the following Federal Constitution:

Article I

The people of the twenty-two sovereign Cantons of Switzerland, united by the present alliance, to wit: Zurich, Bern, Lucerne, Uri, Schwyz, Unterwalden, (Upper and Lower) Glarus, Zug, Freyburg, Soleiure, Basel, (City and Country) Schaffhausen, Appenzell, (both Rhodes) St. Gallen, Grisons, Argau, Thurgau, Tessin, Vaud, Valais, Neuchatel, Geneva, constitute collectively the Swiss Confederation.

Article II

The objects of the Confederacy are: to insure the independence of the country against foreign power; to maintain tranquillity and order in the interior; to protect the liberty and rights of the Confederates, and to promote the common welfare.

Article III

The Cantons are sovereign, so far as their sovereignty is not limited by the Federal Constitution, and accordingly they exercise all rights which are not delegated to the Federal Power.

Article IV

All Swiss are equal in the eye of the law. Among the Swiss there are no subjects, no local privileges or privileges of birth, whether of persons or of families.

Article V

The Confederacy guarantees to the Cantons their Territory, their Sovereignty, within the limits prescribed by Article III, their Constitutions, the liberty and rights of the people, the constitutional rights of the citizens, as well as the rights and powers which the people have conferred on the authorities.

Article VI

To this end the Cantons are bound to require of the Confederation the guarantee of their Constitutions.

This guarantee is granted, provided:

a. That these Constitutions contain nothing contrary to the provisions of the Federal Constitution.

b. That they secure the exercise of political rights according to Republican forms—representative or democratic.

c. That they have been accepted by the people, and that they can be revised whenever an absolute majority of the citizens demand it.

Article VII

All special alliances and treaties of a political character between Cantons are interdicted.

On the other hand, the Cantons have the right of concluding, among themselves, conventions for matters of legislation, administration, or justice; however, the Federal Authority must be informed of the same, which Authority, should these Conventions contain anything contrary to the Confederation or to the rights of the other Cantons, is authorized to prevent their being carried into execution. Where there is no such incompatibility, the contracting Cantons are granted the right to ask the cooperation of the Federal Authorities for their execution.

Article VIII

The Confederacy has the sole right of declaring War, and of concluding Peace, as well as of forming Alliances with Foreign Countries, and of making Treaties with them, especially such as relate to custom-house duties and to commerce.

Article IX

The Cantons, however, reserve the right of concluding, with Foreign Countries, treaties on matters of public economy, neighborly intercourse, and police; nevertheless these treaties must contain nothing contrary to the Articles of Confederation, nor to the rights of other Cantons.

Article X

Official communications between the Cantons and Foreign Governments or their Representatives, are made through the instrumentality of the Federal Council.

Concerning the matters mentioned in the preceding Article IX, the Cantons can, however, have direct communication with the subordinate Authorities and Functionaries of a Foreign State.

Article XI

Military contracts (capitulations) are not allowed to be concluded.

Article XII

The members of the Federal Authorities, Civil and Military Functionaries of the Confederacy, and the Federal Representatives or Commissioners, are not permitted to receive from Foreign Governments pensions, salaries, titles, presents, or decorations.

If they are already in possession of pensions, titles, or decorations, they must relinquish the enjoyment of their pensions, the bearing of their titles, and the wearing of their decorations, during the continuance of their functions.

Subordinate functionaries and employees may, however, be permitted by the Federal Council to continue in receipt of their pensions.

Article XIII

The Confederacy has no right to maintain Standing Armies.

Without consent of the Federal Authorities, no Canton, or, in divided Cantons, no part thereof, is allowed to have more than three hundred regular soldiers, exclusive of the police (gendarmerie).

Article XIV

The Cantons are bound, when contentions arise among them, to abstain from arming themselves or employing individual force; and they shall submit themselves to the Federal decision.

Article XV

Should a Canton be suddenly threatened with danger from abroad, the government of said Canton is bound to notify other Cantons that their assistance is required; at the same time giving the Federal Authorities notice thereof, and submitting itself entirely to their further orders. The notified Cantons are bound to render aid. The expenses are borne by the Confederacy.

Article XVI

If civil disturbances take place, or if one Canton is threatened with danger from another, the government of the threatened Canton is immediately to apprize the Federal Council thereof, in order that the latter, within the limits of their instructions (Article XC, Nos. 3, 10, and 11), may adopt the requisite measures, or convene the Federal Assembly. In pressing cases, the government in question is privileged, when notifying the Federal Council, also to inform other Cantons, that their assistance is required, and such as are called upon are in duty bound to render aid.

If it is out of the power of the Cantonal Government to apply for assistance, then may, and if the safety of Switzerland be placed in jeopardy, then shall, the properly constituted Federal Authorities interpose of their own accord. In case of intervention, the Federal Authorities will see to the observance of instructions contained in Article V.

The expenses are borne by the Canton for assistance or causing the Federal intervention, unless, owing to peculiar circumstances, the Federal Assembly determine otherwise.

Article XVII

In cases designated by Articles XV and XVI, every Canton is bound to allow free passage to the troops. These are forthwith to be placed under Federal command.

Article XVIII

Every Swiss is subject to military duty.

Article XIX

The Federal Army, which is composed of the contingents of the Cantons, consists:

(a) Of the Elite, to which each Canton is to contribute three men in every hundred of its Swiss population.

(b) Of the Reserve, which consists of half the number of the Elite.

In times of danger the Confederacy has also the disposition of the Second Reserve, which consists of all the remaining military forces of the Cantons.

The census, which, according to the designated rate, determines the contingent of each Canton, is to be subjected to a revision every twenty years.

Article XX

In order to secure in the Federal Army the requisite uniformity and fitness for service, the following principles are established:

1. A Federal statute determines the general organization of the Army.

2. The Confederacy assumes:

   a. The instruction of the Engineer Corps, of the Artillery and Cavalry; the delivery of horses, however, being left optional with the Cantons which are to furnish these branches of the service.

   b. The education of instructors for the remaining military branches.

   c. The erection of Institutes and the gathering of troops for instruction in all the higher branches of military service.

   d. The furnishing of part of the materials of war.

The centralization of the military education can, if needed, be further developed by Federal Legislation.

3. The Confederacy exercises surveillance over the military instruction of the Infantry and Rifle Corps, and likewise over the purchase, construction, and maintenance of the Ordnance which the Cantons are to furnish to the Federal Army.

4. The military regulations of the Cantons are not allowed to contain anything contrary to the Federal military organization, nor to the Federal

obligations incumbent upon them, and must therefore be laid before the Federal Council for approval.

5. All military divisions in service of the Confederacy, bear exclusively the Federal Standard.

Article XXI

The Confederacy is empowered, when conducive to the interests of the Swiss people, or a considerable part of them, to erect or assist the erection of public works at the expense of the Confederation.

To this end, in condemning private property, it must award a just indemnity. The more definite provisions relating to this subject are entrusted to Federal Legislation.

The Federal Assembly can prohibit the erection of public works which would be detrimental to the military interests of the Confederation.

Article XXII

The Confederacy is empowered to erect a University and a Polytechnic School.

Article XIII

The Customs and all relating thereto are affairs of the Confederacy.

Article XXIV

To the Confederacy is delegated the right to abolish, wholly or in part, all land and water customs, road and bridge tolls, obligatory mercantile and other similar imposts, granted or recognized by the Diet, be they levied by Cantons, Communes, Corporations or private individuals, after justly indemnifying the recipients. Those customs and tolls which burden the transit, are, at all events, to be redeemed throughout the whole circuit of the Confederation.

The Confederacy has the right to levy, on the frontiers of Switzerland, import, export, and transit duties.

It is empowered, after proper indemnification, to take possession, either as property of its own or under lease, of certain buildings on the frontiers of Switzerland at present in use for the business appertaining to customs.

Article XXV

When levying duties, the following principles are to be taken into consideration:

1. Import duties:
    a. Materials used in domestic manufacture are to be taxed as lightly as possible in the tariff schedule.
    b. Also such articles as constitute the necessities of life.

c. Articles of luxury are subject to the highest rates of tariff.

2. Transit, and in general also export duties, are to be made as moderate as possible.

3. The custom laws will make more definite provisions for the security of frontier and commercial intercourse.

The Confederacy is, nevertheless, always empowered, in extraordinary circumstances, to deviate from the preceding rules, and adopt special temporary measures.

Article XXVI

The revenue of the import, export, and transit customs are to be appropriated as follows:

a. Every Canton receives four batz per head, according to the ratio of the entire population as taken in the census of 1838.
b. Should a Canton thus not be sufficiently reimbursed for the abolished imposts mentioned in Article XXIV, it will then be further entitled to draw according to the nett average receipts of the five years, 1842 to 1846 inclusive, such an amount as will be necessary to indemnify it for those revenues.
c. The surplus receipts go into the Treasury of the Confederacy.

Article XXVII

If customs, road and bridge tolls have been granted for the redemption of capital employed in building, or for a part thereof, the receipt or indemnification for such ceases, as soon as the capital or part in question, including interest, is obtained.

Article XXVIII

Such dispositions as relate to transit duties which may have been already determined upon in railroad contracts are to remain uimpaired. On the other hand, the Confederacy assumes those rights relative to contracts concerning transit duties, which heretofore had been reserved to the Cantons.

Article XXIX

Freedom to buy and sell, free import, export, and transit from one Canton to another, is guaranteed to the necessaries of life, to cattle and merchandise, to products of the soil, and of mechanic arts of every description.

Exceptions are:

a. The Federal statute concerning the selling and purchasing of salt and gunpowder.
b. The police ordinances of the Cantons in regard to the exercise of mercantile pursuits, trades, and the use of roads.

    c. Regulations against forestalling.

    d. Temporary sanitary police enactments during epidemics.

The regulations contained in letters b and c must apply alike to the Cantonal citizens and the Swiss citizens of other Cantons. They are to be laid before the Federal Council for inspection and are not allowed to take effect without previously having received its approval.

    e. Those duties which were granted or recognized by the Diet, and not revoked by the Confederacy. (Articles XXIV and XXXI.)

    f. Duties on the consumption of wine and other spiritous liquors, according to instructions of Article XXXII.

Article XXX

It is reserved for Federal legislation, so far as deemed conducive to the interests of the Confederation, to adopt the requisite measures in regard to the abolishing of existing privileges on transportation of individuals and goods of every description, on water or land, between Cantons or in their interior.

Article XXXI

The collection of duties, denoted in Article XXIX, letter e, is supervised by the Federal Council. They are not allowed to be increased; and the collection thereof, if limited to a certain time, cannot be continued without the concurrence of the Federal Assembly.

The Cantons are on no account permitted to introduce new duties, road and bridge tolls. The Federal Assembly, however, can grant, for a limited period, the imposing of duties, in order thus to assist the erection of public works embraced in the intent of Article XXI, as being of general interest to commerce, and which, without said grant, could not be accomplished.

Article XXXII

The Cantons are invested with the right to impose taxes on the consumption of wine and other spiritous liquors, exclusive of the privileges reserved in Article XXIX, letter e, under the following restrictions, however:

    a. When levying the same, the transit thereof shall in no way be burdened, and the traffic in general shall be checked as little as possible, and not subjected to any other duties.

    b. Should articles, which are imported into a Canton for consumption, be again exported, the duties paid thereon are to be refunded, without any additional exactions.

    c. The native products of Switzerland are to be taxed less than those of Foreign Countries.

    d. Taxes on the consumption of wine and other spiritous liquors of Swiss production are not allowed, where they already exist, to be increased, and in Cantons where none at present are levied, are not permitted to be established.

e. The laws and regulations of the Cantons concerning the levying of taxes on the consumption of articles, are to be submitted for approval to the Federal Authorities, previous to their going into effect, in order that disregard for previously established principles may be avoided.

Article XXXIII

The Mail arrangements throughout the whole extent of the Swiss dominions are taken in charge by the Confederacy, under the following conditions:

1. The mail routes at present existing are not, on the whole, to be lessened, unless with the assent of the Cantons interested therein.

2. The rates of postage throughout the whole of Switzerland are to be fixed on as low and equitable a scale as possible.

3. To mail matter inviolable secrecy is guaranteed.

4. For the relinquishment of the mail revenue, the Confederacy indemnifies under the following conditions:

a. The Cantons receive annually the average amount of the net income which was yielded them by the mail service on their Cantonal territory in the years 1844, 1845, and 1846.

   Should, however, the net revenue which is yielded to the Confederacy by the mail service not be sufficient to cover these indemnities, then the above amount awarded to the Cantons will be diminished in proportion to the average receipts.

b. If a Canton as yet has received no direct revenue from the mail system, or, in consequence of a concluded letting to another Canton, has been in receipt of considerably less than the exercise of the mail service had evidently yielded on the territory of the Canton which had thus let the same, then circumstances of this kind are to receive due consideration when determining the amount of indemnification.

c. Where the exercise of the mail service has been ceded to private individuals, the Confederacy assumes their indeminification.

d. The Confederacy is empowered and obligated to make use of such materials as appertain to the mail service, so far as they are fit and requisite, granting in return therefore to the owners a fair compensation.

e. By indemnifying, the Federal Administration is entitled, either by purchase or lease, to occupy such buildings as are at present in use for mail purposes.

Article XXXIV

In conducting the custom and postal systems, the employees are to be principally selected from among the inhabitants of the Cantons in which their services are made use of.

Article XXXV

The Confederacy exercises supervision over the roads and bridges in whose preservation the Confederation is interested.

The sums mentioned in Articles XXVI and XXXIII as accruing to Cantons for duties and postal revenues, will be withheld by the Federal Authorities, should these roads and bridges not be kept in good repair by the Cantons, Corporations, or individuals having control of them.

Article XXXVI

The Confederacy exercises all prerogatives relative to coinage.

Coinage by the Cantons is discontinued, and is carried on solely by the Confederacy.

It is an affair of Federal Legislation to determine a standard of coinage, to rate the existing kinds of coin, and decide upon more particular designations according to which the Cantons are obligated to have melted or recoined such coin as they may already have issued.

Article XXXVII

The Confederacy will introduce, according to the basis of the existing Federal Concordat, uniform Weights and Measures for the whole Confederation.

Article XXXVIII

The manufacture and sale of gunpowder within the extent of the Confederation is the exclusive privilege of the Confederacy.

Article XXXIX

The expenses of the Confederacy are defrayed:
    a. Out of the interests accruing on the Federal War Funds.
    b. Out of the revenue obtained from Customs on the frontiers of Switzerland.
    c. Out of the revenue yielded by the mail service.
    d. Out of the revenue arising from the manufacture of gunpowder.
    e. Out of contributions from the Cantons, which, however, can only be levied in accordance with acts passed by the Federal Assembly.

Contributions of this kind are to be made by the Cantons according to a proportionate quota of their wealth, which quota is to be subjected every twenty years to a revision. Partly the population, partly the financial and industrial circumstances of a Canton, are to furnish the basis for such a revision.

Article XL

There shall be specie on hand in the Federal Treasury, at all times, double the amount of the contingent fund, in order to defray military expenses which may be occasioned by the Federal summons of troops.

Article XLI

The Confederacy guarantees to all Swiss belonging to one of the Christian professions, the right of free settlement within the whole extent of the Confederation, according to the following more definite stipulations:

1. No Swiss belonging to a Christian profession can be denied the right to settle in any one of the Cantons, provided he is in possession of the following vouchers:

   a. A certificate of nativity or its equivalent.
   b. A certificate of good moral conduct.
   c. A certificate that he enjoys the rights and honors of citizenship; and if on demand he can prove that, by means of possessed wealth, profession, or occupation, he is enabled to support himself and family.

   Naturalized citizens must also add a certificate, proving, that for at least five years they have been in possession of a Cantonal citizenship.

2. The settler is not allowed to be subjected, on part of the Canton granting him permission to settle, to any bonds or other special burdens in lieu of his settlement.

3. A Federal statute will determine the duration of grants to settle, and likewise, also the maximum of Chancery fees to be paid to the Canton in order to obtain the same.

4. The settler enjoys all the rights and privileges of a citizen of the Canton in which he has settled, with exception of the right to vote on Municipal affairs, and of being joint owner of the Commonwealth and Corporation property. In particular, free exercise of industrial pursuits, and the acquisition and sale of real estate, are secured to him in accordance with the laws and ordinances of the Canton, which, in all these respects, shall consider the settler as being on an equality with its own citizens.

5. Settlers of other Cantons cannot be subjected, on part of Municipalities, to greater Corporation taxes than settlers of their own Canton.

6. The settler can be ordered out of the Canton in which he has settled:

   a. By the penal sentence of a court.
   b. By order of the Police Authorities, on his having forfeited the rights and honors of citizenship, or been guilty of an improper

course of conduct, or through impoverishment having become a public burden, or having frequently been fined for transgressions of the police ordinances.

Article XLII

Every Cantonal citizen is likewise a citizen of Switzerland. As such he can exercise in Federal and Cantonal affairs the political rights of any Canton in which he has settled. He can, however, only [exercise] these privileges under the same restrictions as the citizens of the Canton, and, as regards Cantonal affairs, only after a residence of a certain time, the length of which is designated by Cantonal legislation, and which cannot exceed two years.

No one can exercise political rights in more than one Canton.

Article XLIII

No Canton can deprive a citizen of his rights of citizenship.

No Canton is permitted to grant citizenship to foreigners unless they have been released from their former State allegiance.

Article XLIV

The free exercise of religious worship is guaranteed to the acknowledged Christian professions throughout the whole extent of Switzerland.

To the Cantons, as well as the Confederacy, is reserved the right to adopt measures necessary for maintaining public order and peace among the different denominations.

Article XLV

The Freedom of the Press is guaranteed: In regard to abuse of the same, Cantonal legislation determines the requisite prescriptions, which, however, require the assent of the Federal Council.

The Confederacy is empowered to designate penalties for abuse of the press, when the same is directed against the Confederation and its Autonomies.

Article XLVI

Citizens have the right to form Associations, provided there is nothing illegal or treasonable contained in their proceedings and objects. Cantonal legislation determines the requisite regulations concerning the abuse of this privilege.

Article XLVII

The Right of Petition is guaranteed.

Article XLVIII

All Cantons are in duty bound to consider every citizen of Switzerland, professing Christianity, in an equality with their own citizens in legislative as well as judicial proceedings.

Article XLIX

Legally rendered judgments in Cantons on civil cases can be enforced throughout Switzerland.

Article L

The solvent Swiss debtor who possesses a permanent residence must, for personal claims, be summoned before the judge of the place where he resides, and on arrest is therefor allowed to be made for demands on the property of such a person out of the Canton of which he is a resident.

Article LI

The import and export prerogative (Abzugsrechte) in the interior of Switzerland, as also the pre-emption rights (Zugrechte) existing between citizens of one Canton and those of another, are absolished.

Article LII

Towards Foreign States which extend a like privilege, there exist on import and export prerogatives, (Freizuegigkeit).

Article LIII

No one is allowed to be debarred the benefit of his Constitutional Tribunal, and no privileged Courts of Justice are therefore permitted to be established.

Article LIV

No sentence inflicting capital punishment for political offences is permitted to be passed.

Article LV

A Federal Statute will determine stipulations between Cantons in regard to the extradition of any one accused. The extradition for political offences and misuse of the press cannot, however, be made obligatory.

Article LVI

To establish the citizenship of homeless persons (Heimathlosen) and to adopt measures for preventing the recurrence of similar cases, are affairs of Federal Legislation.

Article LVII

The Confederacy is empowered to expel from Swiss Territory foreigners who compromise, at home or abroad, the security of the Swiss people.

Article LVIII

The Order of Jesuits, and societies affiliated thereto, are not permitted to be domiciliated in any part of Switzerland.

Article LIX

The Federal Authorities are empowered to issue sanitary police regulations during epidemics threatening general danger.

CHAPTER SECOND: FEDERAL AUTHORITIES

I. FEDERAL ASSEMBLY

Article LX

The Supreme Power of the confederacy is exercised by the Federal Assembly, which is composed of two divisions:
A. Of the National Council.
B. Of the States Council.

A. NATIONAL COUNCIL

Article LXI

The National Council is composed of Delegates from the Swiss people. One member is elected to every 20,000 inhabitants of the gross population.
A fractional number of inhabitants exceeding 10,000 is rated as 20,000.
Every Canton, and, in divided Cantons, each part thereof is to elect at least one member.

Article LXII

The elections for the National Council are direct. They take place in Federal Election Districts, which, however, cannot embrace sections of different Cantons.

Article LXIII

Every Swiss is entitled to vote who is twenty years of age, and who, in other respects, according to the laws of the Canton wherein he resides, is not excluded from active citizenship.

Article LXIV

Every citizen of Switzerland belonging to the laity and possessing a vote, is eligible as a member of the National Council. Naturalized Swiss citizens must have possessed their acquired citizenship at least five years in order to be eligible.

Article LXV

The National Council is elected for the term of three years, and at stated times an entire renewal of Delegates takes place.

Article LXVI

Members of the States Council, of the Federal Council, and the functionaries elected by the latter, cannot at the same time be members of the National Council.

Article LXVII

The National Council elects from among its number, for every regular or extra session, a President and Vice President.

The member who, during a regular session, occupies the position of President, is ineligible either as President or Vice President for the following regular session. The same member cannot be Vice President at two successive regular sessions.

The President decides in case of ties. At elections he exercises the elective franchise the same as every other member.

Article LXVIII

The members of the National Council are indemnified out of the Federal Treasury.

B. STATES COUNCIL

Article LXIX

The States Council consists of forty-four Delegates from the Cantons. Each Canton elects two Delegates; in divided Cantons, each part, one.

Article LXX

Members of the National Council, and of the Federal Council, cannot at the same time be members of the States Council.

Article LXXI

The States Council elects from its midst, for every regular or extra session, a President and Vice President.

Neither President or Vice President can be elected for a succeeding

regular session from among the delegation of a Canton, one of whose
members served as President during the regular session immediately preceding.

Delegates of the same Canton cannot, during two successive regular
sessions, occupy the position of Vice President.

The President decides in case of ties. At elections he exercises the
elective franchise the same as every other member.

Article LXXII

The members of the States Council are indemnified by the Cantons.

C. DUTIES INCUMBENT UPON THE FEDERAL ASSEMBLY

Article LXXIII

The National Council and the States Council have the management
of all affairs, which, according to the contents of the present Constitution,
come within jurisdiction of the Confederacy, and are not assigned to other
Federal Authorities.

Article LXXIV

The subjects which the business department of the two Councils embrace, are, in particular, as follows:

1. Laws and Decrees to carry into effect the Federal Constitution,
especially Laws for the establishing of Election Districts, concerning the
manner of voting, in regard to the organization and business routine of
the Federal Authorities, and the formation of Juries.

2. Salaries and compensation of members of the Federal Authorities,
and Federal Secretarial Department, (Bundeskanzlei) creating permanent
civil offices and determining their emoluments.

3. Election of the Federal Council, of the Federal Tribunal, (Bundesgericht) of the Secretary, (Kantzler) of the General, of the Chief of the
Staff, and of the Federal Representatives.

4. Recognizing Foreign States and Governments.

5. Alliances and Treaties with Foreign Countries, as also the approv-
ing of Treaties concluded by Cantons with each other or with Foreign
Powers. Such Treaties of the Cantons, however, only come before the
Federal Assembly when the Federal Council or a Canton enters protest
against them.

6. Measures for security against foreign aggression, for maintaining
the independence and neutrality of Switzerland, declaring war, and concluding treaties of peace.

7. The guarantee of the Constitutions of the Cantons and of their
territory; intervention consequent upon the guarantee; measures for do-

mestic security, for the maintenance of tranquillity and order; amnesty and pardon.

8. Measures whose object is to secure a proper observance of the Federal Constitution, of the guarantee of the Cantonal Constitutions, the fulfilment of Confederate obligations, and the protection of rights guaranteed by the Confederacy.

9. Ordinances concerning the organization of the Confederate Military System, the instruction of troops, and the contributions of the Cantons; the disposal of the Federal Army.

10. Determining the Confederate quota according to which troops and funds are to be furnished; legal provisions regarding the administration and disposition of the Federal War Fund; levying direct contributions upon Cantons; Loans; Estimates and Accounts.

11. Laws and ordinances concerning Duties, Postal System, Coinage, Weights and Measures, manufacture and sale of Gunpowder, Arms, and Ammunition.

12. Erection of public works and institutions, and the consequent expropriations.

13. Legal provisions regarding the relation of settlers; regarding persons destitute of any citizenship, (Heimathlose) Foreign Police, and Sanitary Regulations.

14. Supreme supervision of the Federal Administration and Courts of Justice.

15. Complaints of Cantons or citizens against enactments of the Federal Council.

16. Disputes among Cantons in relation to States Rights.

17. Contentions in regard to legal power, as, particularly:
   a. Whether a subject is under the jurisdiction of Federal or Cantonal Sovereignty.
   b. Whether a question should properly go before the Federal Council or the Federal Tribunal.

18. Revision of the Federal Constitution.

Article LXXV

The two Councils assemble once a year in regular session, on a day to be determined upon in their rules.

They are convened for extra session by resolution of the Federal Council, or by request of one-fourth of the members of the National Council, or of five Cantons.

Article LXXVI

In order that their transactions may be valid, the presence of the absolute majority of members of the Council in question is required.

Article LXXVII

In the National and States Councils a majority of the votes cast decide.

Article LXXVIII

Federal Laws and Decrees require the concurrence of both Councils.

Article LXXIX

The members of both Councils vote without instructions.

Article LXXX

Each Council deliberates separately. At elections (Article LXXIV, No. 3), in the exercise of the pardoning power, and decisions in regard to legal authority, the two Councils, however, unite, under direction of the President of the National Council, for joint deliberation, so that the absolute majority of the vote cast by the members of both Councils effects a decision.

Article LXXXI

Each of the two Councils, and each member thereof, is privileged to offer propositions.

Cantons are at liberty to exercise the same privilege by correspondence.

Article LXXXII

The sessions of the two Councils are generally public.

II. FEDERAL COUNCIL

Article LXXXIII

The highest Executive and Directing Authority of the Confederation is the Federal Council, which is composed of seven members.

Article LXXXIV

The members of the Federal Council are appointed for the term of three years from among any citizens of Switzerland who are eligible as members of the National Council. Only one member, however, is allowed to be chosen from the same Canton. A total renewal of the Federal Council takes place after each total renewed of the National Council.

Such vacancies as may occur during the intervening time are filled for the remaining term of office by the Federal Assembly next in session.

Article LXXXV

Members of the Federal Council are not allowed to hold any other office, be it in the service of the Confederacy or of a Canton, or be in the pursuit of any other vocation or business.

Article LXXXVI

The President of the Confederation is the presiding officer of the Federal Council, who, as well as the Vice President, is elected from among that body, for the term of one year, by the Federal Assembly.

The retiring President is not eligible, either as President or Vice President, for the succeeding year. The same member cannot officiate for two successive years as Vice President.

Article LXXXVII

The President and remaining members of the Federal Council constitute a quorum for the transaction of business.

Article LXXXVIII

Not less than four members of the Federal Council constitute a quorum for the transaction of business.

Article LXXXIX

The members of the Federal Council may enter into consultation at transactions of either branch of the Federal Assembly, and also have the right to submit propositions in behalf of subjects under deliberation.

Article XC

According to the intent of the present Constitution, the following duties, in particular, are incumbent upon the Federal Council:

1. It directs the affairs of the Confederacy in accordance with the Federal Statutes and Decrees.

2. It sees to the proper observance of the Constitution, Federal Statutes and Decrees, as also of the provisions contained in Federal Concordats; it issues, of its own accord, or on rendered complaints, the requisite orders for their enforcement.

3. It exercises surveillance over the guarantee of the Cantonal Constitutions.

4. It suggests to the Federal Assembly Laws and Regulations, and pays due regard to the propositions which are communicated to it by the Councils of the Councils of the Confederacy or by Cantons.

5. It executes the Federal Laws and Decrees, the sentences of the Federal Tribunal (Bundesgericht), as also the compromise or arbitration decrees concerning disputes between Cantons.

6. It is to determine upon such provisions and appointments as are not delegated to the Federal Assembly or Federal Tribunal by the Constitution, or have not been by legislation entailed upon some other subordinate Authority.

7. It examines the treaties made by Cantons between themselves or with Foreign Powers, and approves of the same, provided they are admissible (Article LXXIV, No. 5).

. . . It makes the appointment for missions at home and abroad.

8. It protects the interests of the Confederacy abroad, particularly its international rights, and attends to its Foreign Affairs in general.

9. It provides for security against dangers threatened from abroad, and takes measures for asserting the independence and neutrality of Switzerland.

10. It provides for the security of the Confederation in the interior, and for the preservation of quiet and order.

11. In cases of emergency the Federal Council is empowered, when the National and States Councils are not in session, to call out the requisite number of troops, and make disposition of the same, with the proviso of an immediate convening of the Federal Assembly, should the call for troops exceed two thousand in number, or continue longer than three weeks.

12. It attends to the Confederate Military Affairs, and all branches of Administration connected therewith, which are within the province of the Confederacy.

13. It examines the Statutes and Ordinances of the Cantons which require its approval; has surveillance over those branches of Cantonal Administration which are placed by the Confederacy under its supervision, such as military affairs, duties, roads, and bridges.

14. It provides for the proper disposition of the Finances of the Confederacy, for a plan of computation, and the auditing of accounts concerning the receipts and expenses of the Confederacy.

15. It supervises the management of affairs by all officials and employees of the Federal Administration.

16. It renders an account of its transactions to the Federal Assembly at each of the latter's regular sessions, as likewise a report in regard to the condition of affairs of the Confederation at home and abroad, and will recommend to its notice such measures as it deems would conduce to the advancement of the general welfare.

It has also to render special reports, should the Federal Assembly, or a part thereof, make such request.

Article XCI

The business of the Federal Council is divided into Departments among the respective members. This division, however, has only in view to expedite the auditing and transaction of business. Each decision emanates from the Federal Council as authority.

Article XCII

The Federal Council and its Departments are empowered to call into requisition, for special business, the aid of individuals versed in affairs of the kind.

III. THE FEDERAL SECRETARYSHIP (BUNDESKANZLEI)

Article XCIII

A Federal Secretarial Department (Bundeskanzlei) which is presided over by a Secretary, (Kanzler) attends to the Secretarial business of the Federal Assembly, and to that of the Federal Council.

The Secretary is elected by the Federal Assembly for the term of three years, simultaneously with the Federal Council.

The Secretarial Department is under special supervision of the Federal Council.

The details of organization of the Secretarial Department remain subject to Federal legislation.

IV. THE FEDERAL TRIBUNAL (BUNDESGERICHT)

Article XCIV

In order to facilitate the Administration of Justice, so far as it lies within the jurisdiction of the Confederacy, a Federal Tribunal of Justice is established.

For trials of Penal cases, Juries are empanneled.

Article XCV

The Federal Tribunal consists of eleven members exclusive of deputies, whose number is fixed by Federal Legislation.

Article XCVI

The members of the Federal Tribunal and their deputies are appointed by the Federal Assembly. Their term of office is three years. After the total renewal of the National Council, also an entire renewal of the Federal Tribunal takes place.

Vacancies which may occur during the intervening time, are filled for the remaining term by the Federal Assembly at its next session.

Article XCVII

Any citizen of Switzerland who is eligible to the National Council, is eligible to the Federal Tribunal.

The members of the Federal Council and its appointees cannot simultaneously be members of the Federal Tribunal.

Article XCVIII

The President and Vice President of the Federal Tribunal are chosen from among the members thereof, by the Federal assembly, for the term of one year.

Article XCIX

The members of the Federal Tribunal are remunerated per diem from the Federal Treasury.

Article C

The Federal Tribunal appoints its own clerks.

Article CI

The Federal Tribunal decides on such civil cases:
1. As disputes which do not pertain to public law.
   a. Between Cantons themselves.
   b. Between the Confederacy and Canton.
2. As disputes between the Confederacy, on the one part, and corporations or individuals, on the other, when such corporations or individuals are plaintiffs, and the object in dispute is of considerable importance, which latter Federal legislation determines.
3. As contentions in regard to homeless persons (Heimathlose). Cases comprised in No. 1, letters a and b, are presented to the Federal Tribunal through the Federal Council. Should this Council pronounce an application to be beyond the jurisdiction of the Federal Tribunal, then the Federal Assembly decides thereon.

Article CII

It is obligatory upon the Federal Tribunal, also, to accept other cases for trial, when the same is appealed to by both parties, and the object in dispute is of considerable importance, which latter is determined by Federal legislation. In such cases, however, the costs accrue exclusively to the account of the parties.

Article CIII

The co-operation of the Federal Tribunal in trials of penal cases will be determined by Federal legislation, which fixes the details regarding the transfer of bills of indictment, and concerning the organization of the Courts of Assizes and Appeals (Kassationsgericht).

Article CIV

The Court of Assizes, having empaneled a jury which pronounces upon the matter in question, tries:

a. Cases where the appointed officials of a Federal Authority are bound over to be adjudged for some penal offence.
b. Cases of high treason against the Confederation; of rebellion and acts of violence against the Federal Authorities.
c. Cases of transgression against and breaches of international law.
d. Cases involving political offences and transgressions, which are causes or consequences of such disturbances as have necessitated an armed intervention of the Confederacy.

The Federal Assembly is empowered, in regard to such offences and transgressions, to grant amnesty or pardon.

Article CV

The Federal Tribunal, in addition, passes judgment upon the violation of rights guaranteed by the Federal Constitution, if complaints of this kind are referred to it by the Federal Assembly.

Article CVI

It remains optional with Federal legislation to place, exclusive of those cases denoted in Articles CI, CIV, and CV, also others within the jurisdiction of the Federal Tribunal.

Article CVII

Federal legislation will determine the details:

a. In regard to the establishing of an Attorney Generalship.
b. As to the crimes and transgressions which come under the jurisdiction of the Federal Tribunal, and in regard to the penalties which are inflicted.
c. Concerning the proceedings, which are to be verbal and public.
d. Regarding court charges.

V. MISCELLANEOUS PROVISIONS

Article CVIII

Everything relating to the seat of the Federal Government officials is a subject for Federal Legislation.

Article CIX

The three prevailing languages of Switzerland, the German, French, and Italian, are the national languages of the Confederacy.

Article CX

The officials of the Confederation are responsible for the faithful performance of their duties. A Federal Statute will define this accountability more particularly.

CHAPTER THIRD: REVISION OF THE FEDERAL CONSTITUTION

Article CXI

The Federal Constitution can at any time be revised.

Article CXII

The revision is performed according to the manner prescribed by Federal Legislation.

Article CXIII

If a portion of the Federal Assembly determines upon a revision, and the remainder do not acquiesce, or if fifty thousand Swiss citizens legally entitled to vote, demand a revision of the Federal Constitution, then, in either case, the question whether or not a revision shall take place, must be subjected to the vote of the Swiss People.

Should, in either of the above cases, the voting citizens of Switzerland express themselves in the affirmative, then both Councils are to be elected anew, in order to take in hand the revision.

Article CXIV

The revised Federal Constitution goes into effect when accepted by the majority of the voting Swiss citizens and by a majority of the Cantons.

TRANSITIONARY PROVISIONS

Article I

In regard to the acceptance of the present Federal Constitution, the Cantons are to express themselves according to the prescribed regulations of the Cantonal Constitutions, or, where such Constitutions contain provisions in regard thereto, in a manner to be determined upon by the Supreme Authority of the Canton in question.

Article 2

The results of the balloting are to be transmitted to the seat of government, in order to be placed in the hands of the Diet, which decides whether the new Constitution is adopted.

Article 3

If the Diet declares the Federal Constitution accepted, it immediately adopts the necessary measures for carrying it into effect.

The duties of the Federal War Council, and of the Council administrating the Confederate war funds, devolve upon the Federal Council.

Article 4

The provisions contained in the Preamble and letter c of Article VI of the present Federal Constitution do not apply to Cantonal Constitutions already in force.

Such article of Cantonal Constitutions as conflict with the remaining provisions of the Federal Constitution are annulled from the day of the adoption of the latter.

Article 5

The collection of Swiss Frontier Duties continues until the new tariff of the future frontier duties is established.

Article 6

The Resolutions of the Diet and the Concordats continue in force, so far as they do not conflict with the Federal Constitution, until they are cancelled or altered.

On the other hand, those Concordats become void, whose contents have been decared a subject of Federal legislation, and that from the time the latter dates its existence.

Article 7

As soon as the Federal Assembly and the Federal Council are organized, the Federal Compact of the 7th of August, 1815, ceases to exist.

Japanese Constitution of 1889

Because Japan's current constitution, promulgated in 1947, was so influenced by American ideas, there exists the mistaken notion that Japan's constitutional predecessor was somehow "oriental" in character. On the contrary, that constitution was also influenced by the ideas of western constitutionalism. That predecessor and the only other Japanese constitution—the famous Meiji Constitution of 1889—was based on a study of then-existing world constitutions. One of its leading draftsman, Ito Hirobumi, led a mission to Europe where they studied the constitutions of Prussia and France's Third Republic, attended lectures in Vienna, and journeyed to London to hear Herbert Spencer lecture on the theory of representative government. Yet another mission was to visit in the United States.

Even though the Meiji Constitution continued the dominance of the emperor and created a new nobility, this charter was an important step in the westernization of Japan. The monarchy under Emperor Meiji was a modernizing force, unlike the reactionary influence of European monarchies. The Japanese monarchy had replaced the feudalism of the Tokugawa Shogunate, in the coup d'etat of 3 January 1868.

From 1868 until 1881 when the final decision was reached to promulgate a constitution, Japan was ruled by a series of oligarchs who ruled in the name of the emperor. There was factional fighting among them, and the decision to have a constitution had been thwarted and delayed by those who feared the growth of popular government. Finally, in October 1881, the emperor promised the people a constitution and a parliament.

The eight-year hiatus in promulgating the constitution was based partly on the delaying tactics of the oligarchs, as they sought to dominate the constitution-making process to limit power sharing. No prior experience in constitutionalism and time required to study the constitutional systems already in existence also contributed to delays in declaring the Japanese Constitution.

Before the actual writing of the constitution, Ito sought three administrative measures to facilitate the shift to constitutional government. The first was the creation of a 500-member new nobility, based on the German system. The nobility established an elite from which members would be drawn for an upper house that would be called a House of Peers. This measure would not only be a check on the popularly elected lower house but also would serve to institutionalize the support of former feudal families. The second reform was the establishment of a modern cabinet system, which was similar to the traditional Japanese practice of having a group of ministers in attendance to advise the emperor. The third reform was the formation in 1885 of a civil service system to replace the old "spoils" system.

Drafting the constitution under Ito (and with negligible popular consultations) began in 1886, and, after two years of deliberations, it was ready for ratification. Such ratification became the task of a privy council established by imperial ordinance on 28 April 1888; approval came in January 1889. On 11 February 1889, the anniversary of the accession of Emperor Jimmu in the twenty-third year of Meiji, the emperor "granted" the constitution to the people of Japan.

Under the Meiji Constitution, the supreme political power rested in the emperor by virtue of his divine descent, which, as stated in the Preamble, was "unbroken for ages eternal." According to Article 73, the emperor alone had the power to initiate constitutional change. He was also protected by his own House budget which was not subject to the control of the Imperial Diet (parliament). However, the emperor did not have absolute power; his authority was specifically detailed in Articles 11 to 16, giving him the basic powers usually accorded a strong executive.

The limit on the emperor's absolute powers (and the principal provision promising popular sovereignty) was described in Article 5. This article stated that, "The Emperor exercises the legislative power with the consent of the Imperial Diet." However, Article 6 gave the emperor an effective veto over all laws passed by the Imperial Diet. Further, although the constitution invested all these powers in the emperor, his ministers conducted the administration of government in his name. The privy council, which had been created in 1888 to ratify the constitution, was continued to "deliberate upon important matters of state, when they have been consulted by the Emperor" (Article 56).

Chapter II of the Constitution, enumerating the "Rights and Duties of Subjects," contained many of the freedoms generally found in Western constitutions. These included freedom of speech, press, assembly, and religion; elements of due process of law; and so forth. However, such rights could only be exercised within the limits of the law. And at least one expert has expressed the view that Japanese citizens never enjoyed an unimpeded freedom to challenge or criticize the government.[1]

The Meiji Constitution was the oligarch's ultimate solution to the general problem of government that faced Japan after the collapse of the Tokugawa feudal system. In this broad context, the Meiji Constitution was a political highpoint in the destruction of feudalism and the rise of capitalism as well as in the emergence of a fervent nationalism during the nineteenth century. In a narrower political sense, the Meiji Constitution was basically a compromise embodying a feudal-based authoritarian political philosophy and the democratic movement's demand for representative government. Thus, in the final analysis, through their dominant position in the government, cabinet, military, and Privy Council, the oligarchs sought to maintain their power in modern political forms sanctioned by a written constitution and buttressed by a renewed emphasis upon Shinto and Emperor worship.[2]

Nevertheless, the Meiji Constitution stands as the major attempt to incorporate Western constitutional ideas into a non-Western context.

KENNETH R. RUSH
School of Law
Rutgers University
Camden, New Jersey

NOTES

1. Dan F. Henderson, *The Constitution of Japan* (Seattle: University of Washington Press, 1968), 7.
2. George M. Beckman, *The Making of the Meiji Constitution* (Lawrence, Kansas: University of Kansas Press, 1957), 95.

CONSTITUTION OF THE EMPIRE OF JAPAN, 1889 [MEIJI CONSTITUTION]*

Promulgated on February 11, 1889; Put into effect on November 29, 1890 (based upon the 4th paragraph of the Edict); Superseded by the Constitution of Japan on May 3, 1947.

IMPERIAL OATH SWORN IN THE SANCTUARY IN THE IMPERIAL PALACE (TSUGE-BUMI)

We, the Successor to the properous Throne of Our Predecessors, do humbly and solemnly swear to the Imperial Founder of Our House and to Our other Imperial Ancestors that, in pursuance of a great policy co-extensive with the Heavens and with the Earth, We shall maintain and secure from decline the ancient form of government.

In consideration of the progressive tendency of the course of human affairs and in parallel with the advance of civilization, We deem it expedient, in order to give clearness and distinctness to the instructions bequeathed by the Imperial Founder of Our House and by Our other Imperial Ancestors, to establish fundamental laws formulated into express provisions of law, so that, on the one hand, Our Imperial posterity may possess an express guide for the course they are to follow and that, on the other, Our subjects shall thereby be enabled to enjoy a wider range of action in giving Us their support, and that the observance of Our laws shall continue to the remotest ages of time. We will thereby to give greater firmness to the stability of Our country and to promote the welfare of all the people within the boundaries of Our dominions; and We now establish the Imperial House Law and the Constitution. These Laws come to only an exposition of grand precepts for the conduct of the government, bequeathed by the Imperial Founder of Our House and by Our other Imperial Ancestors. That we have been so fortunate in Our reign, in keeping with the tendency of the times, as to accomplish this work, We owe to the glorious Spirits of the Imperial Founder of Our House and of Our other Imperial Ancestors.

We now reverently make Our prayers to Them and to Our Illustrious Father, and implore the help of Their Sacred Spirits, and make to Them

* H. Quigley and J. Turner, *The New Japan: Government and Politics.* Minneapolis: University of Minnesota Press, 1956.

solemn oath never at this time nor in the future to fail to be an example to Our subjects in the observance of the Laws hereby established.

May the heavenly Spirits witness this Our solemn Oath.

IMPERIAL RESCRIPT OF THE PROMULGATION OF THE CONSTITUTION

Whereas We make it the joy and glory of Our heart to behold the prosperity of Our country and the welfare of Our subjects, We do hereby, in virtue of the supreme power We inherit from Our Imperial Ancestors, promulgate the present immutable fundamental law, for the sake of Our present subjects and their descendants.

The Imperial Founder of Our House and Our other Imperial Ancestors, by the help and support of the forefathers of Our subjects, laid the foundation of Our Empire upon a basis, which is to last forever. That this brilliant achievement embellishes the annals of Our country, is due to the glorious virtues of Our Sacred Imperial Ancestors, and to the loyalty and bravery of Our subjects, their love of their country and their public spirit. Considering that Our subjects are the descendants of the loyal and good subjects of Our Imperial Ancestors, We doubt not but that Our subjects will be guided by Our views, and will sympathize with all Our endeavours, and that, harmoniously cooperating together, they will share with Us Our hope of making manifest the glory of Our country, both at home and abroad, and of securing forever the stability of the work bequeathed to Us by Our Imperial Ancestors.

PREAMBLE [OR EDICT] (JOYU)

Having, by virtue of the glories of Our Ancestors, ascended the Throne of a lineal succession unbroken for ages eternal; desiring to promote the welfare of, and to give development to the moral and intellectual faculties of Our beloved subjects, the very same that have been favoured with the benevolent care and affectionate vigilance of Our Ancestors; and hoping to maintain the prosperity of the State, in concert with Our people and with their support, We hereby promulgate, in pursuance of Our Imperial Rescript of the 12th day of the 10th month of the 14th year of Meiji, a fundamental law of the State, to exhibit the principles, by which We are guided in Our conduct, and to point out to what Our descendants and Our subjects and their descendants are forever to conform.

The right of sovereignty of the State, We have inherited from Our Ancestors, and We shall bequeath them to Our descendants. Neither We nor they shall in the future fail to wield them, in accordance with the provisions of the Constitution hereby granted.

We now declare to respect and protect the security of the rights and of the property of Our people, and to secure to them the complete enjoyment of the same, within the extent of the provisions of the present Constitution and of the law.

The Imperial Diet shall first be convoked for the 23rd year of the Meiji and the time of its opening shall be the date, when the present Constitution comes into force.

When in the future it may become necessary to amend any of the provisions of the present Constitution, We or Our successors shall assume the initiative right, and submit a project for the same to the Imperial Diet. The Imperial Diet shall pass its vote upon it, according to the conditions imposed by the present Constitution, and in no otherwise shall Our descendants or Our subjects be permitted to attempt any alteration thereof.

Our Ministers of State, on Our behalf, shall be held responsible for the carrying out of the present Constitution, and Our present and future subjects shall forever assume the duty of allegiance to the present Constitution.

CHAPTER I. THE EMPEROR

Article 1. The Empire of Japan shall be reigned over and governed by a line of Emperors unbroken for ages eternal.

Article 2. The Imperial Throne shall be succeeded to by Imperial male descendants, according to the provisions of the Imperial House Law.

Article 3. The Emperor is sacred and inviolable.

Article 4. The Emperor is head of the Empire, combining in Himself the rights of sovereignty, and exercises them, according to the provisions of the present Constitutions.

Article 5. The Emperor exercises the legislative power with the consent of the Imperial Diet.

Article 6. The Emperor gives sanction to laws, and orders them to be promulgated and executed.

Article 7. The Emperor convokes the Imperial Diet, opens, closes, and prorogues it, and dissolves the House of Representatives.

Article 8. The Emperor, in consequence of an urgent necessity to maintain public safety or to avert public calamities, issues, when the Imperial Diet is not sitting, Imperial Ordinances in the place of law.

(2) Such Imperial Ordinances are to be laid before the Imperial Diet at its next session, and when the Diet does not approve the said Ordinances, the Government shall declare them to be invalid for the future.

Article 9. The Emperor issues or causes to be issued, the Ordinances necessary for the carrying out of the laws, or for the maintenance of the public peace and order, and for the promotion of the welfare of the subjects. But no Ordinance shall in any way alter any of the existing laws.

Article 10. The Emperor determines the organization of the different branches of the administration, and salaries of all civil and military officers, and appoints and dismisses the same. Exceptions especially provided for in the present Constitution or in other laws, shall be in accordance with the respective provisions (bearing thereon).

Article 11. The Emperor has the supreme command of the Army and Navy.

Article 12. The Emperor determines the organization and peace standing of the Army and Navy.

Article 13. The Emperor declares war, makes peace, and concludes treaties.

Article 14. The Emperor declares a state of siege.

(2) The conditions and effects of a state of siege shall be determined by law.

Article 15. The Emperor confers titles of nobility, rank, orders and other marks of honor.

Article 16. The Emperor orders amnesty, pardon, commutation of punishments and rehabilitation.

Article 17. A Regency shall be instituted in conformity with the provisions of the Imperial House Law.

(2) The Regent shall exercise the powers appertaining to the Emperor in His name.

CHAPTER II. RIGHTS AND DUTIES OF SUBJECTS

Article 18. The conditions necessary for being a Japanese subject shall be determined by law.

Article 19. Japanese subjects may, according to qualifications determined in laws or ordinances, be appointed to civil or military or any other public offices equally.

Article 20. Japanese subjects are amenable to service in the Army or Navy, according to the provisions of law.

Article 21. Japanese subjects are amenable to the duty of paying taxes, according to the provisions of law.

Article 22. Japanese subjects shall have the liberty of abode and of changing the same within the limits of the law.

Article 23. No Japanese subject shall be arrested, detained, tried or punished, unless according to law.

Article 25. Except in the cases provided for in the law, the house of no Japanese subject shall be entered or searched without his consent.

Article 26. Except in the cases mentioned in the law, the secrecy of the letters of every Japanese subject shall remain inviolate.

Article 27. The right of property of every Japanese subject shall remain inviolate.

(2) Measures necessary to be taken for the public benefit shall be provided for by law.

Article 28. Japanese subjects shall, within limits not prejudicial to peace and order, and not antagonistic to their duties as subjects, enjoy freedom of religious beliefs.

Article 29. Japanese subjects shall, within the limits of law, enjoy the liberty of speech, writing, publication, public meetings and associations.

Article 30. Japanese subjects may present petitions, by observing the proper forms of respect, and by complying with the rules specially provided for the same.

Article 31. The provisions contained in the present Chapter shall not affect the exercises of the powers appertaining to the Emperor, in times of war or in cases of a national emergency.

Article 32. Each and every one of the provisions contained in the preceding Articles of the present Chapter, that are not in conflict with the laws or the rules and discipline of the Army and Navy, shall apply to the officers and men of the Army and of the Navy.

CHAPTER III. THE IMPERIAL DIET

Article 33. The Imperial Diet shall consist of two Houses, a House of Peers and a House of Representatives.

Article 34. The House of Peers shall, in accordance with the Ordinance concerning the House of Peers, be composed of the members of the Imperial Family, of the orders of nobility, and of those who have been nominated thereto by the Emperor.

Article 35. The House of Representatives shall be composed of Members elected by the people, according to the provisions of the Law of Election.

Article 36. No one can at one and the same time be a Member of both Houses.

Article 37. Every law requires the consent of the Imperial Diet.

Article 38. Both Houses shall vote upon projects of law submitted to it by the Government, and may respectively initiate projects of law.

Article 39. A Bill, which has been rejected by either the one or the other of the two Houses, shall not be brought in again during the same session.

Article 40. Both Houses can make representations to the Government, as to laws or upon any other subject. When, however, such representations are not accepted, they cannot be made a second time during the same session.

Article 41. The Imperial Diet shall be convoked every year.

Article 42. A session of the Imperial Diet shall last during three months. In case of necessity, the duration of a session may be prolonged by the Imperial Order.

Article 43. When urgent necessity arises, an extraordinary session may be convoked in addition to the ordinary one.

(2) The duration of an extraordinary session shall be determined by Imperial Order.

Article 44. The opening, closing, prolongation of session and prorogation of the Imperial Diet, shall be effected simultaneously for both Houses.

(2) In case the House of Representatives has been ordered to dissolve, the House of Peers shall at the same time be prorogued.

Article 45. When the House of Representatives has been ordered to dissolve, Members shall be caused by Imperial Order to be newly elected, and the new House shall be convoked within five months from the day of dissolution.

Article 46. No debate can be opened and no vote can be taken in either House of the Imperial Diet, unless not less than one-third of the whole number of Members thereof is present.

Article 47. Votes shall be taken in both Houses by absolute majority. In the case of a tie vote, the President shall have the casting vote.

Article 48. The deliberations of both Houses shall be held in public. The deliberations may, however, upon demand of the Government or by resolution of the House, be held in secret sitting.

Article 49. Both Houses of the Imperial Diet may respectively present addresses to the Emperor.

Article 50. Both Houses may receive petitions presented by subjects.

Article 51. Both Houses may enact, besides what is provided for in the present Constitution and in the Law of the Houses, rules necessary for the management of their internal affairs.

Article 52. No Member of either House shall be held responsible outside the respective Houses, for any opinion uttered or for any vote given in the House. When, however, a Member himself has given publicity to his opinions by public speech, by documents in print or in writing, or by any other similar means, he shall, in the matter, be amenable to the general law.

Article 53. The Members of both Houses shall, during the session, be free from arrest, unless with the consent of the House, except in cases of flagrant delicts, or of offenses connected with a state of internal commotion or with a foreign trouble.

Article 54. The Ministers of State and the Delegates of the Government may, at any time, take seats and speak in either House.

CHAPTER IV. THE MINISTERS OF STATE AND THE PRIVY COUNCIL

Article 55. The respective Ministers of State shall give their advice to the Emperor, and be responsible for it.

(2) All Laws, Imperial Ordinances, and Imperial Rescripts of whatever kind, that relate to the affairs of the State, require the countersignature of a Minister of State.

Article 56. The Privy Councillors shall, in accordance with the provisions for the organization of the Privy Council, deliberate upon important matters of State, when they have been consulted by the Emperor.

CHAPTER V. THE JUDICATURE

Article 57. The Judicature shall be exercised by the Courts of Law according to law, in the name of the Emperor.

(2) The organization of the Courts of Law shall be determined by law.

Article 58. The judges shall be appointed from among those who possess proper qualifications according to law.

(2) No judge shall be deprived of his position, unless by way of criminal sentence or disciplinary punishment.

(3) Rules for disciplinary punishment shall be determined by law.

Article 59. Trials and judgments of a Court shall be conducted publicly. When, however, there exists any fear, that such publicity may be prejudicial to peace and order, or to the maintenance of public morality, the public trial may be suspended by provisions of law or by the decision of the Court of Law.

Article 60. All matters, that fall within the competency of a special Court, shall be specially provided for by law.

Article 61. No suit at law, which relates to rights alleged to have been infringed by the illegal measures of the administrative authorities, and which shall come within the competency of the Court of Administrative Litigation specially established by law, shall be taken cognizance of by a Court of Law.

CHAPTER VI. FINANCE

Article 62. The imposition of a new tax or the modification of the rates (of an existing one) shall be determined by law.

(2) However, all such administrative fees or other revenue having the nature of compensation shall not fall within the category of the above clause.

(3) The raising of national loans and the contracting of other liabilities

to the charge of the National Treasury, except those that are provided in the Budget, shall require the consent of the Imperial Diet.

Article 63. The taxes levied at present shall, in so far as they are not remodelled by a new law, be collected according to the old system.

Article 64. The expenditure and revenue of the State require the consent of the Imperial Diet by means of an annual Budget.

(2) Any and all expenditures overpassing the appropriations set forth in the Titles and Paragraphs of the Budget, or that are not provided for in the Budget, shall subsequently require the approbation of the Imperial Diet.

Article 65. The Budget shall be first laid before the House of Representatives.

Article 66. The expenditures of the Imperial House shall be defrayed every year out of the National Treasury, according to the present fixed amount for the same, and shall not require the consent thereto of the Imperial Diet, except in case an increase thereof is found necessary.

Article 67. Those already fixed expenditures based by the Constitution upon the powers appertaining to the Emperor, and such expenditures as may have arisen by the effect of law, or that appertain to the legal obligations of the Government, shall be neither rejected nor reduced by the Imperial Diet, without the concurrence of the Government.

Article 68. In order to meet special requirements, the Government may ask the consent of the Imperial Diet to a certain amount as a Continuing Expenditure Fund, for a previously fixed number of years.

Article 69. In order to supply deficiencies, which are unavoidable, in the Budget, and to meet requirements unprovided for in the same, a Reserve Fund shall be provided in the Budget.

Article 70. When the Imperial Diet cannot be convoked, owing to the external or internal condition of the country, in case of urgent need for the maintenance of public safety, the Government may take all necessary financial measures, by means of an Imperial Ordinance.

(2) In the case mentioned in the preceding clause, the matter shall be submitted to the Imperial Diet at its next session, and its approbation shall be obtained thereto.

Article 71. When the Imperial Diet has not voted on the Budget, or when the Budget has not been brought into actual existence, the Government shall carry out the Budget of the preceding year.

Article 72. The final account of the expenditures and revenues of the State shall be verified and confirmed by the Board of Audit, and it shall be submitted by the Government to the Imperial Diet, together with the report of verification of the said Board.

(2) The organization and competency of the Board of Audit shall be determined by law separately.

CHAPTER VII. SUPPLEMENTARY RULES

Article 73. When it has become necessary in future to amend the provisions of the present Constitution, a project to the effect shall be submitted to the Imperial Diet by Imperial Order.

(2) In the above case, neither House can open the debate, unless not less than two-thirds of the whole number of Members are present, and no amendment can be passed, unless a majority of not less than two-thirds of the Members present is obtained.

Article 74. No modification of the Imperial House Law shall be required to be submitted to the deliberation of the Imperial Diet.

(2) No provision of the present Constitution can be modified by the Imperial House Law.

Article 75. No modification can be introduced into the Constitution, or into the Imperial House Law, during the time of a Regency.

Article 76. Existing legal enactments, such as laws, regulations, Ordinances, or by whatever names they may be called, shall, so far as they do not conflict with the present Constitution, continue in force.

(2) All existing contracts or orders, that entail obligations upon the Government, and that are connected with expenditure, shall come within the scope of Article 67.

Russian Constitution
of 1906

The Russian Constitution of 23 April 1906, the last constitution of the Russian Empire, was issued by a government in distress. Political and social discontent had grown in intensity following a series of economic crises. National unrest grew in the wake of the disastrous Russo-Japanese War. The Empire was collapsing, and its people were in misery.

By 1905, everyday life was dominated by a series of workers' demonstrations, strikes, mutinies, peasant insurrections, pogroms, and the murderous reactionary violence of armed bands, such as the Black Hundred. Disorder spread over great parts of Russia and then to Poland, Latvia, Georgia, and the Ukraine. Government suppression of the workers' societies culminated in Bloody Sunday, 22 January 1905, when several hundred demonstrators were killed or injured on the square in front of the Winter Palace in St. Petersburg, now Leningrad.

A revolutionary movement gathered momentum. Nationwide strikes began on 11 October, leading to a continuing wave of industrial unrest in the principal cities and to the formation in St. Petersburg of the first Soviet of Workers' Deputies. Political parties and various other groups called for a constituent assembly to write a new constitution. The reply of the czar was the Imperial Manifesto of 17 October; this delaying tactic eventually led to the promulgation of the monarchial constitution of 1906—a last-ditch stand of autocracy in the face of the peoples' demands.

The concept of constitutionalism, as first developed in the United

Prepared by Marc Szeftel, from *Studies Presented to the International Commission for the History of Representation and Parliamentary Institutions* (Brussels: Les Editions de la Librairie Encyclopedique, 1976).

States and soon thereafter featured in the governments of Western Europe, had been unknown in Russia. Political opposition to the czar used the idea of a constitution as a unifying symbol. Until 1906 the idea of a constitution had been taboo in autocratic circles; at this time, the czarist government attempted to preempt this concept as a method of thwarting the revolution. However, instead of promulgating a constitution in the American–West European pattern—which respected the sovereignty of the people and guaranteed certain basic human rights—this was the epitome of a constitution designed to preserve imperial power. Therefore, the word "constitution" was strictly avoided, and the document was entitled the "Code of Fundamental State Laws."

The most striking features of this Constitution are the sections dealing with the imperial family. Three-fifths of the document deals with the nature, rights, and privileges of the autocratic power as well as related issues. The underlying theme of this Constitution is the preservation of monarchical power and privilege. Chapter One is entitled "On the Nature of the Supreme Autocratic Power," and every article in this chapter refers to "Our Sovereign, the Emperor." Article 4 reads: "To the All-Russian Emperor belongs the Supreme Autocratic Power. To obey his power, not only through fear, but also for the sake of conscience, is commanded by God Himself."

The response to the demands of the people is found in Chapter Eight, bearing the title "On the Rights and Duties of Russian Subjects." However, the chapter is dominated by the prescribed "duties," and all of the "rights" are qualified by such phrases as "except in the cases determined by law."

Some of these constitutionally created conditional rights include freedom from search, seizure, and arbitrary detention as well as freedom of travel and occupation. But even the provision dealing with religious freedom is subject to contrary legislation. No such limitations are attached to the specified "duties," which include the obligation of military service and the payment of taxes.

The only real political concession of the czarist government was the creation of a new state Duma (parliament), which for the first time was based on national representation. This gesture at least gave the appearance of shared power in which a peoples' assembly might initiate legislation on their behalf. However, the imperial-controlled state council was a constitutionally retained organ of government that not only had similar legislative authority but also could veto the acts of the state duma. Because the czar retained veto power over the acts of both bodies, autocratic power essentially was preserved.

The Constitution of 1906 served as the framework of Russian government until its collapse in the first revolution of 1917 and the abdication of the czar. During the eleven years of its existence, there were four state Dumas as well as numerous political parties and factions. However, there was no unified opposition. The Socialist revolutionaries on the left fought with the Cadets and Octobrists on the right. Despite outcries from the opposition, the czar continued to dominate the government.

Whether the machinery of the Constitution of 1906 would have permitted evolution to a democratic government is still a matter of debate. Any efforts made in that direction ended with the revolution of October 1917, the installation of a Marxist-Leninist state, and the first Marxist-Leninist Constitution of 1918.

The nondemocratic similarities between the Constitutions of 1906 and 1918 are noteworthy in constitutional study. Although no one could claim that Lenin's Constitution was based on the czarist model, they shared the "family resemblance" of Russian political tradition. Both manifested distrust of the people, limited the scope of popular representation, connected all power to the central government, and sharply restricted the protection of human rights.

GER F. VAN DER TANG
Professor
Erasmus University
Rotterdam, The Netherlands

CONSTITUTION OF RUSSIA
CODE OF FUNDAMENTAL STATE LAWS
APRIL 23, 1906

FIRST DIVISION: THE FUNDAMENTAL STATE LAWS

Article 1. The Russian State is one and indivisible.

Article 2. The Grand Duchy of Finland, which constitutes an indivisible part of the Russian State, shall be governed in its domestic affairs by special institutions on the basis of a special legislation.

Article 3. The Russian language is the common language of the State and its use is obligatory in the Army, in the Navy, and in all State and public institutions. The use of the local languages and dialects in State and public institutions shall be determined by special laws.

Translated from official Russian government text by Ger F. van der Tang, Professor of Law, Erasmus University, Rotterdam, The Netherlands, for this volume.

CHAPTER ONE

On the Nature of the Supreme Autocratic Power

Article 4. To the All-Russian Emperor belongs the Supreme Autocratic Power. To obey his power, not only through fear, but also for the sake of conscience, is commanded by God Himself.

Article 5. The person of our Sovereign the Emperor is sacred and inviolable.

Article 6. The same Supreme Autocratic Power shall belong likewise to our Sovereign the Empress when the succession to the Throne, according to the order established for it, reaches a woman; her consort, however, shall not be considered as a Sovereign: he shall enjoy honors and prerogatives equal to those of the Emperors' consorts except the title.

Article 7. Our Sovereign the Emperor shall exercise the legislative power in conjunction with the State Council and the State Duma.

Article 8. To our Sovereign the Emperor shall belong the initiative in all matters of legislation. Solely upon his initiative may the Fundamental State Laws be subjected to a revision in the State Council and in the State Duma.

Article 9. Our Sovereign the Emperor shall sanction the laws and without his sanction no law may go into effect.

Article 10. The administrative power in all its extent shall belong to our Sovereign the Emperor within the boundaries of the whole Russian State. He shall exercise his power directly in matters of supreme administration; in matters of subordinate administration a limited amount of power may be entrusted by him, in accordance with the law, to competent organs and persons acting in his name and following his orders.

Article 11. Our Sovereign the Emperor, in the exercise of the supreme administrative power, shall issue, in conformity with the laws, ukases for the organization and setting in motion of various parts of the State administration, as well as orders necessary for the implementation of the laws.

Article 12. Our Sovereign the Emperor shall be the supreme leader of all external relations of the Russian State with foreign powers. He shall likewise determine the course of the international policy of the Russian State.

Article 13. Our Sovereign the Emperor shall declare war and conclude peace as well as treaties with foreign states.

Article 14. Our Sovereign the Emperor shall be the supreme chief of the Russian Army and Navy. To him shall belong the supreme command of all armed forces of the Russian State on land and sea. He shall determine the organization of the Army and the Navy and issue ukases and orders concerning distribution of the troops, their placing on a war footing, their training, the course of service to follow by the various ranks of the Army and the Navy, and, generally, everything bearing on the organization of the armed forces and the defence of the Russian State. Our Sovereign the Emperor shall likewise determine, by act of supreme administration, restrictions with regard to the right to reside and acquire real estate in localities constituting fortress zones and points of support for the Army and the Navy.

Article 15. Our Sovereign the Emperor shall declare localities to be in a state of war or in a state of emergency.

Article 16. To our Sovereign the Emperor shall belong the right to coin money and to determine its external pattern.

Article 17. Our Sovereign the Emperor shall appoint and discharge the President of the Council of Ministers, the Ministers, and the Chief Adminstrators of separate agencies as well as other officials, if for the latter no other mode of appointment and discharge has been established by law.

Article 18. Our Sovereign the Emperor, by act of supreme administration, shall determine with regard to those in service, the limitations imposed by the requirements of government service.

Article 19. Our Sovereign the Emperor shall grant titles, orders and other State distinctions, as well as rights of status. He shall likewise determine the conditions and the procedure for the granting of titles, orders and distinctions.

Article 20. Our Sovereign the Emperor shall directly issue ukases and orders, both with regard to the estates forming his personal property and with regard to those called the Sovereign's estates, which, while they always belong to the reigning Emperor, cannot be bequeathed, submitted to partition, or subjected to any other form of transfer. Neither the former nor the latter estates shall be subject to taxation and contributions.

Article 21. Our Sovereign the Emperor, as head of the Imperial House, shall make, according to the Organic Law of the Imperial Family, provisions with regard to the appanage estates. He shall likewise determine the organization of establishments and institutions within the province of the Minister of the Imperial Court, as well as the form of their administration.

Article 22. The judicial power shall be exercised on behalf of our Sovereign the Emperor by courts, established by law, whose judgments shall be carried out in the name of the Imperial Majesty.

Article 23. To our Sovereign the Emperor shall belong the pardon of convicts, the commutation of penalties, and general forgiveness of those who have committed criminal actions, with cessation of prosecution against them and freeing them from trial and punishment. To him also shall belong the remission, by way of the Monarch's mercy, of claims to be levied by the Treasury and, in general, the granting of favors in special cases which do not fall under the operation of general laws, provided that no legally protected interests or civil rights are infringed by it.

Article 24. Our Sovereign the Emperor's ukases and orders, issued by him either by act of supreme administration or directly, shall be countersigned by the President of the Council of Ministers or the competent Minister or by the Chief Administrator of a separate agency, and they shall be promulgated by the Ruling Senate.

CHAPTER TWO

On the Order of Succession to the Throne

Article 25. The Imperial All-Russian Throne shall be hereditary in the now happily reigning Imperial House.

Article 26. From the Imperial All-Russian Throne shall be inseparable the Thrones of the Kingdom of Poland and of the Grand Duchy of Finland.

Article 27. Both sexes shall have the right of succession to the Throne; but in preference this right shall belong to the male sex by order of primogeniture; however, should the last male branch die out, the succession to the Throne shall be transferred to the female line by right of substitution.

Article 28. Accordingly, the succession to the Throne shall belong, first of all, to the oldest son of the reigning Emperor, and after him to all his male progeny.

Article 29. After the extinction of this male line, the succession shall pass to the line of the Emperor's second son and to the latter's male progeny; and after extinction of the second male line, the succession shall pass to the line of the third son, and so forth.

Article 30. If the last male branch of the Emperor's sons dies out, the succession shall remain in the same line, but pass to the female branch of the last reigning Emperor, as being the nearest to the Throne, and within this branch it shall follow the same order, preference being given to a man over a woman, provided that the woman, from whom the right directly originated, never loses this right.

Article 31. After the extinction of this line, the succession shall pass to the line of the oldest son of the Emperor-Progenitor, in its female issue, in which the nearest kinswoman of the last reigning male belonging to his son's line succeeds to the Throne, following the oldest branch descending from him or from his son, or, if there are no descending branches, following a lateral branch. In the absence of such a kinswoman, the man or the woman who steps into her place shall succeed to the Throne, preference being given to the male sex over the female sex as stated above.

Article 32. After the extinction also of these lines, the succession shall pass to the female line of the remaining sons of the Emperor-Progenitor, following the same order, and afterwards to the line of the oldest daughter of the Emperor-Progenitor, in its male issue; and after the extinction of the latter, to its female issue, following the order fixed for the female branches of the Emperor's sons.

Article 33. After the extinction of the male and female branches of the oldest daughter of the Emperor-Progenitor, the succession shall pass to the male branch, and afterwards, to the female branch of the second daughter of the Emperor-Progenitor, and so forth.

Article 34. The younger sister, even if she had sons, does not take away the right to succession from the older sister, even if the latter were unmarried; but a younger brother succeeds to the Throne before his older sisters.

Article 35. If the succession reaches a female branch which already reigns on another Throne, it shall be left to the person who succeeds to the Throne to choose the faith and the Throne, and to abdicate jointly with the Heir-to-the-Throne the other faith and the other Throne, in case such a Throne is connected with another religious law; if there is no renunciation of faith, the person thereupon closest according to the order of succession shall succeed to the Throne.

Article 36. Children issuing from the conjugal union of a person of the Imperial Family with a person who does not have a corresponding rank, i.e., does not belong to any reigning or sovereign house, shall have no right of succession to the Throne.

Article 37. Under the operation of the rules on the order of the succession to the Throne stated above, freedom is left to a person having the right to the Throne to renounce this right, provided that no difficulty in the further succession to the Throne is created.

Article 38. Such a renunciation, when it is promulgated and transformed into law, shall thereafter be considered as irrevocable.

Article 39. The Emperor, or the Empress, succeeding to the Throne, at his, or her, accession to the latter and anointment, shall pledge themselves to a sacred observance of the above established laws on the succession to the Throne.

CHAPTER THREE

On our Sovereign the Emperor's Majority,
on Regency and Guardianship

Article 40. Majority of age is fixed at sixteen for the Sovereigns of both sexes and the Heir to the Imperial Throne.

Article 41. If the Emperor succeeds to the Throne before this age, regency and guardianship shall be established until his majority.

Article 42. The regency and the guardianship shall be either vested jointly in one person, or established separately, so that the regency is entrusted to one, the guardianship to another.

Article 43. The appointment of the Regent and the Guardian, either jointly in one person or separately in two persons, shall depend on the wish and discretion of the reigning Emperor, who, for better security, should make this selection in anticipation of his decease.

Article 44. If such an appointment were not made during the Emperor's life, then, after his decease, the regency of the State and the guardianship with regard to the new Emperor's person during his minority shall belong to his father or his mother; but stepfather and stepmother shall be excluded.

Article 45. When there is no father and no mother, the regency and the guardianship shall belong to the adult, of either sex, who is closest to the succession to the Throne among the kinsfolk of the underaged Emperor.

Article 46. Legal causes of incapacity to regency and guardianship shall be: 1) insanity, even if it is temporary; 2) second marriage contracted by a widower or a widow during the regency and the guardianship.

Article 47. The Regent of the State must have a Council of Regency, and just as a Regent cannot be without a Council, there shall be no Council without a Regent.

Article 48. The Council shall be composed of six persons of the two first ranks; they shall be selected by the Regent, who also shall appoint other persons should vacancies occur.

Article 49. Persons of the Imperial Family of the male sex may sit on this Council, if selected by the Regent, but not before their majority of age, and they shall not be included in the number of the six persons constituting the Council.

Article 50. All cases without exception, subject to the personal decision of the Emperor, shall be brought before the Council of Regency, as well as all cases submitted both to him and his Council. The Council, however, shall not be concerned with guardianship.

Article 51. The Regent shall have deciding vote.

Article 52. The appointment of the Council and the selection of its members shall take place only in the absence of a different decision by the deceased Emperor, for the latter should have best knowledge of circumstances and people.

CHAPTER FOUR

On the Accession to the Throne and on the Subjects' Oath

Article 53. After the Emperor's decease, his Heir shall ascend the Throne by the sole virtue of the law on the succession, which attributes this right to him. The Emperor's accession to the Throne shall be reckoned from the day of his predecessor's decease.

Article 54. In the manifesto on the accession to the Throne shall also be proclaimed the lawful Heir-to-the-Throne, if there exists a person to whom the succession belongs by law.

Article 55. An all-national oath shall be taken to confirm the subjects' fidelity to the Emperor who has ascended the Throne and to his lawful Heir, even if the latter was not named in the manifesto.

Article 56. Everyone shall take an oath according to his faith and religious law.

Note 1. The Ruling Senate, having printed the oath of fidelity according to the established form (Annex V), shall distribute it in a sufficient number of copies to all authorities generally, both military and civil; information shall also be sent to the Most Holy Synod for a smiliar arrangement on their part (a).—Everyone shall be sworn in by his superior in cathedrals, monasteries, or parish churches, as is convenient; while those under guard, but not yet sentenced to the loss of civil rights, shall be sworn in by the authorities of the places where they are kept (b).—Those of heterodox denominations, where there is no church of their confession, shall be sworn in in the administration hall, in the presence of the members of that administration (c).—Everyone who takes the oath of fidelity, if he is literate, shall sign the printed sheet according to which he swore. These sheets shall later be conveyed by all the authorities and administrations to the Ruling Senate.

Note 2. All subjects of the male sex in general, of whatever rank and calling, who have reached the age of twelve, shall be sworn in.

CHAPTER FIVE

On the Sacred Coronation and Anointment

Article 57. After the accession to the Throne, the sacred coronation and anointment shall be performed according to the ritual of the Orthodox Greek-Russian Church. The time for this solemn rite shall be appointed by the Emperor at his discretion and announced beforehand for all-national information.

Article 58. Following the Emperor's desire, his Most August wife shall be associated with him in this sacred celebration. But if the Emperor's coronation takes place before his marriage, his wife's coronation shall be performed afterwards only with the Emperor's special permission.

Note 1. The sacred rite of coronation and anointment shall be performed in the Moscow Cathedral of the Assumption, in the presence of the highest state authorities and estates summoned for this purpose by the Emperor (a).—The Coronation of All-Russian Emperors as Kings of Poland shall be included in the same sacred rite; deputies from the Kingdom of Poland shall be called to participate in this solemnity together with the deputies from the other parts of the Empire (b).

Note 2. The Emperor, before this sacred rite is performed, shall utter aloud for his faithful subjects the Creed of the Orthodox-Catholic faith according to the custom of Old Christian Sovereigns and his God-crowned ancestors; and afterwards, having donned the purple, placed upon his head the crown, and received the sceptre and the orb, he shall invoke on his knees the King of Kings in a prayer composed for the occasion, to wit: May God edify him, make him wise, and direct him in his great service as Tsar and Judge of the All-Russian Tsardom; may Wisdom seated on the Divine Throne be with him; may his heart be in God's hand in order that he may conduct everything for the benefit of the people entrusted to him to the glory of God, that on the day of God's judgment he may give answer to Him without shame.

CHAPTER SIX

On His Imperial Majesty's Title and the State Emblem

Article 59. The full title of the Imperial Majesty shall be as follows: "By God's propitiative grace, We, NN, Emperor and Autocrat of All-Russia, Moscow, Kiew, Vladimir, Novgorod; Tsar of Kazan, Tsar of Astrakhan, Tsar (King) of Poland, Tsar of Siberia, Tsar of Chersonesus Taurica, Tsar of Georgia; Sovereign of Pskov and Grand Prince of Smolensk, Lithuania, Volhynia, Podolia and Finland; Prince of Esthonia, Livonia, Courland and Semigalia, Samogitia, Belostok, Karelia, Tver, Iugra, Perm, Viatka, Bolgaria and others; Sovereign and Grand Prince of Novgorod of the Down land, Chernigov, Riazan, Polotsk, Rostov, Yaroslavl, Beloozero, Udora, Obdoria, Kondia, Vitebsk, Mstislavl and Lord of all the Northern Region; and Sovereign of the land of Iveria, Kartalinia, and Kabarda and of the Armenian territory; Hereditary Sovereign and Master of the Circassian and the Mountain Princes and others; Sovereign of Turkestan; Heir of Norway, Duke of Schleswig-Holstein, Stormarn, Dithmarschen and Oldenburg, etc., etc., etc."

Article 60. In certain cases defined by law this title of Imperial Majesty shall be expressed in abbreviation: "By God's propitiative grace, We, NN, Emperor and Autocrat of All Russia, Moscow, Kiev, Vladimir, Novgorod; Tsar of Kazan, Tsar of Astrahkan, Tsar (King) of Poland, Tsar of Siberia, Tsar of Chernosesus Taurica, Tsar of Georgia, Grand Prince (Duke) of Finland, etc., etc., etc." In other cases, also defined by law, the brief title of Imperial Majesty shall be used, of the following form: "By God's grace, We, NN, Emperor and Autocrat of All Russia, Tsar (King) of Poland, Grand Prince (Duke) of Finland, etc., etc., etc."

Article 61. The Russian State emblem is a black, two-headed eagle on a golden escutcheon, crowned with two Imperial crowns, above which there is a third identical crown, of a bigger shape, with two streaming ribbon-ends of the Order of the Apostle Saint Andrew the First-Called.

The State eagle holds golden scepter and orb. On the eagle's breast there is the emblem of Moscow; on a scarlet escutcheon, the great martyr Saint George the Victorious, on horseback, striking a dragon with a golden spear. On the great State seal, the escutcheon with the above described two-headed eagle is crowned with the helm of the Grand Prince Saint Alexander Nevsky and girded with the chain of the Order of the Apostle Saint Andrew the First-Called; on one side of the eagle is an image of the Archistrategus Saint Michael, and on the other one that of the Archangel Saint Gabriel. Above all this is placed a golden canopy studded with two-headed eagles and lined with ermine, with the inscription: "God is with us"; above the canopy the Imperial Crown and the State banner are displayed. Around the escutcheon are pictured the Family arms of His Imperial Majesty and the emblems of the Tsardoms of Kazan, Astrakhan, Poland, Siberia, Chersonesus Taurica and Georgia, and of the Grand Principalities of Kiev, Vladimir, Novgorod and Finland. Above the canopy, on six escutcheons, are the united emblems of all remaining principalities and territories mentioned in the full Imperial title (Art. 59). This full title of Imperial Majesty is placed on the borders of the seal. On the middle State seal are placed the same images as on the Great Seal, with the only exception of the State banner and the six upper escutcheons above the canopy with the united emblems of principalities and territories. On the borders is the Imperial title in abbreviated form (Art. 60, pt. 1). The small State seal is similar in general to the middle one, but there are no images of the Saint Archangels on it and no Family arms of His Imperial Majesty, while the emblems of the Tsardoms and the Grand Principalities which surround the main escutcheon are placed on the eagle's wings. On the borders of the seal is the Imperial title in brief form (Art. 60, pt. 2).

Note. A detailed description of the State emblem and the State seal in all its forms, and the rules on their use shall be stated in a special annex (Annex I).

CHAPTER SEVEN

On Faith

Article 62. Taking precedence and predominating in the Russian Empire shall be the Christian Orthodox Catholic Faith of the Eastern confession.

Article 63. The Emperor, who holds the All-Russian Throne, cannot profess any other faith than the Orthodox faith (Art. 62).

Article 64. The Emperor as a Christian Sovereign shall be the supreme defender and custodian of the dogmas of the predominating faith and the keeper of the true faith and pious discipline in the Holy Church. In this sense the Emperor is called Head of the Church in the Act on the succession to the Throne of April 5, 1797 (17910).

Article 65. In the administration of the Church the Autocratic Power shall act through the Most Holy Ruling Synod, established by this Power.

Article 66. All subjects of the Russian State not belonging to the predominating church, subjects by birth or admitted to be subjects, as well as foreigners who are in Russian service, or staying in Russia temporarily, shall enjoy everywhere the free exercise of their faith and may worship according to its rites.

Article 67. Freedom of religion is granted not only to Christians of foreign confessions, but also to Jews, Moslems and pagans: in order that all races residing in Russia praise God Almighty in different languages according to the religious law and confession of their forefathers, blessing the reign of Russian Monarchs, and beseeching the Creator of the Universe to augment the prosperity of the Empire and to fortify its strength.

Article 68. The ecclesiastical affairs of Christians of foreign confessions and of non-Christians in the Russian Empire shall be administered by their spiritual authorities and the special Government agencies instituted for this purpose by the Supreme Power.

Note. The rules on protection of religious tolerance and its limits shall appear in detail in the appropriate Statutes.

CHAPTER EIGHT

On the Rights and Duties of Russian Subjects

Article 69. The conditions for the acquisition of the rights of Russian citizenship, as well as for their loss, shall be determined by law.

Article 70. The defense of the Throne and of the Fatherland is the sacred duty of every Russian subject. The male population, without distinction of status, shall be liable to military service in accordance with the provisions of the law.

Article 71. Russian subjects are obliged to pay taxes and duties established by law, and to perform services in accordance with the provisions of the law.

Article 72. No one may be prosecuted for a criminal offence otherwise than in a manner determined by law.

Article 73. No one may be held under arrest, except in the cases determined by law.

Article 74. No one may be tried and punished except for criminal offences provided for by penal laws in force at the time they were committed, provided that newly issued laws do not exclude from the category of criminal offences those committed by the culprit.

Article 75. Everyone's domicile shall be inviolable. No search or seizure, without the master's consent, may be carried out in a domicile except in the cases and in the manner prescribed by law.

Article 76. Every Russian subject shall have the right to choose freely his place of residence and his occupation, to acquire and to transfer property and to travel without impediment beyond the limits of the State. Limitations of these rights shall be established by special laws.

Article 77. Property is inviolable. Compulsory expropriation of real estate, when such is necessary for any State or public benefit, is admissible only on the basis of a just and adequate compensation.

Article 78. Russian subjects shall have the right to hold meetings, peacefully and without arms, for purposes not contrary to the laws. The conditions under which meetings may be held, the manner of closing them, as well as restrictions concerning their place, shall be determined by law.

Article 79. Everyone may, within the limits established by law, express his thoughts orally and in writing, as well as disseminate them in print or by other means.

Article 80. Russian subjects shall have the right to form associations and unions for purposes not contrary to the laws. The conditions for forming associations and unions, their mode of functioning, the conditions and the mode of giving to them legal personality, as well as the manner of dissolving associations and unions, shall be determined by law.

Articles 81. Russian subjects shall enjoy freedom of religion. The conditions under which they may enjoy this freedom shall be determined by law.

Article 82. Foreigners sojourning in Russia shall enjoy the rights of Russian subjects within the limitations established by law.

Article 83. Exemptions from the operation of the provisions stated in this chapter with regard to localities declared to be in a state of war, or in a state of emergency, shall be determined by special laws.

CHAPTER NINE

On the Laws

Article 84. The Russian Empire shall be ruled on the firm basis of laws, which are enacted according to established procedure.

Article 85. The laws shall be equally binding upon all Russian subjects without exception, and upon foreigners sojourning in the Russian State.

Article 86. No new law may be passed without the approval of the State Council and the State Duma and come into force without the sanction of our Sovereign the Emperor.

Article 87. When the State Duma is in recess and extraordinary circumstances create the necessity of a measure requiring legislative deliberation, the Council of Ministers shall submit the matter directly to the Emperor. Such a measure, however, may not introduce changes either in the Fundamental State Laws or in the Organic Laws of the State Council or the State Duma or in the provisions on elections to the Council or to the Duma. Such a measure becomes inoperative if a legislative bill, corresponding to the adopted measure, is not introduced by the competent Minister or the Chief Administrator of a separate agency into the State Duma within the first two months after the resumption of the Duma's business, or if the State Duma or the State Council does not adopt the bill.

Article 88. Laws specially enacted for a certain locality or a part of the population shall not be abrogated by a new general law, unless in this law there is a specific provision for such abrogation.

Article 89. Every law shall have force only for the future, except in the cases when in the law itself there is a provision that its force also extends to the foregoing time, or that it is merely a confirmation and clarification of a former law.

Article 90. The general custody of the laws shall belong to the Ruling Senate. Therefore, all laws must be sent to the Ruling Senate in the original or in certified copies.

Article 91. The laws shall be promulgated for general information by the Ruling Senate according to established procedure, and they shall not be enforced before promulgation.

Article 92. Legislative provisions shall not be subject to promulgation if the procedure followed in enacting them does not correspond to the clauses of these Fundamental Laws.

Article 93. After promulgation, the law shall receive binding force from the date specified in the law itself. If, however, such a date should not be fixed—then from the day when the sheet of the Senate's publication in which the law is printed is received in a given locality. It may be stated in the law itself that before its promulgation it will be put into execution by telegraph or by couriers.

Article 94. A law may not be abrogated otherwise than by force of law. Therefore, as long as an existing law has not been expressly abrogated by a new law, the former shall keep its full force.

Article 95. No one may plead ignorance of the law when this law was promulgated in accordance with established procedure.

Article 96. Provisions concerning the service-in-the-rank, technical and economic agencies of the War and Navy Departments, as well as ordinances and instructions to the institutions and officials of these departments, shall be submitted directly to our Sovereign the Emperor, after consideration by the War Council or the Admiralty Council, to whichever they belong, provided these provisions, ordinances and instructions strictly concern the aforementioned institutions alone, do not touch upon matters of general laws and do not call for a new expenditure from the Treasury, or if the new expenditure called for by them is covered by expected savings on the budget of the Ministry of War or Ministry of the Navy, to which it belongs. In case, however, the new expenditure cannot be covered by the savings referred to, submission of the aforementioned provisions, ordinances, and instructions to the Emperor for confirmation is permitted only after the appropriation of a corresponding credit has been solicited in accordance with established procedure.

Article 97. Provisions concerning the tribunals of military and naval justice shall be enacted in accordance with the procedure established in codes of military and naval law.

CHAPTER TEN

On the State Council, the State Duma and the Mode of their Activity

Article 98. The State Council and the State Duma shall be summoned every year by ukases of our Sovereign the Emperor.

Article 99. The duration of the yearly business of the State Council and the State Duma, and the dates of their recess from business in the course of the year shall be determined by ukases of our Sovereign the Emperor.

Article 100. The State Council shall be composed of members appointed by the Emperor and of elective members. The total number of members called by the Supreme Power to sit in the (legislative) Council from among the members of the State Council appointed by the Emperor may not exceed the total number of elective members in that Council.

Article 101. The State Duma shall be composed of members elected by the people of the Russian Empire for five years in accordance with the principles indicated in the legal ordinances on the elections to the Duma.

Article 102. The State Council shall verify the credentials of its elective members. Likewise, the State Duma shall verify the credentials of its members.

Article 103. The same person may not be simultaneously a member of the State Council and a member of the State Duma.

Article 104. The elective membership of the State Council may be replaced by a new group of members before the expiration of the terms of their mandates. This shall be done by ukase of our Sovereign the Emperor, which also shall order new elections of the Council's members.

Article 105. The State Duma may be dissolved by ukase of our Sovereign the Emperor before the expiration of the five-year term of its members' mandates. The same ukase shall order new elections to the Duma, and fix the time of its convocation.

Article 106. The State Council and the State Duma shall enjoy equal rights in matters of legislation.

Article 107. The State Council and the State Duma shall have the right to initiate, in the manner determined by their Organic Laws, proposals concerning the abrogation or amendment of existing laws and the enactment of new laws, with the exception of the Fundamental State Laws, the initiative for the revision of which belongs to our Sovereign the Emperor solely.

Article 108. The State Council and the State Duma shall have the right to address, in the manner determined by their Organic Laws, interpellations to the Ministers and Chief Administrators of separate agencies, who are subordinated to the Ruling Senate in accordance with the law, in connection with apparently illegal actions committed on their part or on that of persons and institutions under their authority.

Article 109. Within the province of the State Council and the State Duma and subject to discussion by them in the manner determined by their Organic Laws shall be the matters indicated in the Organic Laws of the Council and the Duma.

Article 110. Legislative proposals shall be discussed in the State Duma and, after approval by it, shall be brought before the State Council. Legislative proposals, drafted on the initiative of the State Council, shall be discussed in the Council, and, after approval of it, shall be brought before the Duma.

Article 111. Legislative bills not adopted by the State Council or by the State Duma shall be considered as rejected.

Article 112. Legislative bills drafted on the initiative of the State Council or the State Duma and not assented to by the Emperor may not be reintroduced for legislative consideration in the course of the same session. Legislative bills, drafted on the initiative of the State Council or the State Duma and rejected by either of these institutions, may be reintroduced for legislative consideration in the course of the same session if such is the Emperor's command.

Article 113. Legislative bills brought before the State Duma and approved both by it and the State Council, as well as legislative bills on the initiative of the State Council and approved both by it and the State Duma, shall be submitted to our Sovereign the Emperor by the Chairman of the State Council.

Article 114. When the State budget is discussed, the sums appropriated for payments concerning State debts and other obligations contracted by the Russian State shall not be subject to exclusion or reduction.

Article 115. Credits for the expenditures of the Ministry of the Imperial Court, as well as those for the institutions within its province, shall not be subject to discussion by the State Council and the State Duma, when in sums not exceeding the appropriations in the State Budget for 1906. Likewise not subject to discussion by them shall be modifications of the aforementioned credits conditioned by the provisions of the Organic Law of the Imperial Family in connection with changes occurring in this Family.

Article 116. If the State budget is not confirmed at the beginning of the fiscal period, the last budget confirmed in accordance with the established procedure shall remain in force, with only those modifications which are conditioned by carrying out legislative enactments passed after its confirmation. Pending the promulgation of a new budget, credits shall be opened gradually by decisions of the Council of Ministers and placed at the disposal of Ministries and Chief Administrations to the extent of actual need. These credits may not, however, exceed, in their total monthly aggregate, one-twelfth part of the sum total of expenditures according to the budget.

Article 117. Extraordinary credits, exceeding the budget, for the needs of wartime and for special preparations preceding war, shall be opened in all Departments by act of supreme administration in accordance with the principles determined by law.

Article 118. State loans to cover expenditures both within the limits of the budget, as well as those in excess of the budget shall be authorized in the manner established for the confirmation of the State budget of revenues and expenditures. State loans to cover expenditures in the cases and within the limits foreseen in Art. 116, as well as loans to cover the expenditures assigned on the basis of Art. 117, shall be authorized by our Sovereign the Emperor by act of supreme administration. The time and the conditions under which the State loans are contracted shall be determined by act of supreme administration.

Article 119. If after the introduction in the Duma at the proper time of proposals concerning the number of people needed for the reinforcement of the Army and the Navy, a law on this subject should not be enacted by May 1, in accordance with the established procedure, then the necessary number of people shall be called to military service by a ukase of our Sovereign the Emperor, not to exceed, however, that assigned in the previous year.

CHAPTER ELEVEN

On the Council of Ministers, the Ministers and the Chief Administrators of Separate Agencies

Article 120. The direction and unification of the actions of the Ministers and Chief Administrators of separate agencies in matters both of legislation and of the highest administration of the State shall devolve upon the Council of Ministers in accordance with the principles determined by law.

Article 121. The Ministers and Chief Administrators of separate agencies shall have the right of participation in the vote of the State Council and the State Duma only if they are members of these institutions.

Article 122. Compulsory decrees, instructions, and decisions issued by the Council of Ministers, the Ministers and Chief Administrators of separate agencies, as well as by other institutions empowered by law, may not contradict the laws.

Article 123. The President of the Council of Ministers, the Ministers and Chief Administrators of separate agencies shall be responsible to our Sovereign the Emperor for the general course of the administration of the State. Each of them shall be individually responsible for his own actions and decisions.

Article 124. For criminal acts committed in office, the President of the Council of Ministers, the Ministers and Chief Administrators of separate agencies shall be subject to civil and criminal responsibility in accordance with principles determined by law.

Chinese Constitution of 1912

On 12 February 1912, as the result of revolution, the oldest of monarchies became the newest of republics. The settlement that created the Republic of China included among its terms the permanent union of North and South China as well as the abdication of the emperor. Five constitutions of the infant republic were to follow within a few years, of which scholar Tuan-sheng Ch'ien asserted, "the Provisional Constitution of 1912 was the most respected." As he has explained it, "in 1912 the Republic was new, the hopes for the future were high, and the revolutionary spirit [had not ebbed]."[1]

Chosen as provisional president of the new republic was Sun Yat-sen who had inspired the revolution with his Three Principles of the People: those of nationalism, democracy, and the people's livelihood. These principles not only served as guidelines for the Constitution of 1912 but also for Chinese constitutionalism until the abrogation of the Constitution of 1946 by the Communists on the Chinese mainland in 1949. They are still honored, however, by their incorporation into the Preamble and Article 1 of the Chinese Constitution.

The Chinese designation for the Constitution of 1912 was Chung hua min kuo lin shih yueh fa. The inclusion of the term *yueh fa* indicates that it was a provisional constitution as opposed to *hsien fa*, the term for a permanent constitution. The designation also included the adjective *lin shih*, meaning temporary, further emphasizing the original concept that this document was only provisional.

The foundation of the provisional Constitution of 1912 was another legal document dealing with basic law. It was designated Chung hua min kuo lin shih cheng fu tsu chih ta kang (Outline for the Organization of the

Provisional Government of the Republic of China).[2] This outline, which was enacted on 13 October 1911, consisted of twenty-one articles in three chapters. The first chapter (Articles 1–6) dealt with the provisional president, the second chapter (Articles 7–16) concerned the legislature, and the third chapter (Articles 17–21) covered the ministries under the executive branch.

Delegates from seventeen provinces met in Nanking for the drafting of the Constitution of 1912. There were two meetings, the first on 7 February and the second on 8 March. The 1912 document went into effect at the close of the second session, but it was not officially promulgated until 11 March.

There were several reasons why a new document had to be prepared to replace the 1911 outline.[3] First, the outline did not have a bill of rights. Second, the outline provided that the legislature was to meet within six months of its promulgation, and it was impossible to meet such a deadline. Third, the outline was based on a presidential, rather than a cabinet system of government, and the delegates had opted for the latter constitutional arrangement. Finally, it was decided that the outline was not sufficiently comprehensive. As of 11 March—the date of the official promulgation—the outline was no longer in force.

The provisional Constitution, with its fifty-six articles in seven chapters, was a detailed document that had the impact of a full-fledged constitution in the modern sense.[4] For the first time in Chinese history, obligations of the people and government were stated in writing. Delegates made sure that the chapter included "the right to institute proceedings before the judiciary" and "the right of suing officials in the administrative courts for violation of law or gainst their rights." Chapter II on human rights (under the heading "Citizens") provided that all Chinese citizens were to be considered equal, regardless of "racial, class or religious distinctions." In addition, the document specified the right to vote and be voted for as well as the rights of freedom of speech and religion, which are common to most bills of rights. Article 11, uniquely Chinese, gave all citizens "the right of participating in civil examinations."

Article 53 provided for convening a national assembly, which met for the first time on 8 April 1913. One of its tasks was the preparation of a permanent constitution, which was completed in 113 articles and submitted to the two houses of the national assembly on 3 November 1913. But before the draft could be adopted, a number of the members were unseated because of suspected complicity in a rebellion. This upheaval destroyed the quorum in both houses and in effect dissolved the national assembly.

The then-president Yuan Shih-k'ai appointed a council of state, which designated a committee to draw up a new constitution. This second of the early constitutions, also a provisional constitution, was the Constitutional Compact of 1 May 1914, under which Yuan became a virtual dictator.

Yuan died on 6 June 1916, and the first provisional Constitution of 11 March was revived. Note that Article 54 of that document had provided that before a permanent constitution was adopted "the Provisional Constitution shall be as effective as the Constitution itself."

The other three of the early constitutions were the Draft Constitution of the Anfu Parliament of 12 August 1919, the Ts'ao K'un Constitution of 10 October 1923, and the Draft Constitution of Tuan Ch'i-jui's regime of 12 December 1926.

Commenting on these five constitutions, scholar Ch'ien notes that they failed to install constitutionalism in the young republic. In his view, the important provisional Constitution of 1912 "was too often honored in the breach and too often suspended." However, he adds that, despite the problems of implementation, "The Provisional Constitution, representing the spirit of the times, was a symbol of a change and a promise of modernization. It was due to this quality that it was resurrected time and again and was always held in some measure of affection by those who were genuinely republican.[5]

TAO-TAI HSIA
Editor-in-Chief
WENDY ZELDIN
Senior Editor
Far Eastern Law Division
Law Library
Library of Congress
Washington, D.C.

NOTES

1. Tuan-sheng Ch'ien, *The Government and Politics of China*, (Cambridge: Harvard University Press, 1961), Vol 2, 70.
2. See Wu Tsung-tz'u, "The Outline of the Organization of the Provisional Government of the Republic of China and Its Origins," *Min kuo hsien cheng yun tung* [Constitutional Movement of the Republic] Hu Ch'un-hui, comp. (Taipei: Cheng Chung Books, 1978), 23–27.
3. Mentioned in another essay by Wu Tsung-tz'u, "The Provisional Constitution of the Republic of China," supra n. 2, 28.
4. See Hu Ch'un-hui's Preface, in Wu, supra n. 2, 2.
5. Supra n. 1.

CHINA—PROVISIONAL CONSTITUTION OF 11 MARCH 1912

CHAPTER I. GENERAL PROVISIONS

Article 1. The Republic of China is composed of the Chinese people.

Article 2. The sovereignty of the Chinese Republic is vested in the people.

Article 3. The territory of the Chinese Republic consists of 22 provinces, Inner and Outer Mongolia, Tibet and Chinghai.

Article 4. The sovereignty of the Chinese Republic is exercised by the Advisory Council, the Provisional President, the Cabinet and the Judiciary.

CHAPTER II. CITIZENS

Article 5. Citizens of the Chinese Republic are all equal, and there shall be no racial, class or religious distinctions.

Article 6. Citizens shall enjoy the following rights:

1. The person of the citizens shall not be arrested, imprisoned, tried or punished except in accordance with law.

2. The habitations of citizens shall not be entered or searched except in accordance with law.

3. Citizens shall enjoy the right of the security of their property and the freedom of trade.

4. Citizens shall have the freedom of speech, of composition, of publication, of assembly and of association.

5. Citizens shall have the right of the secrecy of their letters.

6. Citizens shall have the liberty of residence and removal.

7. Citizens shall have the freedom of religion.

Article 8. Citizens shall have the right of petitioning the executive officials.

Article 9. Citizens shall have the right to institute proceedings before the judiciary and to receive its trial and judgments.

Article 10. Citizens shall have the right of suing officials in the administrative courts for violation of law or gainst their rights.

Translated from the Peking Daily News, verified by the Chinese Secretary of the American Legation, Peking, China, and published in *American Journal of International Law* 6 (Suppl): 149-154, (1912). A French translation is in the *Annuaire de legislation etrangere* 12: 598-602, (1912).

Article 11. Citizens shall have the right of participating in civil examinations.

Article 12. Citizens shall have the right to vote and to be voted for.

Article 13. Citizens shall have the duty to pay taxes according to law.

Article 14. Citizens shall have the duty to enlist as soldiers according to law.

Article 15. The rights of citizens as provided in the present chapter shall be limited or modified by laws provided such limitation or modification shall be deemed necessary for the promotion of public welfare, for the maintenance of public order or on account of extraordinary exigency.

CHAPTER III. THE ADVISORY COUNCIL

Article 16. The legislative power of the Chinese Republic is exercised by the Advisory Council.

Article 17. The Advisory Council shall be composed of members elected by the several districts as provided in Article 18.

Article 18. The Provinces, Inner and Outer Mongolia and Tibet shall each elect and depute five members to the Advisory Council and Chinghai shall elect one member.

Article 18. The election districts and methods of elections shall be decided by the localities concerned.

During the meeting of the Advisory Council each member shall have one vote.

Article 19. The Advisory Council shall have the following powers:

1. To pass all law bills.

2. To pass the budgets of the provisional government.

3. To pass laws of taxation, of currency, and of weights and measures for the whole country.

4. To pass measures for the calling of public loans and to conclude contracts affecting the national treasury.

5. To give consent to matters provided in Articles 34, 35 and 40.

6. To reply to inquiries from the provisional government.

7. To receive and consider petitions of citizens.

8. To make suggestions to the government on legal or other matters.

9. To introduce interpellations to members of the cabinet and to insist on their being present in the Council in making replies thereto.

10. To insist on the government investigating into any alleged bribery and infringement of laws by officials.

11. To impeach the Provisional President for high treason by a majority vote of three fourths of the quorum consisting of more than four fifths of the total number of the members.

12. To impeach members of the cabinet for failure to perform their

official duties or for violation of the law, by majority votes of two thirds of the quorum consisting of over three fourths of the total number of the members.

Article 20. The Advisory Council shall itself convoke, open and adjourn its own meetings.

Article 21. The meetings of the Advisory Council shall be conducted publicly, but secret meetings may be held at the instigation of members of the cabinet or by the majority vote of its quorum.

Article 22. Matters passed by the Advisory Council shall be communicated to the Provisional President for promulgation and execution.

Article 23. If the Provisional President should veto matters passed by the Advisory Council, he shall, within ten days after he received such resolutions, return the same with stated reasons to the Council for reconsideration. If the same matter should again be passed by a two-thirds vote of the quorum of the Council, it shall be dealt with in accordance with Article 22.

Article 24. The President of the Advisory Council shall be elected by ballots signed by the voting members, and the one who receives more than one half of the total number of votes cast shall be elected.

Article 25. Members of the Advisory Council shall not, outside the Council hall, be responsible for their opinions expressed and votes cast in the Council.

Article 26. Members of the Council shall not be arrested without the permission of the President of the Council, except for crimes committed at the time of arrest and for crimes pertaining to civil and international warfare.

Article 27. Procedures of the Advisory Council shall be decided by its own members.

Article 28. The Advisory Council shall be dissolved on the day of the convocation of the National Assembly and its powers shall be exercised by the latter.

CHAPTER IV. THE PROVISIONAL PRESIDENT
AND VICE-PRESIDENT

Article 29. The Provisional President and Vice-President shall be elected by the Advisory Council, and he who receives two thirds of the total amount of votes cast by a sitting of the Council consisting of over three fourths of the total number of members shall be elected.

Article 30. The Provisional President represents the provisional government as the fountain of all executive powers and for promulgating all laws.

Article 31. The Provisional President may issue or cause to be issued orders for the execution of laws and of powers delegated to him by the laws.

Article 32. The Provisional President shall be the commander-in-chief of the army and navy of the whole of China.

Article 33. The Provisional President shall ordain and establish the administrative system and official regulations, but he must first submit them to the Advisory Council for its approval.

Article 34. The Provisional President shall appoint and remove civil and military officials, but in the appointment of members of the Cabinet, ambassadors and ministers, he must have the concurrence of the Advisory Council.

Article 35. The Provisional President shall have power, with the concurrence of the Advisory Council, to declare war and conclude treaties.

Article 36. The Provisional President may, in accordance with law, declare a state of siege.

Article 37. The Provisional President shall, representing the whole country, receive ambassadors and ministers of foreign countries.

Article 38. The Provisional President may introduce bills into the Advisory Council.

Article 39. The Provisional President may confer decorations and other insignia of honor.

Article 40. The Provisional President may declare general amnesty, grant special pardon, commute a punishment and restore rights, but, in the case of a general amnesty, he must have the concurrence of the Advisory Council.

Article 41. In case the Provisional President is impeached by the Advisory Council, he shall be tried by a special court consisting of nine judges elected among the justices of the Supreme Court of the realm.

Article 42. In case the Provisional President vacates his office for various reasons, or is unable to discharge the powers and duties of the said office, the Provisional Vice-President shall take his place.

CHAPTER V. MEMBERS OF THE CABINET

Article 43. The premier and the chiefs of the government departments shall be called members of the Cabinet.[1]

Article 44. Members of the Cabinet shall assist the Provisional President in assuming responsibilities.

Article 45. Members of the Cabinet shall countersign all bills intro-

[1] Literally, secretaries of state affairs.

duced by the Provisional President and all laws and orders issued by him.

Article 46. Members of the Cabinet and their deputies may be present and speak in the Advisory Council.

Article 47. After members of the Cabinet have been impeached by the Advisory Council, the Provisional President may remove them from office, but such removal shall be subject to the reconsideration of the Advisory Council.

CHAPTER VI. THE JUDICIARY

Article 48. The judiciary shall be composed of those judges appointed by the Provisional President and the Chief of the Department of Justice.

The organization of the courts and the qualifications of judges shall be determined by law.

Article 49. The judiciary shall try civil and criminal cases, but cases involving administrative affairs or arising from particular causes shall be dealt with according to special laws.

Article 50. The trial of cases in the law courts shall be conducted publicly, but those affecting public safety and order may be in camera.

Article 51. Judges shall be independent and shall not be subject to the interference of higher officials.

Article 52. Judges during their continuance in office shall not have their emoluments decreased and shall not be transferred to other offices, nor shall they be removed from office except when they are convicted of crimes, or of offences punishable according to law by removal from office.

Regulations for the punishment of judges shall be determined by law.

CHAPTER VII. SUPPLEMENTARY ARTICLES

Article 53. Within ten months after the promulgation of this Provisional Constitution, the Provisional President shall convene a national assembly, the organization of which and the laws for the election of whose members shall be decided by the Advisory Council.

Article 54. The Constitution of the Republic of China shall be adopted by the National Assembly, but before the promulgation of the Constitution, the Provisional Constitution shall be as effective as the Constitution itself.

Article 55. The Provisional Constitution may be amended by the assent of two thirds of the members of the Advisory Council or upon the application of the Provisional President, and being passed by over three fourths of the quorum of the Council consisting of over four fifths of the total number of its members.

Article 56. The present Provisional Constitution shall take effect on the date of its promulgation and the fundamental articles for the organization of the provisional government shall cease to be effective on the same date.

Mexican Constitution
of 1917

The Mexican Constitution of 1917 (not the Russian Socialist Federal Soviet Republic Constitution of 1918—see following section) was the first revolutionary constitution of the twentieth century. It was revolutionary as the first constitution that emphasized economic and cultural rights as opposed to political and civil rights. In addition, this document was revolutionary as a nationalistic constitution designed to protect its citizens against foreign economic exploitation as well as political neocolonialism. It has been a landmark secular constitution, the first to restrict and deny the privileges of a majority religion—in this case, the Catholic Church. Seventy years later and much amended, it is still recognized as the model of a radical, but not Marxist, constitution.

The Mexican Constitution of 1917 is an original, distinctive product. Although shorter than today's encyclopedic constitutions of India, Yugoslavia, and Papua New Guinea, it was at the time of its promulgation the longest constitution in the world. Criticized now as well as then for its length and prolixity, it represented an attempt to solve the nation's ills as then perceived. If it resembled a code rather than the typical constitution, this charter manifested in detail the desires and aspirations of its draftsmen who did not provide for practical implementation.

The Mexican Constitution of 1917 was both the result and the end of a revolution that had dominated the life of the country since the overthrow of the Porfirio Diaz dictatorship in 1910. The most important response to the political instability of the period was the formation of the Constitutionalist movement. This movement was headed by Venustiano Carranza, one of the many revolutionary generals, who became president in 1915. It was his proposed constitutional draft that led to the election of a constituent assembly to meet at Queretaro in 1916/17 to prepare a new constitution. Its product has been called "the legal triumph of the Mexican Revolution, the first great social upheaval of the twentieth century. To some it is the Revolution."[1] To other commentators this document marked the end of the years of revolution.

Article 123 is regarded as the most innovative and influential component of the 1917 constitution.[2] Incorporated into the constitution as a separate title labeled "Of Labour and Social Welfare," it focused on the special position in Mexico of "skilled and unskilled workmen, employees, domestic servants and artisans. . . ." It guaranteed the eight-hour day, minimum wages, equal pay without regard to sex and nationality, double pay for overtime, and the right to strike. Unusual were the special provisions that required employers to install safety devices, guarantee one day's rest per week, furnish low-cost housing, and, in some instances, install profit-sharing plans.

The longest and most nationalistic part of this Constitution was Article 27, adopted by the unanimous vote of the constituent assembly during its last two weeks. This article was the major response to the goals of the revolution—a new program dealing with land ownership and its redistribution. Here is the operative language: "Necessary measures shall be taken to divide large landed holdings; to develop small holdings; [and] to establish new centers of rural population with such land and waters as may be indispensable to them."

Land ownership was further restricted in other ways. The constitution established as a basic principle that "in each state and territory there shall be fixed the maximum area of land which any one individual or legally organized corporation may own." Expropriation of private land was permitted when land owners refused to comply with the policies of government. Finally, "all contracts and concessions made by former governments . . . which shall have resulted in the monopoly of lands, waters, and natural resources of the nation by a single individual or corporation, are declared subject to revision, and the executive is authorized to declare those null and void which seriously prejudice the public interest."

Most controversial were the provisions dealing with the Catholic Church, especially Article 130. The state legislatures were given "the exclusive power of determining the maximum number of ministers of religious creeds according to the needs of each locality." Clergy were not permitted to "criticize the fundamental laws of the country, the authorities in particular or the government in general." They were denied the vote and were made ineligible for public office. Article 27 also denied religious institutions the "legal capacity to acquire, hold, or administer real property." In addition, Article 3 prohibited religious education at the elementary school level.

Structurally, the Constitution of 1917 borrowed much from earlier

Mexican charters, especially the Constitution of 1857. These, in turn, were modeled in large part on the U.S. Constitution. The federal pattern developed to divide power between the central government and states was closely followed in the Mexican Constitution. A reading of the powers given to the Mexican Congress in Chapter II indicates the strong precedent of Article I, Section 8, of the U.S. Constitution.

Still in force today, the Mexican Constitution is one of the ten oldest in the world. Because of frequent amendments to the Constitution of 1917, students of Mexican constitutionalism are compelled to return to the original document to understand its full significance.

ROBERT PHILIP PAYNE, JR.
School of Law
Rutgers University
Camden, New Jersey

NOTES

1. E. V. Niemeyer, Jr., *Revolution at Queretaro* (Austin: University of Texas Press, 1974), 352.
2. Charles C. Cumberland, *Mexican Revolution: The Constitutional Years* (Austin: University of Texas Press, 1972), 348.

POLITICAL CONSTITUTION
OF THE
UNITED STATES OF MEXICO,
ADOPTED ON THE 31ST JANUARY, 1917,
AMENDING THAT OF THE 5TH FEBRUARY, 1857

TITLE I

CHAPTER I. OF PERSONAL GUARANTEES

Article 1. Every person in the United States of Mexico shall enjoy all guarantees granted by this Constitution; these shall neither be abridged nor suspended except in such cases and under such conditions as are herein provided.

Article 2. Slavery is forbidden in the United States of Mexico. Slaves who enter the national territory shall, by this act alone, recover their freedom, and enjoy the protection of the law.

Article 3. Instruction is free; that given in public institutions of learning shall be secular. Primary instruction, whether higher or lower, given in private institutions shall likewise be secular.

No religious corporation nor minister of any religious creed shall establish or direct schools of primary instruction.

Primary instruction in public institutions shall be gratuitous.

Article 4. No person shall be prevented from engaging in any profession, industrial or commercial pursuit or occupation of his liking, providing it be lawful. The exercise of this liberty shall only be forbidden by judicial order when the rights of a third person are infringed, or by executive order, issued under the conditions prescribed by law, when the rights of society are violated. No one shall be deprived of the fruit of his labour except by judicial decree.

Each State shall determine by law what professions shall require licenses, the conditions to be complied with in obtaining the same, and the authorities empowered to issue them.

Article 5. No one shall be compelled to render personal services without due compensation and without his full consent, excepting labour imposed as a penalty by judicial decree, which shall conform to the provisions of Clauses 1 and 2 of Article 123.

Only the following public service shall be obligatory, subject to the conditions set forth in the respective laws:—Military service, jury service, service in municipal and other public elective office, whether this election be direct or indirect, and service in connection with elections, which shall be obligatory and without compensation.

The State shall not permit any contract, covenant or agreement to be carried out having for its object the abridgment, loss or irrevocable sacrifice of the liberty of man, whether by reason of labour, education, or religious vows. The law, therefore, does not permit the establishment of monastic orders of whatever denomination, or for whatever purpose contemplated.

Nor shall any person legally agree to his own proscription or exile, or to the temporary or permanent renunciation of the exercise of any profession or industrial or commercial pursuit.

A contract for labour shall only be binding to render the services agreed upon for the time fixed by law and shall not exceed one year to the prejudice of the party rendering the service; nor shall it in any case whatsoever embrace the waiver, loss or abridgment of any political or civil right.

In the event of a breach of such contract on the part of the party pledging himself to render the service, the said party shall only be liable civilly for damages arising from such breach, and in no event shall coercion against his person be employed.

Article 6. The expression of ideas shall not be the subject of any judicial or executive investigation, unless it offend good morals, impair the rights of third parties, incite to crime, or cause a breach of the peace.

Article 7. Freedom of writing and publishing writings on any subject is inviolable. No law or authority shall have the right to establish censorship, require bond from authors or printers, nor restrict the liberty of the press, which shall be limited only by the respect due to private life, morals, and public peace. Under no circumstances shall a printing press be sequestered as the corpus delicti.

The organic laws shall prescribe whatever provisions may be necessary to prevent the imprisonment, under pretext of proceedings against offences of the press, of the vendors, newsboys, workmen, and other employees of the establishment publishing the writing which forms the subject matter of the proceedings, unless their responsibility be previously established.

Article 8. Public officials and employees shall respect the exercise of the right of petition, provided that the petition be in writing and in a peaceful and respectful manner; but this right may be exercised in political matters solely by citizens.

To every petition there shall be given an answer in writing by the official to whom it may be addressed, and the said official shall be bound to inform the petitioner of the decision taken within a brief period.

Article 9. The right peaceably to assemble or to come together for any lawful purpose shall not be abridged; but only citizens shall be permitted to exercise this right for the purpose of taking part in the political affairs of the country. No armed assembly shall have the right to deliberate.

No meeting or assembly shall be deemed unlawful, nor may it be dissolved, which shall have for its purpose the petitioning of any authority or the presentation of any protest against any act, provided no insults be proffered against the said authority, nor violence resorted to, nor threats used to intimidate or to compel the said authority to arrive at a favourable decision.

Article 10. The inhabitants of the United States of Mexico are entitled to have arms of any kind in their possession for their protection and legitimate defence, excepting such as are expressly prohibited by law, and such as the nation may reserve for the exclusive use of the army, navy and national guard; but they shall not bear such arms within inhabited places, except subject to the police regulations thereof.

Article 11. Everyone has the right to enter and leave the Republic, to travel through its territory, and to change his residence, without necessity of a letter of security, passport, safe conduct, or any other similar requirement. The exercise of this right shall be subordinated to the powers of the judiciary, in the event of civil or criminal responsibility, and to those of the executive, in so far as relates to the limitations imposed by law in regard to emigration, immigration, and the public health of the country, or in regard to undesirable foreigners resident in the country.

Article 12. No titles of nobility, prerogatives, or hereditary honours shall be granted in the United States of Mexico, nor shall any effect be given to those granted by other countries.

Article 13. No one shall be tried according to private laws or by special tribunals. No person or corporation shall have privileges nor enjoy emoluments which are not by way of compensation for public services and established by law. Military jurisdiction shall be recognised for the trial of criminal cases having direct connection with military discipline, but the military tribunals shall in no case and for no reason extend their jurisdiction over persons not belonging to the army. Whenever a civilian shall be implicated in any military crime or offence, the cause shall be heard by the appropriate civil authorities.

Article 14. No law shall be given retroactive effect to the prejudice of any person whatsoever.

No person shall be deprived of life, liberty, property, possessions, or rights without due process of law instituted before a duly created court, in which the essential elements of procedure are observed, and in accordance with previously existing laws.

In criminal cases no penalty shall be imposed by mere analogy or even by a priori evidence, but the penalty shall be decreed by a law in every respect applicable to the crime in question.

In civil suits the final judgment shall be according to the letter or the juridical interpretation of the law; in the absence of the latter, the general legal principles shall govern.

Article 15. No treaty shall be authorised for the extradition of political offenders, or of offenders of the common class, who have been slaves in the country where the offence was committed. Nor shall any agreement or treaty be entered into which abridges or modifies the guarantees and rights which this Constitution grants to the individual and to the citizen.

Article 16. No one shall be molested in his person, family, domicile, papers, or possessions except by virtue of an order in writing of the competent authority setting forth the legal ground and justification for the action taken. No order of arrest or detention shall be issued against any person other than by competent judicial authority, nor unless preceded by a charge, accusation or complaint for a specific offence punishable by imprisonment, supported by an affidavit of a credible party or by such other evidence as shall make the guilt of the accused probable; in cases flagrante delicto any person may arrest the offender and his accomplices, placing them at once at the disposal of the judicial authority. Only in urgent cases instituted by the authorities, when there is no judicial authority available, may the administrative authorities, on their strictest accountability, order the detention of the accused, placing him at the disposal of the judicial authorities. Every search warrant, which may only be issued by the judicial authority, and which must be in writing, shall specify the place to be searched, the person or persons to be arrested, and the objects sought, to which the proceeding shall be strictly limited; at the conclusion of which a detailed written statement shall be drawn up in the presence of two witnesses proposed by the occupant of the place to be searched, or in his absence or on his refusal, by the official making the search.

Administrative officials may enter private houses solely for the purpose of determining that the sanitary and police regulations have been complied with; they may likewise demand the exhibition of books and documents necessary to prove that the fiscal regulations have been obeyed, subject to the respective laws, and to the formalities prescribed for cases of search.

Article 17. No one shall be imprisoned for debts of a purely civil character. No one shall take the law into his own hands, nor resort to violence in the enforcement of his rights. The courts shall be open for the administration of justice at such times and under such conditions as the law may establish; their services shall be gratuitous, and all judicial costs are accordingly prohibited.

Article 18. Preventive detention shall be exercised only for offences meriting punishment inflicted on the person. The place of detention shall be different and completely separated from that set apart for the serving of sentences.

The Federal and State Governments shall, in their respective territories, organize the penal system—penal colonies or prisons—on the basis of labour as a means of regeneration.

Article 19. No preventive detention shall exceed three days except for reasons specified in the formal order of commitment, which shall set forth the offence charged, the substance thereof, the time, place, and circumstances of its commission, and the facts disclosed in the preliminary examination; these facts must always be sufficient to establish the wrongful act and the probable guilt of the accused. All authorities ordering any detention or consenting thereto, as well as all agents, subordinates, wardens, or jailors executing the same, shall be liable for any breach of this provision.

The trial shall take place only for the offence or offences set forth in the formal order of commitment. If it shall develop in the course of trial that another offence different from that charged has been committed, a separate accusation must be brought. This, however, shall not prevent the joinder of both proceedings, if deemed desirable.

Any maltreatment during apprehension or confinement, any molestation inflicted without legal justification, and any exaction or contribution levied in prison are abuses which the law shall correct and the authorities repress.

Article 20. In every criminal trial the accused shall enjoy the following guarantees:—

I. He shall be at liberty on demand and upon giving a bond up to ten thousand pesos,* according to his status and the gravity of the offence charged, provided, however, that the said offence shall not be punishable with more than five years' imprisonment; he shall be set at liberty without any further requirement than the placing of the stipulated sum at the disposal of the proper authorities, or the giving of an adequate mortgage or personal security.

II. He may not be forced to be a witness against himself; wherefore isolation or other means working towards this end is hereby strictly prohibited.

III. He shall be publicly notified within forty-eight hours after being handed over to the judicial authorities of the name of his accuser, and of the nature of and cause for the accusation, so that he may be familiar with the offence with which he is charged, may reply thereto, and make his preliminary statement.

IV. He shall be confronted with the witnesses against him, who shall testify in his presence if they are to be found in the place where the trial is being held, so that he may cross-examine them in his defence.

V. All witnesses which he shall offer shall be heard in his defence, as well as all evidence received, for which he shall be given such time as the law may prescribe; he shall furthermore be assisted in securing the presence of any person or persons whose testimony he may request, provided they are to be found at the place of trial.

VI. He shall be entitled to a public trial by a judge or jury of citizens who can read and write, and are also citizens of the place and district where the offence shall have been committed provided the penalty for such offence be greater than one year's imprisonment. The accused shall always be entitled to trial by jury for all offences committed by means of the press against the public peace or against the internal or external security of the Republic.

VII. He shall be furnished with all information of record needed for his defence.

VIII. He shall be tried within four months, if charged with an offence the maximum penalty for which does not exceed two years' imprisonment, and within one year, if the maximum penalty be greater.

IX. He shall be heard in his own defence, either personally or by

* Equivalent to about £1,000 at peace-time rates.

counsel, or by both, as he may desire. In case he shall have no one to defend him a list of official counsel shall be submitted to him in order that he may choose one or more to act in his defence. If the accused shall not desire to name any counsel for his defence, after having been called upon to do so at the time of his preliminary examination, the court shall appoint counsel to defend him. The accused may name his counsel immediately on arrest, and shall be entitled to have him present at every stage of the trial; and shall be bound to have him appear as often as required by the court.

X. In no event may imprisonment or detention be extended through failure to pay counsel fees or through any other pecuniary charge, by virtue of any civil liability or other similar cause. Nor shall detention be extended beyond the time set by law as the maximum for the offence charged.

The period of detention shall be reckoned as a part of the final sentence.

Article 21. The imposition of all penalties is an exclusive power of the judiciary. The prosecution of offences is the duty of the Public Prosecutor and of the judicial police, who shall be under the immediate command and authority of the public prosecutor. The punishment of violations of municipal and police regulations belongs to the administrative authorities, and shall consist only of a fine or of imprisonment not exceeding thirty-six hours. Should the offender fail to pay the fine this shall be substituted by the corresponding period of arrest, which shall in no case exceed fifteen days.

Should the offender be a workman or unskilled labourer, he shall not be punished with a fine greater than the amount of his weekly pay or salary.

Article 22. Punishments by mutilation and infamy, by branding, flogging, beating with sticks, torture of any kind, excessive fines, confiscation of property and any other unusual or extraordinary penalties are prohibited.

Attachment of the whole or part of the property of any person made under judicial authority to cover any civil liability arising out of the commission of any offence, or by reason of the imposition of any tax or fine, shall not be deemed a confiscation of property.

Article 23. Capital punishment is likewise forbidden for all political offences; in the case of offences other than political it shall only be imposed for high treason committed during a foreign war, parricide, murder with malice aforethought, arson, abduction, highway robbery, piracy, and grave military offences.

Article 24. Every one is free to embrace the religion of his choice, and to practice all ceremonies, devotions, or observances of his particular creed, either in places of public worship or at home, provided that such practices do not constitute offences punishable by law.

Every religious act of public worship shall be performed strictly within the places of public worship, which shall be at all times under governmental supervision.

Article 25. Sealed correspondence sent through the mails shall be free from search, and its violation shall be punishable by law.

Article 26. No member of the army shall in time of peace be quartered in private dwellings, without the consent of the owner; nor shall any other exaction be demanded. In time of war the military forces may demand lodging, equipment, provisions, and other assistance, in the manner provided by the military law relating thereto.

Article 27. The ownership of lands and waters comprised within the limits of the national territory is vested originally in the Nation, which has had, and has, the right to transmit title thereof to private persons, thereby constituting private property.

Private property shall not be expropriated except for reasons of public utility, and upon payment of compensation.

The Nation shall have at all times the right to impose on private property such limitations as the public interest may demand, as well as the right to regulate the development of natural resources, which are susceptible of appropriation, in order to conserve them and equitably to distribute the public wealth. For this purpose necessary measures shall be taken to divide large landed holdings; to develop small holdings; to establish new centres of rural population with such lands and waters as may be indispensable to them; to encourage agriculture, and to prevent the destruction of natural resources, and to protect property from damage detrimental to society. Settlements, hamlets situated on private property and communes which lack lands or water or do not possess them in sufficient quantities for their needs shall have the right to be provided with them from the adjoining properties, always having due regard for small landed holdings. Wherefore, all grants of lands made up to the present time under the decree of January 6, 1915, are confirmed. Private property the acquisition of which is necessary for the said purposes shall be considered as taken for public utility.

To the Nation belongs direct authority over all minerals or substances which in veins, layers, masses, or beds constitute deposits whose nature is different from the components of the land, such as minerals from which metals and metalloids used for industrial purposes are extracted; beds of precious stones, rock salt and salt mines formed directly by marine waters, products derived from the decomposition of rocks, when their exploitations requires underground work; phosphates which may be used for fertilizers; solid mineral fuels; petroleum and all hydrocarbons—solid, liquid, or gaseous.

In the Nation is likewise vested the ownership of the waters of territorial seas to the extent and in the term fixed by International Law; the waters of the lagoons and marshes along the coast; those of inland lakes of natural formation which are directly connected with continually flowing waters; those of principal rivers or tributaries from the points at which there is a permanent current of water in their beds to their mouths, whether they flow to the sea or cross two or more States; those of intermittent streams which traverse two or more States in their main body; the waters of rivers, streams, or torrents, when they bound the national territory or that of the States; waters extracted from mines; and the beds and banks of the lakes and streams hereinbefore mentioned, to the extent fixed by law. Any other stream of water not comprised within the foregoing enumeration shall be considered as an integral part of the private property through which it flows; but the use of the waters when they pass from one landed property to another shall be considered of public utility and shall be subject to the provisions prescribed by the States.

In the cases to which the two foregoing paragraphs refer, the ownership of the Nation is inalienable, and may not be lost by prescription; concessions shall be granted by the Federal Government to private parties or civil or commercial corporations organised under the laws of Mexico, only on condition that said resources be regularly developed, and on the further condition that the legal provisions be observed. Legal capacity to acquire ownership of lands and waters of the Nation shall be governed by the following provisions:

I. Only Mexicans by birth or naturalisation and Mexican companies have the right to acquire authority over lands, waters, and their appurtenances, or to obtain concessions to develop mines, waters or mineral fuels in the Republic of Mexico. The Nation may grant the same right to foreigners, provided they agree before the Department of Foreign Affairs to be considered Mexicans in respect to such property, and accordingly not to invoke the protection of their Governments in respect to the same, under penalty, in case of breach, of forfeiture to the Nation of property so acquired. Within a zone of 100 kilometres from the frontiers, and of 50 kilometres from the sea coast, no foreigner shall under any conditions acquire direct authority over lands and waters.

II. The religious institutions known as churches, irrespective of creed, shall in no case have legal capacity to acquire, hold, or administer real property or loans made on such real property; all such real property or loans as may be at present held by the said religious institutions, either on their behalf or through third parties, shall vest in the Nation, and any one may give information as to property so held. Presumptive proof shall be sufficient to declare the information well-founded. Places of public worship are the property of the Nation, as represented by the Federal Government, which shall determine which of them may continue to be devoted to this purpose. Episcopal residences, rectories, seminaries, asylums or collegiate establishments of religious institutions, convents or any other buildings built or designed for the administration, propaganda, or teaching of the tenets of any religious creed shall forthwith vest, as of full right, directly in the Nation, to be used exclusively for the public services of the Federation or of the States, within their respective jurisdictions. All places of public worship which shall later be erected shall be the property of the Nation.

III. Public and private charitable institutions for the assistance of the necessitous, for scientific research, or for the diffusion of knowledge, mutual aid societies or organisations formed for any other lawful purpose shall in no case acquire more landed property than is indispensable for their object, and is directly or indirectly destined for that purpose, but they may acquire, hold, or administer loans made on real property unless the mortgage terms exceed ten years. In no case shall institutions of this character be under the patronage, direction, or administration, charge, or supervision of religious corporations or institutions, nor of ministers of any religious creed or of their dependants even though either the former or the latter shall not be in the exercise of their office.

IV. Commercial stock companies shall not acquire, hold, or administer rural properties. Companies of this nature which may be organised to develop any manufacturing, mining, petroleum or other industry, excepting only agricultural industries, may acquire, hold, or administer lands only in an area absolutely necessary for their establishments or adequate to serve the purposes indicated, which the Executive of the Union or of the respective State in each case shall determine.

V. Banks duly organised under the laws governing credit institutions may hold capital invested in rural or urban property in accordance with the provisions of the said law, but they may not own nor administer more real property than that absolutely necessary for their brief purposes.

VI. Properties held in common by co-owners, hamlets, towns, congregations, tribes, and other settlements which, as a matter of fact or law, conserve their communal character, shall have legal capacity to enjoy in common the waters, woods, and lands belonging to them, or which may have been or shall be restored to them according to the law of January 6, 1915. The law shall determine only the method of carrying out the allocation of the lands.

VII. Excepting the corporations to which Clauses III., IV., V., and VI. hereof refer, no other civil corporation may hold or administer on its own behalf real estate or capital invested therein, with the single exception of buildings designed directly and immediately for the purposes of the Institution. The States, the Federal District, and the Territories, as well as the municipalities throughout the Republic, shall enjoy full legal capacity to acquire and hold all real estate necessary for public services.

The Federal and State laws shall determine within their respective jurisdictions those cases in which the occupation of private property shall be considered of public utility; and in accordance with the said laws the administrative authorities shall make the proper declarations. The amount fixed as compensation for the expropriated property shall be based on the sum at which the said property shall be valued for fiscal purposes in the land tax registry or revenue offices, whether this value be that manifested by the owner or merely impliedly accepted by reason of the payment of his taxes on such a basis, to which there shall be added ten per cent. The increased value which the property in question may have acquired through improvements made subsequent to the date of the fixing of the fiscal value shall be the only matter subject to expert opinion and to judicial determination. The same procedure shall be observed in respect to objects whose value is not recorded in the revenue offices.

All proceedings, findings, decisions and all operations of demarcation, concession, composition, judgment, compromise, alienation, or auction which may have deprived co-owners, hamlets, settlements, congregations, tribes, and other settlement organisations still existing since the law of June 25, 1856, of the whole or a part of their lands, woods and waters, are declared null and void; all findings, resolutions, and operations which may subsequently take place and produce the same effects shall likewise be null and void. Consequently, all lands, forests, and waters of which the above-mentioned settlements may have been deprived shall be restored to them according to the decree of January 6, 1915, which shall remain in force as a constitutional law. In any case in which the adjudication upon lands applied for by any of the communities mentioned does not, under the provisions of the said decree, result in restitution, they shall receive such lands by way of grant and in no case shall they fail to receive such lands as are essential to them. Only such lands, title to which may have been acquired in the divisions made by virtue of the said law of June 25, 1856, or such as may be held in undisputed ownership for more than ten years are excepted from the provision of nullity, provided their area does not exceed fifty hectares.* Any excess over this area shall be returned to the commune, and the owner shall be indemnified. All laws of restitution enacted by virtue of this provision shall be immediately carried into effect by the administrative authorities. Only members of the commune shall have the right to the lands destined to be divided, and the rights to these lands shall be inalienable so long as they remain undivided; the same provision shall govern the right of ownership after the division has been made.

The exercise of the functions belonging to the Nation by virtue of this article shall follow judicial process; but as a part of this process and by order of the proper tribunals, which order shall be issued within the maximum period of one month, the administrative authorities shall proceed

* About 125 acres.

without delay to the occupation, administration, auction, or sale of the lands and waters in question, together with all their appurtenances, and in no case may the acts of the said authorities be revoked until an execution order has been issued.

During the next constitutional term, the Congress and the State Legislatures shall enact laws within their respective jurisdictions, for the purpose of carrying out the division of large landed estates, subject to the following basic principles:—

(a) In each State and Territory there shall be fixed the maximum area of land which any one individual or legally organised corporation may own.

(b) The excess over the area thus fixed shall be subdivided by the owner within the period set by the laws of the respective locality; and these subdivisions shall be offered for sale on such conditions as the respective governments shall approve, in accordance with the said laws.

(c) If the owner shall refuse to make the subdivision, this shall be carried out by the local government, by means of expropriation proceedings.

(d) The value of the subdivisions shall be paid in annual amounts sufficient to redeem the principal and interest within a period of not less than twenty years, during which the person acquiring them may not alienate them. The rate of interest shall not exceed five per cent per annum.

(e) The owner shall be bound to accept bonds of a special issue to guarantee the payment of the property expropriated. With this end in view, the Congress shall issue a law authorising the States to issue bonds to meet their land debt.

(f) The local laws shall regulate the family patrimony and determine what property shall constitute the same on the basis of its inalienability; it shall not be subject to attachment nor to any charge whatever.

All contracts and concessions made by former governments from and after the year 1876 which shall have resulted in the monopoly of lands, waters, and natural resources of the Nation by a single individual or corporation, are declared subject to revision, and the Executive is authorised to declare those null and void which seriously prejudice the public interest.

Article 28. There shall be no monopolies of any kind whatsoever in the United States of Mexico; nor exemption from taxation; nor any prohibition even under cover of protection to industry, excepting only those relating to the coinage of money, to the postal, telegraphic, and radio-telegraphic services, to the issuing of notes by a single banking institution to be controlled by the Federal Government, and to the privileges which for a limited period the law may concede to authors and artists for the reproduction of their work, and, lastly, to those granted inventors for the exclusive use of their inventions or improvements.

The law will accordingly severely punish, and the authorities diligently prosecute, any accumulating or cornering by one or more persons of necessaries for the purpose of bringing about a rise in prices; any act or measure which shall stifle or endeavour to stifle free competition in any production, industry, trade, or public service; any agreement or combination of any kind entered into by producers, manufacturers, merchants, common carriers, or any other public service, to stifle competition, and to compel the consumer to pay exorbitant prices; and in general whatever constitutes an unfair and exclusive advantage in favour of one or more specified persons to the detriment of the public in general or of any special class of society.

Associations of labour organised to protect their own interests shall not be deemed a monopoly.

Nor shall co-operative associations or unions of producers be deemed monopolies when, in defence of their own interests or of the general public, they sell directly in foreign markets national or industrial products which are the principal source of wealth of the region in which they are produced, provided they be not necessaries, and provided further that such associations be under the supervision or protection of the Federal Government or of that of the States, and provided further that authorisation be in each case obtained from the respective legislative bodies. These legislative bodies may, either on their own initiative or on the recommendation of the Executive, revoke, whenever the public interest shall so demand, the authorisation granted for the establishment of the associations in question.

Article 29. In cases of invasion, grave disturbance of the public peace, or any other emergency which may place society in grave danger or conflict, the President of the Republic of Mexico, and no one else, with the concurrence of the Council of Ministers, and with the approval of the Congress, or if the latter shall be in recess, of the Permanent Committee, shall have power to suspend throughout the whole Republic or in any portion thereof, such guarantees as shall be a hindrance in meeting the situation promptly and readily; but such suspension shall in no case be confined to a particular individual, but shall be made by means of a general decree, and only for a limited period. If the suspension occur while the Congress is in session, this body shall grant such powers as in its judgment the executive may need to meet the situation; if the suspension occur while the Congress is in recess, the Congress shall be convoked forthwith for the granting of such powers.

CHAPTER II. OF MEXICANS

Article 30. A Mexican shall be such either by birth or by naturalisation.

I. Mexicans by birth are those born of Mexican parents, within or without the Republic, provided in the latter case the parents be also Mexicans by birth. Persons born within the Republic of foreign parentage shall likewise be considered Mexicans by birth, if within one year after they come of age they shall declare to the Department of Foreign Affairs that they elect Mexican citizenship, and shall furthermore prove to the said Department that they have resided within the country during the six years immediately prior to the said declaration.

II. Mexicans by naturalisation are:—

(a) The children of foreign parentage born in the country, who shall elect Mexican citizenship in the manner prescribed in the foregoing clause, but who have not the residence qualification required in the said section.

(b) Those persons who shall have resided in the country for five consecutive years, have an honest means of livelihood, and shall have obtained naturalisation from the said Department of Foreign Affairs.

(c) Those of mixed Indian and Latin descent who may have established residence in the Republic, and shall have manifested their intention to acquire Mexican citizenship.

In the cases stipulated in these sections, the law shall determine the manner of proving compliance with the requirements therein demanded.

Article 31. It shall be the duty of every Mexican:—

I. To compel the attendance at either private or public schools of their children or wards, when under fifteen years of age, in order that they may receive primary instruction and military training for such periods as the law of public instruction in each State shall determine.

II. To attend on such days and at such hours as the town council shall in each case prescribe, to receive such civic instruction and military training as shall fit them to exercise their civic rights, shall make them skillful in the handling of arms and familiar with military discipline.

III. To enlist and serve in the national guard, pursuant to the organic law relating thereto, for the purpose of preserving and defending the independence, territory, honour, rights, and interests of the country, as well as domestic peace and order.

IV. To contribute in the proportionate and equitable manner prescribed by law toward the public expenses of the Federation, the State and the municipality in which he resides.

Article 32. Mexicans shall be preferred under equal circumstances to foreigners for all kinds of concessions and for all public employments, offices or commissions, when citizenship is not indispensable. No foreigner shall serve in the army nor in the police corps nor in any other department of public safety during times of peace.

Only Mexicans by birth may belong to the national navy, or fill any office or commission therein. The same qualification shall be required for captains, pilots, masters, and chief engineers of Mexican merchant ships, as well as for two-thirds of the members of the crew.

CHAPTER III. OF ALIENS

Article 33. Aliens are those who do not possess the qualifications prescribed in Article 30. They shall be entitled to the guarantees granted by Chapter I, Title I, of the present Constitution; but the Executive shall have the exclusive right to expel from the Republic forthwith, and without judicial process, any foreigner whose presence he may deem inexpedient.

No foreigner shall meddle in any way whatsoever in the political affairs of the country.

CHAPTER IV. OF MEXICAN CITIZENS

Article 34. Mexican citizenship shall be enjoyed only by those Mexicans who have the following qualifications:—

I. Are over 21 years of age, if unmarried, and over 18 if married.

II. Have an honest means of livelihood.

Article 35. The prerogatives of citizens are:—

I. To vote at popular elections.

II. To be eligible for any elective office and be qualified for any other office or commission, provided they have the other qualifications required by law.

III. To assemble for the purpose of discussing the political affairs of the country.

IV. To serve in the army or national guard for the defence of the Republic and its institutions, as by law determined.

V. To exercise the right of petition in any matter whatever.

Article 36. It shall be the duty of every Mexican citizen:—

I. To register in the land tax register of the municipality, setting forth any property he may own, and his professional or industrial pursuit, or occupation; and also to register in the electoral registration list, as by law determined.

II. To enlist in the national guard.

III. To vote at popular elections in the electoral district to which he belongs.

IV. To discharge the duties of the Federal or State offices to which he may be elected, which service shall in no case be gratuitous.

V. To serve on the Town Council of the municipality wherein he resides, and to perform all electoral and jury service.

Article 37. Citizenship shall be lost:—

I. By officially serving the Government of another country, or accepting its decorations, titles, or employment without previous permission of the Federal Congress, excepting literary, scientific and humanitarian titles, which may be accepted freely.

III. By compromising themselves in any way before ministers of any religious creed or before any other person not to observe the present Constitution, or the laws arising thereunder.

Article 38. The rights or prerogatives of citizenship shall be suspended for the following reasons:—

I. Through failure to comply, without sufficient cause, with any of the obligations imposed by Article 36. This suspension shall last for one year, and shall be in addition to any other penalties prescribed by law for the same offence.

II. Through being subjected to criminal prosecution for an offence punishable with imprisonment, such suspension to be reckoned from the date of the formal order of commitment.

III. Throughout the term of imprisonment.

IV. Through vagrancy or habitual drunkenness, declared in the manner provided by law.

V. Through being a fugitive from justice, the suspension to be reckoned from the date of the order of arrest until the prescription of the criminal action.

VI. Through any final sentence which shall decree as a penalty such suspension.

The law shall determine the cases in which they may be regained.

TITLE II

CHAPTER I. OF THE NATIONAL SOVEREIGNTY AND FORM OF GOVERNMENT

Article 39. The national sovereignty is vested essentially and originally in the people. All public power emanates from the people, and is instituted for their benefit. The people have at all times the inalienable right to alter or modify the form of their government.

Article 40. It is the will of the Mexican people to constitute themselves into a democratic, federal, representative Republic, consisting of States, free and sovereign in all that concerns their internal affairs, but united in a federation according to the principles of this fundamental law.

Article 41. The people exercise their sovereignty through the Federal powers in the matters belonging to the Union, and through those of the States in the matters relating to the internal administration of the latter. This power shall be exercised in the manner respectively established by the Constitution, both Federal and State. The Constitutions of the States shall in no case contravene the stipulations of the Federal Constitution.

CHAPTER II. OF THE INTEGRAL PARTS OF THE FEDERATION AND THE NATIONAL TERRITORY

Article 42. The national territory comprises the integral parts of the Federation and the adjacent islands in both oceans. It likewise comprises the Island of Guadalupe, those of Revillagigedo, and that of La Pasion, situated in the Pacific Ocean.

Article 43. The integral parts of the Federation are:—The States of Aguascalientes, Campeche, Coahuila, Colima, Chiapas, Chihuahua, Durango, Guanajuato, Guerrero, Hidalgo, Jalisco, Mexico, Michoacan, Morelos, Nayarit, Nuevo Leon, Oaxaca, Puebla, Queretaro, San-Luis-Potosi, Sinaloa, Sonora, Tabasco, Tamaulipas, Tlaxcala, Vera Cruz, Yucatan, Zacatecas, the Federal District, the Territory of Lower California, and the Territory of Quintana Roo.

Article 44. The Federal District shall embrace its present territory; in the event of the removal of the Federal Powers to some other place it shall be created into the State of the Valley of Mexico with such boundaries and area as the Federal Congress shall assign to it.

Article 45. The States and Territories of the Federation shall keep their present boundaries and areas, provided that no boundary question shall exist between them.

Article 46. The States having pending boundary questions shall arrange or settle them as provided by this Constitution.

Article 47. The State of Nayarit shall have the territorial area and boundaries at present comprising the territory of Tepic.

Article 48. The Islands in both Oceans embraced within the national territory shall depend directly on the Federal Government, excepting those over which the States have up to the present time exercised jurisdiction.

TITLE III

CHAPTER I. OF THE DIVISION OF POWERS

Article 49. The Supreme Power of the Federation is divided for its exercise into legislative, executive, and judicial.

Two or more of these powers shall never be united in one person or corporation, nor shall the legislative power be vested in one individual, except in the case of extraordinary powers granted to the Executive, in accordance with the provisions of Article 29.

CHAPTER II. OF THE LEGISLATIVE POWER

Article 50. The Legislative power of the United States of Mexico is vested in a general Congress, which shall consist of a House of Representatives and a Senate.

Section I. Of the Election and Installation of the Congress

Article 51. The House of Representatives shall consist of representatives of the Nation, all of whom shall be elected every two years by the citizens of Mexico.

Article 52. One Representative shall be chosen for each 60,000 inhabitants or for any fraction thereof exceeding 20,000 on the basis of the general Census of the Federal District and of each State and Territory. Any State or Territory in which the population shall be less than that fixed by this Article shall, nevertheless, elect one representative.

Article 53. There shall be elected a substitute for each Representative.

Article 54. The election of Representatives shall be direct, in accordance with the provisions of the electoral law.

Article 55. Representatives shall have the following qualifications:—

I. They shall be Mexican citizens by birth and in the enjoyment of their rights.

II. They shall be over 25 years of age on the day of election.

III. They shall be natives of the States or Territories respectively electing them, or domiciled and actually resident therein for six months immediately prior to the election. The domicile shall not be lost through absence in the discharge of any elective office.

IV. They shall not be on active service in the Federal Army, nor have any command in the police corps or rural constabulary in the district in which the election takes place, for at least ninety days prior to the election.

V. They shall not hold the office of Secretary nor Assistant Secretary of any Executive Department, nor of Justice of the Supreme Court, unless they shall have resigned therefrom ninety days immediately prior to the election.

No State Governor, Secretary of State of the several States, nor State Judge shall be eligible in the Districts within their several jurisdictions, unless they shall have resigned from their office ninety days immediately prior to the day of election.

VI. They shall not be ministers of any religious creed.

Article 56. The Senate shall consist of two Senators from each State, and two from the Federal District, chosen in direct election.

Each State Legislature shall certify to the election of the candidate who shall have obtained a majority of the total number of votes cast.

Article 57. There shall be elected a substitute for each Senator.

Article 58. Each Senator shall serve four years. The Senate shall be renewed by half every two years.

Article 59. The qualifications necessary to be a Senator shall be the same as those necessary to be a Representative, excepting that of age, which shall be at least thirty-five years on the day of election.

Article 60. Each House shall be the judge of the election of its members, and shall decide all questions arising therefrom. Its decisions shall be final.

Article 61. Representatives and Senators are inviolable in respect of opinions, expressed by them in the discharge of their duties, and shall never be called to account for them.

Article 62. Representatives and Senators shall be disqualified, during the terms for which they have been elected, from holding any Federal or State commission or office for which any emolument is received without previous permission of the respective House; in the event of their accepting such commission or office they shall forthwith lose their representative character for such time as they hall hold such appointive office. The same provision shall apply to substitute Representatives and Senators, when on active service. The violation of this provision shall be punished by forfeiture of the office of Representative or Senator.

Article 63. The Houses shall not open their sessions nor exercise their functions without a quorum, in the Senate of two-thirds, and in the House of Representatives of a majority of the total membership; but the members present of either House shall meet on the day appointed by law, and compel the attendance of the absentees within the next thirty days, and they shall warn them that failure to comply with this provision shall be taken to a refusal of office, and the corresponding substitutes shall be summoned forthwith; the latter shall have a similar period within which to present themselves, and on their failure to do so the seats shall be declared vacant and new elections called.

Representatives or Senators who shall be absent during ten consecutive days without proper cause or without leave of the President of the respective House, notice of which shall be duly communicated to the House, shall be understood as waiving their right to attend until the next session, and their substitutes shall be summoned without delay.

If there shall be no quorum to constitute either of the Houses, or to continue their labours, once constituted, the substitutes shall be ordered to present themselves as soon as possible for the purpose of taking office until the expiration of the thirty days hereinbefore mentioned.

Article 64. No Representative or Senator who shall fail to attend any daily session without proper cause or without previous permission of the respective House, shall be entitled to the daily salary corresponding to the day on which he shall have been absent.

Article 65. The Congress shall meet on the first day of September of each year in regular session for the consideration of the following matters:—

I. To audit the accounts of the previous year, which shall be submitted to the House of Representatives not later than ten days after the opening of the session. The audit shall not be confined to determining whether the expenditures do or do not conform with the respective items in the Budget, but shall comprise an examination of the exactness of, and authorisation for, payments made thereunder, and of any liability arising from such payments.

No other secret items shall be permitted than those which the Budget for that year may consider necessary as such; these amounts shall be paid out by the Secretaries of Executive Departments under written orders of the President.

II. To examine, discuss and approve the Budget for the next fiscal year, and to levy such taxes as may be needed to meet the expenditures.

III. To study, discuss, and vote on Bills presented and to discuss all other matters incumbent upon the Congress by virtue of this Constitution.

Article 66. The regular session of the Congress shall last the period necessary to deal with all of the matters mentioned in the foregoing article, but it may not be extended beyond the thirty-first day of December of the same year. Should both Houses fail to agree as to adjournment prior to the above date, the matter shall be decided by the Executive.

Article 67. The Congress shall meet in extraordinary session whenever so summoned by the President, but in such event it shall consider only the matter or matters submitted to it by the President, who shall specify such matter or matters in the notice convening the meeting. The President shall have power to convene in extraordinary session only one of the Houses when the matter to be referred to it pertains to its exclusive jurisdiction.

Article 68. Both Houses shall hold their meetings in the same place, and shall not move to another without having first agreed upon the moving and the time and manner of accomplishing it, as well as upon the place of meeting, which shall be the same for both Houses. If both Houses agree to change their meeting place, but disagree as to the time, manner, and place the President shall settle the question by choosing one of the two proposals. Neither House may suspend its sessions for more than three days without the consent of the other.

Article 69. The President of the Republic shall attend at the opening of the Sessions of the Congress, whether regular or extraordinary, and shall submit a report in writing; this report shall, in the former case, relate to the general state of the Union; and in the latter, it shall explain to the Congress or to the House addressed the reasons or causes which rendered the summons necessary, and the matters requiring immediate attention.

Article 70. Every measure of the Congress shall be in the form of a law or decree. The laws or decrees shall be communicated to the Executive after having been signed by the Presidents of both Houses, and by one of the Secretaries of each. When promulgated, the enacting clause shall read as follows:—

"The Congress of the United States of Mexico decrees (text of the law or decree)."

Section II. Of the Initiation and Passage of the Laws

Article 71. The right to originate legislation pertains:—

I. To the President of the Republic;

II. To the Representatives and Senators of the Congress;

III. To the State Legislatures.

Bills submitted by the President of the Republic, by State Legislatures, or by delegations of the States shall be at once referred to committee. Those introduced by Representatives or Senators shall be subject to the rules of procedure.

Article 72. Bills, action on which shall not pertain exclusively to one of the Houses, shall be discussed first by one and then by the other, according to the rules as to the form, intervals, and the mode of procedure as to discussions and votes.

(a) After a Bill has been approved in the House where it originated it shall be sent to the other House for consideration. If passed by the latter it shall be transmitted to the President who, if he has no observations to make thereon, shall immediately promulgate it.

(b) Bills not returned within ten working days by the President with his observations to the House in which they originated, shall be considered approved, unless during the said ten days the Congress shall have adjourned or suspended its sessions, in which event they shall be returned on the first working day after the Congress shall have reassembled.

(c) Bills rejected in whole or in part by the President shall be returned with his observations to the House where they originated. They shall be discussed anew by this House, and if confirmed by a two-thirds majority of the total votes shall be sent to the other House for reconsideration. If approved by it, also by the same majority vote, the Bill shall become law and shall be returned to the President for promulgation.

The voting on a law or decree shall be by name.

(d) A Bill totally rejected by the revising chamber shall be returned with the proper observations to the Huose of origin. If examined anew and approved by an absolute majority of the members present, it shall be returned to the House rejecting it, which shall once again take it under consideration, and if approved by it, likewise by the same majority vote, it shall be sent to the President for the purposes of Clause (a); but if the said House fail to approve it, it shall not be reintroduced in the same session.

(e) If a Bill is rejected in part or modified or amended by the House of revision, the new discussion in the House of origin shall be confined to the portion rejected, or to the amendments or additions, without the approved articles being altered in any respect. If the additions or amendments made by the House of revision be approved by an absolute majority of the members present in the House of origin, the Bill shall be transmitted to the President for the purpose of Clause (a); but if the amendments or additions by the House of revision be rejected by a majority vote of the House of origin they shall be returned to the former House in order that the reasons set forth by the latter may be taken into consideration. If in this second revision the said additions or amendments be rejected by an absolute majority of the members present, the portions of the Bill which have been approved by both Houses shall be sent to the President for the purposes of Clause (a). If the House of revision insist by a majority vote of the members present upon the additions or amendments, no action shall be taken on the whole Bill until the next session, unless both Houses agree, by a majority vote of the members present, to the promulgation of the law without the articles objected to, which shall be left till the next session, when they shall be then discussed and voted upon.

(f) The same formalities as are required for the enactment of laws shall be observed for their interpretation, amendment, or repeal.

(g) No Bill rejected in the House of origin before passing to the other House shall be re-introduced during the session of that year.

(h) Legislative measures may be originated in either House, excepting Bills dealing with loans, taxes, or imposts, or with the raising of troops, which must have their origin in the House of Representatives.

(i) The opening stages of a Bill shall be discussed preferably in the House where it was introduced, unless one month shall have elapsed since it was referred to committee, and not reported on, in which event an identical Bill may be presented and discussed in the other House.

(j) The President of the Union shall not make any observations touching the resolutions of the Congress, or of either House, when acting as an electoral body or as a grand jury, nor when the House of Representatives shall declare that there are grounds to impeach any high federal authority for official offences.

Nor shall he make any observances touching the convocation decree issued by the Permanent Committee as provided in Article 84.

Section III. Of the Powers of the Congress

Article 73. The Congress shall have power:

I. To admit new States or Territories into the Federal Union.

II. To establish Territories as States which have a population of eighty thousand inhabitants, and the necessary means to provide for their political existence.

III. To form new States within the boundaries of existing ones, provided the following conditions are complied with:

(1) That the section or sections wishing to be established as States have a population of one hundred and twenty thousand inhabitants at least;

(2) That proof be given to the Congress that it has sufficient means to provide for its political existence;

(3) That the Legislatures of the States affected be heard as to the advisability or inadvisability of granting such Statehood, which opinion shall be given within six months reckoned from the day on which the particular application is forwarded;

(4) That the opinion of the President of the Federal Government be also heard on the subject; this opinion shall be given within seven days after the date on which it is requested.

(5) That the creation of the new State be voted upon favourably by two-thirds of the Represenatatives and Senators present in their respective Houses.

(6) That the resolution of the Congress be ratified by a majority of the State Legislatures, upon examination of a copy of the record of the case, provided that the Legislatures of the States to which the section belongs shall have given their consent.

(7) That the ratification referred to in the foregoing clause be given by two-thirds of the Legislatures of the States, if the Legislatures of the States to which the section belongs have not given their consent.

IV. To settle finally the limits of the States, terminating the differences which may arise between them relative to the demarcation of their respective territories, at least when the differences are of a contentious nature.

V. To change the seat of the Supreme Powers of the Federation.

VI. To legislate in all matters, relating to the Federal District and the Territories, as hereinafter provided:—

(1) The Federal District and the Territories shall be divided into municipalities, each of which shall have the area and population sufficient for its own support and for its contribution towards the common expenses.

(2) Each municipality shall be governed by a town council elected by direct vote of the people.

(3) The Federal District and each of the Territories, shall be administered by governors under the direct orders of the President of the Republic. The Governor of the Federal District shall report to the President, and the Governor of each Territory shall report to the President through the channels prescribed by law. The Governor of the Federal District and the Governor of each Territory shall be appointed by the President, and may be removed by him at will.

(4) The Superior Judges and the Judges of First Instance of the Federal District as well as of the Territories shall be named by the Congress, acting in each case as an electoral college. In the temporary or permanent absences of the said Superior Judges these shall be replaced by appointment of the Congress, and in recess by temporary appointments of the Permanent Committee. The organic law shall determine the manner of filling temporary vacancies in the case of judges, and shall designate the authority before whom they shall be called to account for any dereliction, without prejudice to the provisions of this Constitution with regard to the responsibility of officials. From and after the year 1923 the Superior Judges and those of First Instance to which this clause refers may only be removed from office for misconduct and after judicial enquiry, unless removed for promotion to the next higher grade. From and after the said date the salary enjoyed by the said officials shall not be diminished during their term of office.

(5) The office of the Public Attorney (Ministerio Publico) of the Federal District and of the Territories, shall be in charge of an Attorney-General, who shall reside in the City of Mexico, and of such Public Attorney or Attorneys as the law may determine; the said Attorney-General shall be under the direct orders of the President of the Republic, who shall appoint and remove him at will.

VII. To levy the taxes necessary to meet the expenditures of the Budget.

VIII. To establish the bases upon which the Executive may make loans on the credit of the nation; to approve the said loans and to acknowledge and order the payment of the national debt.

IX. To enact tariff laws on foreign commerce and to prevent restrictions from being imposed on interstate commerce.

X. To legislate for the entire Republic in all matters relating to mining, commerce, and credit institutions, and to establish the sole bank of issue, as provided in Article 28 of this Constitution.

XI. To create or abolish Federal offices, and to fix, increase, or decrease the salaries assigned thereto.

XII. To declare war, upon examination of the facts submitted by the Executive.

XIII. To regulate the manner in which letters of marque may be issued; to enact laws according to which prizes on sea and land shall be adjudged valid or invalid; and to frame the admiralty law for times of peace and war.

XIV. To raise and maintain the army and navy of the Union, and to regulate their organisation and service.

XV. To make rules for the organisation and discipline of the National Guard, reserving for the cities from which it is formed the right of appointing their respective commanders and officers, and to the States the power of instructing it in conformity with the discipline prescribed by the said regulations.

XVI. To enact laws on citizenship, naturalisation, colonisation, emigration, immigration, and public health of the Republic.

(1) The Public Health Council shall depend directly upon the President of the Republic, without the intervention of any Secretary of State, and its general provisions shall be binding throughout the Republic.

(2) In the event of serious epidemics or of the risk of introduction of diseases from abroad, the Public Health Department shall put into force without delay the necessary preventive measures, subject to their subsequent sanction by the President of the Republic.

(3) The sanitary authorities shall have executive powers, and their decisions shall be obeyed by the administrative authorities of the country.

(4) All measures which the Council shall have put into effect in its campaign against alcoholism and the sale of substances injurious to man and tending to degenerate the race shall be subsequently revised by the Congress, in such cases as fall within its powers.

XVII. To enact laws on general means of communication, postroads and post offices, and to enact laws as to the use and development of the waters subject to the Federal jurisdiction.

XVIII. To establish mints, regulate the monetary system, fix the value of foreign moneys, and adopt a general system of weights and measures.

XIX. To make rules for the occupation and alienation of uncultivated lands and the prices thereof.

XX. To enact laws as to the organisation of the diplomatic and consular services.

XXI. To define the crimes and offences against the Federation, and to fix the penalties therefor.

XXII. To grant pardons for offences subject to federal jurisdiction.

XXIII. To make rules for its internal government, and to enact the necessary provisions to compel the attendance of absent Representatives and Senators, and to punish the acts of commission or omission of those present.

XXIV. To issue the organic law of the office of the Comptroller of the Treasury.

XXV. To sit as an electoral college, and to name the Justices of the Supreme Court, and the Superior and Inferior Judges of the Federal District and Territories.

XXVI. To accept the resignation of the Justices of the Supreme Court, Justices of the Nation, and of the Superior and Inferior Judges of the Federal District and Territories, and to name substitutes in their absence, and to appoint their successors.

XXVII. To establish professional schools of scientific research and fine arts, vocational, agricultural, and trade schools, museums, libraries, observatories and other institutes of higher learning, until such time as these establishments can be supported by private funds. These powers shall not pertain exclusively to the Federal Government.

All degrees conferred by any of the above institutions shall be valid throughout the Republic.

XXVIII. To sit as an electoral college and to choose the person to asssume the office of President of the Republic, either as a substitute President or as a President ad interim in the terms established by Articles 84 and 85 of this Constitution.

XXIX. To accept the resignation of the President of the Republic.

XXX. To audit the accounts which shall be submitted annually by the Executive; this audit shall comprise not only the checking of the items disbursed under the Budget, but the exactness of and authorisation for the expenditures in each case.

XXXI. To make all laws necessary for carrying into execution the foregoing powers and all other powers vested by this Constitution in the several branches of the Government.

Article 74. The House of Representatives shall have the following exclusive powers:—

I. To sit as an electoral college to exercise the powers conferred by law as to the election of the President.

II. To watch by means of a committee appointed from among its own members the faithful performance of the duties of the Comptroller of the Treasury.

III. To appoint all the higher officials and other employees of the office of the Comptroller of the Treasury.

IV. To approve the annual Budget, after a discussion as to what taxes must in its judgment be levied to meet the necessary expenditures.

V. To take cognisance of all charges brought against public officials, as herein provided, for official offences, and should the circumstances so warrant to impeach them before the Senate; and further to act as a grand jury to decide whether there is or is not good ground for proceeding against any official enjoying constitutional privileges, whenever accused of offences of the common order.

VI. To exercise such other powers as may be expressly vested in it by this Constitution.

Article 75. The House of Representatives, in passing the budget, shall not fail to assign a definite salary to every office created by law, and if for any reason such salary shall not be assigned, the amount fixed in the preceding Budget or in the law creating the office shall be presumed to be assigned.

Article 76. The Senate shall have the following exclusive powers:—

I. To approve the Treaties and diplomatic conventions concluded by the President with foreign powers.

II. To confirm the nominations made by the President of diplomatic ministers or agents, consuls-general, higher officials of the Treasury, colonels and other superior officers of the army and navy, in the manner and form by law provided.

III. To authorise the giving of permission for national troops to go beyond the limits of the Republic, or to permit foreign troops to pass through the national territory, and to consent to the presence of fleets of another nation for more than one month in Mexican waters.

IV. To consent to the President of the Republic disposing of the National Guard outside the limits of its respective States or Territories, and to fix the amount of the force to be used.

V. To declare, when all the constitutional powers of any State have disappeared, that the occasion has arisen to give to the said State a provisional governor, who shall arrange for elections to be held according to the Constitution and laws of the said State. The appointment of such a governor shall be made by the Senate with the approval of two-thirds of its members present or during recess by the Permanent Committee by the same two-thirds majority, from among three names submitted by the President. The official thus selected shall not be chosen constitutional governor in the elections to be held under the summons which he shall issue. This provision shall govern whenever the State Constitutions do not provide for the contingencies.

VI. To sit as a grand jury to take cognisance of such official offences of functionaries as are expressly prescribed by this Constitution.

VII. To exercise such other powers as may be expressly vested in it by this Constitution.

VIII. To adjust all political questions arising between the powers of the State whenever one of them shall appeal to the Senate, or whenever by virtue of such differences a clash of arms has arisen to interrupt the constitutional order. In this event the Senate shall decide in accordance with the Federal Constitution and the Constitution of the State involved.

The exercise of this power and of the foregoing shall be regulated by law.

Article 77. Each House may, without the intervention of the other:—

I. Pass resolutions upon matters exclusively relating to its own interior government.

II. Communicate with the other House and with the Executive, through committees appointed from among its members.

III. Appoint the employees in the office of its secretary and make all rules and regulations for the said office.

IV. Issue writs for extraordinary elections to fill any vacancies which may occur in its membership.

Section IV. Of the Permanent Committee

Article 78. During the recess of the Congress there shall be a Permanent Committee consisting of twenty-nine members, fifteen of whom shall be Representatives and fourteen Senators, appointed by the respective Houses on the eve of the day of adjournment.

Article 79. In addition to the powers expressly vested in it by this Constitution, the Permanent Committee shall have the following powers:—

I. To give its consent to the use of the National Guard as provided in Article 76, Clause IV.

II. To administer the oath of office, should the occasion arise, to the President, to the Justices of the Supreme Court, to the Superior Judges of the Federal Districts and Territories, on such occasions as the latter officials may meet in the city of Mexico.

III. To report on all pending matters, so that they may be considered in the next session.

IV. To call extraordinary sessions in the case of official or ordinary offences committed by Secretaries of State or Justices of the Supreme Court, and official offences committed by State governors, provided the case shall have been already instituted by the Committee of the Grand Jury, in which event no other business of the Congress shall be considered, nor shall the sessions be prolonged beyond the time necessary for a decision.

CHAPTER III. OF THE EXECUTIVE POWER

Article 80. The exercise of the Supreme Executive power of the Union is vested in a single individual, who shall be called "President of the United States of Mexico."

Article 81. The election of the President shall be direct, in accordance with the terms of the electoral law.

Article 82. The president of the Republic shall have the following qualifications:—

I. He shall be a Mexican citizen by birth, in the full enjoyment of his rights, and he must be the son of Mexican parents by birth.

II. He shall be over thirty-five years of age at the time of election.

III. He shall have resided in the country during the entire year prior to the election.

IV. He shall not belong to the ecclesiastical state, nor be a minister of any religious creed.

V. In the event of belonging to the army, he shall have retired from active service 90 days prior to the election.

VI. He shall not be a Secretary or Assistant Secretary of any Executive Department, unless he shall have resigned from office 90 days prior to the election.

VII. He shall not have taken part, directly or indirectly, in any uprising, riot, or military coup.

Article 83. The President shall enter upon the duties of his office on the first day of December, shall serve four years, and shall never be re-elected.

The citizen who shall replace the constitutional President in the event of his permanent disability shall not be elected President for the ensuing term.

Nor shall the person designated as Acting President during the temporary disabilities of the constitutional President be re-elected President for the ensuing term.

Article 84. In the event of the permanent disability of the President of the Republic, if this shall occur within the first two years of his term of office, the Congress, if in session, shall forthwith act as an electoral college, and with the attendance of at least two-thirds of its total membership shall choose a President by secret ballot and by a majority vote; and the same Congress shall issue the summons for Presidential elections, and shall endeavour to have the date set for this event as far as possible coincident with the date of the next election of Representatives and Senators to Congress.

Should the disability of the President occur while Congress is in recess, the Permanent Committee shall forthwith designate a President ad interim, who shall call Congress together in extraordinary session, in order that it may in turn issue the summons for Presidential elections in the manner provided in the foregoing paragraph.

Should the disability of the President occur in the last two years of his term of office, the Congress, if in session, shall choose the substitute to conclude the period of the Presidential term; if Congress shall not be in session the Permanent Committee shall choose a President ad interim, and shall summon Congress in extraordinary session, in order that it may act as an electoral college and proceed to the election of the substitute President.

The citizen designated as President ad interim for the purpose of calling elections, in the event of the disability, of the President within the two first years of the respective term, shall not be chosen in the elections held to fill such vacancy and for which he was designated.

Article 85. If the President-Elect shall fail to present himself at the beginning of the constitutional term, or if the election shall not have been held and the result made known by the 1st of December, the outgoing President shall nevertheless vacate office and the President ad interim chosen by the Congress, or in its recess by the Permanent Committee, shall forthwith assume the executive power. All action taken hereunder shall be governed by the provisions of the foregoing article.

In case of a temporary disability of the President, the Congress, or the Permanent Committee if the Congress shall not be in session, shall designate an Acting President during such disability. If a temporary disability shall become permanent, the action prescribed in the preceding article shall be taken.

In the event of a leave of absence being granted to the President of the Republic, the person acting in his stead shall not be disqualified from being elected in the ensuing period, provided he shall not have been in office during the holding of elections.

Article 86. The President shall not resign office except for grave cause, which shall be authorised by Congress, to which body the resignation shall be tendered.

Article 87. The President, before entering upon the discharge of the duties of his office, shall make the following affirmation before the Congress, or in its recess before the Permanent Committee:—

I do solemnly affirm that I will defend and enforce the Constitution of the United States of Mexico and the laws enacted thereunder, and that I will faithfully and conscientiously perform the duties of President of the United States of Mexico, to which I have been chosen by the people, having ever in mind the welfare and prosperity of the Nation; if I shall fail to do so, may the Nation call me to account.

Article 88. The President shall not absent himself from the national territory without the permission of the Congress.

Article 89. The President shall have the following powers and duties:—

I. To promulgate and execute the laws enacted by the Congress, providing within the executive sphere for their faithful observance.

II. To appoint and remove at will the Secretaries of Executive Departments, the Attorney General of the Republic, the Governor of the Federal District, the Governors of Territories, the Attorney General of the Federal District and Territories; and to appoint and remove at will all other Federal employees whose appointment or removal is not otherwise provided for by law or in this Constitution.

III. To appoint, with the approval of the Senate, all ministers, diplomatic agents and consuls general.

IV. To appoint, with the approval of the Senate, the colonels and other superior officers of the army and navy and the superior officials of the treasury.

V. To appoint all other officers of the national army and navy, as by law provided.

VI. To dispose of the permanent land and sea forces for the domestic safety and external defence of the Union.

VII. To dispose of the National Guard for the same purposes, as provided by Article 76, Clause IV.

VIII. To declare war in the name of the United States of Mexico, after the passage of the corresponding resolution by the Congress of the Union.

IX. To grant letters of marque, upon the terms and conditions fixed by the Congress.

X. To conduct diplomatic negotiations and to make treaties.

XI. To call Congress, or either of the Houses, in extraordinary session, whenever in his judgment it may be advisable.

XII. To afford the judiciary the assistance necessary for the expeditious exercise of its functions.

XIII. To open all kinds of posts, establish maritime and frontier custom houses and designate their location.

XIV. To grant, according to law, pardons to criminals sentenced for offences within the jurisdiction of the Federal tribunals, and to all persons sentenced for offences of the common order in the Federal District and Territories.

XV. To grant exclusive privileges for a limited time, and according to the laws relating thereto, to persons making discoveries, inventions and improvements in any branch of industry.

XVI. Whenever the Senate shall not be in session the President may temporarily make the nominations enumerated in Clauses III and IV hereof, but these nominations shall be submitted to the Senate as soon as it re-convenes.

XVII. To exercise such other rights and duties as are expressly conferred upon him by this Constitution.

Article 90. For the transaction of administrative matters of the Federal Government there shall be the number of Secretaries of Executive Departments which the Congress may by law establish, which law shall likewise assign among the various departments the several matters with which each shall be charged.

Article 91. No person shall be appointed Secretary of an Executive Department who is not a Mexican citizen by birth, in the enjoyment of his rights, and who has not attained the age of thirty years.

Article 92. All regulations, decrees and orders of the President shall be signed by the Secretary of the Executive Department to which the matter pertains. They shall not be binding without this requisite. All regulations, decrees, and orders of the President touching the government of the Federal District and the administrative departments shall be transmitted directly by the President to the Governor of the district and to the chief of the respective department.

Article 93. The Secretaries of Executive Departments shall on the opening of each regular session report to the Congress as to the state of their respective Departments. Either House may summon a Secretary of an Executive Department to inform it, whenever a bill or other matter pertaining to his department is under discussion or consideration.

CHAPTER IV. OF THE JUDICIAL POWER

Article 94. The judicial power of the Federation is vested in a Supreme Court and in Circuit and District Courts, whose number and powers shall be fixed by law. The Supreme Court of Justice shall consist of eleven members; it shall sit only as a body and its hearings shall be public, except in the cases where public interest or morality shall otherwise require. It shall meet at such times and under such conditions as by law prescribed. No sittings of the Court shall be held without the attendance of at least two-thirds of its total membership, and all decisions rendered shall be by a majority vote.

The Justices of the Supreme Court chosen to this office in the forthcoming elections shall serve two years; those elected at the conclusion of this first term shall serve four years, and from and after the year 1923, the Justices of the Supreme Court, the Circuit and District Judges may only be removed for malfeasance and after impeachment proceedings, save in the case of the promotion of Circuit and District Judges to the next higher grade.

The same provision shall apply, in so far as it be applicable, to the terms of two and four years, respectively, to which this Article refers.

Article 95. The Justices of the Supreme Court shall have the following qualifications:

I. They shall be Mexican citizens by birth, in the full enjoyment of their civil and political rights.

II. They shall be over thirty-five years of age at the time of election.

III. They shall be graduates in law of some institution or corporation authorised by law to confer such degrees.

IV. They shall be of good repute and not have been convicted of any offence punishable with more than one year's imprisonment; but conviction of larceny, deceit, forgery, embezzlement or any other offence seriously impairing their good name in public mind shall disqualify them from office, whatever may have been the penalty imposed.

V. They shall have resided in the country for the last five years, except in the case of absence due to public service abroad for a period not exceeding six months.

Article 96. The members of the Supreme Court of Justice shall be chosen by the Congress, acting as an electoral college; the presence of at least two-thirds of the total number of Representatives and Senators shall be necessary for such action. The election shall be by secret ballot and by a majority vote, and shall be held as among the candidates previously proposed, one being nominated by each State Legislature, as provided in the respective State laws.

Should no candidate receive a majority on the first ballot, the balloting shall be repeated between the two candidates receiving the highest number of votes.

Article 97. All Circuit and District Judges shall be appointed by the Supreme Court of Justice; they shall have such qualifications as are by law required, shall serve four years and shall not be removed except by impeachment proceedings or for incapacity to discharge their duties, in accordance with the law.

The Supreme Court of Justice may remove the District Judges from one District to another, or it may fix their seats in another locality, as it may deem most advantageous to the public business. A similar procedure shall be observed in the case of Circuit Judges.

The Supreme Court of Justice may likewise appoint auxiliary Circuit and District Judges to assist in the labours of such courts as have excessive amount of business, in order that the administration of justice may be speedy; it shall also name one or more of its members or some District or Circuit Judge or shall designate one or more special commissioners, whenever it shall deem it advisable or on the request of the President or of either House or of any State Governor, solely for the purpose of inquiring into the behaviour of any Judge or Federal Justice or into any fact or facts which amount to a violation of any individual rights or to the subversion of the popular will or of any other offence punishable by Federal statute.

The Circuit and District courts shall be assigned among the several Justices of the Supreme Court who shall visit them periodically, shall observe the conduct of their judges, listen to any complaint presented against them and perform all such other acts as the law may require. The Supreme Court shall appoint and remove at will its Clerk of the Court and other employees on the roster established by law. The Circuit and District Judges shall likewise appoint and remove at will their respective clerks and employees.

The Supreme Court shall choose each year one of its members to act as Chief Justice, with the right of re-election.

Each Justice of the Supreme Court on assuming office shall make an affirmation before the Congress, or if it is in recess, before the Permanent Committee, as follows:—

The Presiding Officer shall say:—"Do you promise to perform faithfully and conscientiously the duties of Justice of the Supreme Court with which you have been charged, and to defend and enforce the Constitution of the United States of Mexico and the laws enacted thereunder, having ever in mind the welfare and prosperity of the Nation?" To which the Justice shall reply, "I do." On which the Presiding Officer shall answer; "If you fail to do so, may the Nation call you to account."

The Circuit and District Judges shall make the affirmation of office before the Supreme Court or before such other authority as the law may determine.

Article 98. No vacancy arising from temporary disability of a Justice of the Supreme Court not exceeding one month shall be filled, provided there be otherwise a quorum. In the absence of a quorum the Congress, or in its recess the Permanent Committee, shall name a substitute selected from among the candidates submitted by the States for the election of the Justice in question and not chosen, to serve during such disability.

If the disability does not exceed two months, the Congress, or during its recess, the Permanent Committee, shall choose at will a temporary justice.

In the event of the death, resignation or disqualification of any justice of the Supreme Court, a new election shall be held by the Congress to fill this vacancy as provided in Article 96.

If the Congress shall not be in session, the Permanent Committee shall make a temporary appointment until such time as the Congress shall convene and proceed to the corresponding election.

Article 99. The resignation of a justice of the Supreme Court shall only be accepted for grave cause, approved by the Congress, to whom the resignation shall be tendered. In the recesses of the Congress the power to act in this matter belongs to the Permanent Committee.

Article 100. The Supreme Court shall grant all leaves of absence of its members, when they do not exceed one month; such as do exceed this period shall be granted by the House of Representatives; or during its recess by the Permanent Committee.

Article 101. No justice of the Supreme Court, Circuit or District judge, nor clerk of any of these Courts shall under any circumstances accept any State, Federal or private commission or office, excepting honorary titles from scientific, literary or charitable associations. The violation of this provision shall result in a forfeiture of office.

Article 102. The office of the Public Attorney shall be organised in accordance with the law, and its officers shall be appointed and removed at will by the Executive. They shall be under the direction of an Attorney General who shall possess the same qualifications as are required for the office of Justice of the Supreme Court.

The Public Attorneys shall be charged with the judicial prosecution of all Federal offences; they shall accordingly sue out all orders of arrest, collect and present all evidence as to the responsibility of the accused, see that the trials are conducted in due order so that the administration of justice may be speedy, pray the imposition of sentence, and in general take part in all matters required by law.

The Attorney General of the Republic shall personally intervene in matters to which the Federal Government is a party, in cases affecting ministers, diplomatic agents and consuls general, and in all controversies between two or more States of the Union, between the Federal Government and a State or between the several powers of a State. The Attorney General may either personally or through one of the Public Attorneys take part in all other cases in which the public attorneys are called upon to act.

The Attorney General shall be the legal adviser of the Government, and both he and the Public Attorneys under his orders shall faithfully obey the law and shall be liable for all breaches or for any violation which they may incur in the discharge of their duties.

Article 103. The Federal Tribunals shall take cognisance of:—

I. All controversies arising out of laws or acts of the authorities which shall infringe guarantees of personal liberty.

II. All controversies arising out of laws or acts of the Federal authorities which limit or encroach upon the sovreignty of the States.

III. All controversies arising out of laws or acts of the State authorities which invade the sphere of the Federal authorities.

Article 104. The Federal Tribunals shall have jurisdiction over:—

I. All controversies of a civil or criminal nature arising out of the application and enforcement of the Federal laws, or out of treaties concluded with foreign powers. Whenever such controversies affect only private rights, the regular local court of the States, the Federal District and Territories shall, at the election of the plaintiff, assume jurisdiction. Appeal may be had from all judgments of first instance to the next higher tribunal of the same which the case was first heard. Appeal may be taken from sentences of second instance to the Supreme Court of Justice, which appeal shall be prepared, submitted and prosecuted, in accordance with the procedure provided by law.

II. All cases pertaining to admiralty law.

III. All cases to which the Federation may be a party.

IV. All cases arising between two or more States, or between any State and Federal Government, as well as those arising between the courts of the Federal District and those of the Federal Government or of a State.

V. All cases arising between a State and one or more citizens of another State.

VI. All cases concerning diplomatic agents and consuls.

Article 105. The Supreme Court of Justice shall have exclusive jurisdiction in all controversies arising between two or more States, between the powers of Government of any State as to the constitutionality of their acts, or between one or more States and the Federal Government, and in all cases to which the Federal Government may be a party.

Article 106. The Supreme Court of Justice shall likewise have exclusive jurisdiction to determine all questions of jurisdiction between the Federal Tribunals, betwen these and those of the States, or between those of one State and those of another.

Article 107. All controversies mentioned in Article 103 shall be prosecuted by the injured party in accordance with the judicial forms and procedure which the law shall establish, subject to the following conditions:—

I. The judgment shall always be so drawn as to affect exclusively private individuals and shall confine itself to affording them redress in the special case to which the complaint refers; but it shall make no general statement as to the law or the act that may have formed the basis of the complaint.

II. In civil or penal suits, excepting those mentioned in Clause XI hereof, the writ of "amparo"* shall issue only against final judgments when no other ordinary recourse is available by which these judgments may be modified or amended, if the violation of the law shall have occurred in the judgment or if, although committed during the course of the trial, objection was duly noted and protest entered against the denial of reparation, and provided further that if committed in the first instance it shall have been invoked in second instance as a violation of the law.

Notwithstanding the foregoing provision, the Supreme Court may in

---

* Amparo. This unique feature of Mexican jurisprudence combines the essential elements of the extraordinary writs of habeas corpus, certiorari and mandamus. It is a federal procedure designed to give immediate redress when any of the fundamental rights of man are infringed by any authority, irrespective of category, or to excuse the obedience of a law or decree which has invaded the federal or local sphere. Its use is most extensive, embracing minors, persons absent abroad acting through a "next friend," corporations, etc. An important feature is that it merely gives redress to a specific person or entity, and never makes any general statement of law. It could, hence, never declare a law unconstitutional, though it would give immediate relief, so soon as the law in question acted upon any person.

(Note to "The Mexican Constitution of 1917," *Annals of the American Academy of Political and Social Science* (Suppl., May 1917) penal cases waive any defects in the petition when there has been a manifest violation of the law which has left the petitioner without recourse, or when he has been tried by a law not strictly applicable to the case, provided failure to take advantage of this violation has been merely an oversight.

III. In similar penal suits the writ of "amparo" shall issue only if substantial portions of the rules of procedure have been violated, and provided further that the said violation shall deprive the petitioner of means of defence.

IV. In addition to the case mentioned in the foregoing paragraph, the writ of "amparo" shall issue only on a final judgment in a civil suit— provided the requirements set forth in Clause II hereof have been complied with,—when the judgment shall be contrary to the letter of the law applicable to the case or contrary to its legal interpretation, when it includes persons, actions, defences, or things which have not been the object of the suit, or finally when all these have not been included either through omission or express refusal.

When the writ of "amparo" is sought against judgments which are not definitive in accordance with the provisions of the foregoing Clause, these rules shall be observed, as far as applicable.

V. In penal suits, the authorities responsible shall stay the execution of final judgment against which the writ of "amparo" has been sought; for this purpose the petitioner shall within the period set by law, give notice, under oath, to the said authorities of the interposition of this proceeding, accompanying it with two copies of the petition, one of which shall be delivered to the opposing party and the other filed.

VI. The execution of a final judgment in civil suits shall only be stayed when the petitioner shall give bond to cover damages occasioned thereby, unless the other party shall give a counter bond (1) to guarantee that the normal conditions and relations previously existing shall be restored, and (2) to pay the corresponding damages, in the event of the granting of the "amparo." In such event the interposition of the proceeding by "amparo" shall be communicated as provided in the foregoing Clause.

VII. If a writ of "amparo" be sought against a final judgment, a certified copy of such portions of the record as the petitioner may desire shall be requested from the authority responsible for the violation; to this there shall be added such portions as the other party may desire and a clear and succinct statement by the said authority of the justification of the act protested; note shall be made of this on the record.

VIII. When a writ of "amparo" is sought against a final judgment, the petition shall be brought before the Supreme Court; this petition, together with the copy required by Clause VII, shall be either presented to the Supreme Court or sent through the authority responsible for the violation or through the District Court of the corresponding State. The Supreme Court shall render judgment without any other formality or procedure than the petition, the document presented by the other party and that of the Attorney General or the Public Attorney he may name in his stead, and shall comprise no other legal question that that contained in the complaint.

IX. When the acts of an authority other than the judicial are involved or the acts of the judiciary exercised outside of the suit or after the termination thereof, or acts committed during the suit whose execution is of impossible reparation, or which affect persons not parties to the suit, the writ of "amparo" shall be sought before the District Court within whose jurisdiction is located the place where the act protested was committed or attempted; the procedure in this case shall be confined to the report of the authority and to a hearing, the summons for which shall be issued in the same order of the court as that calling for the report. This hearing shall be held at as early a date as possible, the testimony of both parties offered, arguments heard, which shall not exceed on hour for each side, and finally the judgment given, which shall be pronounced at the same hearing. The judgment of the District Court shall be final, if the interested parties do not appeal to the Supreme Court within the period set by law and in the manner prescribed by Clause VIII.

In case of a violation of the guarantees of Articles 16, 19 and 20, recourse shall be had to the appellate court of the court committing the breach or to the corresponding District Court. An appeal against the decision of any of these Courts may be taken to the Supreme Court.

If the District Judge shall not reside in the same locality as the official guilty of the violation, the judge before whom the petition of "amparo" shall be submitted shall be determined by law; this judge shall be authorised to suspend temporarily the execution of the act protested, in accordance with the terms established by law.

X. Any official failing to suspend the execution of the act protested, when in duty bound to do so, or when he admits an insufficient or improper bond, shall be turned over to the proper authorities; the civil and penal liability of the official shall in these cases be a joint liability with the person offering the bond and his surety.

XI. If after the granting of an "amparo," the guilty official shall persist in the act or acts against which the petition of "amparo" was filed, or shall seek to render of no effect the judgment of the Federal authority, he shall be forthwith removed from office and turned over for trial to the appropriate District Court.

XII. Wardens and jailers who fail to receive a duly certified copy of the formal order of commitment within the seventy-two hours granted by Article 19, reckoned from the time the accused is placed at the disposal of the court, shall bring this fact to the attention of the court, immediately upon expiration of this period; and if the proper order be not received within the next three hours the accused shall be set at liberty.

Any official who shall violate this provision and the Article referred to in the foregoing paragraph shall be immediately handed over to the proper authorities. Any official or agent thereof who, after an arrest has been made, shall fail to place the accused at the disposal of the court within the next twenty-four hours shall himself be handed over to the proper authority.

If the detention be effected outside the locality in which the court is situated, there shall be added to the period mentioned in the preceding sentence the time necessary to travel from the said locality to that where the detention took place.

TITLE 4: OF THE RESPONSIBILITY OF OFFICIALS

Article 108. Senators and Representatives of Congress, Justices of the Supreme Court, Secretaries of Executive Departments, and the Attorney General of the Republic shall be liable for all common offences committed during their term of office, as well as for all official offences or acts of commission or omission of which they may be guilty in the discharge of their duties.

Governors of States and members of State Legislatures shall be liable for violation of the Constitution and the Federal laws.

The President of the Republic may only be impeached during his term of office for high treason and common offences of a serious character.

Article 109. If the offence belongs to the common order the House of Representatives, acting as a grand jury, shall determine by a majority vote of its total membership whether there is or is not any ground for proceeding against the accused.

If the finding be favourable to the accused, no further action shall be taken; but such findings shall not be a bar to the prosecution of the charge so soon as the constitutional privilege shall cease, since the finding of the House does not in any way determine the merits of the charge.

If the finding be adverse, the accused shall ipso facto be removed from office and be placed at the disposition of the ordinary courts of justice, except in the case of the President of the Republic, who may only be impeached before the Senate, as in the case of an official offence.

Article 110. No constitutional privilege shall be extended to any high Federal functionary when tried for official offences, misdemeanours, or omissions committed by him in the discharge of any public function or commission, during the time in which, according to law, the privilege is enjoyed. This provision shall be applicable to cases of common offences committed under the same circumstances. In order that the proceedings may be instituted when the functionary returns to the exercise of his own functions, the rules set forth in Article 109 of the Constitution shall be observed.

Article 111. The Senate acting as a grand jury shall try all cases of impeachment; but it may not institute such proceedings without a previous accusation brought by the House of Representatives.

If the Senate should, after hearing the accused and conducting such proceedings as it may deem advisable, determine by a majority vote of two-thirds of its total membership removed from office by virtue of such decision, or he may be disqualified from holding any other office for such time as the law may determine.

When the same office is punishable with an additional penalty, the accused shall be placed at the disposition of the regular authorities who shall judge and sentence him in accordance with the law.

In all cases embraced by this Article and in those included by the preceding, both the decisions of the Grand Jury and the findings of the House of Representatives shall be final.

Any person shall have the right to denounce before the House of Representatives offences of a common order or of an official character committed by high Federal functionaries; and whenever the said House of Representatives shall determine that there exists good grounds for impeachment proceedings before the Senate, it shall name a committee from among its own members to sustain the charges brought.

The Congress shall as soon as possible enact a law as to the responsibility of all Federal officials and employees which shall fix as official offences all acts of commission or omission, which may prejudice the public interest and efficient administration, even though such acts may not heretofore have been considered offences. These officials shall be tried by a jury in the same manner as provided for trials by jury in Article 20.

Article 112. No pardon shall be granted the offender in cases of impeachment.

Article 113. The responsibility for official breaches and offences may only be enforced during such time as the functionary shall remain in office and one year thereafter.

Article 114. In civil cases no privilege or immunity in favour of any public functionary shall be recognised.

TITLE 5: OF THE STATES OF THE FEDERATION

Article 115. The States shall adopt for their internal government the popular, representative, republican form of government; they shall have as the basis of their territorial division and political and administrative organisation, the free municipality, in accordance with the following provisions:—

I. Each municipality shall be administered by a town council chosen by direct vote of the people, and no authority shall intervene between the municipality and the State government.

II. Municipalities shall freely administer their own revenues which shall be derived from the taxes fixed by the State Legislatures, which shall at all times be sufficient to meet their needs.

III. The municipalities shall be regarded as enjoying corporate existence for all legal purposes.

The Federal Executive and State Governors shall have command over all public forces of the municipalities wherein they may permanently or temporarily reside.

State Governors under the Constitution shall not be re-elected, nor shall their term of office exceed four years.

The prohibitions of Article 83 are applicable to substitute or ad interim Governors.

The number of Representatives in the State Legislatures shall be in proportion to the inhabitants of each State, but in no case shall the number of representatives in any State Legislature be less than fifteen.

Each electoral district of the States shall choose a Representative and a substitute to the State Legislature.

Every State Governor shall be a Mexican citizen by birth and a native of the State, or resident therein not less than five years immediately prior to the date of election.

Article 116. The States shall have the power to fix among themselves, by friendly agreements, their respective boundaries; but these agreements shall not be carried into effect without the approval of the Congress.

Article 117. No State shall in any circumstances:—

I. Enter into alliances, treaties, or coalitions with another State or with foreign powers.

II. Grant letters of marque or reprisal.

III. Coin money, issue paper money, stamps or stamped paper.

IV. Levy taxes on persons or property passing through its territory.

V. Prohibit or tax, directly or indirectly, the entry into its territory, or the withdrawal therefrom, of any merchandise, foreign or domestic.

VI. Burden the circulation or consumption of domestic or foreign merchandise with taxes or duties to be collected by local custom houses or subject to inspection the said merchandise, or require it to be accompanied by documents.

VII. Enact or maintain in force laws or fiscal regulations discriminating, by taxation or otherwise, between merchandise, foreign or domestic, on account of its origin, whether this discrimination be established with regard to similar products of the locality or between similar products of separate places of origin.

VIII. Issue bonds of the public debt payable in foreign coin or outside the Federal territory; contract loans, directly or indirectly, with any foreign government, or assume any obligation in favour of any foreign corporation or individual, requiring the issuance of certificates or bonds payable to bearer or negotiable by endorsement.

The Federal Congress and the State Legislatures shall forthwith enact laws against alcoholism.

Article 118. No State shall, without the consent of the Congress:—

I. Establish tonnage dues or other port charges, or impose taxes or other duties upon imports or exports; or

II. Keep at any time permanent troops or vessels of war.

Article 119. Every State shall be bound to deliver without delay to the demanding authorities the fugitives from justice from other States or from foreign nations.

In such cases the writ of the court granting the extradition shall operate as a sufficient warrant for the detention of the accused for one month, in the case of extradition from one State to another, and for two months in the case of international extradition.

Article 120. The State Governors are bound to publish and enforce the Federal laws.

Article 121. Full faith and credit shall be given in each State of the Federation to the public acts, records and judicial proceedings of all the other States. The Congress shall by general laws prescribe the manner of proving the said acts, records and proceedings and the effect thereof.

I. The laws of a State shall only be binding within its own confines, and shall therefore have no extra-territorial force.

II. Movable and immovable property shall be governed by the lex sitae.

III. Judgments of a State Court as to property and property rights situated in another State shall only be binding when expressly so provided by the law of the latter State.

Judgments relating to personal rights shall only be binding in another State provided the person shall have expressly, or impliedly by reason of domicile, submitted to the jurisdiction of the court rendering such judgment, and provided further that personal service shall have been secured.

IV. All acts of civil status performed in accordance with the laws of one State shall be binding in all other States.

V. All professional licences issued by the authorities of one State in accordance with its laws shall be valid in all other States.

Article 122. The Powers of the Union are bound to protect the States against all invasion or external violence. In case of insurrection or internal disturbance they shall give them the same protection, provided the Legislature of the State, or the Executive thereof if the Legislature is not in session, shall so request.

TITLE 6: OF LABOUR AND SOCIAL WELFARE

Article 123. The congress and the State Legislatures shall make laws relative to labour with due regard for the needs of each region, and in conformity with the following principles, and these principles and laws shall govern the labour of skilled and unskilled workmen, employees, domestic servants and artisans, and in general every contract of labour.

I. Eight hours shall be the maximum limit of a day's work.

II. The maximum limit of night work shall be seven hours. Unhealthy and dangerous occupations are forbidden to all women and to children under sixteen years of age. Night work in factories is likewise forbidden to women and to children under sixteen years of age; nor shall they be employed in commercial establishments after ten o'clock at night.

III. The maximum limit of a day's work for children over twelve and under sixteen years of age shall be six hours. The work of children under twelve years of age shall not be made the subject of a contract.

IV. Every workman shall enjoy at least one day's rest for every six days' work.

V. Women shall not perform any physical work requiring considerable physical effort during the three months immediately preceding parturition; during the month following parturition they shall necessarily enjoy a period of rest and shall receive their salaries or wages in full and retain their employment and the rights they may have acquired under their contracts. During the period of lactation they shall enjoy two extraordinary periods of rest of one-half hour each, in order to nurse their children.

VI. The minimum wage to be received by a workman shall be that considered sufficient, according to the conditions prevailing in the respective region of the country, to satisfy the normal needs of the life of the workman, his education and his lawful pleasures, considering him as the head of a family. In all agricultural, commercial, manufacturing or mining enterprises the workman shall have the right to participate in the profits in the manner fixed in Clause IX of this Article.

VII. The same remuneration shall be paid for the same work, without regard to sex or nationality.

VIII. The minimum wage shall be exempt from attachment, set off or discount.

IX. The determination of the minimum wage and of the rate of profit-sharing described in Clause VI shall be made by special commissions to be appointed in each municipality and to be subordinated to the Central Board of Conciliation to be established in each State.

X. All wages shall be paid in legal currency and shall not be paid in merchandise, orders, counters or any other representative token with which it is sought to substitute money.

XI. When owing to special circumstances it becomes necessary to increase the working hours, there shall be paid as wages for the overtime one hundred per cent more than those fixed for regular time. In no case shall the overtime exceed three hours nor continue for more than three consecutive days; and no women of whatever age nor boys under sixteen years of age may engage in overtime work.

XII. In every agricultural, industrial, mining or other class of work employers are bound to furnish to their workmen comfortable and sanitary dwelling-places, for which they may charge rents not exceeding one-half of one per cent per month of the assessed value of the properties. They shall likewise establish schools, dispensaries and other services necessary to the community. If the factories are located within inhabited places and more than one hundred persons are employed therein, the first of the above-mentioned conditions shall still be complied with.

XIII. Furthermore, there shall be set aside in these labour centres, whenever their population exceeds two hundred inhabitants, a space of land not less than five thousand square meters for the establishment of public markets and the construction of buildings designed for municipal services and places of amusement. No saloons nor gambling houses shall be permitted in such labour centres.

XIV. Employers shall be liable for labour accidents and occupational diseases arising from work; therefore, employers shall pay the proper compensation, according to whether death or merely temporary or permanent disability has ensued, in accordance with the provisions of law. This liability shall remain in force even though the employer contract for the work through an agent.

XV. Employers shall be bound to observe in the installation of their establishments all the provisions of law regarding hygiene and sanitation and to adopt adequate measures to prevent accidents due to the use of machinery, tools and working materials, as well as to organise work in such a manner as to assure the greatest guarantees possible for the health and lives of workmen, compatible with the nature of the work, under penalties which the law shall determine.

XVI. Workmen and employers shall have the right to unite for the defence of their respective interests, by forming syndicates, unions, etc.

XVII. The laws shall recognise the right of workmen and employers to strike and to lock-out.

XVIII. Strikes shall be lawful when by the employment of peaceful means they shall aim to bring about a balance between the various factors of production, and to harmonise the rights of capital and labour. In the case of public services, the workmen shall be obliged to give notice ten days in advance to the Board of Conciliation and Arbitration of the date set for the suspension of work. Strikes shall only be considered unlawful when the majority of the strikers shall resort to acts of violence against persons or property, or in case of war when the strikers belong to establishments and services dependent on the government. Employees of military manufacturing establishments of the Federal Government shall not be included in the provisions of this Clause, inasmuch as they are a dependency of the national army.

XIX. Lock-outs shall only be lawful when the excess of production shall render it necessary to shut down in order to maintain prices reasonably above the cost of production, subject to the approval of the Board of Conciliation and Arbitration.

XX. Differences or disputes between capital and labour shall be submitted for settlement to a Board of Conciliation and Arbitration to consist of an equal number of representatives of the workmen and of the employers and of one representative of the Government.

XXI. If the employer shall refuse to submit his differences to arbitration or to accept the award rendered by the Board, the labour contract shall be considered as terminated, and the employer shall be bound to indemnify the workman by the payment to him of three months' wages, in addition to the liability which he may have incurred by reason of the dispute. If the workman rejects the award, the contract will be held to have terminated.

XXII. An employer who discharges a workman without proper cause or for having joined a union or syndicate or for having taken part in a lawful strike shall be bound, at the option of the workman, either to perform the contract or to indemnify him by the payment of three months' wages. He shall incur the same liability if the workman shall leave his service on account of the lack of good faith on the part of the employer or of maltreatment either as to his own person or that of his wife, parents, children or brothers or sisters. The employer cannot evade this liability when the maltreatment is inflicted by subordinates or agents acting with his consent or knowledge.

XXIII. Credits in favour of workmen for salary or other remuneration accrued during the past year shall be preferred over any other claims, in cases of bankruptcy or composition.

XXIV. Debts contracted by workmen in favour of their employers or their employers' associates, subordinates or agents, may only be charged against the workmen themselves and cannot under any circumstances be collected from the members of his family. Nor shall such debts be paid by the taking of more than the entire wages of the workman for any one month.

XXV. No fee shall be charged for finding work for workmen which is done by municipal offices, employment bureaus or other public or private agencies.

XXVI. Every contract of labour between a Mexican citizen and a foreign principal shall be legalised before the competent municipal authority and vise by the consul of the nation to which the workman is undertaking to go, on the understanding that, in addition to the usual clauses, special and clear provisions shall be inserted for the payment of the cost of repatriation to the labourer by the foreign principal making the contract.

XXVII. The following stipulations shall be null and void and shall not bind the contracting parties, even though embodied in the contract:

- (a) Stipulations providing for inhuman day's work on account of its notorious excessiveness, in view of the nature of the work.
- (b) Stipulations providing for a wage rate which in the judgement of the Board of Conciliation and Arbitration is not remunerative.
- (c) Stipulations providing for a term of more than one week before the payment of wages.
- (d) Stipulations providing for the assigning of places of amusement, eating places, cafes, taverns, saloon or shops for the payment of wages, when employees of such establishments are not involved.
- (e) Stipulations involving a direct or indirect obligation to purchase articles of consumption in specified shops or places.
- (f) Stipulations permitting the retention of wages by way of fines.
- (g) Stipulations constituting a waiver on the part of the workman of the indemnities to which he may become entitled by reason of labour accidents or occupational diseases, damages for breach of contract or for discharge from work.
- (h) All other stipulations implying the waiver of any right vested in the workman by labour laws.

XXVIII. The law shall decide what property constitutes the family patrimony. These goods shall be inalienable and shall not be mortgaged, nor attached, and may be transmitted by a title of inheritance with simplified formalities in the succession proceedings.

XXIX. Institutions of popular insurance established for old age, sickness, life, unemployment, and accident and others of a similar character, are considered of social utility; the Federal and State Governments shall therefore encourage the organisation of institutions of this character in order to instil and inculcate popular habits of thrift.

XXX. Co-operative associations for the construction of cheap and sanitary dwelling houses for workmen shall likewise be considered of social utility whenever these properties are designed to be acquired in ownership by the workmen within specified periods.

TITLE 7: GENERAL PROVISIONS

Article 124. All powers not expressly vested by this Constitution in the Federal authorities are understood to be reserved to the States.

Article 125. No person shall hold at the same time two Federal offices or one Federal and one State elective office; if elected to two he shall choose between them.

Article 126. No payment shall be made which is not included in the budget or authorised by a law subsequent to the same.

Article 127. The President of the Republic, the Justices of the Supreme Court, Representatives and Senators and other public officials of the Federation who are chosen by popular election shall receive a remuneration for their services, which shall be paid by the Federal Treasury and determined by law. This compensation may not be waived and any law increasing or decreasing it shall have no effect during the period for which the functionary holds office.

Article 128. Every public official, without exception, shall before entering on the discharge of his duties, make an affirmation to maintain this Constitution and the laws arising thereunder.

Article 129. In time of peace no military authorities shall exercise other functions than those bearing direct relation to military discipline. No permanent military posts shall be established other than in castles, forts and arsenals depending directly upon the Federal Government, or in camps, barracks, or depots, established outside of inhabited places for the stationing of troops.

Article 130. The Federal authorities shall have power to exercise in matters of religious worship and outward ecclesiastical forms such intervention as the laws prescribe. All other officials shall act as auxiliaries to the Federal authorities.

The Congress shall not enact any law establishing or forbidding any religion whatsoever.

Marriage is a civil contract. Marriage and all other acts relating to the civil status of individuals shall appertain to the exclusive jurisdiction of the civil authorities in the manner and form by law provided, and they shall have the force and validity given them by said laws.

A simple promise to tell the truth and to comply with obligations contracted shall subject the promisor, in the event of a breach, to the penalties established therefor by law.

The law recognises no juridic personality in the religious institutions known as churches.

Ministers of religious creeds shall be considered as persons excercising a profession, and shall be directly subject to the laws enacted on the matter.

The State legislatures shall have the exclusive power of determining the maximum number of ministers of religious creeds, according to the needs of each locality. Only a Mexican by birth may be a minister of any religious creed in Mexico.

No ministers of religious creeds shall, either in public or private meetings, or in acts of worship or religious propaganda, criticise the fundamental laws of the country, the authorities in particular or the government in general; they shall have no vote, nor be eligible to office, nor shall they be entitled to assemble for political purposes.

Before dedicating new places of worship for public use, permission shall be obtained from the Department of the Interior (Gobernacion); the opinion of the Governor of the respective State shall be previously heard on the subject. Every place of worship shall have a person charged with its care and maintenance, who shall be legally responsible for the faithful performance of the laws on religious observances within the said place of worship, and for all the objects used for purposes of worship.

The caretaker of each place of public worship, together with ten citizens of the place, shall promptly advise the municipal authorities as to the person charged with the care of the said place of worship. Every change shall be notified by the outgoing minister, together with the incoming minister and ten other citizens of the palace. The municipal authorities, under penalty of dismissal and fine not exceeding 1,000 pesos for each breach, shall be responsible for the exact performance of this provision; they shall keep a register of the places of worship and another of the caretakers thereof, subject to the same penalty as above provided. The municipal authorities shall likewise give notice to the Department of the Interior, through the State Governor, of any permission to open to the public use a new place of worship, as well as of any change in the caretakers. Gifts of personalty may be received in the interior of places of public worship.

Under no conditions shall studies carried on in institutions devoted to the professional training of ministers of religious creeds be given credit or granted any other dispensation of privilege which shall have for its purpose the accrediting of the said studies in official institutions. Any authority violating this provision shall be punished criminally, and all such dispensation of privilege be null and void, and shall invalidate wholly or entirely the professional degree toward the obtaining of which the infraction of this provision may in any way have contributed.

No periodical publication which either by reason of its programme, its title or merely by its general tendencies, is of a religious character, shall comment upon any political affairs of the nation, nor publish any information regarding the acts of the authorities of the country or of private individuals in so far as the latter have to do with public affairs.

Every kind of political association whose name shall bear any word or any indication relating to any religious belief is hereby forbidden. No assemblies of any political character shall be held within places of public worship.

No minister of any religious creed may inherit, either on his own behalf or by means of a trustee or otherwise, any real property occupied by any association for religious propaganda or religious or charitable purposes. Ministers of religious creeds are incapable legally of inheriting by will from ministers of the same religious creed or from any private individual to whom they are not related by blood within the fourth degree.

All real and personal property pertaining to the clergy or to religious institutions shall be governed, in so far as their acquisition by private parties is concerned, by Article 27 of this Constitution.

No trial by jury shall ever be granted for the infraction of any of the preceding provisions.

Article 131. The Federal Government shall have exclusive power to levy duties on merchandise imported, exported or passing in transit through the national territory, as well as to regulate at all times, and if necessary to forbid for the sake of public safety or good government, the circulation in the interior of the Republic of all kinds of goods, regardless of their origin; but the Federal Government shall have no power to establish or decree in the Federal District and Territories the taxes and laws to which Clauses VI and VII of Article 117 refer.

Article 132. All forts, barracks, warehouses, and other real property destined by the Federal Government for public service or common use, shall be under the jurisdiction of the Federal authorities, in accordance with the law which the Congress shall issue on the subject; any of these establishments which may subsequently be acquired within the territory of any State shall likewise be subject to Federal jurisdiction, provided consent thereto shall have been obtained from the respective State Legislature.

Article 133. This Constitution and the laws of the United States of Mexico which shall be made in pursuance hereof and all treaties made or which shall be made under the authority of the President of the Republic, with the approval of the Congress, shall be the supreme law of the land. And the judges in every State shall be bound by this Constitution and by these laws and treaties, anything in the Constitution or laws of any State to the contrary notwithstanding.

Article 134. Tenders shall be invited for all contracts which the Government may have occasion to enter into for the execution of any public works; these tenders shall be submitted under seal and shall only be opened publicly.

TITLE 8: OF THE AMENDMENTS TO THE CONSTITUTION

Article 135. The present Constitution may be added to or amended. No amendment or addition shall become part of the constitution until agreed to by the Congress of the Union, by a two-thirds vote of the members present, and approved by a majority of the State Legislatures. The Congress shall count the votes of the Legislatures and make the declaration that the amendments or additions have been adopted.

TITLE 9: OF THE INVIOLABILITY OF THE CONSTITUTION

Article 136. This constitution shall not lose its force and vigour, even though its observance be interrupted by rebellion. In case that through any public disturbance a Government contrary to the priniciples which it sanctions be established, its force shall be restored so soon as the people shall regain their liberty, and those who have participated in the government emanating from the rebellion or have co-operated with it shall be tried in accordance with its provisions and with the laws arising under it.

TRANSITORY ARTICLES

Article 1. This Constitution shall be published at once and a solemn affirmation made to defend and enforce it throughout the Republic; but its provisions, except those relating to the election of the supreme powers, Federal and State, shall not go into effect until the first day of May, 1917, at which time the Constitutional Congress shall be so solemnly convened and the oath of office taken by the citizen chosen at the forthcoming elections to discharge the duties of President of the Republic.

The provisions of Clause V of Article 82 shall not be applicable to the elections to be held in accordance with Article 2 of the Transitory Articles, nor shall active service in the Army act as a disqualification for the office of Representative or Senator, provided the candidate shall not have active command of troops in the respective electoral district.

Nor shall the Secretaries nor Assistant Secretaries of Executive Departments be disqualified from election to the next Federal Congress, provided they shall definitively resign from office on or before the day on which the respective writ is issued.

Article 2. The person charged with the executive power of the Nation shall immediately, upon the publication of this Constitution, issue writs for elections to fill the Federal offices; he shall see that these elections be held so that Congress may be constituted within a reasonable time, in order that it may count the votes cast in the presidential elections and make known the name of the person who has been elected President of the Republic; this shall be done in order that the provisions of the foregoing Article may be complied with.

Article 3. The next constitutional term shall be computed, in the case of Senators and Representatives, from the first of September last, and in the case of the President of the Republic, from the first of December, 1916.

Article 4. Senators who in the coming election shall be classified as "even" shall serve only two years, in order that the Senate may be renewed by half every two years.

Article 5. The Congress shall in the month of May next choose the Justices of the Supreme Court in order that this tribunal may be constituted on the first day of June, 1917.

In these elections, Article 96 shall not apply in so far as the candidates proposed by the State Legislatures are concerned; but those chosen shall be designated for the first term of two years prescribed by Article 94.

Article 6. The Congress shall meet in extraordinary session on the fifteenth day of April, 1917, to act as an electoral college, for the computing of the ballots and the determination of the election of President of the Republic, at which time it shall make known the results; it shall likewise enact the organic law of the circuit and district Courts, the organic law of the Tribunals of the Federal District and Territories, in order that the Supreme Court of Justice may immediately appoint the Inferior and Superior District and Circuit Judges; at the same session the Congress shall choose the Superior Judges and Judges of First Instance of the Federal District and Territories, and shall also enact all laws submitted by the Executive. The Circuit and District Judges and the Superor and Inferior Judges of the Federal District and Territories shall take office not later than the first day of July, 1917, at which time such as shall have been temporarily appointed by the person now charged with the executive power of the nation shall cease to act.

Article 7. For this occasion only, the votes for the office of Senator shall be counted by the Board of the First Electoral District of each State or of the Federal District which shall be instituted for the counting of the votes of Representatives. This Board shall issue the respective credentials to the Senators-elect.

Article 8. The Supreme Court shall decide all pending petitions of "amparo," in accordance with the laws at present in force.

Article 9. The First Chief of the Constitutional Army, charged with the executive power of the nation, is hereby authorised to issue the electoral law according to which, on this occasion, the elections to fill the various Federal offices shall be held.

Article 10. All persons who shall have taken part in the Government emanating from the rebellion against the legitimate Government of the Republic, or who may have given aid to the said rebellion and later taken up arms or held any office or commission of the factions which have opposed the Constitutional Government, shall be tried in accordance with the laws at present in force, unless they shall have been previously pardoned by the said Constitutional Government.

Article 11. Until such time as the Congress of the Union and the State Legislatures shall legislate on the agrarian and labour problems, the bases established by this Constitution for the said laws shall be put into force throughout the Republic.

Article 12. All Mexicans who shall have fought in the ranks of the Constitutional Army, and their children and widows and all other persons who shall have rendered service to the cause of the revolution, or to public instruction, shall be preferred in the acquisition of lots to which Article 27 refers, and shall be entitled to such rebates as the law shall determine.

Article 13. All debts contracted by working men on account of work up to the date of this Constitution with masters, their subordinates and agents, are hereby declared wholly and entirely discharged.

Article 14. The Departments of Justice and of Public Instruction and Fine Arts are hereby abolished.

Article 15. The citizen at present charged with the executive power is hereby authorised to issue the law of civil responsibility applicable to all promoters, accomplices and abettors of the offences committed against the constitutional order in the month of February, 1913, and against the Constitutional Government.

Article 16. The Constitutional Congress in the regular period of sessions, to begin on the first day of September of the present year, shall issue all the organic laws of the Constitution which may not have been already issued in the extraordinary session to which Transitory Article number 6 refers; and it shall give preference to the laws relating to personal guarantees and to Articles 30, 32, 33, 35, 36, 38, 107, and the latter part of Article 111 of this Constitution.

Signed at Queretaro de Arteago, January 31, 1917.

Russian Socialist Federal Soviet Republic Constitution of 1918

The Russian Socialist Federal Soviet Republic (RSFSR) Constitution of 1918 was the first of the Marxist-Leninist constitutions. As such, it was oriented toward a new society and future objectives derived from that ideology. Article 9 of that Constitution encompassed the ultimate aims of the Communist Revolution. These included the complete crushing of the bourgeoisie, the abolition of the exploitation of a person by another, and the establishment of socialism. According to theory, socialism would eliminate class divisions, and the coercion of the state would cease to exist.

The RSFSR Constitution did not establish a Socialist state. Instead, it formulated a dictatorship "for the period of transition." This was, according to Article 9, "a dictatorship of the urban and rural workers, combined with the poorer peasantry." According to Leninist theory, the "powerful All-Russian Soviet Government," which had been created under this 1918 Constitution, eventually would "wither away," and true socialism would emerge.

Non-Russian Soviet republics were not affected by this Constitution. Similar Constitutions were imposed only after Communist Russian armies defeated these republics. Patterned after the RSFSR model in the first years after the 1918 Revolution were the five constitutions of the Soviet republics of the Ukraine, Byelorussia, Azerbaijan, Armenia, and Georgia.

In 1925, 1937, and 1978 this Soviet constitutional pattern has continued. First, an RSFSR Constitution was created. Later, its structure and principle provisions were adopted in the other Soviet republics—now twenty-six in number.

Many of the features of Communist regimes can be traced to the RSFSR Constitution of 1918. Most noteworthy is the assembly-type government with power placed (at least theoretically) in the hands of a Congress of Soviets. However, as a practical matter, the real power is given to an executive committee elected by this Congress. In addition, a Council of People's Commissars in Article 37 was "charged with the general direction of the affairs" of the republic.

The concept of democratic centralism, now found in all Soviet-style constitutions, is evident in the 1918 document. Set forth in Article 62, this duty implements instructions from higher organs of government as well as the power of revision and nullification of decisions.

Entirely absent was any recognition of the ruling position of the Bolshevik party—renamed the Russian Communist party in May 1918. Many critics have said that this omission demonstrated the gap between the formal constitution and the real power structure of the RSFSR. Later Soviet-style constitutions have given prominence to the Communist party, completing the constitutional transformation into a one-party state. (In 1918 the Communist party had not as yet established its control over the population.)

Another distinction between this document and the succeeding Communist-style constitutions can be found in their references to human rights. Today's Soviet constitutions are known for their attention to cultural and social rights. However, this first communist constitution provides only limited political rights, in its Chapter V, and then only to "all the toilers of Russia." Guaranteed are certain rights connected with speech, press, and assembly as well as "freedom of religious and anti-religious propaganda." Missing are personal rights and freedoms such as freedom from arbitrary arrest, and procedural safeguards in criminal proceedings. However, according to Article 23, even the rights granted may be taken away if they are exercised "to the detriment of the interests of the Socialist revolution."

The RSFSR Constitution of 1918 was prepared by a revolutionary committee, the Third All-Russian Congress of Soviets, dominated by Bolsheviks and the other followers of Vladimir Lenin. On 28 January 1918, this committee adopted a "Resolution on the Federal Institutions of the Russian Republics," which involved the appointment of a Central Executive Committee to prepare a draft of the "Fundamental Principles of the Constitution of the Russian Federal Republic." Significantly, the provisional government of Russia, which had been formed after the assassination of the czar, was not involved.

On 1 April 1918, a constitutional commission was appointed to prepare the final version. Among the fifteen members of this commission were Joseph Stalin, representing the Centralists, and Nikolay Bukharin, representing the so-called Left-Communists. Although the commission also included three anarchists, their views carried little weight. After the promulgation of this Constitution, non-Communists ceased to have any influence in Soviet government affairs.

It was the Stalin Centralists who were to emerge victorious in the constitutional debates. In the internecine battles that followed the overthrow of the czar, a number of Soviets had arisen representing the various revolutionary interests. They were opposed by the Bolshevik Centralists who had actually used the Russian army to destroy them. Thus when a majority of the commission accepted Stalin's General Proposals of the Constitution of the Russian Soviet Federative Republic, it represented a significant victory for the forces of centralization. This victory was the mark of future Communist governments and constitutions throughout the world.

On 3 July 1918, Lenin, now chairman of a special commission of the central committee of the Bolshevik Party, introduced a number of additions. They included the freedom of antireligious propaganda, the right of asylum, and the equality of rights irrespective of race or nationality. In addition, restrictions on freedom of association were also included.

Constitutionalism was not among Lenin's major concerns. His pamphlet on "How the Socialist Revolutionaries Sum-Up the Revolution and How the Revolution Summed Them Up" expressed his doubts that the conditions of the working class could ever be improved by a constitution. In his view, only "vulgar democrats" believed such ideas.

The Fifth All-Russian Congress of Soviets unanimously approved the revised text on 10 July 1918. At the same time, it instructed the People's Commissariat of Education to introduce in all schools and educational institutions a study of the basic principles of the constitution. Russia was declared a "Republic of Soviet of Workers', Soldiers' and Peasants' Deputies."

GER F. VAN DER TANG
Professor
Erasmus University
Rotterdam,
The Netherlands

CONSTITUTION (FUNDAMENTAL LAW) OF THE RUSSIAN SOCIALIST FEDERAL SOVIET REPUBLIC

Adopted by the Fifth All-Russian Congress of Soviets, at the Session of July 10, 1918

The Declaration of the Rights of the Toiling and Exploited People, adopted by the Third All-Russian Congress of Soviets in January 1918, together with the Constitution of the Soviet Republic, adopted by the Fifth All-Russian Congress, shall constitute a single Fundamental Law of the Russian Socialist Federal Soviet Republic.

This Fundamental Law shall come into force upon the publication of the same in final form in Izvestiya Vserossiiskogo Tsentral'nogo Ispolnitel'nogo Komiteta Sovetov. It shall be republished by all local organs of Soviet power and shall be prominently displayed in all Soviet institutions.

The Fifth All-Russian Congress of Soviets instructs the People's Commissariat of Education to introduce in all schools and educational institutions without exception the study of the basic provisions of this Constitution, as well as their explanation and interpretation.

PART I: DECLARATION OF RIGHTS OF THE TOILING AND EXPLOITED PEOPLE

Chapter I

Article 1. Russia is declared a Republic of Soviets of Workers', Soldiers' and Peasants' Deputies. All central and local power shall be vested in these Soviets.

Article 2. The Russian Soviet Republic is established on the basis of a free union of free nations, as a federation of national Soviet Republics.

Chapter II

Article 3. Its fundamental aim being the abolition of all exploitation of man by man, the complete elimination of the division of society into classes, the ruthless suppression of all exploiters, the establishment of the Socialist organization of society and the triumph of Socialism in all coun-

---

Translated from original official Russian text by Ger F. van der Tang. Professor of Law, Erasmus University, Rotterdam, The Netherlands.

tries, the Third All-Russian Congress of Soviets of Workers', Soldiers' and Peasants' Deputies further decrees;

(a) In order to establish the socialization of land, private ownership of land is abolished; all land is declared the property of the people, and is handed over to the toilers without compensation on the basis of equal rights to its use.

(b) All forests, underground mineral wealth, and waters of national importance, all live stock and appurtenances, together with all model-farms and agricultural enterprises, are declared national property.

(c) As a first step towards the complete transfer to the Workers' and Peasants' Soviet Republic of all factories, workshops, mines, railroads, and other means of production and transport, and in order to ensure the supremacy of the toilers over the exploiters, the Congress endorses the Soviet laws on Workers' control of industry and on the Supreme Council of National Economy.

(d) The Third All-Russian Congress of Soviets regards the Soviet law repudiating the debts contracted by the government of the Tsar, the landlords, and the bourgeoisie as a first blow . to international banking and financial capitalism; and it expresses its full confidence that the Soviet Government will continue firmly this course, until the international revolt of the workers against the yoke of capitalism shall have secured a complete victory.

(e) The Congress endorses the transfer of all banks to the ownership of the Workers' and Peasants' Government, as one of the conditions for the emancipation of the toiling masses from the yoke of capitalism.

(f) In order to destroy all parasitic elements of society, and to organize the economic life of the country, work useful to the community shall be obligatory upon all.

(g) In order to secure the complete supremacy of power for the toiling masses and to eliminate any possibility of the exploiters regaining power, the Congress decrees the arming of the toilers, the formation of a Socialist Red Army of Workers and Peasants, and the complete disarmament of the propertied classes.

Chapter III

Article 4. Expressing its inflexible determination to wrest mankind from the grip of capitalism and imperialism, which during this the most criminal of all wars have drenched the world with blood, the Third All-Russian Congress of Soviets wholeheartedly endorses the policy of the

Soviet Government in its abrogation of secret treaties, in its organization of the widest possible fraternization between the workers and peasants in the ranks of the belligerent armies, and in its efforts to attain at all costs, by revolutionary means, a democratic peace of toilers—a peace without annexations or indemnities, on the basis of the free self-determination of nations.

Article 5. With the same object, the Third All-Russian Congress of Soviets insists on the complete repudiation of the barbarous politics of bourgeois civilisation, which built the prosperity of the exploiters in a few privileged nations upon the enslavement of hundreds of millions of toilers in Asia, in the colonies, and in small countries.

Article 6. The Third All-Russian Congress of Soviets cordially welcomes the policy of the Council of People's Commissars in proclaiming the complete independence of Finland, in beginning the withdrawal of troops from Persia, and in proclaiming the right of self-determination for Armenia.

Chapter IV

Article 7. The Third All-Russian Congress of Soviets of Workers', Soldiers' and Peasants' Deputies considers that now, at the decisive moment in the struggle of the proletariat against its exploiters, there can be no place for the latter in any organ of power. Power must belong completely and exclusively to the toiling masses and their true representatives, the Soviets of Workers', Soldiers', and Peasants' Deputies.

Article 8. At the same time, striving to bring about a really free and voluntary, and therefore all the more complete and lasting union of the toiling classes of all the various nations in Russia, the Third All-Russian Congress of Soviets confines itself to establishing the fundamental principles of the federation of the Soviet Republics of Russia, leaving to the workers and peasants of each nation the right to decide freely, at their own plenipotentiary Congresses of Soviets, whether, and on what conditions, they desire to participate in the federal government and in other federal Soviet institutions.

PART II: GENERAL PROVISIONS OF THE CONSTITUTION OF THE RUSSIAN SOCIALIST FEDERAL SOVIET REPUBLIC

Chapter V

Article 9. The fundamental aim of the Constitution of the Russian Socialist Federal Soviet Republic, designed for the present period of transition, is to establish (in the form of a powerful All-Russian Soviet Government) the dictatorship of the urban and rural workers, combined with the poorer peasantry, in order to secure the complete crushing of the bourgeoisie, the abolition of the exploitation of man by man, and the establishment of Socialism, under which neither class divisions nor state coercion arising therefrom will any longer exist.

Article 10. The Russian Republic is a free Socialist community of all the toilers of Russia. All authority within the Russian Socialist Federal Soviet Republic shall belong to the entire working population of the country, organized in urban and rural Soviets.

Article 11. Soviets of regions with special usages and national characteristics of their own may unite in autonomous regional unions, governed (like all other regional unions which may be formed) by regional Congresses of Soviets and their executive organs. These autonomous regional unions shall enter into the Russian Socialist Federal Soviet Republic on a federal basis.

Article 12. Supreme power in the Russian Socialist Federal Soviet Republic shall belong to the All-Russian Congress of Soviets and, during the period between Congresses, to the All-Russian Central Executive Committee of Soviets.

Article 13. In order to ensure for the toilers real freedom of conscience, the church shall be separated from the state and the school from the church; and freedom of religious and anti-religious propaganda shall be assured to every citizen.

Article 14. In order to ensure for the toilers real freedom of expression of opinion, the Russian Socialist Federal Soviet Republic shall put an end to the dependence of the press on capital, transfer to the working class and the poor peasantry all technical and material resources necessary for the publication of newspapers, pamphlets, books and all other printed matter, and guarantee their unobstructed circulation throughout the country.

Article 15. In order to ensure for the toilers real freedom of assembly, the Russian Socialist Federal Soviet Republic, recognizing the right of its citizens freely to organize assemblies, meetings, processions, etc., shall place at the disposal of the workers amd poor peasantry all premises convenient for public gatherings, together with lighting, heating, and furniture.

Article 16. In order to ensure for the toilers real freedom of association, the Russian Socialist Federal Soviet Republic, having destroyed the economic and political power of the propertied classes, and thus removed the obstacles which hitherto, in bourgeois society, prevented the workers and peasants from enoying freedom of association and action, lends to the workers and peasants all assistance, material and otherwise, to help them to unite and organize themselves.

Article 17. In order to ensure for the toilers real access to knowledge, the Russian Socialist Federal Soviet Republic shall undertake to provide for the workers and poorer peasants a complete, comprehensive, and free education.

Article 18. The Russian Socialist Federal Soviet Republic shall consider work the duty of all citizens, on the principle "He who does not work, neither shall he eat."

Article 19. In order to safeguard in every possible way the conquests of the great workers' and peasants' revolution, the Russian Socialist Federal Soviet Republic shall consider it the duty of all citizens of the Republic to defend the Socialist fatherland, and shall establish universal military service. The honour of bearing arms in defence of the revolution shall be granted only to the toilers. Non-toiling elements of the population shall have to perform other military duties.

Article 20. Recognizing the solidarity of the toilers of all nations, the Russian Socialist Federal Soviet Republic shall extend all political rights enjoyed by Russian citizens to foreigners resident within the territory of the Russian Republic, provided that they belong to the working class or to the peasantry working without hired labour. It shall authorize the local Soviets to confer upon such foreigners, without any annoying formalities, the rights of Russian citizenship.

Article 21. The Russian Socialist Federal Soviet Republic shall grant the right of asylum to all foreigners persecuted for political and religious offences.

Article 22. The Russian Socialist Federal Soviet Republic, recognizing the equality of rights of all citizens, irrespective of race or nationality, declares it contrary to the fundamental laws of the Republic to institute or tolerate any privileges or prerogatives based upon such grounds, or to repress national minorities, or to limit their equality of rights in any way.

Article 23. In the interest of the working class as a whole, the Russian Socialist Federal Soviet Republic shall deprive individuals and sections of the community of any rights used by them to the detriment of the interests of the Socialist revolution.

PART III: THE STRUCTURE OF SOVIET POWER

THE ORGANIZATION OF CENTRAL POWER

Chapter VI. The All-Russian Congress of Soviets of Workers', Peasants', Cossacks' and Red Army Deputies

Article 24. The All-Russian Congress of Soviets shall be the highest authority of the Russian Socialist Federal Soviet Republic.

Article 25. The All-Russian Congress of Soviets shall consist of representatives of town Soviets on the basis of one deputy for every 25,000 electors, and of representatives of Provincial Congresses of Soviets on the basis of one deputy for every 125,000 inhabitants.

Note 1. If a provincial congress of Soviets has not been held before the All-Russian Congress of Soviets, delegates to the latter shall be sent directly by the county congresses of Soviets.

Note 2. If a regional congress of Soviets immediately precedes the All-Russian Congress of Soviets, delegates to the latter may be sent by the regional congress.

Article 26. The All-Russian Congress of Soviets shall be convened by the All-Russian Central Executive Committee of Soviets at least twice a year.*

Article 27. An extraordinary All-Russian Congress may be convened by the All-Russian Central Executive Committee of Soviets, either on its own initiative, or upon the demand of local Soviets representing at least one-third of the total population of the Republic.

Article 28. The All-Russian Congress of Soviets shall elect an All-Russian Central Executive Committee of Soviets, consisting of not more than 200 members.

Article 29. The All-Russian Central Executive Committee of Soviets shall be responsible in all matters to the All-Russian Congress of Soviets.

Article 30. In the period between the Congresses, the All-Russian Central Executive Committee of Soviets shall be the highest authority of the Republic.

Chapter VII. The All-Russian Central Executive Committee of Soviets

Article 31. The All-Russian Central Executive Committee of Soviets shall be the highest legislative, executive, and supervisory organ of the Russian Socialist Federal Soviet Republic.

Article 32. The All-Russian Central Executive Committee of Soviets shall have the general direction of the Workers' and Peasants' Government, and of all Soviet organs throughout the country; it shall unify and coordinate legislative and administrative work; and supervise the application of the Soviet Constitution, the decisions of the All-Russian Congresses of Soviets and the central organs of Soviet power.

Article 33. The All-Russian Central Executive Committee of Soviets shall examine and approve draft decrees and other proposals submitted by the Council of People's Commissars or by individual departments; it shall also issue its own decrees and regulations.

* Amended to once a year by the Ninth All-Russian Congress of Soviets, on December 28, 1921.

Article 34. The All-Russian Central Executive Committee of Soviets shall convene the All-Russian Congress of Soviets, to which it shall submit an account of its activities, together with reports on general policy and on specific questions.

Article 35. The All-Russian Central Executive Committee of Soviets shall form the Council of People's Commissars for the general direction of the affairs of the Russian Socialist Federal Soviet Republic; it shall also form departments (People's Commissariats) for the direction of the various branches of administration.

Article 36. The members of the All-Russian Central Executive Committee of Soviets shall either work in the departments (People's Commissariats), or carry out special assignments of the All-Russian Central Executive Committee of Soviets.

Chapter VIII. The Council of People's Commissars

Article 37. The Council of People's Commissars shall be charged with the general direction of the affairs of the Russian Socialist Federal Soviet Republic.

Article 38. In the execution of this task the Council of People's Commissars shall issue decrees, regulations and instructions, and take all general measures necessary to secure prompt and orderly administration of state affairs.

Article 39. The Council of People's Commissars shall immediately inform the All-Russian Central Executive Committee of Soviets of all its orders and decisions.

Article 40. The All-Russian Central Executive Committee of Soviets shall have power to annul or suspend any order or decision of the Council of People's Commissars.

Article 41. All orders and decisions of the Council of People's Commissars of major political importance shall be submitted to the Central Executive Committee of Soviets for examination and approval.

Note. Measures of extreme urgency may be put into effect directly by the Council of People's Commissars.

Article 42. The members of the Council of People's Commissars shall be in charge of the various People's Commissariats.

Article 43. Eighteen People's Commissariats shall be formed, as follows: Foreign Affairs; War; Marine; Home Affairs; Justice; Labour; Social Security; Education; Posts and Telegraphs; Nationalities; Finance; Transport; Agriculture; Trade and Industry; Food Supplies; State Control; Supreme Council of National Economy; Public Health.

Article 44. Attached to each People's Commissar, and under his chairmanship, a collegium shall be formed, the members of which shall be confirmed in their appointments by the Council of People's Commissars.

Article 45. The People's Commissar shall have the power to decide personally all matters under the jurisdiction of his department, but shall inform the collegium of his decisions. Should the collegium disagree with any decision of the People's Commissar, it may, without suspending the execution of the decision, appeal to the Council of People's Commissars or the Presidium of the All-Russian Central Executive Committee of Soviets. The same right of appeal shall belong to individual members of the collegium.

Article 46. The Council of People's Commissars shall be responsible in all matters to the All-Russian Congress of Soviets and to the All-Russian Central Executive Committee of Soviets.

Article 47. The People's Commissars and the collegia of the People's Commissariats shall be responsible to the Council of People's Commissars and to the All-Russian Central Executive Committee of Soviets.

Article 48. The title of 'People's Commissar' shall belong exclusively to the members of the Council of People's Commissars, in charge of the general affairs of the Russian Socialist Federal Soviet Republic, and no other representative of Soviet power either in the central or local government it may be conferred upon.

Chapter IX. The Jurisdiction of the All-Russian Congress of Soviets, and of the All-Russian Central Executive Committee of Soviets

Article 49. The All-Russian Congress of Soviets and the All-Russian Central Executive Committee of Soviets shall have jurisdiction over all matters of general state importance, namely:

- (a) The approval and amendment of the Constitution of the Russian Socialist Federal Soviet Republic.
- (b) The general direction of the foreign and domestic policy of the Russian Socialist Federal Soviet Republic.
- (c) The determination and alteration of frontiers, as well as the alienation of parts of the territory of the Russian Socialist Federal Soviet Republic, or of the rights of the Republic in respect thereof.
- (d) The establishment of the boundaries and competences of regional unions of Soviets which are part of the Russian Socialist Federal Soviet Republic, and the settlement of disputes which may arise between them.
- (e) The admission of new members into the Russian Socialist Federal Soviet Republic, and the recognition of the secession of different parts from the Russian Federation.
- (f) The determination of the administrative divisions of the territory of the Russian Socialist Federal Soviet Republic, and the approval of regional unions.

(g) The establishment and modification of the system of weights, measures, and currency within the territory of the Russian Socialist Federal Soviet Republic.

(h) Relations with foreign powers, declaration of war and conclusion of peace.

(i) The concluding of loans, customs and trade treaties, and financial agreements.

(j) The establishment of the fundamentals and the general outline for the entire national economy and its different branches within the territory of the Russian Socialist Federal Soviet Republic.

(k) The approval of the budget of the Russian Socialist Federal Soviet Republic.

(l) The levying of taxes and imposition of duties.

(m) The establishment of the fundamentals of organization of the armed forces of the Russian Socialist Federal Soviet Republic.

(n) General legislation, judicial organization and procedure, civil and criminal legislation.

(o) The appointment and dismissal both of the individual members and of the Council of People's Commissars as a whole, and the confirmation of the appointment of the chairman of the Council of People's Commissars.

(p) The issuing of general regulations concerning the acquisition or loss of civic rights by Russian citizens, and the rights of foreigners within the territory of the republic.

(q) The granting of complete or partial amnesty.

Article 50. In addition to the above matters, the All-Russian Congress of Soviets and the All-Russian Central Executive Committee of Soviets may decide on any other matter which they deem within their jurisdiction.

Article 51. The following shall be within the exclusive jurisdiction of the All-Russian Congress of Soviets:

(a) The establishment and amendment of the fundamental elements of the Soviet Constitution.

(b) The ratification of peace treaties.

Article 52. Decisions on matters within the scope of clauses (c) and (h) of Article 49 shall be taken only by the All-Russian Central Executive Committee of Soviets when the All-Russian Congress of Soviets cannot be convened.

THE ORGANIZATION OF LOCAL SOVIET POWER

Chapter X. The Congresses of Soviets

Article 53. The Congresses of Soviets shall be composed as follows:
  (a) Regional (Oblast) Congresses. These shall be composed of representatives of town Soviets and of country congresses; in the case of the latter, in the proportion of one deputy for every 25,000 inhabitants, and in the case of the former, in the proportion of one deputy for every 5,000 electors, with a maximum of 500 deputies for the whole region. They may also be composed of deputies to the provincial congresses of Soviets, elected in the same proportion, if such congresses are held immediately before the regional congress.
  (b) Provincial (Gubernia) Congresses. These shall consist of representatives of town Soviets and of rural district congresses of Soviets; in the proportion of one deputy for every 10,000 inhabitants in the case of the latter, and in the proportion of one deputy for every 2,000 electors in the case of the former; with a maximum of 300 deputies for the whole province. If a county congress of Soviets be held immediately before the provincial congress, the election shall take place on the same principle, not by the rural district congress but by the county congress of Soviets.
  (c) County (Uyezd) Congresses. These shall be composed of representatives of village Soviets, in the proportion of one deputy for every 1,000 inhabitants, with a maximum of 300 deputies for the whole county.
  (d) Rural District (Volost) Congresses. These shall be composed of representatives of all the village Soviets of the rural district, in the proportion of one deputy for every ten members of the Soviet.

Note 1. The Soviets of towns of not more than 10,000 inhabitants shall be represented in the County congresses of Soviets. Soviets of villages of less than 1,000 inhabitants shall meet together to elect deputies to the County Congress of Soviets.

Note 2. Village Soviets of less than ten members shall send one representative to the Rural District Congress of Soviets.

Article 54. The Soviet congresses shall be convened by the corresponding executive organs of Soviet power, that is to say, the executive committees, either upon the initiative of the latter or at the demand of local Soviets, if these represent at least one third of the population of the territory. In any case, regional congresses must be held not less than twice a year, provincial and county congresses at least once in three months, and rural district congresses at least once a month.*

Article 55. Each congress of Soviets (regional, provincial, county, rural district) shall elect its own executive committee with a membership not exceeding (a) for regions and provinces, 25; (b) for counties, 20, and (c) for rural districts, 10. The executive committee shall be responsible in all matters to the congress of Soviets by which it was elected.†

Article 56. Within the limits of its jurisdiction, the congress of Soviets (regional, provincial, county, rural district) shall be the highest authority within the given territory; between the congresses this authority shall be vested in its executive committee.

Chapter XI. The Soviets of Deputies

Article 57. Soviets of Deputies shall be formed as follows:

- (a) In towns in the proportion of one deputy for every 1,000 inhabitants, with a minimum of 50 and a maximum of 1,000 members.
- (b) In rural localities (farms, villages, hamlets, stanitsa's, townships, small towns with a population of less than 10,000, auls, khutors) in the proportion of one deputy for every 100 inhabitants, with a minimum of three, and a maximum of fifty members for each locality. Deputies shall be elected for a period of three months.

Note. In rural localities, wherever it is considered possible, matters of administration shall be directly decided by the general assembly of the electors of the locality concerned.

Article 58. For the conduct of current work, the Soviet of Deputies shall elect from its members an executive committee, consisting of not more than five members in the villages, and in the towns consisting of a number of members in the proportion of one for every fifty deputies, but

---

* This Article was amended by the Ninth All-Russian Congress of Soviets on 28 December 1921, as follows:

(1) All ordinary Congresses of Soviets of the autonomous republics, regions, provinces, counties, and rural districts shall be convened once a year.

(2) Elections for town, settlement, and village Soviets shall be held once a year.

† With regard to Provincial Congresses, this Article was supplemented by the Ninth All-Russian Congress of Soviets, on December 28, 1921, as follows: "Provincial congresses of Soviets shall have the right to appoint members to the provincial executive committees in excess of the number fixed by the Constitution, these appointments being made in order that the provincial executive committee should include not less than one representative from each county and from each industrial district. Such enlarged sessions of the provincial executive committees shall be convened at the time fixed by the provincial executive committees."

with a minimum of three and a maximum of fifteen (In Petrograd and Moscow, the maximum is forty). The executive committee shall be responsible in all matters to the Soviet by which it was elected.

Article 59. The Soviet of Deputies shall be convened by the executive committee on the initiative of the latter, or at the demand of at least half the members of the Soviet, at least once a week in the towns, and twice a week in the country.

Article 60. Within the limits of its jurisdiction, the Soviet or, in the case described in the note to paragraph 57, the general assembly of the electors, shall be the highest authority in the locality.

Chapter XII. The Jurisdiction of the Local Organs of Soviet Power

Article 61. The regional, provincial, county, and rural district organs of Soviet power, as well as the Soviets of Deputies, shall take cognizance of the following:

(a) The implementation of all instructions issued by the corresponding higher organs of Soviet authority;

(b) The adoption of all appropriate measures for developing the cultural and economic life of their territories;

(c) The settlement of all questions of purely local importance;

(d) Coordination of all Soviet activity within the limits of their territories.

Article 62. The congresses of Soviets and their executive committees shall have the right of control over the activities of the local Soviets, i.e., the regional congress shall exercise control over all Soviets of the region, the provincial congress shall have control over all Soviets of the province, with the exception of town Soviets, not forming part of county congresses etc. The regional and provincial congresses together with their executive committees, shall have, in addition, the right of cancelling decisions of Soviets within their respective areas, provided they notify the central Soviet government in important cases.

Article 63. In order to ensure the execution of the tasks entrusted to the organs of Soviet power there shall be formed, in every Soviet (town and village) and every executive committee (regional, provincial, county, and rural district), appropriate departments, under the charge of departmental directors.

PART IV: ACTIVE AND PASSIVE ELECTORAL RIGHTS

Chapter XIII

Article 64. The right to vote and to be elected to the Soviets shall belong to all citizens, of both sexes, of the Russian Socialist Federal Soviet Republic, without distinction as to religion, nationality, and without any residential qualification, provided that on the day of the election they have reached the age of eighteen, and are in one of the following categories:

(a) All those who earn their living by productive work useful to society, and also those who are engaged in domestic occupations which enable the former to undertake productive work, such as workers and employees of all kinds and categories in industry, trade, agriculture etc.; and to peasants and Cossack farmers not employing hired labour for profit;

(b) Soldiers in the army and navy of the Soviet Republic;

(c) Citizens coming under the above categories who are in any degree incapacitated for work.

Note 1. Local Soviets may, with the approval of the central government, lower the age limit set by this article.

Note 2. In addition to Russian citizens, persons mentioned in article 20 (Part II, Chapter V) shall also enjoy active and passive electoral rights.

Article 65. The following persons shall have neither the right to vote nor the right to be elected, even if they are included within one of the above-mentioned categories:

(a) Those who employ others for the sake of profit;

(b) Those who live on income not arising from their own labour, such as interest on capital, revenue from enterprises, landed property, etc.;

(c) Private traders, agents, commercial middlemen, etc.;

(d) Monks and priests of all religious denominations;

(e) Agents and employees of the former police, special corps of gendarmerie, and secret service, as well as members of the former ruling dynasty of Russia;

(f) Persons recognized, under established procedure, as mentally deranged or imbecile; together with persons under wardship.

(g) Persons convicted of infamous or mercenary crimes, and sentenced to a term set by law or by the judgement of a court.

Chapter XIV. Electoral Procedure

Article 66. Elections shall be conducted according to established custom, on days fixed by the local Soviets.

Article 67. Elections shall take place in the presence of an electoral commission and a representative of the local Soviet.

Article 68. In cases where the presence of a representative of the local Soviet is impossible, his place shall be taken by the chairman of the electoral commission, and, in his absence, by the chairman of the electoral assembly.

Article 69. A record of the proceedings and the results of the election shall be drawn up and signed by the members of the electoral commission and the representative of the local Soviets.

Article 70. Details of electoral procedure, and the participation of trade unions and other labour organizations in the elections, shall be determined by the local Soviets, in accordance with instructions issued by the All-Russian Central Executive Committee of Soviets.

Chapter XV. Verification and Annulment of Elections, and Recall of Deputies

Article 71. All materials relating to the conduct of an election shall be handed over to the Soviet concerned.

Article 72. Verification of the elections shall be entrusted to a credentials commission appointed by the Soviet.

Article 73. The credentials commission shall report its findings to the Soviet.

Article 74. The Soviet shall decide election results in the case of a dispute.

Article 75. In the event of the non-confirmation of any candidate, the Soviet shall order a new election.

Article 76. In the event that the election as a whole was carried out irregularly, the question of its annulment shall be decided by the immediately superior organ of Soviet power.

Article 77. The All-Russian Central Executive Committee of Soviets shall be the final court of appeal in matters of Soviet elections.

Article 78. The electors shall have the right to recall at any time the deputy they have sent to the Soviet, and to proceed to new elections in accordance with the law.

PART V: THE BUDGET

Chapter XVI

Article 79. The Russian Socialist Federal Soviet Republic, during the present transitory period of the proletarian dictatorship, shall adopt a financial policy auxiliary to its fundamental aim of the expropriation of the bourgeoisie and the creation of conditions which will secure the equality of all citizens of the Republic in the production and distribution of wealth. To this end it aims at placing at the disposal of the organs of Soviet power all resources necessary to satisfy the local and national requirements of the Soviet Republic, encroaching without fear upon the rights of private property.

Article 80. The revenues and expenditures of the Russian Socialist Federal Soviet Republic shall be incorporated in the general state budget.

Article 81. The All-Russian Congress of Soviets, or the All-Russian Central Executive Committee of Soviets, shall determine the allocation of the public revenues and expenditures to the general state budget and to the local Societs and shall also establish the limits of taxation.

Article 82. The Soviets shall levy taxes and duties exclusively for purely local needs; requirements of a general and national character shall be met by allocations from the State Treasury.

Article 83. No expenditure may be made of money from the funds of the State Treasury without an authorized credit in respect thereof in the State budget, or a special order of the central government.

Article 84. Credits of the State Treasury, required for purposes of national importance, shall be placed at the disposal of the local Soviets by order of the appropriate People's Commissariats.

Article 85. All credits granted to the Soviets out of the State Treasury, as well as those allocated for purely local requirements, must be spent strictly within the limits, by paragraphs and clauses, laid down in the estimates; and they cannot be diverted to any other purpose without a special order of the All-Russian Central Executive Committee of Soviets or the Council of People's Commissars.

Article 86. The local Soviets shall prepare semi-annual and annual estimates of their revenues and expenditures. The estimates of village Soviets and rural district Soviets as well as the estimates of the county organs of Soviet power, shall be approved by the respective provincial and regional congresses, or their executive committees. The estimates of the town, provincial, and regional organs of Soviet power shall be approved by the All-Russian Central Executive Committee of Soviets and the council of People's Commissars.

Article 87. In the event of the need for expenditure not provided for in the estimates, and in cases where the sum allocated by the estimates is insufficient, the Soviets shall apply for supplementary credits to the appropriate People's Commissariats.

Article 88. Should local resources prove insufficient to meet local needs, subsidiaries or loans from the State Treasury to the local Soviets to cover urgent expenditures shall be authorized by the All-Russian Central Executive Committee of Soviets and the Council of People's Commissars.

PART VI: THE ARMS AND FLAG OF THE
RUSSIAN SOCIALIST FEDERAL SOVIET REPUBLIC

Chapter XVII

Article 89. The arms of the Russian Socialist Federal Soviet Republic shall consist of a sickle and a hammer, gold upon a red field and in the rays of the sun, the handles crossed and turned downward, the whole surrounded by a wreath of ears of grain, with the inscriptions:

(a) "RUSSIAN SOCIALIST FEDERAL SOVIET REPUBLIC" and

(b) "PROLETARIANS OF ALL COUNTRIES, UNITE!"

Article 90. The commercial, naval, and military flag of the Russian Socialist Federal Soviet Republic shall consist of red (scarlet) material, on the upper left corner of which, near the staff, are the letters in gold "RSFSR" or the inscription "Russian Socialist Federal Soviet Republic."

Note 1. In cases of necessity, provincial executive committees may convene extraordinary county congresses of Soviets, and county executive committees, rural district congresses of Soviets, at which new executive committees may be elected.

Note 2. The Presidium of the All-Russian Central Executive Committee of Soviets may decide that extraordinary congresses of Soviets of autonomous republics, regions, and provinces shall be convened, and that, when necessary, new elections for their executive committees be held.

German Constitution
of 1919

Better known as the Weimar Constitution because of the small town where the German Reich Constitution of 1919 was prepared, this document has been widely proclaimed as one of the most democratic constitutions of the world. It was among the first to feature universal adult suffrage, proportional representation, popular referenda, petition and recall, along with a generous formulation of human rights.

However, the Weimar Republic created by this constitution had been launched under extremely unfavorable circumstances. Defeat and national humiliation, revolutionary activity, severe economic and social disloca- tions, and an inexperienced political leadership were the major birth defects of Germany's first democracy. The new state never surmounted these ob- stacles. By 1932 the weaknesses of the Weimar republic facilitated the rise of Hitler and the demise of this model constitution.

The World War I peace settlement saddled Germany with a huge war debt, deprived it of 15 percent of its arable land, 10 percent of its popu- lation, and all of its foreign colonies. Most of its merchant fleet and its railroad stock had been seized by the conquering Allies.

The framers of the Weimer Constitution were for the most part dem- ocratic Socialists and liberals. Many of their conservative and Nationalist opponents therefore regarded the Weimar Constitution as a betrayal of the German people. Communists also regarded the system as hostile, be- cause their attempted coups in 1918 and 1919 had been suppressed by the Weimar government. In 1920 the republic also had to confront an at- tempted military coup, the Kapp Putsch. In 1923, the Communists at- tempted revolution in the state of Saxony. In the same year, Hitler made another unsuccessful attempt to take over the government in Munich.

The German middle class was severely threatened by inflation that depleted their savings in 1922 and 1923. In addition, the worldwide depression, which had been touched off by the collapse of the American stock market in 1929, was a further blow from which the Weimer government never rallied. By 1931 about half of all German families were directly affected by unemployment. Voters began to desert the democratic political forces. However, the Nazis and Communists profited from these problems. By 1932 these two antidemocratic elements had a majority of seats in the Reichstag (parliament), and by 1933 Hitler had eliminated all opposition.

The collapse of the Weimar government and the abrogation of its constitution is a major subject of study in today's democratic Federal Republic of Germany. Whether any democratic constitution could have withstood the problems of Germany from 1918 to 1933 is questionable, but Weimar's complex constitutional arrangements inevitably contributed to its demise.

Although the Weimar Constitution is properly praised for its many democratic features, the basic political and structural organization was faulty. The complicated arrangements for power sharing intensified friction among social, economic, religious, and political factions. It contained unworkable compromises between a unitary and federal state, between a parliamentary and presidential system, and between representative and direct democracy. Commentators have expressed the view that the system of proportional representation—designed to make the nation more democratic—resulted in a proliferation of political parties that made government unstable and ineffective.

There were two other constitutional flaws that undermined the document itself. The first was the dual executive system. This system created a strong president, independent of parliament, whose power conflicted with that of the other executive, the chancellor, who was the leader of parliament. The other flaw was in the antidemocratic provision for emergency powers set forth in Article 48. In 1925, World War I hero Paul von Hindenburg, a man who held ambivalent attitudes toward democracy, was elected president. With the rise of antidemocratic forces he invoked Article 48, giving him the power to rule by decree. This position further weakened the nation and facilitated the take-over by Hitler.

Despite these structural defects, the Weimar Constitution is praised for its contributions to human rights. The real legacy and lasting effect of the document is its democratic influence throughout the world. Although it may not be a direct model for the constitutions that followed, it is a constitution that is studied for its original ideas, pioneering features, and value in providing democratic guidelines. A half century later, it is praised as a constitution ahead of its time that had more elements of democratic thought than most contemporary constitutions. This document is a constitution that still has lessons to teach.

Individual rights set forth in this charter included free emigration; secrecy of correspondence in the postal, telegraph, and telephone services; and freedom of expression—not only regarding government but also the the workplace. The right to form and join unions was guaranteed, as well as the right to address a written petition to competent authorities. As a restriction on the power of the state, no provision was more significant than Article 114: "Persons who have been deprived of their liberty shall be informed—at the latest on the following day—by what authority and on what grounds the deprivation of liberty has been ordered; opportunity shall be given them without delay to make legal complaint against such deprivation."

Two other areas of human rights protections are in the fields of religion and education. In addition to guarantees of church-state separation, the Constitution provides that the property rights of religious bodies are protected, although "Sundays and holidays recognized by the state . . . remain under legal protection as days of rest." According to this document, non-religious bodies devoted "to the common protection of a world philosophy" and religious organizations have equal rights. Article 144 places the entire system of education under the general supervision of the state, and Article 145 makes school attendance compulsory. Nevertheless, "upon the request of persons responsible for the education of children," religious and private schools may serve as "a substitute for public schools."

Other guarantees include the right to property, freedom of contract, and the right of inheritance. Comprehensive insurance for medical needs is also provided for throughout one's lifetime. According to Article 163: "Every German must be afforded an opportunity to gain his livelihood by economic labor. Where no suitable opportunity of work can be found for him, provision shall be made for his support."

JAY A. SIGLER
Professor of Law
Rutgers University
Camden, New Jersey

CONSTITUTION
OF
THE GERMAN REICH
OF 11th AUGUST, 1919

The German people, united in every branch and inspired by the determination to renew and establish its realm in freedom and justice, to be of service to the cause of peace at home and abroad, and to further social progress, has given itself this Constitution.

PART I

ORGANISATION AND FUNCTIONS OF THE REICH

Section I. The Reich and the States

Article 1. The German Reich is a Republic.

All state authority emanates from the people.

Article 2. The territory of the Reich consists of the territories of the German States. Other territories may, by a law of the Reich, be incorporated in the Reich if their population so desires in virtue of the right of self-determination.

Article 3. The colours of the Reich are black, red and gold. The commercial flag is black, white and red, with the colours of the Reich in the upper inside corner.

Article 4. The generally recognised rules of International Law are valid as binding constituent parts of the Law of the German Reich.

Article 5. State authority is exercised in the affairs of the Reich through the institutions of the Reich on the basis of the Constitution of the Reich and in State affairs by the institutions of the States on the basis of the Constitutions of the States.

Article 6. The Reich has exclusive legislative power as regards:—

1. Foreign relations;

2. Colonial affairs;

3. Nationally, freedom of domicile, immigration and emigration, and extradition;

4. Military organisation;

Select Constitutions of the World, prepared for presentation to Dail Eireann, by order of the Irish Provisional Government, 1922 (Dublin: Stationery Office, 1922).

5. The monetary system;

6. Customs, as well as uniformity in the sphere of customs and trade, and freedom of commercial intercourse;

7. Posts and telegraphs, including telephones.

Article 7. The Reich has legislative power as regards:—

1. Civic rights;

2. Penal law;

3. Judicial procedure, including the carrying out of sentences, as well as official co-operation between public authorities;

4. Passports and the police supervision of foreigners;

5. Poor-relief and vagrancy;

6. The Press, associations and assemblies;

7. Population questions and the care of motherhood, infants, children and young persons;

8. Public health and veterinary matters, and the protection of plants against disease and pests;

9. Labour laws, the insurance and protection of workers and employees, together with Labour Bureaux;

10. The institution of vocational representative bodies for the territory of the Reich;

11. The care of persons who took part in the war, and of their dependants;

12. The law of expropriation;

13. The formation of associations for dealing with natural resources and economic undertakings, as well as the production, preparation, distribution and determination of prices of economic commodities for common use;

14. Commerce, the system of weights and measures, the issue of paper money, banking affairs and the system of exchange;

15. Traffic in foodstuffs and luxuries, as well as in articles of daily necessity;

16. Industry and mining;

17. Insurance matters;

18. Navigation, deep sea and coastal fishery;

19. Railways, inland navigation, motor traffic by land, water and air, as well as the construction of high-roads, so far as this is concerned with general traffic and home defence;

20. Theatres and cinemas.

Article 8. Further, the Reich has legislative power as regards taxes and other revenues in so far as they are appropriated wholly or in part to its purposes. Should the Reich appropriate taxes or other revenues hitherto appertaining to the various States, it must take into consideration the maintenance of the vitality of those States.

Article 9. Where there is need for the issue of uniform regulations, the Reich has legislative power as regards:—

1. Sanitary administration;

2. The maintainence of public order and security.

Article 10. The Reich may by legislation lay down fundamental principles governing:—

1. The rights and duties of religious associations;

2. Education, including higher education and scientific literature:

3. The law as to the conditions of service of officials of all public bodies;

4. The land laws, the distribution of land, land settlement and small holdings, the tenure of landed property;

5. Burial of the dead.

Article 11. The Reich may by legislation lay down fundamental principles governing the admissibility and mode of collection of State taxes, in so far as they requisite either for the purpose of preventing:—

1. Loss of revenue or injury to the commercial relations of the Reich;

2. Double taxation;

3. Charges for the use of public means of communication and their accessories, which are excessive and constitute a hindrance to traffic;

4. Assessments which are prejudicial to imported goods, as opposed to home products, in dealings between the separate States and parts of a State, or

5. Bounties on exportation; or for the purpose of protecting important social interests.

Article 12. So long and in so far as the Reich does not make use of its legislative power, the States retain that power for themselves. This does not apply to the exclusive legislative power of the Reich.

The Government of the Reich has the right of veto in respect of any laws of a State which refer to subjects included in Article 7, Number 13, in so far as the welfare of the Reich as a whole is thereby affected.

Article 13. The law of the Reich overrides the law of a State.

Where there exists any doubt or difference of opinion as to whether any provision of State law is compatible with the law of the Reich, an appeal may be made by the competent Reich or State authorities to the decision of the Supreme Court of the Reich in accordance with the more detailed provisions to be prescribed by a law of the Reich.

Article 14. Laws of the Reich are carried into execution by the State authorities, unless these laws decree otherwise.

Article 15. The Government of the Reich exercises control in those affairs in which the Reich has legislative power.

In so far as laws of the Reich are carried into execution by State authorities, the government of the Reich may issue general instructions.

For the purpose of supervision of the execution of laws of the Reich, the Government is empowered to despatch commissioners to the State central authorities, and, with their consent, to the subordinate authorities.

It is the duty of the State Governments, at the request of the Government of the Reich, to remedy defects observed in the execution of laws of the Reich. In case of difference of opinion, both the Government of the Reich and the State Government may appeal to the decision of the Supreme Court, save there appeal to another Court has been prescribed by law of the Reich.

Article 16. Officials entrusted with the direct administration of the Reich in the various States shall, as a rule, be citizens of the State in question. Officials, employees and workmen of the administration of the Reich shall, if they desire it, be employed as far as possible in their native districts, unless considerations of training or the exigencies of the service are opposed to this course.

Article 17. Each State must have a republican constitution. The representatives of the people must be elected by the universal equal, direct and secret suffrage of all men and women of the German Reich, upon the principles of proportional representation. The State Government must enjoy the confidence of the people's representatives.

The principles governing elections of the people's representatives apply also to elections to local bodies. By a State law the qualification for a vote may, however, be declared conditional upon a year's residence in the district.

Article 18. The organisation of the Reich into States shall serve the highest economic and cultural interests of the people with all due consideration for the will of the population concerned. Alteration of the territory of the States, and the formation of new States within the Reich, shall be effected by means of a law of the Reich amending the Constitution.

Where the States concerned give their consent, a simple law of the Reich suffices.

A simple law of the Reich suffices also, in a case where the consent of one of the States concerned has not been obtained, but where an alteration of territory or reorganisation is demanded by the will of the population and required by paramount interests of the Reich.

The will of the population is ascertained by plebiscite. The Government of the Reich orders the taking of a plebiscite when demanded by one-third of those inhabitants of the territory to be separate who are entitled to vote for the Reichstag.

For the determination of an alteration or reorganisation of territory, the proportion of votes required is three-fifths of the number cast, or, at least, a majority of the votes of persons qualified. Even when it is a question only of the separation of a portion of a Prussian administrative area (Regierungsbezirk), a Bavarian district (Kreis) or of a corresponding administrative district (Verwaltungsbezirk) in other States, the will of the population of the whole district in question shall be ascertained. Should the area of the territory to be separated and that of the whole district (Bezirk) not coincide, the will of the population of the former may by means of a special law of the Reich be declared sufficient.

The consent of the population having been obtained, the Government of the Reich shall lay before the Reichstag a law in accordance with the decision.

In the case of union or separation, should any dispute arise on the question of arrangements as to property, the decision on such points shall be given, upon an application from one party, by the Supreme Court of the German Reich unless another Court of the Reich is competent.

The President of the Reich carries out the decision of the Supreme Court.

Section II. The Reichstag

Article 20. The Reichstag is composed of the Deputies of the German people.

Article 21. The Deputies are representatives of the whole people. They are subject to their conscience only, and are not bound by any instructions.

Article 22. The Deputies are elected by the universal, equal, direct and secret suffrage of all men and women above the age of twenty, upon the principles of proportional representation. Elections must take place on a Sunday, or a public holiday.

Details are determined by the election law of the Reich.

Article 23. The Reichstag is elected for four years. New elections must take place not later than sixty days after the expiration of its term of office.

The Reichstag must hold its first meeting not less than thirty days after the election.

Article 24. The Reichstag assembles annually on the first Wednesday in November at the seat of the Government of the Reich. The President of the Reichstag must summon it earlier if requested by the President of the Reich or by at least one-third of the members.

The Reichstag determines the conclusion of the session and the day of reassembly.

Article 25. The President of the Reich may dissolve the Reichstag, but only once for any one reason.

The new elections must take place not later than thirty days after the dissolution.

Article 26. The Reichstag elects its Chairman, Deputy-Chairman and Secretaries. It determines its own rules of procedure.

Article 27. Between two sessions or elective periods the Chairman and Vice-Chairman of the last session continue to discharge their duties.

Article 28. The chairman exercises domestic and police authority within the Reichstag buildings. He is responsible for the administration of the House; regulates receipts and expenditure within the limits fixed by the Budget of the Reich, and represents the Reich in all the legal business and legal proceedings connected with his administration.

Article 29. The Reichstag conducts its business in public. Upon the motion of fifty members, supported by a two-thirds majority, the public may be excluded.

Article 30. Accurate reports of deliberations in the public sessions of the Reichstag, of a State Diet, or of their Committees are privileged.

Article 31. A Court of Inquiry into Elections is established in connection with the Reichstag. It also decides the question as to whether a Deputy has forfeited his membership.

The Court consists of members of the Reichstag, chosen by it for the electoral period, and of members of the Administrative Court of the Reich, appointed by the President of the Reich, upon the motion of the presiding officer of that Court.

The Court gives judgment after public viva voce investigation by three members of the Reichstag and two judicial members.

Apart from the investigation before this Court, the proceedings are conducted by an official of the Reich, appointed by the President of the Reich. Further provisions as to procedure are determined by the Court.

Article 32. For a decision of the Reichstag, a simple majority of votes is required, where no other proportion of votes is prescribed by the Constitution. The rules of procedure may permit exceptions in the case of elections to be undertaken by the Reichstag.

The number required to form a quorum is regulated by the rules of procedure.

Article 33. The Reichstag and its Committees may require the attendance of the Chancellor of the Reich and of any Ministers of the Reich.

The Chancellor and the Ministers of the Reich, and officials appointed by them, have access to the sittings of the Reichstag and its Committees. The States are entitled to send plenipotentiaries to these sittings, for the purpose of stating the point of view of their Government with regard to the subject under discussion.

At their request, Government representatives must be heard during the debate, and the representatives of the Government of the Reich must be heard without regard to the Order of the Day.

Such representatives are subject to the authority of the Chair.

Article 34. The Reichstag has the right to appoint Committees of Inquiry and must do so on the motion of one-fifth of its members. These Committees examine in open session such evidence as may be considered necessary by the Committee or by the movers of the motion for their appointment. The public may be excluded by resolution of the Committee of Inquiry supported by a two-third majority. The rules of procedure prescribe the procedure of the Committee and determine the number of its members.

The Courts and administrative authorities are bound to comply with the request of such Committees for the production of evidence; the official documents of the authorities must be laid before them if desired. The regulations as to criminal procedure are applicable in principle to the investigations of the Committees and of the authorities applied to by them, but the privacy of correspondence and of postal, telegraphic and telephonic communications must be respected.

Article 35. The Reichstag appoints a Standing Committee for Foreign Affairs which may also continue its work beyond the sessions of the Reichstag and after the expiration of the term of office or the dissolution of the Reichstag, until the assembly of the new Reichstag. The sittings of this Committee are not public, unless so decided by the Committee upon a two-thirds majority.

The Reichstag also appoints a Standing Committee for the Protection of the Rights of the Representatives of the People as against the Government of the Reich, for the period when the Reichstag is not in session, and after the expiration of its term of office.

These Committees have the same rights as Committees of Inquiry.

Article 36. No judicial or administrative proceedings may be taken at any time against any Member of the Reichstag or of any State Diet, on account of any vote he has given, or of any utterances made in the exercise of his functions, nor may he be called to account in any other way outside the House.

Article 37. No member of the Reichstag or of a State Diet may be summoned for examination or arrested for any action involving criminal proceedings during the period of a session, without the consent of the House of which he is a member, unless the member be apprehended at the time of the act, or, at the least, in the course of the following day.

The same consent is requisite for any other limitation of personal liberty which might hinder a Deputy in the exercise of his functions.

Any criminal proceedings against a Member of the Reichstag or of a State Diet and any arrest or other limitation of personal freedom shall, upon demand of the House of which he is a member, be suspended for the duration of the Session.

Article 38. Members of the Reichstag or a State Diet are entitled to refuse evidence with regard to persons who have confided any facts to them in their capacity as Deputies, or to whom they, in the exercise of their functions as Deputies, have made confidential statements; they may likewise refuse to give evidence as to such facts. With regard also to the sequestration of documents, they are in the position of persons who have a legal right to refuse evidence.

No search or sequestration may be carried out upon the premises of the Reichstag or of a State Diet without the consent of the Chairman.

Article 39. Officials and members of the Military Forces do not require leave of absence in order to exercise their functions as Members of the Reichstag or of a State Diet.

If they are candidates for a seat in these bodies, they shall be granted the requisite leave in order to prepare for the election.

Article 40. Members of the Reichstag are entitled to travel free on all German railways, and to receive allowances as determined by a law of the Reich.

Section III. The President of the Reich and the Government of the Reich

Article 41. The President of the Reich is elected by the whole German people.

Every German who has completed his thirty-fifth year is eligible.

Details shall be determined by a law of the Reich.

Article 42. The President of the Reich when entering upon his office takes the following oath before the Reichstag:—

"I swear to dedicate my powers to the welfare of the German people, to augment their prosperity, to guard them from injury, to maintain the Constitution and the laws of the Reich, to fulfil my duties conscientiously, and to do justice to every man."

The addition of a religious asseveration is permissible.

Article 43. The President of the Reich holds office for seven years. Re-election is permissible.

The President of the Reich may, upon the motion of the Reichstag, be removed from office before the expiration of his term by the vote of the people. The resolution of the Reichstag requires to be carried by a two-thirds majority. Upon the adoption of such a resolution, the President of the Reich is prevented from the further exercise of his office. Refusal to remove him from office, expressed by the vote of the people, is equivalent to re-election, and entails the dissolution of the Reichstag.

Penal proceedings may not be taken against the President of the Reich without the consent of the Reichstag.

Article 44. The President of the Reich may not at the same time be a member of the Reichstag.

Article 45. The President of the Reich represents the Reich in international relations. He concludes alliances and other treaties with Foreign Powers in the name of the Reich. He accredits and receives ambassadors.

The declaration of war and the conclusion of peace are dependent upon the passing of a law of the Reich.

Alliances and treaties with foreign states which refer to matters in which the Reich has legislative power require the consent of the Reichstag.

Article 46. The President of the Reich appoints and dismisses officials and officers of the Reich, where no other system is determined by law. He may delegate his right of appointment and dismissal to other authorities.

Article 47. The President of the Reich has Supreme Command over all the Armed Forces of the Reich.

Article 48. In the event of a State not fulfilling the duties imposed on it by the constitution or the laws of the Reich, the President of the Reich may make use of the armed forces to compel it to do so.

Where public security and order are seriously disturbed or endangered within the Reich, the President of the Reich may take the measures necessary for their restoration, intervening in case of need with the help of armed forces. For this purpose he is permitted, for the time being, to abrogate either wholly or partially the fundamental rights laid down in Articles 114, 115, 117, 123, 124, and 153.

The President of the Reich must, without delay, inform the Reichstag of any measures taken in accordance with paragraph 1 or 2 of this Article. Such measures shall be abrogated upon the demand of the Reichstag.

Where there is danger in delay, the State Government may take provisional measures of the kind indicated in paragraph 2, for its own territory. Such measures shall be abrogated upon the demand of the President of the Reich or the Reichstag.

Details are to be determined by a law of the Reich.

Article 49. The President of the Reich exercises the right of pardon for the Reich.

The grant of amnesty by the Reich requires to be effected by a law of the Reich.

Article 50. All orders and decrees of the President of the Reich, including those relating to the armed forces, require for their validity the counter-signature of the Chancellor or the competent Minister of the Reich. The counter-signature entails the undertaking of responsibility.

Article 51. In case of any disability the President of the Reich is represented in the first instance by the Chancellor of the Reich. Should it be probable that the disability might continue for some time, his representative shall be appointed by a law of the Reich.

The same applies to the case of premature vacancy in the office of President pending the carrying out of the new election.

Article 52. The Government of the Reich consists of the Chancellor of the Reich and the Ministers of the Reich.

Article 53. The President of the Reich appoints and dismisses the Chancellor of the Reich and, on the latter's recommendation, the Ministers of the Reich.

Article 54. The Chancellor of the Reich and the Ministers of the Reich require the confidence of the Reichstag in the administration of their office. Any one of them must resign should the confidence of the Reichstag be withdrawn by an express resolution.

Article 55. The Chancellor of the Reich presides over the Government of the Reich and directs its business, according to rules of procedure drawn up by the Government of the Reich and approved by the President of the Reich.

Article 56. The Chancellor of the Reich determines the main lines of policy, for which he is responsible to the Reichstag. Within these main lines each Minister of the Reich directs independently the department entrusted to him, for which he is personally responsible to the Reichstag.

Article 57. The Ministers of the Reich must submit to the Government for consideration and decision the drafts of all Bills and other matters for which such a course is prescribed by the Constitution or by law, as well as difference of opinion upon questions affecting the sphere of action of more than one Minister of the Reich.

Article 58. The Government of the Reich comes to a decision by a majority of votes. In case of an equality of votes the presiding member gives the casting vote.

Article 59. The Reichstag may arraign the President of the Reich, the Chancellor and the Ministers before the Supreme Court of the German Reich for culpable violation of the Constitution or of a law of the Reich. The motion for the arraignment must be signed by at least one hundred members of the Reichstag, and requires the assent of the majority prescribed for alterations of the Constitution. Details are to be regulated by the law of the Reich as to the Supreme Court.

Section IV. The Reichsrat

Article 60. A Reichsrat is formed in order to represent the German States in the legislation and administration of the Reich.

Article 61. In the Reichsrat, each State has at least one vote. In the larger States, one vote is assigned for each million inhabitants. Any surplus not less than the total population of the smallest State is reckoned as a full million. No State may be represented by more than two-fifths of all votes.

*German Austria will, after her union with the German Reich, acquire the right of participation in the Reichsrat, with the number of votes cor-

---

* According to Article 80 of the Treaty of Peace between the Allied and Associated Powers and Germany, signed at Versailles, June 28th 1919, "Germany acknowledged and will respect strictly the independence of Austria, within the frontiers which may be fixed in a Treaty between that State and the Principal Allied and Associated Powers; she agrees that this independence shall be inalienable, except with the consent of the Council of the League of Nations." A declaration that all provisions of this constitution which are in contradiction with the terms of the Treaty of Peace are null and void was signed on September 22nd, 1919, at Paris, by the acting Head of the German Delegation.

responding to her population. Until that time, the representatives of German Austria have an advisory voice.

The number of votes shall be re-adjusted by the Reichsrat after each general census of the population.

Article 62. In Committees appointed by the Reichsrat from its members no State shall have more than one vote.

Article 63. The States are represented in the Reichsrat by members of their Governments. However, one-half of the Prussian votes shall be assigned, according to a State law, to representatives of Prussian provincial administrations.

The States are entitled to send to the Reichsrat as many representatives as they have votes.

Article 64. The Government of the Reich must convene the Reichsrat upon the demand of one-third of its members.

Article 65. The Reichsrat and its Committees are presided over by a member of the Government of the Reich. The members of the latter are entitled, and, if requested, are bound, to take part in the deliberations of the Reichsrat and its Committees. They must be heard upon their demand at any time during the debate.

Article 66. The Government of the Reich and each member of the Reichsrat are authorised to lay proposals before the Reichsrat.

The Reichsrat regulates the conduct of its business by rules of procedure.

The plenary sessions of the Reichsrat are public. The public may be excluded during the discussion of certain subjects, in accordance with the rules of procedure.

For a decision a simple majority of the votes is required.

Article 67. The Reichsrat shall be kept informed by the Ministries of the Reich of the progress of affairs in the Reich. Upon important subjects the Committees of the Reichsrat concerned shall be called into consultation by the Ministries of the Reich.

Section V. Legislation of the Reich

Article 68. Bills are introduced by the Government of the Reich or by members of the Reichstag.

The laws of the Reich are passed by the Reichstag.

Article 69. The introduction of Bills by the government of the Reich requires the consent of the Reichsrat. Should the Government and the Reichsrat not be in agreement, the former may, nevertheless, introduce the Bill, but, in doing so, must stage the divergent view of the Reichsrat.

Should the Reichsrat adopt a Bill to which the Government does not agree, the latter must introduce the Bill in the Reichstag with a statement of its own point of view.

Article 70. The President of the Reich shall prepare for publication the laws which have been adopted in accordance with the Constitution, and within the period of one month, shall promulgate them in the Journal of Laws, of the Reich (reichsgesetzblatt).

Article 71. Laws of the Reich come into force, unless otherwise provided therein, fourteen days from the day on which the Journal of Laws of the Reich is published in the capital.

Article 72. The promulgation of a law of the Reich shall be deferred for two months, if one-third of the Reichstag so demands. Laws which the Reichstag and the Reichsrat declare to be urgent may, however, be promulgated by the President of the Reich, notwithstanding such a demand.

Article 73. A law by the Reichstag shall, before its promulgation, be submitted to the decision of the people, if the President of the Reich so determines within one month.

A law the promulgation of which is deferred on the motion of at least one-third of the Reichstag shall be submitted to the decision of the people, if desired by one-twentieth of those entitled to the franchise.

There may also be an appeal to the decision of the people if one-tenth of those entitled to the franchise initiate a request for the introduction of a Bill. This popular initiative must be based on a complete draft of the Bill. It shall be submitted to the Reichstag by the Government, accompanied by a statement of the Government's attitude in regard to it. The appeal to the decision of the people shall not take place if the proposed Bill is accepted without amendment by the Reichstag.

The President of the Reich is alone entitled to institute an appeal to the decision of the people on the Budget and on laws dealing with taxation and decrees as to payments to employees.

The procedure in connection with the appeal to any initiative by the people is to be regulated by a law of the Reich.

Article 74. The Reichsrat may enter an objection against a law passed by the Reichstag.

This objection must be lodged with the Government of the Reich within two weeks after the final vote in the Reichstag, and must be supported by reasons, presented at latest within a further two weeks.

When an objection is entered, the law shall be brought before the Reichstag for further consideration. Should the Reichstag and the Reichsrat not arrive at an agreement, the President of the Reich may, within three months, order an appeal to the people upon the subject in dispute. Should the President not make use of this right, the law shall not come into operation. Should the Reichstag decide, by a two-thirds' majority, against the objection of the Reichsrat, the President must, within three months, either promulgate the law in the form approved by the Reichstag or order an appeal to the people.

Article 75. A decision of the Reichstag can be annulled by the decision of the people only when a majority of those entitled to the franchise take part in the vote.

Article 76. The constitution may be amended by legislation. But decisions of the Reichstag as to such amendments come into effect only if two-thirds of the legal total of members be present, and if at least two-thirds of those present have given their consent. Decisions of the Reichsrat in favour of amendments of the Constitution also require a majority of two-thirds of the votes cast. Where an amendment of the Constitution is decided by an appeal to the people as the result of a Popular Initiative, the consent of the majority of the voters is necessary.

Should the Reichstag have decided upon an alteration of the Constitution in spite of the objection of the Reichsrat, the President of the Reich shall not promulgate the law if the Reichsrat, within two weeks, demands an appeal to the people.

Article 77. The Government of the Reich issues the general administrative instructions necessary for the execution of the laws of the Reich, unless otherwise provided by law. For this purpose, the Government needs the assent of the Reichsrat when the execution of the law of the Reich is the business of the Authorities of the States.

Section VI. Administration of the Reich

Article 78. The conduct of foreign affairs is the exclusive concern of the Reich.

In affairs regulated by State legislation, the States may conclude agreement with foreign States. These agreements require the consent of the Reich.

Conventions with foreign States as to the alteration of the frontiers of the Reich are concluded by the Reich, with the consent of the State concerned. Alterations in the frontier may be effected only by a law of the Reich, except in the case of a simple rectification of the borders of uninhabited portions of a district.

In order to guarantee representation of the interests of individual States arising from their special economic relations with foreign States or their proximity thereto, the Reich undertakes the requisite arrangements and measures in agreement with the State concerned.

Article 79. The defence of the Reich is a matter for action by the Reich. The military organisation of the German people is regulated uniformly by means of a law of the Reich, regard being had to the individual conditions of each State.

Article 80. Colonial affairs are exclusively the business of the Reich.

Article 81. All German merchant shipping constitutes a united commercial fleet.

Article 82. Germany forms one customs and commercial district, enclosed by one common customs frontier.

The customs frontier coincides with the foreign frontier. To seaward it is formed by the shore of the mainland, with the islands belonging to the territory of the Reich. On the sea or on other bodies of the water, deviations may be made in the course of the Customs frontier.

The territories or portions of the territories of a foreign State may be included in the customs district by State treaties or by agreement.

In cases of special necessity certain areas may be excluded from the Customs district. In the case of free ports, exclusion can be set aside only by means of a law amending the Constitution.

Places excluded from the Customs district may join a foreign customs district by means of a State treaty or by agreement.

All natural products as well as products of manufacture and industry in which there is free trade within the Reich, may be imported, exported or sent in through transit across the frontiers of the States and local authorities. Exceptions may be allowed by a law of the Reich.

Article 83. Customs and duties upon articles of consumption are administered by authorities of the Reich.

In the administration of taxes by the authorities of the Reich arrangements shall be made so as to ensure to the various States the protection of special State interests within the domain of agriculture, trade, manufacture and industry.

Article 84. The Government of the Reich regulates by law:—

1. The organisation of the administration of taxes in the States, so far is required for the purpose of uniform and equal execution of the laws of the Reich on taxation;

2. The organisation and powers of the authorities entrusted with the superintendence of the execution of the laws of the Reich on taxation;

3. The settlement of accounts with the States;

4. The reimbursement of expenses of administration in the execution of the laws of the Reich on taxation.

Article 85. All receipts and expenditures of the Reich must be estimated for each financial year and be shown in the Budget.

The Budget must be passed into law before the opening of the financial year.

Items of expenditure shall normally be granted for one year; in special cases, they may be granted for a longer period. In general, provisions in the Budget law of the Reich, which extend beyond the financial year or do not refer to the receipts and expenditure of the Reich or their administration, are inadmissible.

The Reichstag may neither increase items of expenditure, nor include new ones, in the draft of the Budget, without the consent of the Reichsrat.

Failing the consent of the Reichsrat the provisions of Article 74 apply.

Article 86. In order to secure discharge of the responsibility of the Government of the Reich, the Minister of Finance for the Reich shall, in the following financial year, submit to the Reichstag and the Reichsrat an account of the expenditure out of all revenues of the Reich. The auditing of accounts shall be regulated by law of the Reich.

Article 87. Funds may be obtained by way of loan in case of special necessity, and, as a rule, only for expenditure on productive undertakings. Such a proceeding, as well as the giving of a security on behalf of the Reich, may be effected only the authority of a law of the Reich.

Article 88. The postal and telegraph services, together with the telephone services, are exclusively the affairs of the Reich.

Postage stamps are uniform for the whole Reich.

The Government of the Reich, with the consent of the Reichsrat, issues the instructions which determine the conditions and charges for the use of the means of communication. With the consent of the Reichsrat, the Government may transfer these powers to the Minister of Posts.

For the purpose of consultative co-operation in matters connected with postal, telegraphic and telephonic communications and the charges therefor, the Government of the Reich shall, with the consent of the Reichsrat, establish an Advisory Council.

Treaties referring to means of communication with foreign countries are concluded only by the Government of the Reich.

Article 89. It is the duty of the Government of the Reich to assume ownership of the railways serving for general traffic, and to manage them on a uniform traffic system.

The rights of States to acquire private railways shall be transferred, upon demand, to the Government of the Reich.

Article 90. With the transfer of the railways, the Reich assumes the power of expropriation and the sovereign rights of the States as regards the railway service. The Supreme Court decides, in case of dispute, as to the extent of such rights.

Article 91. The government of the Reich, with the consent of the Reichsrat, issues orders for regulating the construction, management and working of the railways. With the consent of the Reichsrat, the Government may delegate these powers in the competent Minister of the Reich.

Article 92. Notwithstanding the incorporation of their budget and accounts with the general Budget and accounts of the Reich the railways of the Reich shall be administered as an independent, economic undertaking responsible for defraying its own expenses, inclusive of interest and a sinking-fund for the railway debt, and also for accumulating a reserve. The amount of the sinking-fund and reserve, as well as the purposes to which the reserve is to be applied, shall be regulated by means of a special law.

Article 93. For the purpose of consultative co-operation in matters concerning railway traffic and rates, the Government of the Reich shall, with the consent of the Reichsrat, establish Advisory Councils for the Railways of the Reich.

Article 94. Where the Government of the Reich has taken over in a certain district the railways serving for general traffic, new railways serving the same purpose may be constructed within this district only by the Reich, or with its consent. Should the construction of new or the alteration of existing railways by the Reich affect the sphere of activity of the police authorities of a State, the Railway Administration of the Reich must consult the State Authorities before coming to a decision.

Where the Reich has not yet taken over the railways, it may, on the authority of a law of the Reich, construct at its own expense, or permit another body to construct (subject when necessary to reservation of the right of expropriation), railways considered necessary for general traffic or for the defence of the territory, even without the consent of the States through the territory of which the railway is to run, but without prejudice to the sovereign rights of the States.

Every railway system must permit other railways to make junctions with it at the cost of the latter.

Article 95. Railways for general traffic which are not under the administration of the Reich are subject to its supervision.

Railways subject to such supervision shall be constructed and equipped upon the principles laid down by the Reich. They must be maintained in good working order, and developed in accordance with the requirements of traffic. Both passenger and goods traffic must be attended to and organised in accordance with their needs.

In the supervision of rates, uniform and low railway rates are to be aimed at.

Article 96. All railways, including those not serving for general traffic, must comply with the requirements of the Reich as to the use of railways for the purpose of State defence.

Article 100. For the purpose of meeting the expenses of maintenance and development of inland waterways, a law of the Reich may provide for contributions from those who profit in any other way than by navigation in the construction of dams, in cases where several States have shared in, or where the Reich alone has borne the expenses of construction.

Article 101. It is the duty of the Reich to assume ownership and administration of all navigation marks, particularly lighthouses, light-ships, buoys, barrels and beacons. After such transfer, marks may be constructed and extended only by, or with the consent of, the Reich.

Section VII. Administration of Justice

Article 102. Judges are independent and subject only to the law.

Article 103. The ordinary jurisdiction is exercised by the High Court of the Reich and the Courts of the States.

Article 104. The judges of the ordinary Courts are appointed for life. They may be removed from office, permanently or temporarily transferred to another position or retired only on the authority of a judicial decision, and only upon the grounds and by the methods of procedure fixed by law. Age limits may be fixed by legislation, upon reaching which judges shall retire.

Provisional removal from office when authorised by law is not affected by the above.

In the case of a re-arrangement of the Courts or their circuits, the State Administration of Justice may order compulsory transfer to another court, or removal from office, but only on condition of the retention of full salary.

These provisions do not apply to commercial judges, assessors and juryment.

Article 105. Extraordinary Courts are prohibited. No one may be withdrawn from his legal judge. Legal regulations regarding Courts-Martial and Summary Military Courts are not affected by the above. Military Courts of Honour are abolished.

Article 106. Military jurisdiction is abolished, except in time of war and on board warships. Details are regulated by a law of the Reich.

Article 107. In the Reich and the States administrative courts shall be established by law for the protection of individuals against regulations and decrees of the Administrative authorities.

Article 108. A Supreme Court for the German Reich shall be established by law of the Reich.

PART II

FUNDAMENTAL RIGHTS AND DUTIES OF GERMANS

Section I. The Individual

Article 109. All Germans are equal before the law.

Men and women have fundamentally the same civic rights and duties.

Public legal privileges or disadvantages of birth or rank shall be abolished. Titles of nobility shall be simply a part of the name, and may no longer be conferred.

Titles may be conferred only when they indicate an office or calling; academic degrees are not hereby affected.

Orders and badges of honour may not be conferred by the State.

No German is permitted to accept a title or order from a foreign Government.

Article 110. Nationality in the Reich and the States is acquired and terminated as may be provided by the law of the Reich. Every subject of a State is also a subject of the Reich.

Every German has the same rights and duties in any State of the Reich as the subjects of that State.

Article 111. All Germans enjoy the right of change of domicile within the whole Reich. Everyone has the right to stay in any part of the Realm that he chooses, to settle there, acquire landed property and pursue any means of livelihood. Restrictions may be imposed only by law of the Reich.

Article 112. Every German is entitled to emigrate to countries outside the Reich. Emigration may be restricted only by law of the Reich.

All nationals of the Reich within and beyond its territory are entitled to claim the protection of the Reich in relation to a foreign power.

No German may be handed over to a foreign Government for prosecution or punishment.

Article 113. Sections of the population of the Reich speaking a foreign language may not be restricted, whether by way of legislation or administration, in their free racial development; this applies specially to the use of their mother tongue in education, as well as in questions of internal administrations and the administration of justice.

Article 114. Personal liberty is inviolable. No encroachment on or deprivation of personal liberty by any public authority is permissible except in virtue of a law.

Persons who have been deprived of their liberty shall be informed— at the latest on the following day—by what authority and on what grounds the deprivation of liberty has been ordered; opportunity shall be given them without delay to make legal complaint against such deprivation.

Article 115. The residence of every German is an inviolable sanctuary for him; exceptions are admissible only in virtue of laws.

Article 116. No punishment may be inflicted for any action unless the action was designated by law as punishable, before it was committed.

Article 117. The secrecy of correspondence and of the postal, telegraph and telephone services, is inviolable. Exceptions may be permitted only by law of the Reich.

Article 118. Every German has the right, within the limits of general laws, to express his opinion freely, by word of mouth, writing, printed matter or picture, or in any other manner. This right must not be affected by any conditions of his work or appointment, and no one is permitted to injure him on account of his making use of such rights.

No censorship shall be enforced, but restrictive regulations may be introduced by law in reference to cinematograph entertainments. Legal measures are also admissable for the purpose of combating bad and obscene literature, as well as for the protection of youth in public exhibitions and performances.

Section II. The Life of the Community

Article 119. Marriage, as the foundation of family life and of the preservation and growth of the nation, is under the special protection of the Constitution. It rests upon the equal rights of both sexes.

The preservation of the purity and health of the family and its social advancement is the task both of the State and of the local authorities. Families with a large number of children have a right to corresponding provision.

Motherhood has a claim upon the protection and care of the State.

Article 120. The rearing of the rising generation, in physical, mental and social efficiency, is the highest duty and natural right of the parents, the accomplishment of which is watched over by the community of the State.

Article 121. By means of legislation, opportunity shall be provided for the physical, mental and social nurture of illegitimate children, equal to that enjoyed by legitimate children.

Article 122. Young persons shall be protected against exploitation, as well as against moral, spiritual, or bodily neglect. Both the State and the local authorities must undertake the necessary arrangements.

Protection measures of a compulsory character may only be imposed by virtue of a law.

Article 123. All Germans have the right without notification or special permission to assemble peaceably and unarmed.

Open-air meetings may be made notifiable by a law of the Reich, and in case of direct danger to public security may be forbidden.

Article 124. All Germans have the right to form unions and associations for purposes not in contravention of the penal laws. This right may not be restricted by preventive regulations. The same provisions apply to religious unions and associations.

Every union is at liberty to acquire legal rights in accordance with the provisions of the Civil Code. These rights shall not be refused to a union on the ground that its objects are of political, social-political, or religious nature.

Article 125. The freedom and the secrecy of elections are guaranteed. Details are to be determined by electoral laws.

Article 126. Every German has the right to address written petitions or complaints to the competent authorities or the representatives of the people. This right may be exercised by individuals, and by several persons in common.

Article 127. Communes and associations of Communes have the right to administer their own affairs within the limits of the laws.

Article 128. All citizens of the State, without distinction, are eligible for public offices, as provided by law and in accordance with their qualifications and abilities.

All exceptional provisions against women officials are annulled.

The conditions of employment of officials shall be determined by law of the Reich.

Article 129. Officials are appointed for life, save as may be otherwise provided by law. Pensions and provision for surviving dependants shall be regulated by law. Rights duly acquired by officials are inviolable. Officials may have recourse to legal proceedings in respect of financial claims.

Officials may not be provisionally removed from office, or provisionally or permanently retired, or transferred to another post with a lower salary, save in accordance with and in the manner determined by law.

Every penalty inflicted on an official must be subject to appeal and the possibility of revision. Unfavourable entries may not be made in the personal record of an official, unless he has been given an opportunity to reply to them. Officials have the right to examine their personal records.

The inviolability of duly acquired rights and opportunity to have recourse to legal proceedings in respect of financial. In other respects their status shall be determined by law of the Reich.

Article 130. Officials are servants of the community and not of any party.

Freedom of political opinions and the free right of association are guaranteed to all officials.

Officials have special Service representation, details in regard to which shall be determined by law of the Reich.

Article 131. Should an official, in the exercise of the public authority conferred upon him, neglect an official duty incumbent upon him in relation to a third party, the responsibility as a matter of principle falls upon the State or the corporate body in whose service the official is acting. Their right to take retributory action is reserved. Recourse to the ordinary process of law must not be excluded.

More detailed regulations shall be prescribed by legislation by the appropriate authority.

Article 132. It is the duty of every German to undertake the duties of honorary offices according to the provisions of the laws.

Article 133. All citizens are bound, according to the provisions of the laws, to undertake personal service for the State and the local authorities.

Military service is organised in accordance with the terms of the Military Defence Law of the Reich. This Law determines also to what extent certain fundamental rights must be restricted for members of the armed forces to ensure the fulfilment of their duties and the maintenance of military discipline.

Article 134. All citizens, without exception, contribute in proportion to their means to all public taxes, in accordance with the provisions of the laws.

Section III. Religion and Religious Associations

Article 135. All inhabitants of the Reich enjoy full liberty of faith and of conscience. The undisturbed practice of religion is guaranteed by the Constitution and is under State protection. The general laws of the State shall remain unaffected hereby.

Article 136. Civil and political rights and duties are neither dependent upon nor restricted by the practice of religious freedom.

The enjoyment of civil and political rights, as well as admission to official posts, are independent of religious creed.

No one is found to disclose his religious convictions. The authorities have the right to make enquires as to membership of a religious body only when rights and duties depend upon it or when the collection of statistics ordered by law requires it.

No one may be compelled to take part in any ecclesiastical act or ceremony, or to participate in religious practices or to make use of any religious form of oath.

Article 137. There is no State Church.

Freedom of association is guaranteed to religious bodies. The union of religious bodies within the territory of the Reich is subject to no restriction.

Every religious body regulates and administers its affairs independently, within the limits of the laws applicable to all. It appoints its officers without the co-operation of the State or of the local authorities.

Religious bodies acquire legal status in accordance with the general regulations of the civil code.

Religious bodies remain legal corporations in so far as they have been so up to the present. Equal rights shall be granted to other religious bodies upon application, if their constitution and the number of their members offer a guarantee of permanence. Where several such religious bodies which are legal corporations combine to form one union, this union becomes a legal corporation.

Religious bodies which are legal corporations are entitled to levy taxes on the basis of the civic tax-rolls, in accordance with the provisions of the laws of the States.

Associations devoting themselves to the common promotion of a world-philosophy shall be placed upon an equal footing with religious bodies.

So far as further regulations may be necessary for the carrying-out of these provisions, they shall be prescribed by legislation of the States.

Article 138. Outstanding State liabilities to religious bodies, whether founded upon legislation, contract or exceptional legal title, shall be redeemed by legislation by the States. The governing principles of such legislation shall be prescribed by the Reich.

The property and other rights of religious bodies and unions in respect of their institutions, foundations and other property devoted to public worship, education and social welfare, are guaranteed.

Article 139. Sundays and holidays recognised by the State shall remain under legal protection as days of rest and spiritual improvement.

Article 140. The members of the armed forces are guaranteed the necessary free time for the performance of their religious duties.

Article 141. Religious bodies have the right of entry for religious purposes into the army, hospitals, prisons, or other public institutions, so far as is necessary for the conduct of public worship and religious ministrations, but any form of compulsion is forbidden.

Section IV. Education and Schools

Article 142. Art and science, and the teaching thereof, are free.

The State guarantees their protection and participates in furthering them.

Article 143. Provision shall be made for the education of the young by means of public institutions. The Reich, the States and the local authorities shall co-operate in their organisation. The training of teachers shall be regulated in a uniform manner for the whole Reich, on the general lines laid down for higher education.

Teachers in public schools have the rights and duties of State officials.

Article 144. The whole system of education is under the supervision of the State, which may assign a share in such work to the local authorities. School inspection is carried out by competent, trained and expert officials of high rank.

Article 145. School attendance is compulsory for all. The fulfilment of this obligation is provided for by primary schools, with at least an eight year's course, followed by continuation schools with a course extending to the completion of the eighteenth year of age.

Instruction and all accessories are free of charge in the primary and continuation schools.

Article 146. The public system of education shall be organically developed. Upon the basis of primary schools common to all shall be built up a system of secondary and higher education. The governing consideration in the building up of this system shall be the diversity of vocations and, as regards the admission of a child into any particular school, its capacity and inclination, not the economic and social standing of its parents.

Upon the request of persons responsible for the education of children, however, primary schools in accordance with their religious creed or philosophic views may be established in a locality, so far as is possible without interference with the orderly development of the school system, especially as regards the general principles of the first paragraph of this Article. The wishes of persons responsible for the education of children shall be taken into account as far as possible. Further details shall be determined by legislation by the States in accordance with principles laid down by a law of the Reich.

Public provision shall be made by the Reich, the States and the local authorities, for the admission of persons, of small means to secondary and higher educational institutions; in particular, educational assistance grants shall be provided for the parents of children considered suitable for education in secondary and higher schools until the completion of their education.

Article 147. Private schools, as a substitute for public schools, require the approval of the State, and are subject to the laws of the States. Approval may be granted when the private schools are not inferior to the public schools in their educational aims and organisation, nor in the professional qualifications of their teaching staff; further, there must be no segregation of pupils based upon the means of their parents. Approval shall be refused when the economic and legal position of the teaching staff is not sufficiently assured.

Private primary schools are permissible only when there is in a locality no public primary school corresponding to the religious creed or philosophic views of a minority of persons responsible for the education of children whose desires must be taken into consideration in accordance with Article 146, Paragraph 2, or when the educational administrative authorities recognise that a special educational interest is involved.

Primary preparatory schools are to be abolished.

Private schools not serving as substitutes for public school retain their existing legal rights.

Article 148. All schools shall aim at inculcating moral character, a civic conscience, personal and vocational efficiency, imbued with the spirit of German nationality and international goodwill.

In giving instruction in public schools, care must be taken not to give offence to the susceptibilities of those holding different opinions.

The duties of citizenship and technical education are subjects of instruction in the schools. Upon the completion of the period of school attendance, every pupil receives a copy of the Constitution.

The Reich, the States and the local authorities shall promote the organisation of popular culture, including popular high schools.

Article 149. Religious instruction is a regular subject in schools, with the exception of undenomination (secular) schools. The giving of such instruction shall be regulated in accordance with legislation upon schools. Religious instruction shall be given in accord with the principles of the religious body concerned, without prejudice to the right of State supervision.

The giving of religious instruction and the undertaking of spiritual duties are subject to the declared assent of the teacher; participation in religious instruction and in religious rites and ceremonies is subject to the declared assent of the person responsible for the religious education of the child.

The theological Faculties in the Universities shall continue to be maintained.

Article 150. Monuments of artistic, historic, and natural interest, and exceptional landscapes are under the protection and care of the State.

It is the business of the Reich to prevent the removal of German art treasures into foreign countries.

Section V. Economic Life

Article 151. The organisation of economic life must correspond to the principles of justice, and be designed to ensure for all a life worthy of a human being. Within these limits the economic freedom of the individual must be guaranteed.

Legal compulsion is permissible only in order to enforce rights which are threatened, or to subserve the pre-eminent claims of the common weal.

Article 152. Freedom of contract shall prevail in economic relations, subject to the provisions of the laws.

Usury is forbidden. Contracts which are opposed to morality are void.

Article 153. Property is guaranteed by the Constitution. Its extent and the restrictions placed upon it are defined by law.

Expropriation may be effected only for the benefit of the general community and upon the basis of law. It shall be accompanied by due compensation, save in so far as may be otherwise provided by a law of the Reich. In case of dispute as to the amount of compensation, resort may be had to legal proceedings in the ordinary course, unless a law of the Reich otherwise determines. Property of the States, local authorities and public utility associations may be expropriated by the Reich only on payment of compensation.

The ownership of property entails obligations. Its use must at the same time serve the common good.

Article 154. The right of inheritance is guaranteed in accordance with the provisions of the Civil Law.

The Share in any inheritance which accrues to the State is determined by law.

Article 155. The distribution and use of land shall be supervised by the State in such a way as to prevent abuse and with a view to ensuring to every German a healthy dwelling and to all German families, particularly those with many children, a dwelling and economic homestead suited to their needs. Special consideration shall be given in the framing of the Homestead Laws to persons who have taken part in the war.

Landed property may be expropriated when required to meet the needs of housing, or for the purpose of land settlement, the bringing of land into cultivation or the improvement of husbandry. Testamentary trusts are to be terminated.

The cultivation and full utilization of the land is a duty the landowner owes to the community. Increment in the value of landed property, not accruing from any expenditure of labour and capital upon the land, shall be devoted to the uses of the community.

All riches in the soil and all natural sources of power of economic value shall be under the control of the State. Private-royalties shall be transferred to the State by legislation.

Article 156. The Reich may, by legislation, without prejudice to the payment of compensation and subject to appropriate application of the provisions governing expropriation, transfer to public ownership private economic undertakings which are suitable for socialization. It may itself undertake, or assign to the States or local authorities a share in, the management of such undertakings and associations, or otherwise ensure to itself a determining influence therein.

Further, the Reich may by legislation, in case of pressing necessity and in the economic interests of the community, oblige economic undertakings and associations to combine, on a self-governing basis, for the purpose of ensuring the co-operation of all productive factors of the nation, associating employers and employees in the management, and regulating the production, manufacture, distribution, consumption, prices and the import and export of commodities upon principles determined by the economic interest of the community.

Industrial and argricultural co-operative societies and federations thereof may be incorporated into the public economic system, at their own request and with due regard to their constitution and special characteristics.

Article 157. Labour is under the special protection of the Reich.

The Reich will frame a uniform labour code.

Article 158. Intellectual work, the rights of discoverers, inventors and artists are under the protection and care of the Reich.

By means of international agreements, recognition and protection must be ensured abroad for the products of German science, art, and technical skill.

Article 159. Freedom of association for the maintenance and improvement of labour and economic conditions is guaranteed to everyone and for all occupations. All agreements and measures tending to restrict or obstruct such freedom are illegal.

Article 160. Every person in the position of an employee or workman has a right to such free time as is necessary for the exercise of his civic rights, and, in so far as the business in which he is employed will not be seriously injured thereby, for the discharge of honorary public duties entrusted to him. Legislation shall determine how far such a person may be entitled to claim compensation.

Article 161. The Reich will, with the full co-operation of insured persons, create a comprehensive system of insurance for the maintenance of health and fitness for work, the protection of motherhood and provision for the economic consequences of old age, infirmity, and the vicissitudes of life.

Article 162. The Reich will initiate international regulation of the legal conditions of workers, with a view to securing for the working class of the world a universal minimum of social rights.

Article 163. It is moral duty of every German, without prejudice to his personal liberty, to make such use of his mental and bodily powers as shall be necessary for the welfare of the community.

Every German must be afforded an opportunity to gain his livelihood by economic labour. Where no suitable opportunity of work can be found for him, provision shall be made for his support. Details shall be determined by special law of the Reich.

Article 164. The independent middle class in agriculture, industry and commerce, shall be encouraged by legislative and administrative measures, and shall be protected against exploitation and oppression.

Article 165. Workers and salaried employees are called upon to co-operate with equal rights in common with the employers in the regulation of wages and conditions of labour and in the general economic development of the forces of production. The organisations on both sides and the agreements made by them shall be recognised.

For the protection of their social and economic interests, workers and salaried employees shall have legal representation in Workers' Councils for individuals undertakings and in District Workers' Councils grouped according to economic districts and in a Workers' Council of the Reich.

The District Workers' Council and the Workers' Council of the Reich shall combine with representatives of the employers and other classes of the population concerned so as to form District Economic Councils and an Economic Council of the Reich, for the discharge of their joint economic functions and for co-operation in the carry-out of laws relating to socialization. The District Economic Councils and the Economic Council of the Reich shall be so constituted as to give representation thereon to all important vocational groups in proportion to their economic and social importance.

All Bills of fundamental importance dealing with matters of social and economic legislation shall, before being introduced, be submitted by the Government of the Reich to the Economic Council of the Reich for its opinion thereon. The Economic Council of the Reich shall have the right itself to propose such legislation. Should the Government of the Reich not agree with any such proposal, it must nevertheless introduce it in the

Reichstag, accompanied by a statement of its own views thereon. The Economic Council of the Reich may arrange for one of its own members to advocate the proposal in the Reichstag.

Powers of control and administration in any matters falling within their province may be conferred upon Workers' Councils and Economic Councils.

The constitution and functions of the Workers' and Economic Councils and their relations with other autonomous social organizations are within the exclusive jurisdiction of the Reich.

PROVISIONAL AND CONCLUDING ARRANGEMENTS

Article 166. Until the establishment of the Administrative Court of the Reich its place shall be taken, as regards the formation of the Court of Inquiry into Elections, by the High Court of the Reich.

Article 167. The provisions of Article 18, paragraphs 3 to 6, shall not come into force until two years after the publications of the Constitution of the Reich.

Article 168. Until the promulgation of the State law provided for in Article 63, but at the longest for the period of one year, all Prussian votes in the Reichsrat may be exercised by members of the Government.

Article 169. The date on which the provisions of Article 83, paragraph 1, are to come into force shall be determined by the Government of the Reich.

For a suitable transition period, the collection and administration of customs and excise may, at their request, be left to the States.

Article 170. The administration of the postal and telegraphic services of Bavaria and Wurttemberg shall be transferred to the Reich by 1st April, 1921, at the latest.

Should no agreement as to the conditions of transfer have been attained by 1st October, 1920, the decision shall be given by the Supreme Court.

Up to the date of transfer the existing rights and responsibilities of Bavaria and Wurttemberg shall remain in force. Postal and telegraphic communications with neighbouring foreign States shall, however, be regulated exclusively by the Reich.

Article 171. State railways, waterways and navigation marks shall be transferred to the Reich by 1st April, 1921, at the latest.

Should no agreement as to the conditions of transfer have been attained by 1st October, 1920, the decision shall be given by the Supreme Court.

Article 172. Up to the date at which the law of the Reich as to the Supreme Court comes into force, its functions shall be discharged by a Senate of seven members, four of whom shall be elected by the Reichstag and three by the High Court from its own members. It shall regulate its own procedure.

Article 173. Until the promulgation of a law of the Reich in accordance with Article 138, the hitherto existing State liabilities to religious bodies, founded upon legislation, contract, or exceptional legal titles, shall remain in force.

Article 174. Until the promulgation of the law of the Reich provided for in Article 146, paragraph 2, the existing legal position shall be maintained. The law must give special consideration to those districts of the Reich in which a school is already legally established which is not divided according to religious creeds.

Article 175. The provisions of Article 109 do not apply to orders and decorations conferred for merit during the war years, 1914 to 1919.

Article 176. All public officials and members of the armed forces must take the oath of allegiance to this Constitution. Details shall be determined by decree of the President of the Reich.

Article 177. Where in existing laws the use of a religious formula is required in taking an oath, the person concerned may legally replace the religious formula by the declaration "I swear." Otherwise, the substance of the oath as provided by law remains unaltered.

Article 178. The constitution of the German Reich of 16th April, 1871, and the law of 10th February, 1919, as to the provisional government of the Reich are repealed.

The remaining laws and decrees of the Reich remain in force, so far as they are not in conflict with the present Constitution. The provisions of the Treaty of Peace signed at Versailles on 28th June, 1919, are unaffected by the Constitution.

Regulations of authorities, issued in due legal manner upon the basis of existing laws, remain valid until they are annulled by the issue of further regulations or by legislation.

Article 179. Where, in laws or decrees, reference is made to provisions or institutions abolished by this Constitution, they shall be replaced by the corresponding provisions or institutions of this Constitution. In particular, the National Assembly is replaced by the Reichstag, the Committee of the States by the Reichsrat, and the President of the Reich elected on the basis of the law as to the provisional government of the Reich, is replaced by the President of the Reich elected upon the basis of this Constitution.

The power of issuing decrees vested in the Committee of the States in accordance with hitherto existing regulations is transferred to the Government of the Reich; the consent of the Reichsrat shall be requisite for the issue of decrees, in accordance with the provisions of this Constitution.

Article 180. Until the meeting of the first Reichstag, the National Assembly shall have the status of the Reichstag. Until the first President of the Reich enters upon his office, the duties of his office shall be discharged by the President of the Reich elected under the law as to the provisional government of the Reich.

Article 181. The German people, through their National Assembly, have decreed and prescribed this Constitution. It comes into force upon the day of its promulgation.*

SCHWARZBURG, 11th August, 1919.

---

* The Constitution was published in Berlin in the *Official Journal of Laws* (August 14, 1919).

Esthonian Constitution
of 1920

Distinguished and significant, the Esthonian Constitution of 1920 had a precedent-making position in history. This document is important as a model of popular democracy. More than any other constitution, it provides the best example of guarantees of the sovereignty of the people. At the same time, it provides an extensive formulation of the protection of minority rights.

Esthonians first made claims for autonomy and separatism at the meetings of the Russian Duma of 1905. Then, after the Russian Revolution of 1917, the Russian provisional government under Prince Lvov conferred the desired autonomy. This act was followed by the election of a National Council for Esthonia on 14 July, which established a national government. In November 1917, the Bolshevik Revolution erupted in Russia. The new Russian government declared the Esthonian national council dissolved and, abetted by Russian troops, attempted to create a Soviet republic under the control of local Bolsheviks.

However, on 24 February 1918, the Esthonian national council, which comprised all of the political parties except the Bolsheviks, declared Esthonia an independent republic. In this same month, the Treaty of Brest-Litovsk had been concluded between the Russians and the Germans, providing for both the evacuation of Esthonia by the Russians and an end to occupation by German troops (among other points). However, the Esthonian provisional government contrived to remain in existence, and in May 1918, it secured de facto recognition of its nationhood from the Allied powers. On 20 February 1920, Esthonia and Soviet Russia agreed to a treaty of peace, in which both nations formally recognized each other. De jure recognition by the Allies came on 26 January 1921.

The Esthonian government of 1920 was democratic, liberal, and pro-Western; the Constitution of 15 June 1920 was a reflection of these proclivities. This document lasted until 1935, when it was suspended by a military dictatorship that also abolished all political parties. Although there was a brief return to democratic rule in the years 1938 to 1940, Esthonia was conquered by Soviet forces in 1940 and transformed into the Esthonian Soviet Socialist Republic. Independence movements both inside Esthonia and in refugee communities abroad continue their opposition, and the United States as well as a number of other countries still refuse to recognize Soviet rule.

Popular sovereignty going beyond that of every other constitution in the world is given expression in Articles 29 to 34. The constitution provides for legislative initiative and legislative referenda and even reconciles conflict between parliament and the voters. If one-third of parliament so demands, a law would not take effect for two months to allow for a popular referendum. If the referendum results in popular rejection of such legislation, it remains rejected and elections for a new parliament must then be held within seventy-five days.

The provisions on human rights are similar to those in the Weimar Constitution, which served as a model. But the Esthonian Constitution goes even further. Where the German Constitution of 1919 protects the right to form and join unions, the Esthonian Constitution of 1920 protects the right to strike with no exception of government employees.

It is in the protection of minorities, however, that the Esthonian Constitution is best known and most praised. Racial, ethnic, and linguistic minorities are all given special rights. Significantly, Article 20 gives every citizen the right to declare his or her own nationality. Article 21 gives racial minorities "the right to establish autonomous institutions for the preservation and development of their national culture." According to Article 23, "Citizens of German, Russian, or Swedish nationality have the right to address the central administration of the State in their own language. In addition, Article 12 guarantees all "racial minorities" the right to be taught in their "mother tongue."

JAY A. SIGLER
Professor
Rutgers University
Camden, New Jersey

THE CONSTITUTION
OF THE
ESTHONIAN REPUBLIC

(Adopted by the Constituent Assembly on 15th June, 1920.)

The Esthonian people, with unshaken faith, and the resolute will to create a State based on justice, law, and liberty, to maintain internal and external peace for the general well-being, and to guarantee the social progress of present and future generations, has framed the following Constitution, which has been adopted by the Constituent Assembly.

CHAPTER I. GENERAL PROVISIONS

Article 1. Esthonia is an independent Republic in which the sovereign power is in the hands of the people.

Article 2. The territory of Esthonia includes Harjumaa, Laanemaa, Jarwamaa, Wirumaa, with the town of Narwaa and district, Tartumaa, Wiljandimaa, Parnumaa, the town of Walk, Worumaa, Petserimaa and other border regions inhabited by Esthonians, the islands of Saaremaa (Oesel), Muhumaa (Moon), and Hiiumaa (Dago), and other islands and reefs situated in Esthonian waters.

The delimitation of the Esthonian frontiers shall be determined by International Treaties.

Article 3. The sovereign power of Esthonia cannot be exercised otherwise than on the basis of the Constitution and the laws passed in accordance with the Constitution.

Article 4. Only laws initiated and adopted by the lawful institutions of the country are valid in Esthonia. The universally recognised general rules of international law are an integral part of the Esthonian laws.

No one may be presumed to be ignorant of the law.

Article 5. The State language of the Esthonian Republic is Esthonian.

Select Constitutions of the World, prepared for presentation to Dail Eireann, by order of the Irish Provisional Government, 1922 (Dublin: Stationery Office, 1922).

CHAPTER II. CONSTITUTIONAL RIGHTS
OF ESTHONIAN CITIZENS

Article 6. All citizens of the Republic are equal before the law. Public privileges or prejudices derived from birth, religion, sex, social position, or nationality may not exist. In Esthonia there are no legal class divisions or titles.

Article 7. The Esthonian Republic confers no decorations or marks of distinction on its citizens, excepting members of the defence forces in time of war. Esthonian citizens are likewise forbidden to accept foreign decorations.

Article 8. Personal liberty is guaranteed in Esthonia.

No person may be prosecuted, save in the cases and according to the forms prescribed by law.

No person may be arrested, or in any way deprived of his personal liberty, save by order of a judicial authority, except when apprehended flagrante delicto. The order must be based on stated reasons and must be communicated to the person imprisoned at latest three days after his arrest. Any citizen has the right to require that the order be communicated to the person affected, if this has not been done within the aforesaid period.

No person may be brought against his will before any Court other than that designated by law.

Article 9. No person may be punished for any act, unless a penalty has been attached thereto by a law which came into force before the commission of the said act.

Article 10. The inviolability of the dwelling is guaranteed.

No domiciliary search or investigation may be made, save in cases provided for by law.

Article 11. In Esthonia there is freedom of religion and conscience. No person may be obliged to perform any religious act, to be a member of any religious association, or to pay public taxes for the benefit of any such association.

Every Esthonian citizen may freely practise the rites of his religion, provided they are not contrary to public order or morality.

The religious belief or political opinions of any citizen may not be pleaded in justification of any offence, or of the nonfulfilment of civic duties.

There is no State religion in Esthonia.

Article 12. Science and the arts, and the teaching thereof, are unrestricted in Esthonia. Elementary education is obligatory and free in the primary schools. Instruction in their mother-tongue is guaranteed to racial minorities. Public instruction is placed under the control of the State.

The autonomy of institutions for higher education is guaranteed within the limits laid down by their statutes, which must be approved by legislation.

Article 13. In Esthonia there is liberty for the expression of ideas in speech, writing, print, and pictorial representation and sculpture. This liberty may not be restricted, save for reasons of morality and of the security of the State.

There is no censorship in Esthonia.

Article 14. The secrecy of communications by post, telegraph, telephone, or other general means, is guaranteed. The Courts may authorise exceptions to this rule in cases provided for by law.

Article 15. The right of addressing complaints and requests to public institutions is guaranteed in Esthonia. Such requests may not be accompanied by any compulsion or threat. The institutions concerned are bound to deal with such complaints or requests.

Article 16. State officials may be proceeded against in the Courts without prior authorization.

Article 17. Liberty to establish and change one's place of dwelling is guaranteed in Esthonia. No person may be deprived of this right, save by the Courts.

Restrictions may also be placed upon this right by other authorities, for reasons of public health, in such cases and in such manner as may be prescribed by law.

Article 18. All persons are free to assemble peaceably and unarmed.

All citizens have the right to form associations.

The right to strike is assured.

These rights may be limited only by law and solely in the interests of public safety.

Article 19. Freedom to choose one's occupation as well as to originate enterprises or industries of an agricultural, commercial, industries of an agricultural, commercial, industrial or other nature, is guaranteed in Esthonia. No person may be deprived of this right, save in accordance with and subject to the limits laid down by the law.

Article 20. Each Esthonian citizen is free to declare to what nationality he belongs. In cases where personal determination of nationality is impossible, the decision shall be taken in the mannner prescribed by law.

Article 21. Racial minorities in the country have the right to establish autonomous institutions for the preservation and development of their national culture and to maintain special organisations for their welfare, so far as is not incompatible with the interests of the State.

Article 22. In districts where the majority of the population is not Esthonian, but belongs to a racial minority, the language used in the administration of local self-governing authorities may be the language of that racial minority, but every citizen had the right to use the language of the State in dealings with such authorities. Local self-governing bodies which use the language of a racial minority must use the national language in their communications with governmental institutions, and with other local self-governing bodies which do not make use of the language of the same racial minority.

Article 23. Citizens of German, Russian or Swedish nationality have the right to address the central administration of the State in their own language. The use of these languages in the Courts, and in dealings with the local administrations of the State and of self-governing bodies, shall be the subject of detailed regulation by special laws.

Article 24. The right of private property is guaranteed to every citizen in Esthonia. Property may be expropriated without the consent of the owner only if the public interest so requires, and upon the basis and in the manner prescribed by law.

Article 25. The organisation of economic life in Esthonia must conform to the principles of justice, so as to ensure to all citizens a life worthy of human beings, by means of laws for the encouragement of agriculture, the ensuring of a dwelling and of work for every citizen, the protection of maternity, the safeguarding of labour, the assistance of the aged, and the relief of disablement due to accidents at work.

Article 26. The enumeration of the rights and liberties of citizens in the foregoing articles (6 to 24), does not exclude other rights derived from the Constitutional Law, or in accord therewith.

Restrictions placed upon the liberty of the citizen and his fundamental rights in exceptional circumstances, as when a State of Defence is proclaimed, may not be brought into operation save after the period prescribed by law, and upon the basis of, and within the limits laid down by, the law.

CHAPTER III. THE NATION

Article 27. The nation exercises the sovereign power in Esthonia through citizens who possess the right to vote. Every citizen who has reached the age of twenty years has the right to vote, if he has been an Esthonian subject for a period of not less than one year.

Article 28. The following are not entitled to vote:—

(1) Persons legally declared to be of unsound mind;

(2) Blind and deaf-mute persons, and spendthrifts placed under legal guardianship.

Certain categories of malefactors are deprived of the right to vote by the Organic Electoral Law.

Article 29. The people exercise sovereign power through:—

(1) the Referendum;

(2) the Legislative Initiative; and

(3) their power of electing the members of the State Assembly.

Article 30. Every law passed by the State Assembly (Riigikogu) shall remain unpromulgated for a period of two months, reckoned from the day on which it is passed, if one-third of the members of the State Assembly so demand. If, within this period of two months, 25,000 citizens entitled to vote demand that the adoption or rejection of the said law be submitted to a Referendum of the people, promulgation or non-promulgation of the law shall be determined by the result of the Referendum.

Article 31. In the exercise of the right of the Legislative Initiative, 25,000 citizens entitled to vote may demand the promulgation, amendment or repeal of a law. The Bill for this purpose shall be presented to the State Assembly, which may either pass the Bill into law or reject it. In the latter case the Bill shall be submitted to a Referendum for adoption or rejection by the people. If the majority of the citizens voting accept the Bill, it shall come into force as the law of the State.

Article 32. If the people reject a law passed by the State Assembly, or accept a law rejected by the Assembly, new elections for the Assembly shall be held not later than seventy-five days after the holding of the Referendum.

Article 33. The Referendum of the people shall take place under the control of the officers (bureau) of the State Assembly. The basis and procedure governing the Referendum are prescribed by a special law.

Article 34. The following matters may not be submitted to a Referendum, or be the subject of the Legislative Initiative by the people: The Budget and State loans; laws relating to the payment of taxes; the declaration of war and conclusion of peace; the declaration of a State of Defence and the withdrawal of the same; and treaties with foreign States.

CHAPTER IV. THE STATE ASSEMBLY (RIIGIKOGU)

Article 35. The State Assembly exercises legislative power as the representative of the nation.

Article 36. The State Assembly consists of one hundred members, elected on the principle of proportional representation, by universal, equal, direct and secret suffrage.

The State Assembly may increase the number of its members, but the law providing for an increase in number shall not come into force until the next elections to the State Assembly.

The electoral law for the State Assembly forms a special organic law, distinct from the present law.

Article 37. Every Esthonian elector is entitled to vote at elections for the State Assembly and is eligible for election thereto.

Article 38. Members of the State Assembly, with the exception of the assistants to members of the Government of the Republic, may not become officials of the Government, or of institutions under the control of the Government.

Article 39. The State Assembly is completely renewed by elections every three years. The term of office of the members dates from the day of the publication of the results of the elections.

Article 40. If a member of the State Assembly ceases to be entitled to vote, is placed under arrest with the consent of the State Assembly, resigns or dies, his place shall be filled, in accordance with the rules laid down by the electoral law, by a new member, who shall hold office for the remainder of the period fixed by the preceding article.

Article 41. The ordinary sessions of the State Assembly commence each year on the first Monday in October.

Article 42. The officers of the State Assembly may summon the Assembly in extraordinary session, if circumstances so require, and shall be bound to do so upon request by the Government of the Republic, or by one-fourth of the members of the State Assembly.

Article 43. At its first sitting after the elections, the State Assembly elects its Chairman and other officers (membres du Bureau). The Chairman of the previous State Assembly shall preside over this sitting until the new Chairman is elected.

Article 44. The State Assembly prescribes its own rules of procedure, which shall be promulgated as law.

Article 45. The members of the State Assembly are not bound by any instructions for the electors.

Article 46. The State Assembly can come to valid decisions if at least half of its members are present.

Article 47. The sittings of the State Assembly are public. Only in extraordinary cases, if two-thirds of the members agree, the sitting of the State Assembly may be declared secret.

Article 48. Save as provided in the rules of procedure, no member of the State Assembly may be made answerable for political utterance in the Assembly or its Committees.

Article 49. Members of the State Assembly may not be imprisoned without the consent of the Assembly, save when apprehended flagrante delicto. In such a case, the officers of the State Assembly must, within forty-eight hours at latest, be informed of the imprisonment and of the reasons therefor. The officers shall report the matter to the Assembly at its next sitting.

The State Assembly may defer the imprisonment, or suspend any other restriction placed on the liberty of a member, until the end of the session, or until the expiry of its term of office.

Article 51. The travelling allowances and salaries of members of the State Assembly are fixed by law, and may not be altered by the State Assembly, save for subsequent sessions.

Article 52. The State Assembly passes laws, determines the budget, revenues and expenditure of the State, and decides as to loans and other matters in accordance with the principles of the Constitution.

Article 53. The officers of the State Assembly are responsible for the publication of laws passed by the National Assembly.

Article 54. Every law comes into operation, save as may be otherwise provided by the law itself, on the tenth day after its publication in the Official Gazette, "Riigi Teataja."

Article 55. The State Assembly exercises its powers of control through machinery set up by itself, by means of which it supervises the State Administration, the economic affairs of State undertakings, and the utilization of credits provided for by the State Budget.

Article 56. Every member of the State Assembly has the right to address questions to the Government at sittings of the State Assembly; one-fourth of the members of the State Assembly, as fixed by law, may interpellate the Government, and the Government is bound to reply to such interpellation.

CHAPTER V. THE GOVERNMENT

Article 57. The Government of the Republic exercises executive power in Esthonia.

Article 58. The Government is composed of the Head of the State (Riigiwanem) and the Ministers. The number of the latter, their powers and duties, are determined by a special law.

Article 59. The State Assembly appoints the Government and receives its resignation. If a Minister resigns, his duties are discharged by another member of the Government, designated by the Government, until a new Minister is appointed.

Article 60. The Government of the Republic directs the internal and external policy of the State, and ensures the preservation of internal and external security and the execution of the laws.

The Government—

(1) frames the Budget of receipts and expenditure of the State, and submits it to the State Assembly for confirmation;

(2) appoints and dismisses civil and military officials of the State, save in so far as this right is vested by law in any other authority;

(3) concludes treaties with foreign States in the name of the Esthonian Republic, and submits them to the State Assembly for ratification;

(4) declares war and concludes peace in accordance with the decisions of the State Assembly;

(5) proclaims a State of Defence throughout the whole or a part of

the territory, and submits the proclamation to the State Assembly for ratification;

(6) presents proposals for legislation to the State Assembly;

(7) issues decrees and ordinances in accordance with the laws;

(8) decides appeals for amnesties.

Article 61. The Head of the State acts as representative of the Esthonian Republic, directs and correlates the activities of the Government of the Republic, and presides over the councils of Ministers, and may require each individual Minister to render an account of his actions.

Article 62. The Government of the Republic appoints a substitute for the Head of the State from among its own members.

Article 63. The sittings of the Council of Ministers are private; on exceptional and ceremonial occasions they may be held in public.

Article 64. The Government of the Republic must possess the confidence of the State Assembly. If the Government or any of its members find that the Assembly has withdrawn its support, they must resign.

Article 65. The State Chancellory is attached to the Government of the Republic, and placed under the supervision of the Head of the State. The State Chancellory is directed by the State Secretary appointed by the Government of the Republic.

Article 66. All decisions of the Government must be signed by the Head of the State, the Minister responsible for carrying them into effect, and the State Secretary.

Article 67. The Head of the State and the Ministers may not be impeached for offences committed in the exercise of their functions, save in pursuance of a decision to that effect by the State Assembly, and may be tried only by the Supreme Court of Justice.

CHAPTER VI. THE JUDICIAL POWER

Article 68. The Courts are empowered to administer justice in Esthonia, and are independent in the exercise of that power.

Article 69. The Supreme Court of Justice, the Judges of which are elected by the State Assembly, exercise supreme jurisdiction in Esthonia.

Article 70. The Supreme Court of Justice appoints judges, save as the law may provide that they shall be elected.

The Government of the Republic may order mobilization in the absence of a decision by the State Assembly, if a foreign State has declared war on the Republic, or has commenced hostilities, or has ordered mobilization against the Republic.

CHAPTER VIII. THE DEFENCE OF THE STATE

Article 84. No pension, remuneration or compensation may be paid out of State funds save in accordance with law.

Article 85. The Budget of receipts and expenditure of the State is fixed for each year. The Budget for one year may, by legislation, be given continued effect until the adoption of the Budget for the following year.

CHAPTER X. THE OPERATION OF THE CONSTITUTION AND ITS AMENDMENT

Article 86. The Constitution is the inviolable rule governing the activities of the State Assembly, the Courts, and Governmental organizations.

Article 87. The right of initiative in the amendment of the Constitutional Law may be exercised by the people in the same manner as the Popular Initiative, and by the State Assembly in the ordinary manner.

Article 88. Amendments of the Constitution proposed by the Popular Initiative, or by the State Assembly, are determined by Popular Referendum.

Article 89. Every proposal for the amendment of the Constitutional Law must be published for the information of the people at least three months before being put to the vote.